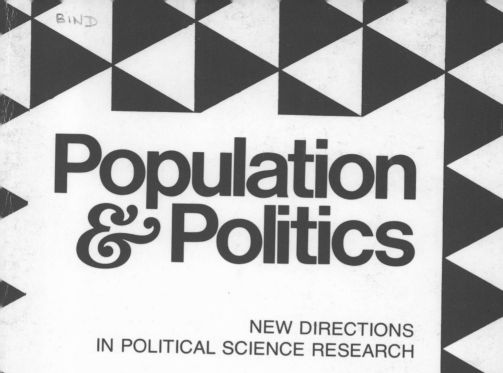

Population
& Politics

NEW DIRECTIONS
IN POLITICAL SCIENCE RESEARCH

Richard L. Clinton

The Carolina Population Center, a part of The University of N
Carolina at Chapel Hill, was created in 1966 to facilitate research, edu
tion, and service devoted to the understanding of population phenomena and
solution of population-related problems. It serves public and private agenc
business and the public directly, in North Carolina and the South, and provi
technical assistance on population matters to more than 20 nations.

This soft-cover edition of Richard L. Clinton's *Population and Politics* is publis
by Lexington Books, D. C. Heath and Company especially for the Carolina Pop
tion Center. In helping to serve the communications needs of the population/far
planning field, the Center seeks to make significant publications available t
wide an audience as possible of students, advanced scholars, leaders of governm
and business, and many other interested persons. Inquiries about this edition
other population/family planning publications should be addressed to:

Population Publications
Carolina Population Center
University of North Carolina at Chapel
Chapel Hill, North Carolina 27514

Population and Politics

Population and Politics

New Directions in Political Science Research

Edited by
Richard L. Clinton
University of North Carolina
at Chapel Hill

Lexington Books
D.C. Heath and Company
Lexington, Massachusetts
Toronto   London

Library of Congress Cataloging in Publication Data

Clinton, Richard L.
 Population and Politics.

 1. Population research — Addresses, essays, lectures. 2. Political science research — Addresses, essays, lectures. 3. Underdeveloped areas — Population — Addresses, essays, lectures. 4. United States — Population — Addresses, essays, lectures. I. Title.
HB850.C54   320'.07'2   73-9655
ISBN 0-669-87203-4

Copyright © 1973 by D.C. Heath and Company

Published simultaneously in Canada.

Printed in the United States of America.

International Standard Book Number: 0-669-87023-4

Library of Congress Catalog Card Number: 73-9655

For Susan, Lara, and Lisa
with apologies for the
many lost hours

Contents

List of Figures

xi

List of Tables

Foreword

The concept that population patterns, including size, distribution, composition, and rates of change, can profoundly influence the quality of human life is now becoming the subject of common awareness and of broad scientific inquiry. A more revolutionary concept, that human societies can consciously influence their own population patterns toward optimizing the achievement of human values under various conditions, still largely awaits development of a sounder scientific base.

These notions have of course been pursued in various ways, off and on, since early history. But the precipitous transformations in the human situation which have recently occurred and which certainly lie ahead now raise the subject of population studies to a level of imperative concern both for scientific research and for public policy.

So far, relative to the needs for knowledge, the stakes involved, and the investments we make in other aspects of life, scientific work in the population field is still at a very early stage. This complex field requires the mobilization and synthesis of insights from many different scientific disciplines. Basic reproductive biology and clinical studies on fertility control were badly neglected until the last decade. General theoretical insights from population biologists and ecologists are only now being related to the human condition. Epidemiological methods are being used to strengthen our knowledge of relationships between family size and family health and to understand "epidemiologic transition". Population geneticists are beginning to acquire basic knowledge which may yet have the profoundest implications for future human population dynamics. Biostatisticians are starting to help improve methods for obtaining primary demographic data and for mathematically modeling population change. Administrative and management sciences have also only recently been focused on problems in this field.

The social sciences are especially needed to illuminate key aspects of population dynamics. Would that they were more ready for this challenge, with a deeper fund of knowledge, methods, and theory. Given that an adolescent stage of isolation may be needed to acquire a certain purification and self-confidence, would that the present social science disciplinary groups could hurry on through this stage to a next level of maturity. As the current boundary defenses relax among such groups, there are rich opportunities for sharing tools, for linking concepts, and for better understanding of natural phenomena which do not organize themselves according to man-made disciplines.

Among the social sciences, in Europe economics has tended so far to dominate the study of population dynamics. Economic methods of analysis, from Adam Smith and Malthus onward, have helped to identify and dramatize the fundamental importance of population factors in national development. However, with some notable exceptions, even modern economists have tended to suffer from the self-imposed limitations which are reflected by references to population and other key factors as "exogenous" and "nontraditional" variables. Recently, this discipline is moving to contribute anew to population studies through system simulation methods, human resource studies, and micro-economic analysis at the family level.

In the United States, sociology has tended to spearhead social science studies in population. It has contributed greatly to descriptive demography and to related survey and statistical methods. However, most sociologists are still humble indeed about their contributions to general population theory. A handy precept for current students in demography is never to make a population prediction testable in your own lifetime! Sociological forays into prescription on population policy matters also merit considerable humility. Furthermore, there is increasing realization that research data collected for sociological studies often is inadequate for testing important hypotheses regarding population dynamics emerging from economics, psychology, and other sources.

Anthropology has recently begun to contribute to this field through deeper studies of the cultural context of population change and by adding comparative and historical perspectives. Psychology as a discipline is now beginning to bring to this field new techniques of measurement and explanatory concepts that can open barriers which have heretofore blocked the work of economists and sociologists. These approaches can provide the deeper roots which population research so much needs.

Amid such ferment, political science has so far remained little involved. This despite the fact that, from Plato onward, the basic links between political and population phenomena have been repeatedly observed. Modern demography, indeed, was born in the study of "political arithmetick" in 17th century England. However, the rites of scientific passage for modern political science are especially difficult. This discipline as no other must face human value questions. It deals with the most complex decision processes, in different settings and at various levels of aggregation. It is trying to learn to apply and wisely orchestrate the collection of methods and concepts available from other disciplines, as well as to build appropriate new ones. With these preoccupations, the lag in rediscovery of the population matrix of political science is unfortunate but understandable.

The present book reflects an important phase in this rediscovery. It can be compared with an earlier volume in this series edited by Professors Clinton, Flash and Godwin, which presented the speculations of senior figures in academic political science regarding the possible applications of their existing knowledge to population problems. The present book, by contrast, represents the Young Turks. Perhaps with less polish but with more sense of personal engagement, they speak to the real problems they now face in active pursuit of such research. They must deal explicitly with their own personal value orientations, and with defensive reactions from their own and other professional groups, in addition to identifying and accounting for value systems of the societies they study. Against this background, they explore and illustrate current research problems, and they help to map possible further needs and priorities for study.

Along with the work of this group, other significant steps have advanced political science studies in the population field during the past year. The Commission on Population Growth and the American Future, through its final report and its associated studies, has helped especially to draw attention to implications of population change on the dynamics of governance at local, state, and national levels. The burgeoning interest in land-use planning in the United States involves questions of optimal population distribution, migration, and related political processes, which offer a particularly interesting arena for political science research. An international population policy studies consortium, currently coordinated by Professor Clinton, is building an international colleagueship of political scientists concerned with this field. A project of the National Academy of Science is also helping to stimulate population policy-oriented studies on a worldwide basis. In connection with the World Population Year in 1974, the United Nations and related international groups are concerned with how to raise knowledge of and responsiveness to population problems above the concerns of nationalism; to advance a global population, as well as peace, ethic.

Aristotle called politics the "master science". His apt description remains yet unfulfilled. This book and other current developments suggest that population research and political science share many increasingly important, substantive interrelationships. They also share an inevitable breadth of approach, a search for strategy and synthesis, and basic concerns for the greatest questions of mankind. The two fields greatly need and can help each other. If they can grow together, they have a magnificent agenda ahead.

Moye W. Freymann

August 22, 1973

Preface

Given the proliferation of "readers" and published proceedings of conferences, it bears mentioning at the outset that this volume consists of original essays written specifically for this book. Moreover, the organziation of the book was worked out collaboratively with the contributors and others well in advance of the time the individual chapters were composed. The way the book developed was, in fact, of sufficient uniqueness to warrant recounting in some detail.

In January 1972, as a part of its effort to expand the involvement of political scientists in population research, the Carolina Population Center provided me with the opportunity to organize a Political Science/Population Workshop[a] as a means for exploring the implications of population dynamics for politics and of the study of population and politics for the discipline of political science. Dissatisfied with the presentation-of-papers-cum-discussant format so often employed at academic conferences, I opted for a round-table discussion approach. To give focus to the discussions and structure to the workshop, however, it was necessary to organize the sessions around a limited number of carefully chosen and well-defined topics. For assistance in the selection of these substantive areas I appealed to my colleagues in the Department of Political Science at the University of North Carolina at Chapel Hill, both faculty and graduate students,[b] and to the dozen or so political scientists around the country who I knew were already working in the population field. The pooling of their insights led to the following format and suggested areas of inquiry for the workshop:

Session I: Normative Concerns

Should political scientists study population?

What, if anything, does political science bring to the study of population-related matters that other disciplines do not?

What role should governments play in population matters?

Is the right to choose the number of one's children an inalienable human right?

Given the inevitably discriminatory nature of incentives, are there nevertheless situations in which a government would be justified in offering them to encourage adoption of contraception, abortion, or sterilization?

[a]The workshop was held in Chapel Hill on May 4-6, 1972 and was generously supported by both the Department of Political Science and the United States Agency for International Development (Contract No. csd/2507 to the University of North Carolina Population Center).

[b]I am particularly indebted to Steven Garland, Dan Gattis, Edward Humberger, Harriet Imrey, and Anne Stubbs for their help at this crucial stage.

What are the conflicts between the academician's research interests (motivations?) and the interests (motivations?) of official agencies as regards the area of population and politics?

What are the criteria by which population policies should be evaluated?

Session II: Methodological Issues

How can the population policy process best be studied? (e.g., elite interviews, organizational structures, decision making, bureaucratic behavior, interest groups, etc.)

What is the potential usefulness of cohort analysis in explaining the political implications of changing age distributions? (Given the possible age-specificity of crime rates, electoral participation, party preference, political radicalization, political conservatism, etc.)

What kind of comprehensive multivariate models of development (which include socioeconomic, political, and population variables) are available?

What are the political uses of large-scale simulations such as the Club of Rome projections, M.I.T.'s World III, etc.?

Is it possible or desirable to construct country-specific models of the impact of population growth and distribution (geographically, by class, by ethnic group) on political stability, political modernization/development, government capability, etc.? (What uses would be made of such models were it possible to construct them? Do the posssible uses justify or militate against the construction of such models?)

What sorts of questions can be answered by large-scale simulations and aggregate-data analyses and what sorts are inappropriate for this type of approach?

Given the sensitivity of population matters and the present state of world tensions, are in-depth case studies in developing countries really feasible?

How serious are the data unreliability and unavailability problems in the population field?

Session III: Developing Countries and Their Relations with Developed Countries

Could population policies obscure the need for more fundamental, structural, socioeconomic changes?

How should the influence of extranational factors be assessed? (Are the concepts of intervention and imperialism relevant? Has aid been tied to the existence of population policies? Have such policies been promoted even where they conflict with local values? Are the motives for population policies as important as the consequences of such policies?)

What are the likely effects of population changes such as rapid growth and urban migration on the ability of governments to fulfill their functions and on political stability? (What are the likely effects on the populations involved, i.e., on human beings?)

What are the implications of current population projections in both the developing and the developed worlds for the future relationships between these two areas? (Are the problems of pollution and ecological imbalance connected with population questions? What are the implications of population dynamics — levels, rates, composition, and movements — for international conflict?)

Session IV: The Developed (Overdeveloped?) Countries, with Special Emphasis on the United States

What does the population policy process "look like"? What do governments do — and what don't they do? How does the advisory process short-circuit some possibilities? Why?

What is a politically optimum growth rate? What size government will be required to manage it? At what point of political centralization do diseconomies of scale arise?

Population distribution: how can political science participate in assessing the consequences of, for example, the regulation of interstate migration, municipal zoning, reconstruction of inner cities, the flight to suburbia, etc.?

What is the likely political reaction of middle-class taxpayers when state or (especially!) municipal diseconomies of scale become very evident? Does the northern backlash vote reflect some of this unease toward mounting welfare payments and more expensive yet less efficient public services?

The Commission on Population Growth and the American Future has recommended that the nation act now to encourage a two-child family norm. By what political means, excluding coercive measures, can this be accomplished?

Consider existing and proposed legislation in regard to legalization of abortion and contraceptive devices, equal job opportunities for women, day-care centers, legalization of homosexuality, etc. How is the political impact of such measures to be evaluated?

How can political scientists participate in evaluation of current population legislation before Congress or the recommendations of the Commission on Population Growth and the American Future?

What are the political implications of the Women's Liberation movement with respect to population policies? How do women participate in and influence the formulation of population policy and its execution? What is the effectiveness of current population policy measures in the light of political and socioeconomic structures shaping women's lives?

Obviously, the four major divisions were neither mutually exclusive nor all inclusive. Nor were the suggested subsidiary questions by any means exhaustive. Nevertheless, the latter were suggestive, and the participants were encouraged to go beyond them to examine any other issues they deemed of importance, while the former did reflect both a logical division between the normative and the methodological and the necessary distinction which must always be drawn when discussing population problems between the situation in the less developed versus that of the more developed areas.

Each of the invited participants was asked to pick one of the four general topics and to prepare a short introductory statement — not to exceed ten minutes — on that subject to get the discussion going. Since the entire panel would have ample opportunity to discuss all four topics, everyone was asked to give some thought to the three other areas in addition to the one for which he or she had primary responsibility. The result, by all accounts, was an extremely lively and stimulating ten hours of intensive discussion.

Basing themselves on the shared ideas of the workshop experience, each participant then devoted several months to writing a chapter on some particular aspect of the general topic wherein his or her expertise was greatest. After these essays were edited and again reviewed by their authors, they were sent to other scholars — one for each of the four sections — who had agreed to reflect upon their content, respond selectively to the ideas they contained, attempt to tie them together, and try to make some reasoned judgment of the directions in which they were pointing. The results of these efforts will be found in the concluding chapter of each section.

Such was the gestation of this volume, which, it is hoped, will be as useful a learning experience for those who read it as it was for those who wrote it.

RICHARD LEE CLINTON

Acknowledgments

This book is the product of the efforts and support of many individuals and several institutions, in particular of the contributors, the Carolina Population Center, and, indirectly but no less importantly, the Agency for International Development. I am also happy to acknowledge my appreciation to my colleagues in the International Population Policy Consortium for their advice and support. A special word of thanks must go to Ms. Beverly Rosser who, because of her exceptional industry and intelligence and in spite of her pay category and job description, has been of inestimable assistance at every phase of the book's development.

**Part One
Normative Concerns**

1

Ethical Issues in Relating Normative Concerns to the Politics of Population

Thomas G. Sanders

The manner of relating ethics to population and political science depends on how we define ethics. Because of its long history, ethics, like political science or any other interpretation of human behavior, has produced different approaches to its subject matter. All ethicists agree, however, on a common object of inquiry, namely, what individuals or collectivities claim *ought to be* or *ought to be done*. This focus on normative thought, statements, or actions differs from that of social sciences like demography or political science, which try to explain by appropriate methods and theory what persons and institutions *actually do.*

The most obvious normative dimension of population and politics would seem to be policy, where the choices are shaped not only by social scientific studies, available resources, and political pressures, but often by the perceived values of the decision maker or of society. Actually, however, normative impulses, often unrecognized, enter at a much more basic stage in the presuppositions underlying social sciences like demography and political science. To select some aspects of experience rather than others, to adopt certain methods, to commit oneself to objectivity and the scientific interpretation of reality, to dedicate one's life to a career in the social sciences all involve judgments of the good, relevant, and proper for oneself, society, or humanity, which are normative rather than descriptive.

Many people believe that the function of ethicists is to decide good and bad aspects of choices in a given problem area. This seems to be one way of doing ethics, since an important segment of population literature does include valuative statements or suggestions, often intertwined with empirical statements. This approach, which we may call *prescriptive* or hortatory, has centered its attention on two basic issues in population.

The first has involved judgments about an appropriate broad response to the effects of unrestrained reproduction on personal and social existence. It begins with empirical observations that rapid population growth causes certain economic and social problems for the nation, or that absence of family planning information encourages abortion and endangers the health of women, and then makes value judgments that societies *should* restrict their rates of population growth, or women *ought* to have the information to plan their children safely.

The second issue concerns a range of policies associated with implementing family planning policies. On the individual level, ethically motivated persons

3

have asked about the impact of family planning programs on values considered intrinsic to human dignity such as freedom of expression, access to information, and freedom from outside control or manipulation. On the broader social and national level, we find discussion of the legitimacy of some policies in contrast with others, especially certain drastic proposals to deal with population growth which in turn restrict individual freedom and voluntariness of response. Finally, certain ethical questions have been raised on the international level, involving the action of developed nations in exerting pressure for particular policies in the developing world, the mode of financing, and the presumed motivations behind these policies.

A distinctive characteristic of the prescriptive approach to ethics is the assumption that its audience shares a common set of values which provide the presuppositions for its suggestions. While the operative values may seem self-evident, the problems in prescriptive ethics provide the object of scrutiny in a second, different approach to ethics.

In this case, ethics becomes *analytical,* an inquiry into other people's normative or value statements, judgments, and presuppositions. The ethicist distinguishes normative from descriptive judgments and clarifies the presuppositions which underlie both. He often discovers that issues which seem to be normative may be only partly so or not at all, or that descriptive propositions are in fact normative.

The analytical ethicist is interested as well in examining the criteria, like the dignity of human life or human survival, on which the value judgments often rest. While we might agree that these goods are obvious and hardly worth questioning, we should also recognize that such a conclusion does not follow from empirical examination. (Some thinkers in history, for example, have questioned the absoluteness of these values in certain contexts.) Rather, they are valuative assumptions based on a different set of presuppositions and a different mental process from those used to discover facts. The analytical ethicist wants to clarify how we arrive at these criteria, whether through consensus, the ethical heritage of civilization, the nature of man, or self-interest in survival.

Once moral criteria have been determined, the ethicist can relate them to policy choices. For instance, the analysis of "Ethics, Population, and the American Tradition" for the Commission on Population Growth and the American Future first isolated moral principles in the American tradition and various interest groups and then evaluated the consistency of policy alternatives with these criteria.

This approach to ethics responds to normative statements rather than initiating them. It is analytical rather than hortatory. It can tell us what we should do, but only after clarifying existent statements which define what we should do.

A third approach to ethics is the so-called *ethical realism* associated with the writings of Hans Morgenthau and Reinhold Niebuhr.[1] This method has been applied principally to international relations and, by Niebuhr, to determining how a relative justice is achieved within a democratic political system. In modern times it has been the most successful attempt to bring into dialogue the interests of ethicists, academic figures, and public policy makers.

Ethical realism has the following important features:

1. While it acknowledges the role of values as both a human aspiration and a social substratum, it also emphasizes self-interest in individual and collective behavior.

2. It argues that the most difficult problem of ethics is not to articulate the good and the bad, but to show how self-interest is related to moral values.

3. It tries to demonstrate the moral implications when groups or nations function according to self-interest.

4. As distinguished from the method previously distinguished, which is strictly analytical, ethical realism is ontological. That is, it claims to base its interpretation on a real pattern of human behavior which it finds defined in the Jewish-Christian view of man.

Utilizing the analytical and the realistic approaches to ethics, we may examine some of the questions that have been suggested as normative issues for our consideration. Our intent will be to demonstrate some of the problems in assuming that issues are normative, since immediately we discover that these questions are much more complicated.

One of the questions is basically methodological rather than normative: What, if anything, does political science bring to the study of population-related matters that other disciplines do not? Political science brings a methodological "perspective" by which population data are ordered and interpreted within such disciplinary interests as political groups, governmental institutions, and policy. (Comparably, demography might utilize the data of politics to help clarify some aspects of its disciplinary interests.) The normative aspect is implicit: to understand population is a good thing; the perspective of political science enhances the understanding of population; therefore, political science should study population. But this does not even appear in the question.

Another question can also be considered methodological: What are the criteria by which population policy should be evaluated? The most obvious answers to this question are not what would usually be called normative. They include such criteria as effectiveness, feasibility, and economy. We could, however, also introduce moral criteria to evaluate population policies, for example, that they do not violate individual rights or that they are presented without deception. If we introduce such criteria, we must be clear about what they are, why we have introduced these rather than others, and the sources of their presumed validity.

Two of the questions refer to behavior predominantly based on self-interest: What role should governments play in population matters? and Is a government justified in offering discriminatory incentives to encourage adoption of contraception, abortion, or sterilization? Nations act on perceived national interest, even though they may be oriented and restrained by values within their culture. It is somewhat abstract to ask what role governments should play in population matters as a moral question, since they will in any event play the role they deem necessary for survival, development, national aggrandizement, or the well-being of the populace. Similarly, they will adopt nondiscriminatory or discriminatory policies to achieve these goals.

Moral values, however, do enter the picture. One might argue that a policy adopted on grounds of national interest has moral implications, if one presupposes certain moral values. Survival, development, national expansion, and responsibility for well-being could be assumed as values themselves or as instruments to achieve other, perhaps humanistic or social values. Nevertheless, the selling of policy to decision makers can best be done, not by moral arguments, but by showing that it corresponds to national interest.

One of the questions is partly methodological, partly self-interest, and partly moral: Should political scientists study population? As we indicated previously, it may be appropriate for political scientists to study population since they have certain disciplinary interests, such as the role of their government, which other disciplines might include in their analyses but not sufficiently to understand the complex area of population politics. This is methodological. Self-interest enters in the following manner. Political scientists are already studying population because they want to stay busy, because this is a wide-open field for political science, and because there is money in it for research and travel.

On the other hand, we would be totally cynical to rest the analysis here. Some political scientists want to study population because they have interests or convictions about it. If so, we must return to some of our former questions. Why do they have these interests and convictions? What values do they presuppose? Where do these values originate, and so forth?

Of similar complexity is the question about the academician's research interests and those of official agencies in the area of population and politics: What are the conflicts between the academician's research interests (motivations?) and the interests (motivations?) of official agencies as regards the area of population and politics? At first glance, it may sound as if the academician's motives are purer than those of official agencies which serve the national interest. In actuality, both fields have morally concerned individuals in them, and, moreover, the interest of the government agency may conflict with the interest of the academician. The government agency distributes its resources on the assumption that population research enhances awareness of the field and thus prevents strains in developing countries that would contradict United States interests. The academic person has his own interest in doing research, but gathering the information he needs may require an environment of confidence among citizens of other countries which is undermined if he is suspected of serving United States interests. Thus we have a conflict of interests. Yet to try to understand another culture is not necessarily more moral than to carry out programs that serve both United States interests and those of other nations. They are just different functions. Both can have broad moral implications for human well-being, and the person or institution doing one or the other with competence is following his or its own interests.

The final question, Is the right to choose the number of one's own children an inalienable human right? hinges on certain assumptions about inalienable rights. What is an inalienable right? Is it something intrinsic to human nature, as the framers of the Declaration of Independence believed and modern Thomism maintains? If so, we must then adopt a particular view of man as a being with intrinsic, hence inalienable, rights, a perspective that many people do not share. Are inalienable rights defined by a consensus such as might be arrived at by the United Nations, the United States, the wisdom of intelligent men, or the governments of various countries? If this is so, we are not talking about inalienable rights, *per se,* but are saying that certain consensus instruments have defined them as such.

I have used the questions in our prospectus to illustrate some problems in the analysis of normative dimensions in the politics of population. Other questions could as well have been used. What I find impressive is the fact that political scientists interested in population recognize that normative questions are an issue they must confront.

We will all be aided in our sensitivity to ethical or valuative aspects of academic research and writing if we realize that these are not outside principles added to a body of scientific material. Rather values can be interpreted as implicit in all human behavior, whether the action under scrutiny is the research of a social scientist, the development of nations, the movement of people from rural to urban areas, or a policy to encourage the adoption of family planning.

Values and value judgments are so inextricably linked to human aspirations and actions that social sciences like demography and political science cannot evade them. The normative begins with the philosophical presuppositions and commitments behind the social scientific quest for knowledge, calls for attention in any objective analysis of human behavior, and pops up in all policy decisions. It is both unscientific and unphilosophical to flee from the value dimension of human existence. The proper response is to acknowledge it, understand its distinctive characteristics, and probe the assumptions behind it.

If the present analysis of the questions has relied on the two approaches to ethics that we call analytical and realistic, this does not imply abandoning the prescriptive approach. Outside analyses of phenomena, whether social scientific or ethical, are a useful intellectual exercise abstracted from life, which is where value-laden motivations and actions express themselves. Almost any scholar in demography or political science holds views on population that are not wholly empirical but normative as well. The common concern with human behavior by the ethicist, the political scientist, and the demographer suggests the usefulness of mutual interchange for furthering our understanding of human nature.

Notes

1. Hans J. Morgenthau, *Politics Among Nations* (New York: Knopf, 1969); Harry R. Davis and Robert C. Good, eds., *Reinhold Niebuhr on Politics* (New York: Scribner, 1960).

2

Population Policy: The Ethical Dimension

Thomas C. Lyons, Jr.

In the past year or so, a number of articles, papers, and books from various disciplines have raised specific issues of a normative nature relative to population policy.[1] Since each discipline comes at a problem in a way befitting, complementing, and contributing to itself, population problems are usually approached through such disciplines as epidemiology, public health, sociology, economics, anthropology, demography, psychology, and so on. By and large the political scientist has not joined this crusade. One might hope that because of symposia such as this, we also will come to have something substantial to say about population matters so that it will not be possible for the American Psychological Association to hear a psychologist discuss ethical issues and population policy with these words:

I recently took part in a discussion that included several eminent political scientists who ruled out the very possibility of policy in this sense, as unworthy of serious consideration; they could only get interested in latent or implicit policy, that is, the unintended consequences of governmental action − or in the effects of predicted population change on the processes of government. To me, this is rank and irresponsible defeatism. The need for explicit social policy in regard to population and a variety of related urgent issues seems to me a principal challenge to our faltering governmental system. We have already gone much too far in reaping the unintended and unwelcome consequences of implicit policy.[2]

It has been my experience that no discussion of population policy advances very far before we are squarely in the middle of *both* political and ethical issues, and more often than not the differences between the two are not readily perceived. It was Rousseau, I believe, who reminded us: "Those who would treat politics and morality apart will never understand the one or the other." In a large measure, the American political scientist strives for a value free discipline. I believe that any social scientist who seeks to deal seriously with population issues is dealing with ethical concerns automatically, and since the methodology of his discipline cannot bail him out, he should face this fact squarely.

The purpose of this chapter is not to argue *which* ethical judgments are necessarily important or critical to the policy process but rather to argue that we

The opinions and views of this paper are those of the author and are not necessarily those of the U.S. Government or any of its agencies.

9

must realize that ethical/moral judgments *are* important, indeed critical, and to suggest that we do not jeopardize our standing as social scientists by accepting this and admitting that ours is not a value free approach. In this sense, then, my remarks can be classed as hortative, explicative, and expositive.

To create the framework within which ethical and political issues of population policy merge, it is instructive to review how the population problem is seen around the world. The value of this exercise is to reaffirm the important fact that one's definition of the problem dictates the suggested solution(s); that is, actual and potential policy responses.

If we were to poll the world's leaders, students, intellectuals, bureaucrats, and masses of people as to the seriousness of population problems, we could roughly classify all replies into five, not always mutually exclusive, groups. In doing so, we would find that no one group is homogenous in its scientific or intellectual makeup; scholars, writers, scientists, political elites, and the like are found in all groups.

Group One. There is no problem, and, moreover, a growing population is necessary to social/political/economic progress. In addition, world technology, intelligently applied and humanely shared, can come to the rescue in many areas until social changes inevitably force a slower population growth. Those who hold this point of view say that no historical or empirical evidence shows rapid population growth necessarily impedes economic progress and human development.

Group Two. Population growth holds an unknown threat to the world's future, but numerous means are at hand to deal effectively with this problem, although the least of these is planned and determined fertility. Indeed, those in this group believe that no antifertility campaign can improve productivity per worker or increase per capita income, the greatest needs of the world's poverty nations. Help for the have-not countries can only be effective by a sharing of the world's wealth and resources. The Roman Catholic Church is among those who accept this point of view. *Humanae Vitae* and other recent encyclicals seem to seek social/economic progress and total sharing of the world's resources as the only answer to man's needs, and it is an interesting footnote that the orthodox Marxist holds a similar view, refined by the doctrine that in the perfectly efficient socialist state overpopulation would be impossible.

Group Three. A serious problem exists, but certain forces have been set in motion which give reason for hope and optimism. This optimism is tempered by the belief that there must be a meaningful promotion of voluntary fertility control and economic, social, and human development in the same package and that the forces now working for amelioration of population problems must be speeded along by positive and humane government decisions. (The author identifies with Group Three.)

Group Four. The population problem is becoming more desperate every day and it is obvious that voluntarism is not the answer. The entire world needs a crash motivational/implementation fertility control program immediately if disaster is to be avoided.

Group Five. The name of the problem is "despair." The world has reached the point of no return. Disaster is eminent. It is now three minutes to midnight. Starvation, social and political disorder, and ecological disruption are nearly upon us. Voluntary family planning is a banal and wasted effort. Massive programs carried out by government fiat hold out some degree of hope — but not much.

Thus, in summary, we find that the same evidence suggests to many scientists that certain rates of population growth affect seriously the prospects for future life on this planet; some will admit that population growth *per se* is not critical but agree that its present rapidity makes the matter serious; to others the evidence suggests that not only rates but ultimate size of the population will have to be determined (some have already made that determination); yet to others the evidence suggests the problem is only partially serious (starvation is bad, but urbanization is not). And so on.

Since a problem is by definition a matter which requires resolution, all definitions of a problem imply that there are right and wrong ways to address it. The way the evidence is evaluated reflects the evaluators' values, interests, and concerns and will have implications for what is recommended or carried out. If one is with the prophets of doom — Group Five — for example, the solutions are clear. As we struggle with this emotion laden subject, it might not be inappropriate to ask ourselves if we do not perhaps decide on the solution and then manipulate the data to create the problem we want to resolve?

Callahan says it another way:

How the problem is defined, and how the different values perceived to be at stake are weighed, will have direct implications for the priority given to population problems in relation to other social problems. People might well agree that population growth is a serious issue but they might (and often do) say that other issues are comparatively more serious. If low priority is given to population problems, this is likely to affect the perception of the ethical issues at stake.[3]

I contend that what kind of ethical/social/value issues arise in the policy process are of serious concern to all social scientists, whether they have a bent in that direction or not. Most especially, however, they are of concern to those who study policy and to those who are in a position to recommend a specific policy posture.

Essentially, in the problem solving process involving policy decisions, the ultimate policy response is conditioned by many factors, three of which are:

1. How is the problem perceived? (Who is doing the perceiving?)
2. How is the problem defined? (Who is doing the defining?)

3. What alternative solutions are available to the policy makers? (Who is recommending solutions?)

Regardless of who is defining what to whom, for an example, those who are in a position to define population problems (development planners, demographers, physicians, ZPGers, public health cadres, urbanologists, muftis, propagandists, etc.) for the policy makers, make value laden definitions, the value content of which is not always apparent or admitted. Often, moreover, the perceivers, the definers, and the recommenders are the same persons.

The difficult ethical issues, as with the basic political issues, arise in the area of alternative solutions. Each society, each polity decides for itself which of all options available for the solution (including technological ones) are ethically and morally acceptable for itself. For example:

Does a particular policy threaten certain values held by a specific society?

Are human values associated with both ends and means taken into account by the legitimate organs of government?

Has the whole range of possible means been taken into account?

As we look at the real world, specific policy issues stem from various policy options which have built-in value implications. In some societies ethical dilemmas may pose serious obstacles for both the policy and the program — or at least raise issues of uncertainty. Thus, a specific policy response may either enhance or undermine national values. I am, therefore, suggesting that just as the anticipated effectiveness of possible policies must be made explicit, so must the values involved or called into question be made explicit. Ethical questions, like some political ones, deal with basic (sometimes ultimate) values, negotiable interests, social compromises, racial equities, group commitments, power relationships, etc.

Based upon the assumption that individual and social behavior — including especially human reproduction — is a function of the *total* life of a people, it is my belief that understanding the social/political/economic/cultural milieu in which people live (and reproduce) is absolutely necessary if acceptable and humane decisions are to be made in the policy sphere. As I have put it elsewhere:

In the years to come, desire on the part of governments to decrease fertility will continue to confront the human desire to reproduce, which is a driving force in the history of civilization, is basic to human nature, and is part of the law governing life itself. Population policy must reconcile the conflicting desire for reproduction with the absolute and sometimes immediate necessity for reduced fertility. Policy decisions will determine if, when, and how this will be done.[4]

The question of if, how, and to what extent a nation needs an explicit population policy cannot escape raising fundamental ethical/social/political/

cultural issues. This is true because such a policy confronts head on the total life of a people — on the individual level, matters of great human concern, and, collectively, matters relating to the common good and social justice.

For example, the pursuit of either a total, integrated population policy or a simple family-planning policy leads to national value structuring (consideration of alternatives) which in turn leads to or strongly suggests possible conflict in the process, for example, economic development vs. protection of large-family norms. Such a pursuit also forces a society to recognize and identify those values that are not negotiable or compromisable.

In addressing the issue of social change that will result in reduced fertility, Veatch writes,

Yet the question must be asked: At what point does advocating such changes for demographic purposes become manipulative? At what point does encouraging social change slide from the enhancement of social freedom to the manipulating of social behavior? Knowing what we do about the power of psycho-social pressures, how are such programs ethically different from physical coercion?[5]

That governments, like people, want to maximize all value preferences at the expense of none is obvious. Maximization may in the end be impossible. It may turn out that a nation will identify an uncompromisable value — e.g., national power, maintenance of church-state relations, etc. It is when value preferences are unclear, misunderstood, or in conflict that tension, even misjudgments, emerge. The point is that we often do not know or understand the social/political consequences of what we do — or do not do. Perhaps it is here that the political scientist has a unique role, by explaining or otherwise making more explicit ethical-*cum*-political concerns of the adviser, advocate, or maker of policy that otherwise may never be made clear. Population policy research and analysis undertaken by political scientists can, in particular:

Make explicit the value implications involved in the process being studied;

assess the degree to which conflicting values are held in a society;

assess how certain values are linked to other policies;

explain — or at least display — the difference between fundamental values and other tradeoffs;

sharpen the difference between basic values and socially expedient values;

help in giving direction to the role of policy in the resolution of social problems;

indicate the potential for the shifting of values over time;

probe, define, or otherwise sharpen the focus of the value implications of future policy alternatives.

More specificity will be found in the literature. These brief pages have tried to make clear that those who study policy as well as those who advocate and make policy cannot escape the recognition of one fundamental point: every policy issue has underlying ethical concerns. Political science is as well equipped to address these concerns as any other profession.

Notes

1. Daniel Callahan, *Abortion: Law, Choice and Morality* (New York: MacMillan Co., 1970); Daniel Callahan, *Ethics and Population Limitation,* an occasional paper of the Population Council, 1971; Arthur J. Dyck, "Population Policies and Ethical Acceptability," pp. 618-38 of National Academy of Sciences, *Rapid Population Growth: Consequences and Policy Implications* (Baltimore: Johns Hopkins Press, 1971); Leon R. Kass, "The New Biology: What Price Relieving Man's Estate?" *Science* 174, no. 4011 (19 November 1971): 779-88; Arnold S. Nash, "Some Thoughts on the Place of the Humanities in Population Studies," unpublished paper, Carolina Population Center, University of North Carolina, Chapel Hill, April 1971; John T. Noonan, Jr., ed., *The Morality of Abortion; Legal and Historical Perspectives* (Cambridge, Massachusetts: Harvard University Press, 1970); Commission on Population Growth and the American Future, *Population and the American Future* (Washington, D.C.: Government Printing Office, 1972), pts. I, II, III; Pierre Pradervand, "The Ideological Premises of Western Research in the Field of Population Policy," paper prepared for the African Population Conference, Accra, Ghana, December 1971; James V. Shall, *Human Dignity and Human Numbers* (New York: Alba House, 1971); "Toward the Year 2000: The Ultimate Goal of a Population Policy," *The Hastings Center Report,* Institute of Society, Ethics and the Life Sciences, no. 3, December 1971.

2. M. Brewster Smith, "Ethical Implications of Population Policies: A Psychologist's View," *American Psychologist* 27, no. 1 (January 1972): 11.

3. Daniel Callahan, "Ethics and Population Limitation," *Science* 175, no. 4021 (4 February 1972): 487.

4. Thomas C. Lyons, Jr., "Population Policies: A World Overview," paper presented at a seminar on population policy, University of Ife, Nigeria, March 1971, p. 28.

5. Robert M. Veatch, "Ethics, Population Policy, and Population Education," *Social Education* 36, no. 4 (April 1972): 364.

3

Political Science in Population Studies: A Disciplinary Perspective

Terry L. McCoy

Two of the principal questions examined by the chapters in part one are: Should political scientists study population, and what, if anything, does political science bring to the study of population that other disciplines do not? This essay approaches these two important questions from a perspective often ignored in the scramble to demonstrate the practical relevance of scholarly activities. It looks at political science in population studies in terms of benefits potentially accruing to the former discipline and then turns to the most effective way of reaping these rewards.

A strong implication of the question – Should political science study population? – is that we have moral and social obligations to tear ourselves away from our more arcane research to help solve one of the major problems of the contemporary era. This of course assumes a positive answer to the second question, that we as political scientists do indeed have something unique to offer the study of population which will facilitate solution of the various demographic problems allegedly plaguing humanity. Because there is a growing tendency to see population, especially population growth, as a political issue, specifically as a problem demanding government attention, political scientists are increasingly expected to apply their accumulated knowledge of politics and government to the problem in question.[1] In essence we are called upon to play the role of political engineers. Parenthetically, it is mildly disconcerting to realize that political science was neither called to action until the problem assumed crisis proportions nor did political scientists become aware of population as a political issue until others called it to our collective attention.

The purpose of this essay is not to deny the moral and social responsibilities of professional political scientists; rather it is to suggest additional disciplinary considerations for those contemplating study of population or any other contemporary problem. I do not pretend to speak for all political science but merely to suggest some of the implications of belonging to a discipline. Thus we shall first reexamine the question of whether political scientists should study population or not in terms of their responsibilities to the discipline of which

Some of the ideas in this essay were developed earlier in "Political Scientists as Problem-Solvers: The Case of Population," *Polity* 5, no. 2 (Winter 1972), pp. 250-59. The author would like to thank Randall Ripley and Donald Van Meter who made suggestions for the earlier article and the Mershon Center of the Ohio State University which has supported his research on population.

they are a part. In considering population related research, we suggest confrontation of a further question: What's in it for political science? Then we move to the task of translating professional and social concerns into valid research efforts. The contributions of political science to population studies and vice versa are hardly self-evident since their interface is so recent, yet the success of any research rests heavily upon definition and conceptualization. Therefore, after developing the case for disciplinary awareness in population studies, we shall explore how the unique contribution of political science might best be realized for the mutual benefit of all involved.

Population Studies and the Advancement of Political Science

The relationship between population studies and political science should be a symbiotic one. The role of problem solver is an accepted one within the social sciences. Political scientists should lend their talents to population studies in order that society better understand the causes and control of demographic trends. Applied research is both useful and a "partial repayment of society's investment in the educational and research enterprise," in the words of a national study of political science.[2] Nevertheless, another primary obligation of all professional social scientists is to advance their disciplines. We often overlook this responsibility in our eagerness to prove the social utility of our chosen profession, but as Eulau and March remind us, "The individual political scientist can serve his community or nation well if he serves well *the demands of his science.*"[3] And, in the final analysis, our value as problem solvers is only as strong as the discipline upon which it is based.

In order to appreciate the argument advanced here, it is necessary to understand the meaning of the term "discipline." In the context of this essay it refers to the body of general knowledge, concepts, and methods developed for interpreting a certain category of phenomena, in this case politics. At the heart of political science are the theories and other intellectual tools utilized to interpret political behavior. Without these tools political scientists would be reduced to particularistic, *ad hoc* explanations in dealing with specific problems. We would be social engineers operating without a scientific base. Therefore, in tackling the issues of the hour we must not only carefully use the theoretical, conceptual, and methodological resources of the discipline but also take advantage of such research opportunities to expand and enrich these resources in order to better confront future problems. How does current political science work on population rate according to this criterion?

Although still relatively new to population studies, political scientists after several years of priority funding are beginning to produce research on population related topics.[4] At best there is a conscientious, systematic attempt to bring existing tools to bear on facets of the population problem. For example,

Theodore Lowi adapts his general framework of public policy for purposes of interpreting the particular case of population policy in the United States.[5] At worst there are a number of atheoretical descriptive case studies which do not even call upon political science for explanation. In some instances the authors may not be political scientists, but interestingly the profession of the author is often not readily distinguishable due to minimum reference to existing knowledge. Neither type of study generates disciplinary payoffs. The Lowi-type effort uses political science but does not exploit population studies to in turn enrich the discipline. In this specific case the policy framework is not systematically improved through its application to population. Such studies do not confront the question, What will we know of a general nature as a result of the proposed work that we do not now know? The other type of research neither uses nor contributes to political science. In fact it is largely devoid of political science, focusing instead almost entirely on population which is ironically not where our expertise lies.

I would now like to suggest several guidelines for maximizing disciplinary inputs and outputs in population studies. First, be self-conscious about being a political scientist. Our training as social scientists is in politics not population. Clearly we must become aware of basic demographic theories and techniques, but we are called to population studies not as demographers but as political scientists. Therefore, we must concentrate on the political-governmental aspects of population issues using the tools of our discipline.

Second, select a research topic which complements your disciplinary training. There is no shortage of interesting unanswered questions about the interaction of politics and population.[6] The fundamental criteria for moving into population studies and choosing a specific topic, however, should be the individual's interests and training as a professional political scientist. Using these criteria he will be able to contribute more both to an understanding of the particular question and to the growth of his discipline.

Third, resist the temptation to engage always in research of immediate policy relevance. Our role as social scientists is to generate the information and theories for social decisions not to make these decisions. This is a mutually beneficial division of labor, and we should not be diverted from the task of building general knowledge about political behavior. Nor should we be misled into jumping from theoretical abstractions to policy prescriptions in every study undertaken. Sometimes this is justified, but there are many valid political science population research topics which are not of direct policy relevance at this time, although their contribution to the policy sciences' infrastructure is important, a fact that should be stressed in project proposals.

Fourth, in preparing a research project, carefully build in an explicit disciplinary feedback loop. Where does this study fit in the context of political science and how will it advance the discipline? Deliberate consideration of these questions not only fulfills disciplinary obligations but it avoids *ad hoc* reasoning in the particular case under consideration. In existing political science studies of population, one does not find many systematic linkages to studies in this narrow field much less to the larger field of political science. For example, there are various definitions and frameworks of population policy — not all developed by political scientists — that do not acknowledge each other's existence. We must become more self-consciously cumulative.

Having laid down some general rules for exploiting research opportunities in population studies, opportunities for which there is ample funding, we now turn to specific ways of slicing the population-politics pie. The framework proposed below is intended to suggest a logical and reciprocally productive approach for political science to take to population research.

The Political Science-Population Studies Interface

Myron Weiner coined the term "political demography" to refer to the study of the political aspects of population dynamics.[7] I shall begin by arguing that there is no such subfield in political science nor should there be, despite the would-be symmetry with allied disciplines. We as political scientists are not population experts. True, those of us interested in studying the political ramifications of population must devote some time to acquiring a working understanding of basic demographic concepts and theories. Otherwise our research is liable to be nonsensical and of little value to population studies. For instance, before launching an analysis of governmental population policies in the developing world, it is necessary to know something about the theory of demographic transition and the historical patterns of fertility decline in order to be aware that traditionally the government has played a minor role in controlling national fertility. This extra effort might be seen as the added price we pay for choosing to work with problems that transcend disciplinary lines. On the other hand, it can be viewed as another opportunity to expand political science since it is perhaps the most synthetic of the social sciences, drawing heavily from sister disciplines for its concepts, theories, and methods. Also the individual researcher stands to gain a broader perspective of his own discipline within the social science enterprise.

While acquiring some knowledge of demography is both necessary and an important supplement to one's primary training, it should not be an end in and of itself. We should not seek to carve out a new subfield of political demography. Professionally it represents a dead end for the individual, as the recent past has taught us that the life cycle of post-World War II controversies is not very long. In the 1960s political scientists and others were called upon to contribute to the "Civil Rights Cause," then the "War on Poverty," and finally the "Demographic-Ecological Crisis." But what happens to the political scientist who has dedicated his career to political demography after interest in, and research funding for, population problems decline? To maintain his expertise within the discipline, the individual researcher must approach population related topics through the existing subfields of political science. It is around them that knowledge about politics is, and will be, arranged.

It is now necessary to become more precise about kinds of population-related research which might appropriately be undertaken by political scientists. Table 3-1 contains a number of potential research topics based upon the intersection of population and politics as structured by accepted subdivisions of the discipline. Depending on how it is defined, "population" can include virtually all aspects of human behavior. As pursued by demographers, however, population research conveniently breaks down into questions regarding size, growth, distribution, and composition.[8] These standard demographic variables constitute the columns in Table 3-1. "Politics . . . refer to the activities of individuals and groups, from the family to the international organization, as they engage in collective decision."[9] Political scientists concern themselves primarily with the "public politics" of the state or government, leaving direct consideration of "private politics" to other social scientists. Therefore, our participation in population studies should be in terms of interpreting the interaction of population dynamics with public processes, structures, and policies. The nation-state is the dominant unit of collective decision making in contemporary politics, and although there is continual debate within the discipline, political science knowledge by and large falls into categories related to it. There are, then, political scientists and a political science literature focusing primarily on relations among nations (International Relations), others dealing with the nation-state as the level of analysis (American and Comparative Politics at the national level), others specializing in the political behavior of subnational entities, and finally those concentrating on the political behavior of individuals. These analytical distinctions, approximating levels of political interaction in the real world, constitute the rows in the table. The final organizing principle in Table 3-1 is the difference between politics as a dependent variable and politics as an independent variable *vis-à-vis* population dynamics. The top half of the table contains research topics dealing with the political consequences of the various demographic situations, while the bottom enumerates projects relevant to the impact of politics and government on population dynamics.

Each cell in the table contains two items. First, there is a suggested research topic for a political scientist in the subfield represented by the particular row. The list of topics is not exhaustive but hopefully indicative of relevant population-related questions and their fit in the discipline. Second, in parenthesis there is the further specification of the kind of research currently underway that is presently treating or might in the future consider such a question. It is a guide to help the population specialist locate his own interests in political science as well as a suggestion to those in these specialties that they might have already generated pertinent knowledge. Now let us briefly explore the interface to illustrate the potential for political science research in population studies.

Table 3-1
Political Science Research in Population Studies

		Population Studies			
		Size	Growth	Distribution	Composition
Political Science	International	World population, world resources and international conflict (Systems Analysis)	Differential growth and international conflict (International Relations Theory)	External migration and international conflict (IR Theory)	Economic and ethnic differences among nations (Peace Research)
Dependent	National	Aggregate demand structure and government (Public Administration)	Growth, economic development, and political unrest (Political Development)	Shifting population and political representation (Legislative Research)	Impact of age structure on government (Political Economics)
	Subnational	Size and party organization (Political Parties)	Reaction of organized groups to low or no growth (Interest Group Analysis)	Political behavior of migrant groups (Parties and Interest Groups)	Ethnic Politics (Political Development)
	Individual	The individual in mass societies (Political Psychology)	Clash of individual rights and social needs (Political Philosophy)	Density and individual political behavior (Political Psychology)	Voting behavior in an aging society (Voting and Public Opinion)

Political Science

Independent

International	External efforts to limit size (Linkage Politics)	International debate and assistance for population control (International Organizations)	International regulation of migration (International Law)	Efforts to lessen gap between rich and poor nations (Peace Research)
National	Foreign policy and size (Foreign Policy)	National growth policy (Policy Analysis)	Colonization and resettlement schemes (Developing Areas)	Internal protection and guarantees for minorities (Minority Research)
Subnational	Interest group activity to control size (Interest Group Analysis)	Private family planning efforts (Interest Groups)	Zoning laws (State and Local Government)	Pressure for differential birth control programs (Political Development)
Individual	Individual attitudes on size (Public Opinion)	Religious affiliation and policy attitudes (Public Opinion)	"Frontier Mentality" (Socialization)	Racial prejudice and policy attitudes (Public Opinion)

The effects of population on politics have been the object of much speculation but relatively little empirical analysis. At the international level, theorists and statesmen alike have long looked upon demographic variables as important determinants of war and peace. Traditionally they viewed large, growing populations as a source of national power, while at the same time differential growth and density were seen as threats to international order. A new school, reflecting concern with the world population explosion, stresses that internal cohesion and development — not increasing numbers — are conducive to success in the international arena. They cite Israel's military superiority in the Middle East as an example. The point is that international relations specialists need to evaluate empirically the relative significance of population variables in the constellation of forces affecting national power and international conflict.[10] In this evaluation they must also consider the impact of migration and distribution, both of which may be more disruptive than either size or growth. Finally, in dealing with the long-run prospects for world peace there are two demographically related phenomena deserving careful analysis: the consumption of nonrenewable resources as a function of demographic factors and the composition of world population with special attention to the gap between the rich and the poor. All of these issues plus others are important, *per se*, but in addition they offer political scientists the opportunity to expand their understanding of international relations.

At the national level recent preoccupation has been with the by now well-known developments of rapid population growth and massive rural-to-urban migration. The former or "population explosion" is most acute in the less developed nations, while the latter or "population implosion" is occurring on a worldwide basis, although somewhat more rapidly once again in the developing world. Specialists in political development, developing areas, and political conflict might well begin to incorporate demographic variables systematically into their analyses of political instability in Asia, Africa, and Latin America. Compared with data on the other independent variables, demographic data are widely available in interval form, and they are relatively reliable. As far as shifting internal population distribution is concerned, we already have some research for the United States done on the policy implications of legislative malapportionment and reapportionment.[11] Looking beyond the current problems of high growth and urbanization, political scientists should begin thinking about the political implications of low or no growth and rapid suburbanization. Analysis of recent fertility trends in the United States projects its population growth rate as approaching zero in the next several generations, while the predominant movement of population in developed societies in general is from center city to suburbs, a future trend perhaps facing developing countries. Such projections pose interesting questions for political scientists. What are the consequences for government of a stable, aging population? Can the interest-group specialist tell us anything about the probable reactions of groups geared to serving the young, such as school teachers and college professors, to a shift of public resources away from the young to the growing sector of retired and aging? Experts in subnational group behavior should also consider extending their research to the effects of suburbanization on political organization. To summarize then, since political scientists are already working at the national and subnational levels with demographic variables, it would be relatively easy and beneficial to expand and systematize research on population, being careful to consider past trends, present tendencies, and future projections.

Students of individual political behavior are already using certain kinds of demographic data to explain aspects of public opinion and political behavior. Relatively little attention has been given, however, to size, growth, and distribution variables such as density. Are people living in densely populated conditions more prone to antisocial political behavior? Or is the political behavior of a recent migrant influenced by the change in residence, itself, or by the demographic characteristics of the new residence? Once again incorporation of demographic variables would strengthen the explanatory power of the existing theory.

An apparent motivation for funding political research in population studies is the desire to strengthen the case for governmental action to control demographic developments. Hence, the concerned demographer and policy maker seek scholarly support for their intuitive feelings that uncontrolled growth causes political unrest and violence, for example. Frequently the ultimate objective is to involve the public sector in the manipulation of demographic variables through the formulation and implementation of official population policies and programs. Advocates of such policies look to political scientists for insights into the mobilization of political support and governmental action — at the international, national, subnational, and even individual levels — for fertility control and population redistribution. Political science provides such insights in some of the policy studies already underway.[12] While we political scientists can serve the specific problem-oriented interests of the population specialist or public official, our work should also contribute generally to policy analysis, a disciplinary activity intersecting all disciplinary subfields. The desired products, then, are public policy studies focusing on population and not simply case studies of population policy.

The impact of politics on population presents a variety of opportunities for illustrating and amplifying the operating principles of international relations. A particularly suitable topic would be "linkage politics" or the study of recurrent patterns of behavior originating in one system and producing reactions in another.[13] Preoccupation with population growth and efforts to control it are largely centered in the developed world but directed at the developing world, with international organizations increasingly playing intermediary roles. The developing nations themselves are primarily concerned not with population growth — certainly they do not perceive their growth as a threat to the rest of the world — but with narrowing the economic gap between themselves and the rich nations. They too turn to international organizations for assistance. We consequently have a complex of political linkages generated by population issues that invites investigation.[14]

As indicated above a number of national and subnational studies of population policy are currently underway.[15] For the future we need to venture beyond the "why country X did or did not enact a national family planning program" genre of research into more penetrating areas of policy research. First, there are important questions about policy implementation and impact. In general political science knows very little about, nor has it devoted much effort to the study of, the effects of government action. Instead, most policy analysis stops with expenditures, giving no attention to how the money was spent or to its impact. Analysis of population policy impact is particularly compelling since demographers disagree among themselves over the efficacy of the various approaches to the all-important question of fertility control. To be sure there are data and methodological obstacles. They are not insurmountable, however, and working them out would have payoffs not only for population studies but for policy analysis in general. A second, related area of needed research deals with the indirect and unintended consequences of policy and politics. There are a number of respected experts who argue that government population policies are relatively insignificant in determining demographic trends. Most governments do not have such policies, and, even where they do, other policies and factors are of more consequence, according to this school of thought. Therefore, in addition to determining the impact of population policies and programs, we must also, once again recognizing the methodological problems, consider the impact on population dynamics of nondemographic policies and nonpolicy variables. Do tax deductions for dependents encourage large families? Or, why do socialist countries have very low growth rates in spite of officially pronatalist policies? Finally, political scientists ought not restrict themselves to national growth policies. Issues of distribution and composition, while not currently subject to public concern, may be more troublesome for the political system in the long run. Students of state and local government have to understand the distributive consequences of differential welfare policies and municipal zoning laws in order to evaluate future policy options. Their research should include analysis of the political dynamics that shape current policies. In the study of black and ethnic politics, we are building the bases for interpreting the governmental actions affecting at least certain aspects of population composition.

We conclude our discussion of the impact of politics on population with reference to another type of linkage research — those studies linking the individual political actor to public policy. Increasingly political scientists are using public opinion, survey, and voting data to get at the complicated question of individual input into policy.[16] While not easy to measure, the Catholicism of Latin Americans and the "Frontier Mentality" of North Americans presumably affect governmental action in the population realm.[17] Once again the resolution of the methodological problems and theoretical puzzles posed by demographic policy would represent major disciplinary contributions.

Conclusion

Returning to the original questions addressed in this chapter, I will conclude that political scientists should indeed study population. In the first place, they do have something unique to offer population studies and public policy makers struggling to understand the effects of demographic developments on politics and the role of government in controlling these developments. But, secondly, population studies properly exploited have a great deal to offer political science. In analyzing the interaction of population and politics within the established disciplinary framework, political scientists can develop knowledge and methods relevant not only to the specific case but to the general interplay of environmental variables with politics. Research on the specific is always justified and desirable as long as it contributes to expansion of the general. With this as our primary objective we will be even more sought out as other social problems assume political proportions.

Notes

1. For example, see Lyle Saunders, "Action Needs: The Relevance of Political Research," pp. 1-14 of Richard L. Clinton, William S. Flash, and R. Kenneth Godwin, eds., *Political Science in Population Studies* (Lexington, Massachusetts: D.C. Heath and Company, 1972).

2. Heinz Eulau and James G. March, eds., *Political Science* (Englewood Cliffs, New Jersey: Prentice-Hall, Inc., 1969), p. 3.

3. Ibid. (Emphasis added.)

4. The following evaluation is based upon the author's personal familiarity with political science work in population, much of it still unpublished, which comes from working in the area since 1968 and attending and participating in conferences, workshops, panels, etc. As a critique it is in part autobiographical.

5. Theodore J. Lowi, "Population Policies and the American Political System," pp. 25-53 of Clinton, Flash, and Godwin (n. 1).

6. See for example the list prepared by the Population and Reproduction Grants Branch, Center for Population Research of the National Institute of Child Health and Human Development entitled "Political Aspects of Population, Family Planning, and Reproductive Research: Research Problem Areas and Research Ideas." The list of possible research topics is over five pages long.

7. Myron Weiner, "Political Demography: An Inquiry into the Political Consequences of Population Change," pp. 567-617 of National Academy of Sciences, *Rapid Population Growth: Consequences and Policy Implications* (Baltimore: Johns Hopkins Press, 1971).

8. Bernard Berelson, "Population Policy: Personal Notes," *Population Studies* 25, no. 2 (July, 1971): 173-82. Each of these broad topics is further subdivided so that there are demographers interested not only in growth, for example, but more specifically in mortality or fertility.

9. Eulau and March (n. 2), p. 14.

10. For examples of efforts currently underway, see A.F.K. Organski, et al, "The Effective Population in International Politics," pp. 79-100 of Clinton, Flash, and Godwin (n. 1), and Nazli Choucri, "Population Dynamics and International Violence: Propositions, Insights, Evidence," paper presented at the annual meeting of the American Political Science Association, Washington, D.C., September 1972.

11. Donald Stuart Van Meter, "The Policy Implications of State Legislative Reapportionment: A Longitudinal Analysis," Ph.D. dissertation, University of Wisconsin, Madison, 1972, summarizes this literature.

12. For examples of the variety of policy studies, see John Corwin Burt, "Decision Networks and the World Population Explosion: The UN and Institutional Innovation for Social Crisis," *Sage Professional Papers in International Studies,* 02-003 (1972); Elihu Bergman and William Flash, "The American Population Policy Process: Some Critical Insights," paper presented at the annual meeting of the American Political Science Association, Chicago, Illinois, September 7-11, 1971; Phyllis Tilson Piotrow, *World Population Crisis: The United States Response* (New York: Praeger, 1972); and Iêda Siqueira Wiarda, "Approaches and Strategies of Population Policy-Mongering in a Democratic Context: The Case of Venezuela," paper presented at the national meeting of the Latin American Studies Association, Austin, Texas, December 2-5, 1971.

13. James N. Rosenau, *Linkage Politics: Essays on the Convergence of National and International Systems* (New York: Free Press, 1969), p. 45.

14. Efforts in this direction include Burt and Piotrow (n. 12) and my own "Linkage Politics and Population Policy in Latin America" in *The Dynamics of Population Policy in Latin America* which I am editing (forthcoming).

15. In addition to the efforts mentioned in note 12, Pi-chao Chen, Aaron Segal, and I are co-authoring a comparative study of population policies in Asia, Africa, and Latin America entitled *Population and Politics in the Developing World* (Free Press, forthcoming).

16. For a recent example, see Richard W. Boyd, "Popular Control of Public Policy: A Normal Vote Analysis of the 1968 Election," *The American Political Science Review* 66, no. 2 (June 1972): 429-70.

17. The policy impact of Latin American Catholicism through individual believers remains questionable since strong Catholics do not differ from weak Catholics or non-Catholics in their reproductive behavior and attitudes toward family planning if other variables are controlled. Furthermore, many Catholics are unaware of, or disagree with, the church's position on contraception. McCoy in McCoy, Chen, and Segal (n. 15).

4

Political Values, Policy Making, and Problem Solving: Political Science Issues in Population Studies

A. E. Keir Nash

My purposes in this essay are three. The first is to venture a few prognostications about the effects upon political science and population studies which might well flow from a substantial investment by political scientists in population research. The second is to sketch out *some*[1] topics of research in population studies about which I suspect that political scientists — the johnny-come-latelys of social science to the area — may find fruitful contributions most readily forthcoming. The third is to hazard a few warnings about possible analytic pitfalls which might be encountered by political scientists as they enter this new substantive area.

Effects of Interactions between Political Science and Population Studies

While it may be a bit rash to predict a sufficient entry of political scientists into population research to affect significantly either domain of inquiry, it seems relatively safe to suggest that if effects are felt they will amount to "pushes" in rather different directions.

To appropriate William James briefly, one might sensibly guess that the major effect of political science in population studies would be to give a thrust toward the more "tender-minded" aspects of the latter domain. The most influential social scientists in setting the contours of population studies traditionally — demographers and population economists — have also been traditionally a good deal "tougher-minded," or if you prefer "harder-headed," than political scientists. Consequently, the "tender-minded" aspects of population analysis are the most neglected. And, in the absence of inrushing angels, political scientists appear the most likely foolish explorers of such tenuous ground.

The effect upon political science may well be more complex, since it would be felt during a time when the discipline is reconsidering the degree of its methodological commitment of the 1960s to behavioralism and beginning,

An earlier and briefer version of this essay was published as the concluding chapter of A.E. Keir Nash, ed. (for Commission on Population Growth and the American Future), *Governance and Population: The Governmental Implications of Population Change* (Washington, D.C.: Government Printing Office, 1972).

29

chiefly under the rubric of public policy, to eye an alternate future objective to "scientism."[2]

By its nature, "giving advice to princes" (for what is, after all, the study of public policy if not the democratic adaptation of that enterprise?) tends to highlight those questions of political values which the pursuit of political studies as science, in the nineteenth-century positivist sense of the word, tends to obliterate. I do not mean, of course, that public policy inevitably brings them out, nor that political scientism inevitably suppresses them — it is simply a question of tendency. Moreover, the suppression that occurs probably does so not because concern with all values is absent but rather because the concern is directed to values pertaining to the nature of the discipline itself, particularly to resolving favorably a dominating question — whether it is becoming "more scientific." The force of concern for this value may, indeed, produce odd results. Thus, when confronted with a nonpositivist view of science from a "respectable source," the political scientist may be led into an attempt to square the circle, to make the source's analysis "fit" the positivist mold. Consider, for example, the "proof" offered by Gabriel Almond on the occasion of his presidential address to the American Political Science Association that the discipline was "becoming a science,"[3] particularly the attempt to square the assertion with the thesis of Thomas S. Kuhn.[4] Almond argued, *inter alia*, "in the last decade or two the elements of a new, more surely scientific paradigm seem to be manifesting themselves rapidly. The core concept of this new approach is that of the political system."[5]

The phrase "more surely scientific paradigm" suggests that Almond's understanding of science is not Kuhn's. For Kuhn, one paradigm is not self-evidently "more scientific" than another. Rather, one paradigm replaces another because its explanatory capacity seems more pleasing to those who adopt it. In this view, there is nothing "finally and unassailably scientific" about natural science's paradigms, and the fact that many political scientists believe the contrary is probably the result of ingenous borrowing from other social sciences (in this case, the values of nineteenth-century sociology's Comtean positivism).

Such borrowed values and consequent circle squaring do not necessarily result in impeccable analytic geometry. Thus Almond's "proof" proceeded:

Let me first develop my theme by the back door, so to speak, through some comments on the sociology of political science, arguing that we are becoming a political science by inference from changes in the magnitude, structure, age distribution, and intellectual environment of the profession. . . . In 1903 the fledgling American Political Science Association numbered a little over 200 members. In 1934 there were 1,800 members of the Association; in 1944, 3,200; in 1954, 6,000; and in 1966, 15,000. The expectation is that the membership will exceed 20,000 in the 1970's. Our Washington office assures us that we are the most rapidly growing discipline in the social sciences.

This growth of the political science profession is primarily an American phenomenon. England has a few hundred members in its Political Studies

Association. Japan has a few hundred political scientists. There are a few hundred more on the European continent and in Asia, Africa, and Latin America. But nine out of every ten political scientists in the world today are American, and probably two out of every three political scientists who have ever lived are alive and practicing today.[6]

At the time, 1966, the proof might well have raised two questions in the mind of the less positivist — and less positive — skeptic. First, did similar growth in membership of the American Federation of Musicians suggest that playing the oboe was becoming a scientific profession? Second, how many natural sciences have displayed such "unbalanced 'one-country' growth"?

The next part of the "proof" might equally well have raised doubts as to how advanced was the scientific metamorphosis, if its degree of advancement be judged by the standard of predictive capacity. Thus: "Furthermore, the growth of departments of political science at a rate exceeding the capacities of our graduate schools to produce Ph.D.'s means that these young men are scarce, are in a seller's market, and are being promoted rapidly, and becoming chairmen and otherwise influential in the affairs of the profession."[7]

It would be rash to suggest that abortive predictions will — or should — entail the burial of the tendency toward favoring the procedural disciplinary values which seem to induce them. However, given the broad contemporary questioning of societal purposes, of which the postpluralist school in political science is a specific disciplinary manifestation, one may plausibly surmise that the larger American climate of opinion within which the study of politics takes place is likely to propel the alternate tendency toward substantive political values more to the foreground.

Equally, however, just as it would be imprudent to envisage a "naive return" to the regnancy of normative theory, as if the behavioral era had never existed and as if the tools of empirical analysis did not lie available for assisting the exploration of basically normative questions,[8] it would be rash to neglect the impetus which political science might receive along behavioral paths from increased attention to demographic studies.

This might occur for several reasons. The one I wish to single out here derives from the observation that if any two things have slowed the movement of political science toward becoming a "harder science"[9] they are: (1) the absence of convenient, thoroughly-agreed-upon, and certain base-units of analysis — such as a currency unit in classical economics or the atom in nineteenth-century chemistry; and (2) the circumstance that "empirical experiments" in political science have been typically *post hoc* and noniterative.[10]

For those who would make political science a "harder science," at least two components of demographic analysis may offer some hopeful potential when taken together. The first is simply "persons" — entities which, treated as demographers generally treat them, have fixed definitions, fixed countable limits, and clear attributes. There is, after all, something extraordinarily tidy about entities whose analytically salient characteristics are being born, marrying, moving, giving birth, divorcing, and dying. And if there are occasional grayer areas such as the ethnic affiliations of the offspring of mixed marriages, still the definitions and characteristics retain a sharpness all too often lacking in much of the contents of political science's conceptual kit-bag — e.g., terms such as power, political development, national integration, political efficacy, and so on. Of course, many political scientists are very well aware of this. Otherwise, they would be engaging in a most peculiar sort of enterprise when they ventured into survey research. But the point appears only when "persons" are conjoined with a second component of demographic analysis — the "projection."

What I have in mind is the potential fruitfulness of that "class"[11] of controlled futurist analysis represented, for example, in a piece by Richard Lehne, which appeared recently in a volume of research essays on politics and population published for the Commission on Population Growth and the American Future.[12] Such a class of "experiments" would be characterized by containing precise "base-units" measurable in cardinal fashion. In Lehne's paper, thus, he took Census Bureau population growth projections B and E, and coupling them with alternate population distribution projections done for the commission by Jerome Pickard,[13] attempted to analyze their import for the distribution of congressional constituencies in 1980, 1990, and 2000, and hence for the relative power in Congress of nonmetropolitan, center city, and suburban areas. Equally well, "experiments" of this sort might utilize other size projections, or various combinations of projections about migration rate, urbanization, ethnic distribution, age-cohort ratios, and so forth. Similarly, one might well imagine that the "other end" of things, the dependent political variables, could be handled in a rather more complex fashion than Lehne's variable of electoral districts. To be sure, at this juncture, one should admit that complexity is likely also to entail venturing into less well-controlled dependent variables — especially those common in the analysis of political opinion. Moreover, the temptation may be to proceed further in projection analysis than is obviously comfortable even with data which are quite "hard" when treated *post hoc,* for example, voting turnouts, court case dispositions, and so on.

But possibly "temptation" is the wrong word. Possibly what we should be thinking is rather "opportunity;" "opportunity" to attempt what political science should be attempting if it is indeed ever to be a "hard science" — attaining predictive capacity. It is not obvious that, with the possible exception of simulation,[14] a better current path is available toward that goal of prediction. Indeed, one might well argue that if empirical statistical studies of political attitudes or behavior are to be worth very many bean hills, then they should have some predictive capacity and should be tested accordingly.

In the absence of space limitations it would be possible to amplify considerably these observations. Here I shall have to rest simply having flagged them, and proceed to my next purpose — noting areas of inquiry in population studies which I suspect may come more naturally to political scientists as a group than to other social scientists longer engaged in the field.

Four Areas for Inquiry

In essence, I have in mind four areas for inquiry besides the one we have been discussing. The first pertains to the adequacy of value assumptions about the goals of "good" population policy typically made by decision makers and advisers active in formulating and executing such policy. The second centers around the question of whether the implications typically drawn from certain kinds of population analysis are in need of the circumscription that might follow from assessing them within a more consciously political framework. As I have argued elsewhere,[15] there are plausible grounds for believing that population studies and population policy in the United States are locked into mutually reinforcing patterns typified both by the failure to scrutinize value assumptions sufficiently and by an inability to relate population analysis adequately to the political process.

The third type of inquiry is delineated by the questions: (1) What are the comparative capacities of various polities for "problem solving" with respect to population matters; (2) What are the sources of the limits to these capacities in one political system as opposed to another; and (3) What are the prospects for change in the limits of such systems? The fourth type of inquiry pertains to improving the analytic utility of a number of demographic concepts which have thus far proved rather troublesome and in some instances almost unproductive in population studies.

Population policy is no exception to the rule that any policy advice rests both upon certain presumptions about the capacity of the political system within which the advised policy would be formulated, and upon a hierarchy of values whose order determines the desirability of the goals being sought through the policy. It is probably more common than not both that the explicitness and rank order of these values are fairly ill-defined and that policy debates tend to be characterized by a number of recurrent value terms forming, as it were, junctions of particularly troublesome disagreement. Typically, I would argue further, the troublesomeness results primarily from two factors: unclear and varying definitions of values, and failure to consider whether the value terms used are indeed really appropriate, given the political system's socio-economic environment and problem-solving capacity.

Any list of such troublesome value terms recurrent in population policy debates should surely include: "survival," "freedom," and "rationality." Of these, "survival," probably the most widely used in the population "agenda-building process,"[16] is intrinsically the least difficult as a concept. Its problematic quality in the population debate is, rather, a political one. Its troublesomeness derives, that is, from ambiguities arising in its political usage — ambiguities either deliberate and for purposes of political mobilization (or if you prefer, for purposes of propaganda[17]) or unintentional and simply the product of unclear thinking by its users.

The resultant confusions are two. One pertains to literalness of meaning; the other leaves unresolved the question of "with respect to whom?" That is to say, does the user really mean "survival" in the literal sense of the existence or nonexistence of the human species? Or does he, as frequently turns out on examination to be the case, really mean something more like "average life expectancy" in a particular country or region of such country? Second, about whose "survival" is he talking: his own, his generation's, his group's, his country's, his civilization's, his species'? In the long run, no individual and no generation survives. Moreover, countries and civilizations generally exhibit at least a strong proclivity in that uneternal direction sooner or later. Hence, the difficulties of "survival" as a political term in population policy debates are reducible to two questions. One is a futurist question about species survival which, though futurist, is still reducible to empirical evidence and to argument about that evidence. The other is a question about the extent to which in political practice as distinct from logic it is in fact so reducible. The former question is, to be sure, political in the sense that one may raise questions about the polity's capacity to produce results in the economy and society which bear satisfactorily upon the issue's resolution. However, it is not a question of political values and political language. Neither it nor the latter question constitute problems of intrinsic difficulty in terms of abstract debate about the meaning of political values.

The case is different with respect to the other two terms, "freedom" and "rationality." Of course, there is at least one grammatically similar aspect of the difficulty — the frequent absence of a clear, qualifying, "with respect to" clause. Just as one frequently needs to ask, "whose survival," one frequently needs to inquire, "whose freedom," "freedom with respect to what," and "rationality with respect to what." In grammar, however, the similarity ends; in both political theory and praxis, difference takes over. Let us examine this briefly.

Not infrequently one hears in discussions of optimal population policy, statements that we need population policies which would maximize freedom or which would increase the number of persons who can exercise "true freedom" in respect to reproductive behavior. Closely related to such statements are assertions about the desirability of "modernizing" or "rationalizing" sexual behavior. The two are used more or less interchangeably, and both appear to mean separating sexual enjoyment from childbearing entirely and without psychological or physical penalty.

Undeniably, there is something very attractive about propositions of this sort. They have much the same attractiveness as Adam Smith's eighteenth-century proposition in economics that the maximal public good is derived from individuals' unfettered pursuit of private gain, and much the same attractiveness as John Locke's seventeenth-century proposition in teleology and psychology that what man should do (God's will) was what man wanted to do anyhow (the pursuit of property).[18]

However, from the standpoint of political theory, and more broadly political science, attractiveness of this sort in which human telos and individualist psychology are equated is not necessarily sufficient justification. On the normative level, the question which immediately arises is: To what extent *should* freedom in this sphere be — as it apparently is — absolutized? To put it a bit differently, one might ask what is the appropriate rank order of this value — freedom in relation to procreation — with respect to other values which ought also to be furthered in the political order?

Of course, this sort of query about the ethics of population policy goals is not peculiarly a province of political theory but should be opened to the scrutiny of normative philosophical analysis generally. However, two propositions about the matter may clarify the particular relevance of normative political theory. The first proposition is that the study of politics, from one angle at least, is the study of the best distribution of scarce values. The second proposition is that the actual distributive characteristics of a political system, including its capacity for change in distributive patterns, place limits upon, and may even affect the normative prescription for, the "best order of values" which a particular population policy is designed to enhance.

Hence, it is at least arguable that a particularly mete concern for political science in population studies lies in the area demarcated by the question: Given the characteristic limits of a particular political system, what is optimal population policy? As Theodore Lowi has argued,[19] certain types of population policy may be judged better or worse not for their demographic or reproductive effects alone but also for their general political results, for the way in which they affect the capacity of a political system to deal with other stresses and strains placed upon it.

So too existing demographic and technological characteristics of a society may affect the population policy "situation" in unforeseen, if unexamined, ways. The point I have in mind is illustrated by adverting to the Holmesian adage: "My freedom to swing my fist stops at your chin." That freedom stops much sooner in a crowded subway than on unsettled plains. Moreover, the accommodations on the subway may vary the results, as may the handling characteristics of the train. Thus it is entirely possible that the carrying capacity of one sociopolitical system may require different population limits than would another. If, for instance, the Lockean American polity is as the postpluralists say,[20] one might sensibly analogize that polity to a "low wattage system" in which population characteristics play the role of "amps" and technology that of "volts." One may vary the amps and the volts, but their socioeconomic product may not exceed a given amount without running into a "crisis of governance" — that is, an incapacity of the political system to deliver the expected output.[21]

This, in a sense, is what the ecological hardliners are telling us is the case today. In their view, it is necessary to decrease certain kinds of freedom in order to maintain others. To permit one set of persons to do A, may be to prohibit another set from doing B. Hence, it is not necessarily "rational" to designate maximizing A as a "rational" goal for the polity if so doing can be shown to have such limiting effects on B. The fact of the matter is that, at present, we know too little along this line of conjecture to be able to make sensible judgments. This is another way of saying that the questions are inherently political — they are left to the distributional patterns of political power because they are irresoluble by policy logic.

The foregoing discussion implies what I earlier suggested as the second of four types of inquiry in which the approaches typical of political science might be useful — that framed by the question of whether a more self-consciously political framework is needed within which to draw properly the policy implications of various types of population analysis.

In the absence of such a framework, at least two "errors" in policy might result. One could stem from too much liberal optimism, an optimism assuming benefits without being sufficiently conscious of costs resulting from such policies. That, of course, describes the situation if — and let me emphasize, if — the postpluralist, or environmentalist, analyses of the results of maximizing "freedom" and reproductive "rationality" should be as accurate as each believes itself to be.

But equally, at least in a democracy, another type of policy "error" might result in the absence of an explicit political framework. It is one that would stem from the opposite sort of a "bias" — a conservative bias leading to overestimating the future's continuity with the past in regard to the nature of citizen desires and the performance of governments. I think one can see this rather clearly if one turns to projections of needed governmental services of the sort which, for instance, RAND did for the Population Commission.[22] Two population growth rates were projected — one with roughly 1 percent growth and the other stable except for immigration — and the two were then compared for expected governmental service demands generated by 1980 and 2000. Accordingly, RAND came to the conclusion with respect to education that by the latter year the higher population growth rate would require something on the order of $120 billion dollars annually more than the lower rate. Furthermore, the higher projection assumed an objective of merely sustaining present standards of education for some 93 percent of the population and an alternate "higher quality" education for only 7 percent. By contrast, the lower projection's cost assumed a "higher quality" education for everyone.[23]

Now it strikes me that a difficulty resides in this kind of projective enterprise. It assumes continuity of present and future on three counts. The first is with respect to the nature of citizens' expectations. Second, roughly the present balance between citizens' satisfactions and dissatisfactions with patterns of formulation and administration of governmental services is assumed to persist. Third, so too continuity is assumed with respect to citizen willingness to accept prevailing patterns of costs and benefits of tax burdens and service outputs. In my judgment this is an area where political scientists ought to be asking sticky questions because with a few exceptions, such as Joseph Spengler and Kenneth Boulding, most population economists seem to be fairly happy about assuming continuity on all these counts — at least in industrialized Western nations.

Similarly, I think we should be asking about three even more basic assumptions typically made at the outset of population economists' analyses. One assumption is that maximizing the nation's gross national product is a very important consideration in assessing the costs and benefits of various future rates of population growth and future patterns of migration and settlement. The second assumption is that at least as important if not more so is maximizing personal income. A third, and closely related, assumption is that the highest possible, or at least a very high, rate of technological innovation is to be preferred to a lower one.

My purpose here is not to argue that these assumptions will prove wrong, but merely to note that we cannot really be certain that they will prove right. They all depend, of course, very much upon a core contention of Western economics — a central proposition about the nature of economic rationality — which holds that the rational economic man maximizes his monetary gain relative to his preferences for work and leisure. In the instant situation of these three assumptions, however, the qualifying last clause is largely dropped.

Another way of stating this is to say that such projections assume a monotonic slope over time in the net of two groups of values. One group is best summed up as the values of affluent material existence. The other group is comprised by everything else. And the assumption is, further, that for the rational man the first group of values always overpowers the second.

The problem with these assumptions is of course that while the historical experiences of many industrializing and industrialized societies appear to bear them out, we do not really know whether they will continue to hold without major qualifications far into the future in postindustrial societies. Surely it is possible that besides a Third-World "revolution of rising expectations" we may encounter a postindustrial "revolution of changing expectations." Certainly it would be foolish to confidently forecast it. But it would be imprudent to overlook the possibilities suggested by the behavior patterns displayed over the past decade or so by increasing numbers of "children of the affluent." It is just possible that a point will come when the expectations of economic behavior on which such projections are based may prove in error.[24] The same may be said about the assumption of maximum rate of technological innovation. Possibly we will reach a point when something akin to "future shock," when "technological-innovation shock" is a manifest phenomenon of some psychological, and therefore of socioeconomic and political, import.

The point is, let me emphasize, not that we know that anything of the sort will happen, but rather that we do not — which is to say again that it is inherently a political question. It is political insofar as the essence of the question is that which comes into play when there is competition between goals and between the values upon which those goals rest.

Furthermore, there is an altogether different future possibility from that of "smoothly changing expectations"; this is a "cacophonic escalation of conflicting expectations." Thus, rather than (to give a specific instance from RAND's education projections) the citizenry being willing to spend 9 to 13 percent of the GNP on education and being willing to accept the educational results of such expenditures, there might be an increasing desire for "output" combined with a diminishing willingness to "put in." Or there might be increasing unwillingness for citizen set A to foot the bills for less fortunate citizen set B. Of course, again, it would be wildly audacious to predict such to the point of causing a breakdown in the political system. It amounts to a prediction that a whole people can become wildly unreasonable. Yet also, it would not do to overlook the possibility: Whole nations — for example, Nazi Germany — have managed something of the sort in this century.

In any event, the point here is to urge that one general area of inquiry for political scientists in population studies is study of the relationships between changes in citizen expectations engendered at least in party by demographic changes, on the one hand, and the capacity of different political systems to cope with such changes on the other hand. Changing patterns of prevailing ideology in political systems, for instance, may make certain areas of "coping" easier and others harder — whether by altering citizens' expectations or by allowing change in the problem-solving modes of the polity itself.

To urge that population studies are in need of the type of analysis which political scientists might be expected to bring to bear is not to suggest that useful fruits are likely to be easily produced. Besides the difficulties we have already discussed — residing both in the "softness" and "ill-definition" of a number of concepts in political science and in the consequent difficulty of making political projections within which to frame economic and demographic projections — there is another. It is a companion to the difficulty we have noted in regard to the prevailing usage of value concepts such as freedom and rationality. It is a question of the difficulty of certain concepts or standards of measurement intrinsic to population studies. They may not lend themselves easily to finding the relationships which are needed in order to sustain analytic linkages between population change and political change. Let me illustrate the point by one example — the concept of population density.

Population density is a concept frequently found in the popular literature on "crises in" population, the environment, and natural resources. Moreover, it is not uncommon to see extrapolations to human behavior from controlled studies in animal (particularly rat) behavior under crowded conditions. Yet, as Jonathan

Freedman has argued,[25] there are two distinct problems with such extrapolations. One is perhaps best summed up by the comment that "rats don't have politics." The other emerges from studies of human behavior in metropolitan settings of crowded living. On balance, the relationships between population density and rates of social pathology among humans are not, at least so far as these studies go, very impressive. When controlled for socioeconomic variables, measures of association between population density, on the one hand, and deviant behavior patterns such as crime, mental illness, and the like, on the other, tend to disappear, or at most in a few instances to remain rather weakly positive.

Results of this sort tend to make population specialists dubious of the import of density in affecting social or political behavior. From the standpoint of social or political analysis this is obviously rather disconcerting — inasmuch as it seems to violate the common sense of the matter. However, before concluding that such is simply so, we might argue that either one of two circumstances may be the case. The first is that, in fact, population density is not significantly related to socially pathological behavior. The other is that the fault lies in the concept or in its measurement. At least four possibilities present themselves with respect to the latter point.

First, it may be that too great crowding does lead to stress but that the relationship between the two is not described by a simple positive slope. Rather one might surmise that the relationship takes the form of a U-shaped curve with a very flat and wide bottom. That is to say, perhaps great extremes of crowding or dispersal are positively correlated with stress while in between lies a broad span of tolerance wherein no relationship is demonstrable.

Second, it may be that personality types vary in their tolerance of crowding or isolation. Hence, possibly, the optimal policy solution may be neither denser settlements nor general dispersal of settlements, but rather minimizing other sorts of "costs" (such as earning power) even while maximizing the choice open to individuals to choose preferred settlement patterns.

Third, it may be that stress arising from discrepancy between "actual" and "comfortable" space is intimately tied in with property. To take a trite example, someone who owns twenty suits and tries to fit them in one small closet may feel more stress than someone with six suits and the same closet. As in the second possibility, the "fit" may be more important than the absolute amount of space.

Fourth and finally, it may be that present measurements fail not only for these reasons but also because of a basic and double flaw in the standard measurement technique, which is to say, persons per square unit of residence area — for example, persons per square mile. There is in fact something peculiar about considering density as a two-dimensional measure anyhow. In the physical sciences, one would not normally seek to ascertain the density of a substance by measuring only the number of molecules contacting the bottom of its container.

In population studies, a two-dimensional measure leads, among other things, to ignoring the "layering" represented by multiple-storied buildings. Is there not indeed something equally funny about a measurement which produces the same quantitative results for two square miles in the same city, each with the same population, but one of which is characterized by three-story tenements and the other by thirty-story apartments capped by penthouses? So too we might surmise that distance between layers makes a difference: Who can doubt that five-foot ceilings would impose stress on most adults?

In addition to the question of whether density can be expected to prove a fruitful measure when calcualted on a two- rather than a three-dimensional basis, there is another question pertaining not to *how* but to *what* is measured. Population density measures are typically based on whole cities or on residential areas. But what does this lead to? It can lead to saying that two couples each with two children and each living in 600 square feet of residential space are experiencing the same density. Yet one couple may consist of an out-of-work husband, a pregnant wife, and two pre-school-age children living in Harlem. The other couple may consist of a junior partner in a Wall Street law firm, a wife in the junior league, and two children in private school. It is a bit much to expect satisfactory results from a density measure which obscures the circumstances that the latter couple's "real living space" includes the husband's offices which may be much less "densely occupied" than his apartment, the restaurants he frequents for business lunches, the first-class lounge of the DC-10 on which he flies to meet a client in Los Angeles, the sweeping snowy slopes at Aspen down which he and his family ski every January, and so on.

What these observations suggest, then, is that the fault may indeed lie in the measure itself — and that rather what is needed is a measure of "personal living space." "Felt density" is where one is and goes to, the "sum" of those places, not where one's bed stays.

Only when, to generalize, we can evolve wholly adequate measures of population characteristics, will it become feasible even to begin answering, in anything like definitive fashion, questions about whether such characteristics do indeed pose significant problems for a polity, if so in what ways, and what, if anything, can be done to cope with them.

Notes

1. Let me emphasize "some." The reader is referred also to Myron Weiner, "Political Demography," pp. 567-617 of National Academy of Sciences, *Rapid Population Growth* (Baltimore: Johns Hopkins Press, 1971).

2. "Scientism," or if you prefer "scientolatry," as distinct from "science." See D.R.G. Owen, *Man, Scientism, and Religion* (Philadelphia: Westminster Press, 1952).

3. Gabriel Almond, "Political Theory and Political Science," *American Political Science Review* 60, no. 4 (December 1966): 869-79.

4. Thomas S. Kuhn, *The Structure of Scientific Revolutions* (Chicago: University of Chicago Press, 1962).

5. Almond (n. 3), p. 369.

6. Ibid.

7. Ibid., p. 370.

8. For example, whether one or more aspects of a particular political system are as they "ought to be" — to the extent that the normative analyst is willing to bring to bear upon the answer such empirical data as the beliefs of members of that system.

9. Or alternately, if one prefers, a "science" at all. The circumstance that alternate formulations are plausible is — like the continuing general debate about the scientific status of the profession — itself a telling argument against the view that political science has yet entered a period of "normal science" with a clearly accepted analytic paradigm. I have yet to see a natural science which bothers to debate whether it is a science, or one which is unduly concerned about its autonomy from other fields. It is tempting to suggest four tests by which political science can short-circuit the debate over the "autonomy" and "scientificness" of the profession. It will be autonomous and scientific when: (1) conferences, panels, and symposia on the question of its autonomy as a discipline cease; (2) similar discussions about "Is political science a science?" come to an end; (3) members of the profession stop criticising each other as being either "unscientific" or "too scientific" (in the sciences, disputes involve other adjectives as epithets — "illogical," "unreasonable," "uneconomical," "unfruitful," "inelegant," "uninteresting," — but rarely "unscientific"); and (4) the formulation of hypotheses is typically made in language more lucid and more elegant than that of everyday speech. This last test suggests a specific question for those political scientists who believe that the "concept of the political system" is becoming the accepted paradigm which will usher in an era of "normal science." Compare Boyle's Law ($p_1 v_1 = p_2 v_2$) with the elegance and lucidity possible about the matter in everyday language. Then compare the elegance and lucidity of a statement in systems language with the same referent. Or for that matter, with the older mode of speaking about "government" and "governments" in presystems political science. See S.E. Finer, "Almond's Concept of the Political System: a Textual Critique," *Government and Opposition* 5 (1970): 3-21.

10. The latter, at least in part, surely because of the "reward structure" of the profession wherein rewards are far greater for "pregnant conceptual suggestions" and "one-shot hypothesis-testing" than for repeating someone else's "experiment." However much, in other words, the disciplinary ideology may have been "scientific," its "economic infra-structure" has not been so.

11. "Class" in the "mathematical" sense of the term. See Kuhn (n. 4) passim, for a discussion of "reasonableness," "economy" (elegance and lucidity?), and "fruitfulness" (in the sense of leading to further experiments) in choosing between competing conceptual schemes in natural science. See also James B. Conant, *Science and Common Sense* (New Haven: Yale University Press, 1951). Generally more helpful to social scientists than the standard social science tomes on the question of what scientific exploration presupposes and or what its procedure is really like are James Bryant Conant, ed., *Harvard Case Histories in Experimental Science* (Cambridge: Harvard University Press, 1950-53) — particularly Case 4, "The Atomic-Molecular Theory," by Leonard K Nash. Illustrative of present-day science's continuing rather messy procedures is Watson's account of his and Krick's race with Pauling to a model for the structure of deoxyribonucleic acid: James D. Watson, *The Double Helix* (New York: Athenaeus, 1968). Note particularly the role of chance in Watson's finding out the "correct" (keto rather than enol) tautomeric forms of guanine and thymine in the base pairs of the helix's core, p. 120 ff. It is sometimes tempting to caricature the difference between natural science and social science as: natural science, inelegant procedures and elegant results; social science elegant procedures and inelegant results.

12. Richard Lehne, "Population Change and Congressional Representation," pp. 83-98 of A.E. Keir Nash, ed. (for Commission on Population Growth and the American Future), *Governance and Population: The Governmental Implications of Population Change* (Washington: G.P.O., 1972).

13. Jerome P. Pickard, "U.S. Metropolitan Growth and Expansion 1970-2000, with Population Projections," in Sara Mills Mazie, ed. (for Commission on Population Growth and the American Future), *Population Distribution and Policy* (Washington: G.P.O., 1973).

14. May I emphasize "possible."

15. See A.E. Keir Nash, "Demographology in U.S. Population Politics," pp 71-94 of Richard L. Clinton and R. Kenneth Godwin, eds., *Research in the Politics of Population* (Lexington, Massachusetts: D.C. Heath and Company 1972); A.E. Keir Nash, "Population Growth and Politics in the United States," in *International Journal of Health Services* (special issue on "Population Growth in International Perspective," forthcoming, 1973); and A.E. Keir Nash, "Making the World Population Problem Safe for American Democracy? — AID, IUD, and the Political Thought of R.T. Ravenholt," paper presented at the annual meeting of the American Political Science Association, Washington, September 1972.

16. See Roger W. Cobb and Charles D. Elder, *Participation in American Politics: The Dynamics of Agenda-Building* (Boston: Allyn and Bacon, 1972) One wonders if "agenda building" — like "nation building" — might not imply too coherent a process.

17. See Frank Notestein, "Zero Population Growth: What Is It?", pp. 31-43

of Daniel Callahan, ed., *The American Population Debate* (New York: Anchor Books, 1971).

18. See particularly Locke's *Second Treatise on Civil Government.*

19. "Population Policies and the American Political System," pp. 283-302 of Nash (n. 12).

20. See A.E. Keir Nash, "Population, Federalism and Democratic Governance," and "Population and State and Local Problems of Governance," pp. 15-24 and 99-108, respectively, of Nash (n. 12).

21. Of course, it is important not to push such a metaphor too hard: so doing may be too recurrent a tendency of "systems analysis," itself after all really an extended metaphor. Nonetheless, in assessing the "system-maintenance" capacities of a particular polity, it is crucial to ask about the nature and degree of strains imposed upon it by the society and the economy. It is entirely possible that, for example, the "pragmatic" American system has — to many American political scientists, at least until recently — "looked good, like a pragmatic system should" because the strains it was "asked to deal with" were not very difficult to deal with. This might have been so both because the societal demands for change were not stridently voiced, and because — due to the Lockean consensus of old, the geographic situation, and the resource-to-population ratio — the changes sought did not fundamentally threaten the system's allocation pattern. The one major exception to this, of course, is the racial problem; and that single serious long-standing problem did — we perhaps too often overlook — shatter the political system in 1860-61. It may be, in short, that the American political system has looked capacious because, until 1945, it did not have to carry a political current of very many "amperes."

Let me note that, here and throughout this essay, I use the phrase "political system" simply as a convenient communicative symbol. Much of the argument over what is and what is not "in" the political system, the party system, or "whatever-you-have" system is silly. "System" is just a convenient mental construct imposed by the analyst upon certain pieces of evidence which interest him in order to create some kind of analytic order in his interpretation of that evidence. The system can be whatever the analyst individually chooses, and hopefully, others will agree with his resulting presentation and interpretation of evidence. Like the radical critic of society who speaks of "the system," the systems analyst too often tends to confuse three entities with each other: (1) his interpretive communication symbols about the evidence about the men; (2) the evidence about the men; and (3) the men.

It is possibly fair to say that political scientists too frequently are excessively optimistic in thinking that, unlike historians, they have "direct access" to the individuals they study — rather than just the evidence about, the tracks left by, those individuals. This seems to be a particularly strong illusion when we employ interview techniques. But — quite apart from the problem of closed-ended survey techniques, which by presetting the choice of responses, bar direct access — even the recordings of open-ended interviews, by the time the interviewer-analyst begins to draw upon them for his study, turn into selective evidence of — rather than, *the* — interviewee himself. Arguably, it does not help the "progress" of the discipline to slight this aspect of the problem of "other minds." Science recedes further the more the analyst grasps after an illusory objectivity.

22. See Jack Applemen, William P. Butz, David H. Greenberg, Paul L. Jordan, and Anthony H. Pascal, "Population Change and Public Resource Requirements: The Impact of Future United States Demographic Trends on Education, Welfare, and Health Care," in Elliott Morss and Ritchie Reed, eds. (for Commission on Population Growth and the American Future), *Economic Aspects of Population Change* (Washington: G.P.O., 1973).

23. It is of course another question whether the "higher quality education" projected by RAND — one emphasizing television aids parateachers and the like — will be so considered when the time arrives.

24. The point may be illuminated by a hypothetical question: Had extensive simulations or projections to the present been made circa 1945 of the British and French economies, how many would have predicted those economies' relative positions as of today?

25. See Jonathan L. Freedman, "Conceptualization and Crowding," and "Population Density, Juvenile Delinquency, and Mental Illness in New York City," in Mazie (n. 13).

5

The Whole-Systems Context of Population and Politics: A Normative Overview

William Ophuls

Population is not something that can be considered in isolation. Population problems are part of a larger environmental crisis that raises the broad question of how man is to survive upon a finite planet. Thus population has to be considered in relation to resources and general ecological constraints such as the limited tolerance of natural systems for toxic compounds, heat, and so on. In other words, population has to be considered in a whole-systems context. This is not, however, how it is done today. Demographers are specialists, and many political scientists who concern themselves with population problems are equally inclined to take a narrow view of their field — defining it, for example, as political demography. The fundamental tenet of human ecology is holism, and to make a meaningful contribution to either the advancement of knowledge or to public policy, scholars are going to have to be generalists who happen to have special interests in particular aspects of the whole rather than, as is the case today, specialists who occasionally consider some of the wider implications of their work.

The necessity for <u>holism</u> is quite frightening to the current generation of academics. Science and rationality of a certain type — based on the Baconian maxim *dissecare naturam,* Cartesian dualism, and Lockean empiricism — have become a species of social religion with us. Asking people to give up the narrow, reductionist, <u>*ceteris paribus*</u> approach is deeply threatening. It threatens our disciplines and the vested interest we have in our peculiar expertise. It threatens to move us from questions that are at least in principle knowable to regimes where certainty is probably not achievable (and thus from science as now defined to philosophy). We are only just beginning to develop the tools for even basic understanding of whole-systems behavior. It is no wonder that any attempt to point out the limitations of reductionist scientific methods provokes fears that we may be headed back to the Dark Ages. Yet we have no choice. We can no longer deal with our problems in a piecemeal fashion. Methodologically, existential need forces us in the direction of general systems theory and computer simulation if we wish to have either intellectual or policy relevance.

Holism will also require a new kind of social vision from us. Population specialists often seem to be remarkably unimaginative. A few honorable exceptions apart, they visualize a homogenous nation with identical 2.11 child families (the children all attending child-care centers so that mothers can have

45

careers just like fathers) as some kind of desirable and unquestioned goal. This is because they are focusing on population control alone in a *ceteris paribus* fashion. If they were to consider population in the context of human ecology (to say nothing of the wider implications of the sexual, social, and psychological consequences of the current nuclear family structure), then it seems to me that they would give much more consideration to the many alternative patterns of childrearing and family formation. What about extended, communal, or tribal families? What about making parenthood a paid profession for those that preferred (and were qualified) to make that their life work, with most of the population remaining childless? I am not pushing for any particular pattern. My aim is to open up a somewhat closed discussion. However, my belief is that both ecology and humanity tell us a wide measure of cultural pluralism, as opposed to monolithic homogeneity, is likely to be the most viable, stimulating, and healthy pattern. On this ground alone, I would not like to see the universal two-child family.

The need for imagination in population policy is underscored when we examine the wider implications of the environmental crisis, of which exponential population growth is only one aspect. The clear consensus among human ecologists and environmentalists is that neither merely technological solutions — even nuclear fusion and other yet-to-be-developed "technological fixes" — nor political reform measures like the National Environmental Protection Act, however beneficial, are sufficient to deal with the fundamental issues raised by the crisis. What is required is a revolution in values, a revolution great enough to overthrow the Enlightenment myths, such as unlimited progress, that underlie the current order. The required changes in our social mythology seem to be so great that almost all those who have seriously examined our problems believe Lynn White is right to say that we need in effect a new religion.[1] Speaking in more political terms, I am convinced that we are faced with a major political crisis. I do not believe that a set of political institutions operating under our assumptions and with our methods can avoid environmental catastrophe.

First, a look at our political methods. As is well known, our political decision making is disjointed and incremental in nature, and it proceeds by way of "partisan mutual adjustment," to use Lindblom's terminology.[2] Political actors acting primarily from self-interest (often a very narrow self-interest), consider only a few of the most intuitively obvious consequences of their policy proposals. They then bargain with actors representing other political interests who have arrived at their policy proposals in the same fashion, to get as much of what they want as they can get. Just as the "invisible hand" is said to regulate the economic market in a way that best allocates scarce resources, the result of partisan mutual adjustment is supposed to be the optimal distribution of political goods.

It is also well known that the political marketplace, like the economic, favors some people and interests over others. However, the human ecologist would not find this to be the crucial objection to our system. For him, the problem is that the biosphere operates under a very different set of rules, in which everything is connected to everything else and many of the most serious consequences of our actions are not intuitively obvious. You do one thing here, and with increasing frequency something surprising and unpleasant happens over there in a counterintuitive fashion. Herman Daly calls this the "invisible foot."[3] The biosphere is a whole system, and we are going to have to learn to play by its rules if we wish to survive.[4]

What this means in practical terms is that the era of partial or single-purpose or incremental decision making is almost over. Only holistic or what Lindblom calls "synoptic" analysis is adequate for environmental management. The practical difficulties of achieving this are enormous, but systems science, for all its faults up to the present, and the computer at least give us the theoretical capability for whole-systems analysis and management. The political difficulties, however, seem even more mind-boggling. If political values are not to be authoritatively allocated by a political marketplace, then how are they to be allocated?

A second problem with our political machinery is that it leaves out of the system of representation a major actor in human affairs — nature. Another fundamental principle of human ecology is that humanity is ultimately and absolutely dependent on nature. However, as things stand now, nature has no institutionalized voice in human affairs. A few persons, motivated by altruism or enlightened self-interest, may occasionally stand up for nature's interests, but there are many legal and procedural barriers, and typically only the rather narrowly defined interests of human beings are effectively represented in our political councils. The ecologist insists on the unity of all being, not in any mystical sense, but as a brute reality of life.[5] How do we make nature, which is part of our own being, a part of our polity as well?[6]

Turning to our political assumptions, let me focus on the problems raised by individualism as a dominant political and social principle. It is becoming widely recognized that the fundamental basis of many of our environmental problems resides in the disjuncture between collective goods and private decisions.[7] The argument has been made in its most provocative form by Garrett Hardin in an essay entitled "The Tragedy of the Commons."[8] Hardin argues that, in the absence of controls, men are driven by rational calculations of self-interest to overexploit or abuse the commons, whether it be a pasture shared by herdsmen or the earth's atmosphere. In Hardin's example, each herdsman will continue to add sheep to his fold, even when a finite common pasture land — a metaphor for the planetary life-support system humanity shares in common — can no longer tolerate any additional grazing without damage, because he gets all the benefit from the additional sheep while damage to the commons is parceled out among all users. But, of course, each herdsman reaches the same conclusion, and competitive overexploitation results in destruction of the commons. Thus "freedom in a commons brings ruin to all." Because there are no technological answers to this problem, says Hardin, we must establish stringent controls ("mutual coercion, mutually agreed upon") to escape the "remorseless working of things" produced by the logic of a free commons.

The fascinating — or should I say appalling? — thing about Hardin's analysis is that it resembles in every major feature that advanced by Thomas Hobbes in *Leviathan*. The "Tragedy of the Commons" is simply a version of the state of nature in which men, seeking gain but unable to agree on rules to protect the common interest, bring disaster on themselves. Hobbes and Hardin agree right down the line in their political analysis and in their prescriptions. For example, Hardin's conclusion that we must have "mutual coercion, mutually agreed upon by a majority of the people affected" describes exactly how Hobbes' sovereign is erected to keep the peace.

What Hobbes and Hardin both assert is that there is a tragic logic buried in the individual pursuit of happiness. We believe that politics should seek no higher values (for example, the good life, salvation, and so forth) than what we as individuals desire. Worse, our reigning epistemology reduces all statements about values to mere personal prejudices. But under current conditions, the aggregation of all our individual desires for children and worldly goods produces environmental degradation and, if current trends continue, eventual collapse. To preserve the commons or to achieve a peaceful commonwealth, a higher logic — one dedicated to the common interests of the whole — must prevail. The political philosophy of Locke, on which our institutions are based, rests on the unspoken assumption that the carrying capacity of the commons is infinite. As long as this is true, Locke works. Now, we have a large population with a high standard of living and a level of technology that can menace our life-support system. We have not yet reached the absolute overall limits, but we are beginning to press very hard against some of them and are rushing rapidly toward the rest. The Lockean system is therefore beginning to break down, and the time will shortly be upon us when people's individual desires will have to be restrained in the interests of the whole. This conclusion is not Hardin's alone but is implicit in virtually all the writings of environmentalists who have examined the requirements of "spaceship earth" or the "steady-state society." The only viable public philosophy is communal rather than individual.[9]

Thus both the American political machinery and the assumptions which underly it are called into question. This being the case, we are back — to use Daniel Bell's words — in an era of "pre-capitalist" modes of social thought in which market decision making will no longer work and in which the classic issues of politics must therefore be reargued.[10] So we as a people are going to have to decide what higher values we shall adopt and what machinery we shall institute for enforcing them. The most fundamental task of our era is to construct a new political philosophy, and it is only in this context that we can meaningfully discuss population policy.[11]

Notes

1. Lynn T. White, "The Historical Roots of Our Ecologic Crisis," *Science* 155 (10 March 1967): 1203-1207.

2. Charles E. Lindblom, *The Intelligence of Democracy* (New York: Free Press, 1965).

3. Herman E. Daly, "Toward a Stationary-State Economy," pp. 226-44 of John Harte and Robert H. Socolow, eds., *Patient Earth* (New York: Holt, Rinehart and Winston, 1971), p. 236.

4. Ian McHarg, *Design with Nature* (Garden City: Doubleday/Natural History Press, 1969), provides an excellent overview of the biosphere's essential rules. For a more detailed and authoritative description, see Eugene P. Odum, *Fundamentals of Ecology* (3rd ed.; Philadelphia: W.B. Saunders, 1971).

5. McHarg (n. 4), p. 117.

6. A first step in this direction might be the adoption of Justice William O. Douglas' position in his dissent on the Mineral King case (*World*, 4 July 1972): give legal personality and standing to voiceless "environmental objects," so that persons could sue in the public interest to uphold the rights of these natural objects against despoilation (instead of having to prove direct economic injury to themselves, as at present).

7. In addition to Daly (n. 3), Kenneth E. Boulding, E.J. Mishan, Edward Dolan, Thomas Schelling, William Kapp, and many others have pointed this out.

8. Garrett Hardin, "The Tragedy of the Commons," *Science* 162 (13 December 1968): 1243-48.

9. For a more detailed comparison of Hobbes and Hardin and a deeper exploration of the Hobbesian implications of the environmental crisis, see my "Leviathan or Oblivion?" pp. 215-30 of Herman E. Daly, ed., *Toward a Steady-State Economy* (San Francisco: W.H. Freeman, 1973).

10. Daniel Bell, "The Corporation and Society in the 1970's," *Public Interest*, no. 14 (Summer 1971): 32.

11. For fuller treatment of the issues above, see my "Prologue to a Political Theory of the Steady State: An Investigation of the Political and Philosophical Implications of the Environmental Crisis," Ph.D. dissertation, Department of Political Science, Yale University, 1973.

6
Population, Politics, and Political Science

*To create a more equal allotment of
property and of rights throughout
the world is the greatest task which
confronts those who lead human affairs.*

Alexis de Tocqueville

Richard Lee Clinton

As noted in the preface, the author of the final chapter in each part of this volume is expected to reflect on the other chapters included in the section, responding selectively to the ideas that had been introduced, attempting to discern any patterns among them, and assaying some reasoned judgment as to the directions indicated for future research.

For three reasons I must preface this discussion of my colleagues' chapters by explaining in some detail how I view contemporary population problems and how I perceive both politics and the discipline of political science intersecting with them. It is a truism that the way one perceives a problem will have a great deal to do with how one chooses to set about solving it. Similarly, the seriousness attributed to a problem will influence the priority assigned to resolving it. It is less well recognized perhaps, although equally obvious upon reflection, that the perceived seriousness of a problem will have an effect on the ethical acceptability of the means considered for implementing solutions.[1] Hence, in a book on population and politics, and particularly in a section dealing explicitly with normative, that is, value, aspects of these questions, it would not do to merely suggest these basic determinants of my value position, although to specify them is to burden the reader with a rather personal and highly complex explication.

My thanks to R. Kenneth Godwin for his comments on an earlier draft of this essay. Had I followed his advice more closely this would have been a far shorter, less involved, and probably more successful exercise.

Portions of this chapter were presented at the Symposium on Afro-Asian World in Transition at North Carolina Central University, April 12-13, 1973, as "The Population Problem in the Third World" and will appear in the published proceedings of that conference.

Population

To begin to understand the nature of population dynamics[2] is to begin to see that the global problem of rapid population growth is not just a temporary imbalance which will shortly be corrected.[3] It is also to recognize that ultimately the solutions to present-day population problems lie in the realm of politics.

This is not the place to describe the characteristics of the modern population explosion or to detail the deleterious effects which rapid population growth can entail for developmental processes, tasks which have been well handled by others.[4] Let me simply ask the reader to reflect for a moment on the information summarized in Table 6-1, pondering in particular the implications of the doubling times inherent in present population growth rates for the efforts to improve the quality of life of human beings around the world. While the doubling times are shortest in the areas of greatest poverty and least productive capacity, thus multiplying the difficulties involved in raising the standard of

Table 6-1
Summary Population Data for Major World Regions

	1972 Population (millions)	Population Growth Rate (% p.a.)	Number Years to Double Population
World	3,782*	2.0	35
Africa	364	2.6	27
Asia	2,154	2.3	30
Latin America	300	2.8	25
Oceania	20	2.0	35
North America	231	1.1	63
Europe	469	0.7	99
USSR	248	0.9	77

Source: Population Reference Bureau, *1972 World Population Data Sheet.*

*Total reflects United Nations adjustments for discrepancies in international migration data.

living of the majority of the human race to some minimally acceptable level, the somewhat slower doubling of population in the more affluent areas can present even more serious problems in terms of resource depletion and environmental deterioration for the planet as a whole. Few slogans convey more truth than the one which asserts that "population is everybody's problem."

Given the universal acceptance of the desirability of lower mortality, in combination with the increasingly effective means of implementing that goal, it should be clear that the force which has precipitated the current worldwide population explosion — declining mortality — is a force that will be with us for as far ahead as projections can reasonably be carried. Certainly there will be areas where mortality will remain high for some time to come, and there will also be areas in which mortality rates, having fallen, will rise again due to particular local conditions. But on the whole, especially in the less advantaged countries where population growth rates are highest and two-thirds of the world's population resides, the tendency for mortality rates to decline will continue into the foreseeable future for the same reasons they have been dropping in the recent past. Perhaps the two most powerful of these reasons are that (1) being high there is considerable potential for their lowering and (2) some of the principal means employed in bringing them down can be implemented by relatively few *for* the many, with little change in the customs or habits or values of the latter being necessary. The classic examples of such means are, of course, public health measures such as water treatment, sewage disposal, mosquito eradication, vaccination campaigns, and the introduction of elementary hygiene.

Continued high fertility, the other force which in combination with declining mortality is responsible for the unparalleled contemporary expansion of population, is also a force that among the less advantaged two-thirds of the world's population will persist far into the future. Such an assertion can be demonstrated by brief reference to the cultural, economic, physiological, and political contexts of today's population explosion.

Even a cursory examination of women's roles and the mechanisms by which status is acquired reveals that most of the cultures of the world are profoundly pronatalist. This is not surprising since cultures are the product of man's interaction with his environment over long periods of time, and for most of man's one-or-two-million-year history high mortality rates made it essential to the survival of the species that birth rates also be high. While, as Polgar and others have pointed out[5], a variety of practices have been employed since prehistoric times to keep the overall numbers of human populations below the biological maximum of reproduction, nevertheless cultural institutions evolved to assure that birth rates would remain in excess of death rates. The problem is the tenacity with which such pronatalist cultural institutions and values persist and the slowness with which they can be modified. In particular the fact that changes in such deep-seated and pervasive values have to be made by the individuals who hold them and cannot be made *for* them makes the process of affecting fertility vastly more complicated and problematic than the process of affecting mortality.

Just as importantly, the economic functions performed by children in the less advantaged areas of the world are such that it would be foolish to expect parents in these areas to limit the size of their families to any great extent in the absence of functional equivalents for the contributions traditionally made by children. For example, it is obvious that in a subsistence-farming situation children begin to provide useful services soon after they are able to walk — running errands, watching younger children, tending animals, and so forth. Often these services are of little importance in themselves except that somebody has to do them and if they can become the responsibility of the younger children then the parents and older children are freed for more productive pursuits. Equally obvious are the ways a large family, especially one with many sons, provides a measure of security for all its members in the event of the incapacitation through illness or accident of any one of them. Similarly, the tradition of care of aged or disabled parents by their children is usually the only way people in most parts of the world can expect to be looked after once their productive years are behind them. Is it rational to expect the masses of the low-income areas to voluntarily reduce their fertility when no surrogates for these vital needs are available? Emphatically it is not, particularly when infant mortality rates remain so high that to have only a few children is to risk having none survive to maturity.

Thus it would appear that the proponents of making family planning clinics accessible to everyone, while to be praised for the humanitarian benefits which would surely result from such an accomplishment, are misguided if they believe that a policy along these lines would bring an end to the population explosion. Certainly universal access to family planning facilities is a noble goal and one to be pursued vigorously. Certainly many women around the world would welcome the opportunity to learn how to space and limit the births of their children and would voluntarily adopt contraceptive practices once they were introduced to them. There can be no question of the benefits of family planning programs for the individuals involved, nor of the practicality of making such programs the first step toward more comprehensive population policies. What I deem unfortunate and misguided is the apparent tendency of many to believe (1) that such programs constitute the major ingredient of adequate population policies and (2) that such programs will suffice to bring population growth rates down to acceptable levels.[6]

One of the principal assumptions underlying these beliefs is that the motivation to have fewer children already exists or can be fairly easily generated through propaganda, educational outreach, and/or incentive programs. While this assumption is doubtless valid in many areas and up to a point, it does not hold in many other areas or beyond certain points. In other words, it might well apply to marginal families in the urban slums of the Third World to the extent that these families have more than three or four children. It has little applicability, however, to subsistence-farming families in rural areas, almost regardless of how many children they have, or in many cases to many middle- and upper-class families in the affluent as well as in the less advantaged countries.[7]

A central confusion in the current population debate, then, is the tendency to assume that enough people around the world want sufficiently fewer children to make population stabilization possible, given universal access to modern means of family planning. A particularly pernicious variant of this unsound assumption manifests itself among those who have placed their faith in a purely technological solution to the problem of excessive population growth.[8] For them the problem is reduced to the comfortingly manageable one of discovering a still cheaper, more effective, and less difficult-to-take contraceptive, preferably with fewer or no possibilities of harmful side effects. The inventor of such a contraceptive will presumably find the women of the world beating a path to his door. The fallaciousness of the family-planning-as-sufficient position is set in bold relief by this technological approach, for the history of the demographic transition[9] has unambiguously demonstrated that the crucial prerequisite to fertility decline is not contraceptive availability but motivation to have fewer children. Where the motivation exists, as in France in the nineteenth century, the absence of modern contraceptive technology does not prevent a decline in fertility from occurring.[10] In the absence of motivation for fewer children, on the other hand, the accessibility of effective means of contraception becomes irrelevant, as our own extended postwar baby boom conclusively proved. In terms of the search for solutions, therefore, the core of the population problem is how to generalize the motivation to have small families.

Three Approaches

Occasionally in the course of the population debate it has been suggested that the motivational problem can be outflanked by administering contraceptive chemicals to entire populations, for instance, by treating the water supply or essentials such as salt which could be distributed through a state monopoly. Such a suggestion, whatever else it reflects, denotes enormous naïveté, both physiologically and politically. Researchers in the field of reproductive physiology agree that the development of temporary sterilants which could be safely ingested not only by both men and women but also by children and animals — all of whom might be exposed to them if they were disseminated indiscriminately — is not even on the horizon.[11] Among the many other strictly technical obstacles such a product would have to surmount would be how to circumvent the dangers inherent in differential dosages, since people's intake of water, salt, and so forth vary widely. On the political side, in addition to the fallacy of assuming that the political systems of the high-fertility areas provide public services such as water treatment to all or even to the majority of their populations, this suggested course of action epitomizes the sort of "proposals for coercive population policies which could cause a nation's government to fall much faster than its birth rate."[12] Moreover, such a proposal seems to assume that many if not most of the governments of the high-fertility areas are in favor of limiting the growth of their populations. Thus the lack of motivation on the part of the masses to have small families is implicitly compensated for by the motivation of governments to limit population growth. Yet few governments can be shown to have even a tenuous commitment to reducing the rate of growth of their populations. As one long-time participant in the population field has recently observed, "Among the twenty-five or so countries that have explicit national policies and active government programs there is probably not one in which political commitment is sufficiently strong or sufficiently widespread to provide an effort consonant with the magnitude of the task of changing the reproductive behavior of a substantial segment of the population."[13]

Another approach to the motivational problem has emphasized education of the illiterate masses of the Third World to inform them of the many advantages inherent in small families both for the individual family and for the nation or the world at large. One can be very much in favor of education of all kinds and still admit to misgivings as to the potential impact on fertility of such an approach unaccompanied by much wider efforts. In the first place, many of the alleged advantages to individual families are probably more apparent in theory than in practice unless other conditions are changed, and, at any rate, the masses in the high-fertility areas will have to be *shown*, not told, that such advantages exist — they have been exploited too long and too consistently by those in more privileged positions to take on faith any advice from these sectors. In the second place, it is doubtful whether any sector of any society would modify its reproductive behavior on the basis of appeals to the national good or world betterment, and certainly it is unreasonable to expect the most disadvantaged sectors to do so. Not only do they have more immediate problems to contend with, but in addition they have the least to gain from promoting the so-called collective good and thereby preserving the present inequitable distribution of the social advantage.[14] This reasoning applies equally to (1) the impoverished and marginalized masses of the Third World *vis-à-vis* their respective political systems, (2) the low-income countries *vis-à-vis* efforts by the wealthier nations to establish international controls for environmental protection, and (3) the discriminated-against minorities which form pockets of poverty and high fertility within the advantaged nations *vis-à-vis* these nations' attempts to deal with problems of environmental quality.

If making family planning facilities available cannot be relied upon because of its neglect of the motivational problem, and if neither the universally-applied-fertility-control-agent approach nor the education-regarding-the-advantages-of-smaller-families approach to the motivational problem seems promising, then perhaps a wider strategy for altering the family-size motivations of whole populations should be considered, one based on altering the conditions which give rise to the motivations regarding family size.

In dealing with the economic context of the population explosion, I noted that children in the less advantaged areas, particularly within the subsistence-farming patterns of existence which dominate in those regions, perform a wide variety of useful services for the family unit. Elsewhere I have tried to indicate how important these services can be for urban middle class families as well under the conditions of inflation, monetary instability, scarce credit, distrust, and unpredictability which characterize Third-World economies.[15] The point I wish to draw out here is that while some of the services performed by children for their parents are merely useful, others under the conditions prevailing in most of the Third World are indispensable. As specialists from many different fields have documented, numerous progeny are the most common form of disability and old-age insurance. Moreover, anthropologists assure us that there is an intricate but direct relationship in most cultures between number of offspring, particularly males, and the status afforded parents, especially mothers. Finally, demographic research has demonstrated time and again that declines in fertility rates are invariably preceded by declines in infant mortality, yet infant mortality rates remain appallingly high in most of the low-income countries. Until they can be fairly sure that the children born to them will survive to adulthood, Third World parents are not likely to risk limiting the number of births they have.

Politics

These three sets of insights into the determinants of high fertility in the less advantaged areas should afford us adequate grasp of the problem to see how unreasonable it is to expect parents in these areas to embrace family planning and small-family norms simply because the means are made available and the ends extolled. Lacking functional equivalents for the services previously provided by their children, in the absence of increased socioeconomic mobility and wider opportunities for women to achieve status, and under circumstances which make significant declines in infant mortality impossible, rational people do not strive for two- and three-child families.

The implications of this line of reasoning for population policy development should be clear. In order for the motivation for small families to be generalized, conditions must be created which make such motivations rational. This means, *inter alia,* that nutritional levels and health care, especially maternal-child health services, must be dramatically improved; that workable forms of social security must be devised to cover entire populations, not just privileged minorities; and that opportunities for education and employment must be created and made available to young women as well as young men.

How can all this be accomplished? In asking this question we are unmistakably confronted by the interface of population and politics. In point of fact we have been in the realm of politics from the moment we began discussing how the motivational enigma might be resolved, for any programs affecting entire populations in ways such as those we discussed — involuntary mass sterilization, public education, creating functional equivalents for the services traditionally provided by children, and so forth — presuppose political means of implementation if not of selection of those means.

To recognize that in seeking viable solutions to the population explosion we are perforce in the realm of politics is itself a first step toward those solutions, for at least we can begin to see how far off target previous efforts have been and where future efforts must be concentrated. The insights into the determinants of high fertility described above make it plain that only sweeping changes in the living conditions and opportunity structures of the masses of the Third World will suffice to alter their family-size motivations sufficiently to make population stabilization a realistic possibility for the twenty-first century. Unquestionably governments are the only feasible mechanisms for bringing about such sweeping changes, although admittedly the likelihood of their making the attempt, much less of their succeeding, is open to serious question.

The means of effecting these sweeping changes will naturally vary from one set of circumstances to another, but the programs adopted will have to address the sorts of matters referred to above, that is improved coverage of health services (probably through extensive reliance on paramedical personnel), creation of social security and care-for-the-aged systems acceptable to the masses (probably through community centers of some kind, perhaps combining them with day-care centers for children), and vastly expanded opportunities for productive employment outside the home for both men and women (probably through labor-intensive agriculture and industries). Before governments can begin initiating such programs, however, at least on anything approaching an adequate scale, three prerequisites would have to be met. In the first place, key elites would have to have a much more adequate recognition of, and substantially greater agreement on, the true magnitude of the population problem and the role of motivation therein than now seems to be the case in any country. Lacking such recognition and relative consensus, it is doubtful that there would be sufficient sense of urgency to justify the necessary programs. Secondly, top priority would have to be given to attacking the problem. Among other things this would mean that other policies and goals would have to be reviewed in terms of their effects on fertility motivations, and some otherwise acceptable programs might have to be modified or postponed. Since the conditions being fostered in the attempt to influence motivations toward small families are so consistently in the direction of enhancing human well-being, it is unlikely that the delay in implementing any of the programs which would have to be held in abeyance would cause widespread hardship. Third, the government would have to be strong enough to resist the objections and weather the opposition of vested interests whose budgetary appropriations and other perquisites will decline as scarce revenues are shifted in line with the new priorities.

Given that key elites are too busy to study population dynamics and, at any rate, are too divided by class, party, and ideological conflicts to agree on hardly anything — particularly when experts themselves are rarely in agreement — the changes that prerequisite number one will be met are not encouraging. In the absence of the sense of urgency which only the elites could galvanize into action, there is no possibility that prerequisite number two could be fulfilled. And in countries where the component parts of government are themselves powerful and voracious vested interests, it is hardly reasonable to expect "the government" to enshrine the general welfare as the principal criterion of public policy.

The hopelessness inspired by this dismal perspective may explain in part the present hyperactivity on the family planning front by most of the population establishment — by focusing on the number of new clinics opened and acceptors serviced, at least they can feel they are accomplishing *something*. One cannot but wonder if another part of the explanation for the continued emphasis on family planning by the major population groups might not lie where their critics often say it is[16] — in their desire not to alter in any significant way the present distribution of the social advantage. This is a serious accusation, entailing the charge that uncompromisingly pro-*status quo* biases are consciously held by many of the dedicated individuals who constitute the population establishment. If the crux of the problem is motivation, as I have been arguing, then it is easy to understand how the persistent and exclusive insistence on family planning on the part of these influential groups leads many to such conclusions. To be fair, however, I would note the possibility that those groups are operating on the practical assumption that such a limited approach is the best that can be implemented under present conditions.

A Critique

Reasoning from entirely different premises, I seem to have reached conclusions basically consistent with those of the many Third-World intellectuals who insist that development, not programs of population limitation, is the answer to their problem of rapid population growth. This coincidence is unfortunate since for many it will make the ideological neutrality — at least in terms of the major ideological blocs — of my position suspect. While a careful reexamination of my argument should demonstrate its empirical as opposed to ideological underpinnings,[17] perhaps a brief critique of the ideological approach would further contribute to clarifying the distinction between it and the position I have been advancing.

There are two principal ideological sources for the antipopulation limitation outlook prevalent among Third-World intellectuals (and the many who pretend to that status in those areas or identify with it in other areas): Marxist thought and anti-imperialism. Marx, perhaps because he recognized that Malthusian insights could undermine crucial aspects of his theorizing,[18] rejected out of hand the idea that population problems could be other than epiphenomena of capitalistic forms of economic, political, and social organization. The anti-imperialist perspective complements Marxist theories nicely, as Lenin discovered, and in terms of present-day population problems the two strains of thought are not only compatible but profoundly mutually reinforcing. In the first place, the anti-imperialist point of view assures that the motives of advantaged countries in their dealings with less advantaged countries are always interpreted in the worst possible light. Moreover, it provides a compelling rationale for why the former would be interested in limiting the population growth of the latter. Since the essence of imperialism is the exploitation of the weaker by the stronger, it is deemed self-evident that the latter will try to prevent any gains in the power of the former. The fact that this argument is grounded on the simplistic and fallacy-laden formula "more people equal more power"[19] seems to detract very little from its wide appeal. A somewhat more sophisticated variant of this rationale focuses on the industrialized nations' need for the primary materials of the less advantaged areas.[20] On this view it is maintained that the "center" states seek to limit the population growth of the "periphery" countries so that growing internal consumption of resources in the latter will not interfere with the export of resources to the former. This formulation of the argument, although flawed by a perhaps exaggerated image of the extent to which the industrialized countries really depend on the raw materials of the less advantaged areas, is probably not entirely wrong and at any rate is widely accepted in the Third World.

The result of the Marxist and anti-imperialist orientation of large segments of, perhaps most, Third-World intellectuals is that foreign assistance in the area of population limitation is decried as an imperialist plot. Unfortunately, as usually happens in ideological disputes, the dogmatism with which this position is espoused leads to serious distortions of perception. From asserting that population growth is not *the* problem of their struggling areas, the exponents of the anti-imperialist line come to insist that population growth is not *a* problem. They ignore the uniqueness of present population trends and overlook the intimate interaction between demographic variables and the process of development.[21] Or worse, they recognize these interactions but refuse to admit to them in hopes that the pressures of rapid population growth, by exposing the contradictions of the capitalist system, will hasten the onset of revolution. Not only does such a strategy rest on the extremely shakey assumption that malnourished, ignorant, and hopeless masses submerged in an animal-like struggle for each day's subsistence are the stuff of which revolutions are made, it reveals a callous willingness to sacrifice countless innocent lives — mostly of children — for the chance to achieve an uncertain future. It also neglects to consider how much more difficult the future would be, even were the revolution to triumph, after a decade or more of continued rapid population growth.

Political Science

My view of how the population explosion in the less advantaged areas should be attacked, then, while similar to that of many Third-World intellectuals, is, I hope, broader than theirs, although it is closer to theirs than to that of the established population agencies. I see current population trends in most of the low-incomes countries as inimical to their present half-hearted efforts to significantly improve the quality of life of their peoples. I reject the argument that economic growth can proceed at a fast enough pace to outstrip population growth to such an extent that the demographic transition which the industrialized countries have experienced will be repeated in the rest of the world. I am convinced that only wide-ranging and profound changes in the basic economic, political, and social structures of the low-income countries *in conjunction with* crash programs of population limitation (propaganda/advertising/education regarding the need for and advantages of small families plus accessible family planning clinics offering abortion and sterilization in addition to contraception plus incentives[22] where appropriate) can bring down population growth rates in the high-fertility areas enough to make population stabilization on a worldwide basis even remotely possible before the end of the twenty-first century. I am equally certain that only through political means can such sweeping changes be effected.

To date two models of such political means with potential generalizability to other low-income, high-fertility countries have been devised and to the extent possible proven successful: that of Taiwan (the Republic of China) — and a similar program in South Korea — and that of the People's Republic of China. Taiwan has had an authoritarian, procapitalist regime; mainland China an authoritarian, Communist government. Taiwan has received massive amounts of foreign aid, including population limitation assistance; mainland China has eschewed foreign aid of all kinds. Taiwan, with only 15 million people as compared with mainland China's nearly 800 million, now has the further marked advantages of having a per capita income more than three times greater than China's and almost three times higher a percentage of its population in an urban environment (cities of over 100,000).

It does not require very great familiarity with the conditions prevailing in most low-income countries nor with the realities of the foreign-assistance programs of the wealthier nations to realize that the Chinese Communist model is the more likely of the two to be generalized. It seems to me that if such a prospect concerns us, we — particularly those of us who have made a profession of the study of politics — should be investing much greater efforts than is currently the case in discovering alternative models of development consonant with the realities of the less advantaged countries.

Given the necessity of substituting labor for capital, any workable alternative to the Chinese model would doubtless also require a high degree of political mobilization, but does that necessarily entail excessive regimentation? Can the sense of dignity and purpose and individual worth so essential to effective mobilization be instilled without reliance on xenophobia, chauvinism, and fear? Are strict controls on the free flow of ideas and information and a conditioned-reflex orthodoxy unavoidable concomitants of rapid political mobilization, or can masses be mobilized in an atmosphere of freedom to know the weaknesses as well as the strengths of their form of political organization and the costly mistakes as well as the accomplishments of their specific government? Is it possible to have the centralized planning and control required for total mobilization and an all-out assault on the root causes of undernourishment, poor health, low productivity, and high fertility without having a self-perpetuating authoritarian regime? Can such monumental undertakings be carried out in accordance with clearly articulated principles of justice and equity and with the participation of the people in decision making, or at least in selection of leaders and priorities, or are these matters as important to full human development as some of us in the West believe?

These are the kinds of questions which, it seems to me, should be of highest priority at least for a significant sector of professional students of politics. Although not lacking in empirical dimensions, they are in no small degree normative questions.

For those of us who wish to see these and related matters occupy a more central position on the agenda of political science research, some encouragement can be derived from the increased attention to the political realities of the less advantaged countries which has resulted from the vogue experienced by the comparative politics subfield during the past decade. Similarly, the post-behavioral trend some have discerned,[23] with its heightened concern for policy analysis and explicitly normative issues, is a welcome sign.

The emergence of the new subfield of political development and the prospect of renewed interest in normative political theory, however, do not imply that the sorts of questions alluded to above will necessarily be dealt with in either a major or a meaningful way by political scientists. The overall orientation of the discipline will continue to be the decisive factor in determining whether these kinds of questions will be asked.[24] Seen in this light the outlook is none too bright, for the three ills which have increasingly plagued all the social sciences in recent times — overspecialization, the emphasis on quantitative analysis, and the premium on the construction of general theories analogous to the laws of the physical sciences — give no indication of abatement. As we continue to know more and more about less and less, as fascination with the neatness and rigor of mathematical manipulations of data leads us to investigate topics for which quantitative data are available or can be generated rather than subjects of substantive importance, as our "physics envy"[25] compels us to strive for general theories of politics even though we have yet to explain adequately most individual political phenomena, there would seem to be scant likelihood that much insight will be gained into the types of questions I raised above. Not only will the reward structures of the profession continue to militate against research of this nature, the training and socialization of new generations of political scientists will tend to inhibit if not practically preclude it.[26]

This is so because to contribute to the design of realistic new models of development demands a certain vision, and such vision is not developed by overspecialization in some narrowly defined and sharply delimited corner of knowledge or by mastering sophisticated methodological techniques — valuable as these things may be in other respects. As used here, vision, like Weber's *Verstehen,* is a uniquely human capacity made up of, but more than the combination of, such elements as: (1) knowledge of as many forms of social organization as possible, their strengths, weaknesses, and fatal flaws; (2) insight into human needs, both physical and psychological; (3) sensitivity to the philosophical and ethical dimensions of human existence; (4) familiarity with the historical and cultural milieu and empathy with the people of the place where the model might be applied.

Those who would seek to expand their vision in order to make a contribution in this area must have a high tolerance for ambiguity, uncertainty, indeterminateness, frustration, and, at times, despair. They must recognize that not only are there no simple answers to many of the questions they will have to ask, often there are no answers at all — or at least no way of knowing whether any particular ones are right or wrong. This means that their self-image as scientists — as professionals dedicated to furthering our knowledge and understanding of some area of experience — must make allowances for the infinite complexity of the subject they have chosen to study; they cannot allow themselves to be constrained by definitions of what constitutes scientific activity in other areas of human endeavor, even though they may be borrowing information, techniques, insights, and inspiration from these other areas.

All this is not asked of the discipline of political science as a whole. What must be asked, however, indeed demanded, of it is that the tendency to establish discipline-wide orthodoxies of approaches, procedures, and areas of inquiry not be allowed to prevail. As Thorson has convincingly argued, "we are rationally obligated to behave as if we are limited with respect to knowledge of matters of fact because we *are* so limited. The examination of our own tools of analysis reveals the limitations."[27] As regards the procedures of scientific investigation, the rule he deduces from this finding is simply "Do not block the way of inquiry." Such a categorical imperative applies especially well, it seems to me, to a field such as political science and most particularly to value-laden subfields such as political development, policy analysis, and the politics of population.

Reflections on Directions

To summarize the foregoing account of my perspective on the population problem and the role of both politics and political science therein, I would list the following more or less empirical considerations: (1) the explosive growth of population is one of the most serious problems facing mankind; (2) there are no simple or short-term solutions to the problem (other than drastic increases in mortality, e.g., through famine, plagues, or war); (3) at the heart of the problem are the family-size motivations of individuals; (4) these motivations are largely a rational response to the conditions of life of the individuals (although there is often considerable lag in adjusting them to changes in these conditions); (5) only by improving these conditions, e.g., living standards and opportunity structures, can small-family norms become widely generalized (as functional equivalents are provided for the services and status traditionally supplied by children); (6) only governments are in a position to effect the sweeping changes required if the living conditions of the masses are to be improved (and, of course, even governments may prove inadequate to the task); (7) the Chinese Communists have thus far provided the most successful model for rapid improvement of the living conditions of an underdeveloped population along with encouragement of small-family norms; (8) a major challenge for political science is to assist in devising alternative models of development which can accomplish these ends without the sacrifice of freedoms essential to full human development (such as freedom of thought and expression, the right to know what is happening in other countries and in other parts of one's own country, and the right of effective participation in the choice of leaders and priorities); (9) the likelihood of substantial attention being given these problems by political scientists is not good (given the obsession with making political science a science on the model of physics or chemistry and the disciplinary reward structures this generates); (10) if these broad, value-laden, policy-relevant problems are to receive attention by political scientists, the tendencies to establish disciplinary orthodoxies as to which research areas and which types of approaches are legitimate for political science must be resisted.

These considerations set the stage for my discussion of the preceding chapters on normative concerns in the politics of population. Without these indications of my particular way of perceiving population, politics, and political science, the following remarks would lack context and might well prove unintelligible.

My own normative assessment of rapid population growth as a problem stems from two value orientations: (1) rapid population growth is a major obstacle (note, however, I do not say *the* major obstacle) to providing all human beings with the necessities for a human, as opposed to an animal-like, existence, which I believe they, as human beings, are entitled to; and (2) unless all human beings enjoy a human level of existence, there is little possibility of enlisting their cooperation in the struggle to prevent ecological imbalances with negative implications for the quality of life on this planet and at some point for the planet's life-support system.

I am fully aware of the problems involved in using terms such as "a human existence," and I am equally aware that the possibility exists of meeting ecological challenges through authoritarian as opposed to cooperative measures and that it is a value preference on my part that I consider the latter to be the means worth striving for. I hope to deal with these matters in detail someday, but here I simply want to make clear that two separate but complementary value orientations are involved. The first, that a human existence is due all human beings, has long been the basis of the rhetorical goals of governments around the world. Little serious commitment on the part of governments has been generated using the first value orientation, which after all assumes something akin to altruism on the part of those whose responsibility it is to implement it, so perhaps the second value orientation should be brought into service since its implementation would be in the self-interest of the implementors. Indeed, I would argue that it is in our own self-interest to see that it *is* brought into service.

It would seem to me, therefore, that in discussing the normative aspects of population and politics and the role of political science therein, the following categories of questions would warrant attention: (1) how can political science research contribute to improved understanding on the part of policy makers, opinion leaders, and mass publics of the necessity for, and urgency of, government involvement in population matters now considered beyond the proper limits of governmental activity? (For example, how could the sphere of acceptability of different population policy measures be expanded?); (2) how can political science research help to clarify the implications of alternative policies so that greater consensus on the priorities and goals of public policy might be promoted? (For example, how can revenue needs be calculated for alternative population futures?); (3) how can political science research demonstrate the areas of our value systems and political institutions where change is essential if effective responses to environmental challenges are to be forthcoming? (For example, how can a value system which exalts individualism be modified to include community needs in conflict with individual preferences or rights? How can anachronistic and increasingly counterproductive concepts such as national sovereignty and historically determined political boundaries be replaced by more functional modes of political organization? How can arms races be ended so resources can be freed for use in development and pollution control?); (4) how can political science as a discipline be convinced of the need to maintain an open perspective as to what constitutes legitimate areas of investigation and acceptable approaches to improved understanding? (For example, how can the discipline's training and socialization of its new members instill an appreciation for the unique instead of *exclusive* emphasis on the general as the proper domain of social science? for understanding instead of prediction as the goal of social science? for viewing the social sciences "as systems of reasoned communication but not exclusively as empirical sciences"[28] so that the larger questions of human experience can become central to the social sciences rather than at the periphery as has largely been the case in recent times?)

Are these sorts of questions raised in the preceding chapters? William Ophuls grapples solidly with aspects of number three and number four as he exposes the inadequacy of our partisan-mutual-adjustment form of political decision making, the absence of institutionalized access to our political councils for natural phenomena threatened by human abuse, "the tragic logic" inherent in the individual-centered assumptions which underlie our political thinking, and the way "our reigning epistemology reduces all statements about values to mere personal prejudices." Indeed, he poses the primordial challenge to political science clearly and succinctly when he concludes that "The most fundamental task of our era is to construct a new political philosophy . . . ."

Keir Nash comes to grips with some of the kinds of issues common to my second category when he asks for clarification of the rank order of values such as "freedom in relation to procreation — with respect to other values which ought also to be furthered in the political order." In asking how "the characteristic limits of a particular political system" put limits on population policy development, he is in the bailiwick of my third category, and he treads the uncertain ground of category four when he suggests that "the discipline is reconsidering the degree of its methodological commitment of the 1960s to behavioralism and beginning, chiefly under the rubric of public policy, to eye an alternate future objective to 'scientism.' "

Thomas Lyons, by noting that we must recognize that we cannot maximize all our value preferences, also deals with the need mentioned in my second category for establishing priorities for public policy. His plea that political scientists not shun population policy questions because they inevitably contain ethical/moral dimensions relates to my fourth category.

Terry McCoy's chapter is directed primarily toward the issues of my fourth category of normative concerns in the politics of population — that is, the role of the discipline. His perspective on the questions raised by this issue, however, differs markedly from my own. While he in principle agrees that "political scientists should lend their talents to population studies in order that society better understand the causes and control of demographic trends," his chapter emphasizes that advancing the discipline is the only really legitimate way in which this can be accomplished since "in the final analysis, our value as problem solvers is only as strong as the discipline upon which it is based."

Because McCoy's chapter is a tightly reasoned statement of what I would say is the dominant attitude within the discipline on this matter,[29] I would like to examine his assumptions in some detail. Perhaps the most important assumption underlying his position is that population problems are not really all that serious.[30] Another important assumption seems to be that left to its own devices the discipline will get around to population-relevant research in due course,[31] that is, by extending its theories to include demographic variables. While the first assumption seems to overlook the complexities I have spent the greater part of this chapter in describing, the second assumption tends to exaggerate the strengths of the discipline and gloss over its weaknesses. For instance, he criticizes the authors of case studies on population policy for their "minimum reference to existing knowledge" as if there were some worth referring to, yet at a later point he admits that "in general political science knows very little about nor has it devoted much effort to the study of the effects of government action."

Fundamentally McCoy and I differ on the long-debated issue of knowledge for knowledge's sake vs. useful knowledge, that is, on basic vs. applied research. He would have political science pursue research as dictated by the state of theory building in the discipline; I would prefer it give priority to issues of compelling current importance in the real world. He would insist that the specific be studied only if it promises to contribute to the expansion of general theories, whereas I applaud the expansion of knowledge itself, however unconnected with what we already know, if that knowledge can help us approach a pressing problem in a more rational manner. He would have us "resist the temptation to engage always in research of immediate policy relevance" and to refrain from making policy prescriptions; I would wonder who, if not professional political scientists, could be expected to concern themselves in a relatively disinterested way with the sort of research policy makers need if they are to make informed and rational decisions in the public interest.

Let me say, although I'm sure it will go unnoticed by those for whom my arguments are most objectionable, that I recognize the merit in McCoy's desire for a discipline more firmly grounded in coherent theory. I share that desire completely. I am far less sanguine than he, however, regarding the likelihood of our substantially fulfilling that desire in the near or even near-distant future. I am not, therefore, prepared to postpone giving whatever benefit our discipline can provide in helping to resolve current problems, particularly when the problems are as serious as those facing the world today. I applaud the efforts of those in the discipline who pursue theory-based research instead of policy-relevant research, and I continue to hope that the two will become increasingly supportive of one another. My plea is that those who choose the former course of action not disparage or seek to discourage the less lofty efforts of those of us whose allegiance to disciplinary progress is outweighed by our concern for immediately useful knowledge.

Only one of the four areas I mentioned above as deserving of attention in a discussion of the normative aspects of population and politics and the role of political science therein failed to be considered by any of the contributors to this section: category one ("how can political science research contribute to improved understanding on the part of policy makers, opinion leaders, and mass publics of the necessity for, and urgency of, government involvement in population matters now considered beyond the proper limits of governmental activity?"). I am not surprised that this topic was neglected, for it was evident at the conference which preceded the writing of these chapters that, even among this exceptionally well-informed group, there was no consensus on the urgent need for priority attention by elites, mass publics, and governments to the implications of rapid population expansion. I confess that I am unable to explain this almost complete lack of any sense of urgency. I can only conjecture that ecological insights have not yet had time to influence the thinking of these busy specialists, with the very notable exception of William Ophuls who has succeeded in directly incorporating them into his specialty.

Without a sense of urgency regarding the need for concerted attention to population growth and the implications it holds for frustrating both developmental efforts and coordinated attempts to avoid ecological imbalance and to improve the quality of life, the question raised in my first category makes little sense. I am afraid it will continue to be looked upon by most political scientists as somehow not relevant to their areas of special competence until a series of disasters involving hideous loss of human life has forced them to reconsider the relationships between population, politics, and political science.

Notes

1. This point is made with specific reference to population problems in *Ethics, Population and the American Tradition: A Study Prepared for the Commission on Population Growth and the American Future* (Hastings-on-Hudson, New York: Institute of Society, Ethics, and the Life Sciences, ca. 1971), pp. 154-59.

2. A good introduction to population dynamics can be gleaned from Ansley J. Coale, "How a Population Ages or Grows Younger," pp. 47-58 of Ronald Freedman, ed., *Population: The Vital Revolution* (Garden City, New York: Doubleday and Company, 1964); Ronald Freedman, "Norms for Family Size in Underdeveloped Areas," *Proceedings* of the Royal Society 159 (1963): 220-34; and David Heer, "Economic Development and the Fertility Transition," *Daedalus* 97, no. 2 (Spring 1968): 447-62.

3. In some industrialized countries, including recently the United States, fertility rates have declined to levels which, if maintained, would result in zero population growth within two or three generations. There is no way of knowing, however, whether fertility in these countries will continue at or below replacement level for the length of time necessary to achieve population stabilization. Moreover, these countries contain less than a third of the population of the planet.

4. Two brief but comprehensive treatments of those subjects are John D. Durand, "The Modern Expansion of World Population," *Proceedings* of the American Philosophical Society 3, no. 3 (June 22, 1967): 136-59; and Richard A. Easterlin, "Effects of Population Growth on the Economic Development of Developing Countries," *The Annals* of the American Academy of Political and Social Science 369 (January 1967): 98-108.

5. Steven Polgar, "Population History and Population Policies from an Anthropological Perspective," *Current Anthropology* 13, no. 2 (April 1972): 203-11.

6. The noted demographers Kingsley Davis and Judith Blake are among the most trenchant critics of these tendencies. See the now classic articles: Kingsley Davis, "Population Policy: Will Current Programs Succeed?" *Science* 158, no. 3802 (10 November 1967): 730-39; and Judith Blake, "Population Policy for Americans: Is the Government Being Misled?" *Science* 164, no. 3879 (2 May 1969): 522-29.

7. Judith Blake, to whom I am indebted for her arguments regarding the importance of family-size motivations, has dealt explicitly with the non-economic utilities of offspring to parents in postindustrial societies. See, for instance, her "Demographic Science and the Redirection of Population Policy," *Journal of Chronic Diseases* 18 (1965): 1181-1200, and "Reproductive Motivation and Population Policy," *Bio-Science* 21, no. 5 (March 1, 1971): 215-20.

8. For a particularly perceptive discussion of this point see Beryl L. Crowe, "The Tragedy of the Commons Revisited," *Science* 166, no. 3909 (28 November 1969): 1103-1107.

9. A clear discussion of this crucial concept may be found in George J. Stolnitz, "The Demographic Transition: From High to Low Birth Rates and Death Rates," pp. 30-46 of Ronald Freedman, ed., *Population: The Vital Revolution* (Garden City, New York: Doubleday and Company, Inc., 1964).

10. There are, of course, a number of methods of fertility control which have been used for centuries and which are still relied upon in many parts of the world, e.g., coitus interruptus, postcoital douche, prolonged lactation, enforced abstinence, abortion, and infanticide.

11. See, for instance, the remarks of Dr. M.C. Shelesnyak at the Smithsonian Institution's Conference on Factors with Impact on the Formulation of Population Policy, Belmont Conference Center, December 3-5, 1972, the edited proceedings of which will appear in 1973.

12. Moye W. Freymann, "Foreword," pp. xiii-xiv of Richard L. Clinton and R. Kenneth Godwin, eds., *Research in the Politics of Population* (Lexington, Massachusetts: D.C. Heath and Company, 1972), p. xiii.

13. Lyle Saunders, "Action Needs: The Relevance of Political Research," pp. 1-14 of Richard L. Clinton, William S. Flash, and R. Kenneth Godwin, eds., *Political Science in Population Studies* (Lexington, Massachusetts: D.C. Heath and Company, 1972), p. 7.

14. "Distribution of the social advantage" is a concept borrowed from Neil W. Chamberlain, *Beyond Malthus: Population and Power* (New York and London: Basic Books, 1970), pp. 16-20 and passim.

15. Richard Lee Clinton, "Opposition to Population Limitation in Latin

America: Some Implications for U.S. Policy," pp. 95-112 of Clinton and Godwin (n. 12), pp. 104-105.

16. Most critics of the population-family planning establishment are unabashedly ideological in their approach, e.g., William Barclay, Joseph Enright, and Reid T. Reynolds, "Population Control in the Third World," *North American Congress on Latin America Newsletter* 4, no. 8 (December 1970): 1-18. A more balanced and much better researched critique may be found in Peter Bachrach and Elihu Bergman, *Power and Choice: Formulation of American Population Policy* (Lexington, Massachusetts: D.C. Heath and Company, 1973).

17. I do not mean to imply that my argument is in any sense value-free, only that it is nonideological.

18. On this point, see the stimulating analyses of William Petersen, "Marx vs. Malthus: The Men and the Symbols," *Population Review* 1, no. 2 (July 1957): 21-32, reprinted in his book *The Politics of Population* (Garden City, New York: Doubleday and Company, 1965); and Herman E. Daly, "A Marxian-Malthusian View of Poverty and Development," *Population Studies* 25, no. 1 (March 1971), pp. 25-37.

19. For a more acceptable alternative to this formula, see the concept of "effective population" elaborated by A.F.K. Organski, Bruce Bueno de Mesquita, and Alan Lamborn, "The Effective Population in International Politics," pp. 79-100 of Clinton, Flash, and Godwin (n. 13).

20. A representative example of this genre is Heather Dean, "Scarce Resources: The Dynamic of American Imperialism," pp. 139-54 of K.T. Fann and D.C. Hodges, eds., *Readings in U.S. Imperialism* (Boston: Porter Sargent Publisher, 1971).

21. Such critics also overlook "that motives for, and consequences of, actions need have little relationship." David Chaplin, "Introduction: The Population Problem in Latin America," pp. 1-22 of David Chaplin, ed. *Population Policies and Growth in Latin America* (Lexington, Massachusetts: D.C. Heath and Company, 1971), p. 6. See also Chaplin's chapter in this volume.

22. Incentives can play an especially important role in family planning programs in countries where mortality rates are falling rapidly, for there is often a considerable lag in the perception of the drop in mortality, hence people continue to conceive offspring on the mistaken assumption that several will die before reaching adulthood.

23. See George J. Graham and George W. Carey, eds., *The Post-Behavioral Era: Perspectives on Political Science* (New York: David McKay Company 1972).

24. Because of its effect on this overall orientation, the selection of the name "political *science*" to denote the discipline which focuses on things political may have been an unhappy choice. Granted the awkwardness of calling oneself a

"student of politics" as opposed to a "political scientist," much internecine strife and wasted effort could be avoided were this less elegant term adopted, and, of even greater importance, the discipline's range of methods and research topics might be considerably expanded.

25. I am indebted to Herman Daly for this apt pun.

26. For more extended discussion of these points, see Richard L. Clinton and R. Kenneth Godwin, "Political Science in Population Studies: Reasons for the Late Start," pp. 141-50 of Clinton, Flash, and Godwin (n. 13) and Richard L. Clinton and R. Kenneth Godwin, "Introduction: The Study of Population by Political Scientists," pp. 1-16 of Clinton and Godwin (n. 12).

27. Thomas Landon Thorson, *Biopolitics* (New York: Holt, Rinehart and Winston, Inc.; 1970), p. 205.

28. Duncan MacRae, Jr., "Commentary on Lindblom's Paper," in James C. Charlesworth, ed., *Integration of the Social Sciences through Policy Analysis* (Philadelphia, Pa.: The American Academy of Political and Social Science, 1972), pp. 20-29.

29. See the lengthier treatment of these issues along similarly "orthodox" lines by James N. Rosenau, *The Dramas of Politics: An Introduction to the Joys of Inquiry* (Boston: Little, Brown and Company, 1973), especially ch. 7.

30. He is somewhat ambiguous in his specific references to population problems, e.g., on the first page of his essay he alludes to "the various demographic problems *allegedly* plaguing humanity" (my emphasis) yet then notes that "the problem has assumed crisis proportions. . . ." Later on he implies that population problems are really only of current interest and will shortly pass, leaving those political scientists who have specialized in them in an unenviable position *vis-à-vis* their profession.

31. Again he offers contradictory evidence, however, for he admits that "it is mildly disconcerting to realize that political science was neither called to action until the problem assumed crisis proportions nor did political scientists become aware of population as a political issue until others called it to our collective attention."

**Part Two
Methodological Issues**

7

Population Dynamics and Social Inquiry: Some Methodological Imperatives

Nazli Choucri

The report of the Commission on Population Growth and the American Future represents a landmark in the analysis of the societal implications of population dynamics.[1] The commission's report is as extensive in its coverage as it is careful and cautious. The breadth of issues examined and the diversity of approaches adopted are indicative of a new dilemma confronting students of population dynamics: Because of increasing public awareness of demographic problems and prospects, it is incumbent upon us to examine more closely than we have done so far the critical methodological and conceptual problems imbedded in systematic inquiry.

It is no longer acceptable to engage in polemical discourse — informed or otherwise — nor is it sufficient simply to acknowledge the complexities involved in demographic investigations. It has become imperative that we address ourselves directly to the issue of method and procedure and to develop ways of recording our observations, the inferences we draw, and the conclusions we reach, in ways that are reliable, consistent, and empirically valid.

This chapter takes one step in the direction of order and precision by addressing itself to some critical methodological problems, basic conceptual distinctions, and alternative ways of analyzing the implications of population dynamics.

The Need for Conceptual Clarity: Statistical Uncertainties and Definitional Ambiguities

Almost everyone recognizes the existence of a population question in the world today, but there are significant differences in the ways by which this issue is defined and the degree to which it is thought to be problematic. We are presently witnessing the cumulative effects of dynamics that were developed at a time when population issues were less salient than they are today. We now realize that in many parts of the world the demographic calculus is becoming increasingly unmanageable, and we now appreciate the need to examine the implications of population-related factors in society. But we still remain fairly ignorant of the procedures by which we might gain insight into the demographic implications of variables that are conventionally viewed as nondemographic in nature.

75

We can no longer ignore the political consequences of population, nor can we ignore the demographic consequences of politics. Unless some clear procedures are undertaken to examine mutual dependencies between population and politics, we will continue to be taken unawares — in turn surprised and disturbed — by the apparent political implications of population variables, by demographic dislocations resulting from imbalances in the global rates of growth, and by imbalances resulting from regional distributions and compositions. It is as imperative that we appreciate the implications of added numbers for increasing demands upon the environment as it is to understand the relationship of added population to regional distributions of resources and to levels of technology, knowledge, and skills.

Different populations make different demands upon their environments. And demands are expressed differently in different contexts. For this reason it is necessary to sharpen the conceptual tools at our disposal so as to capture the intricacies and complexities of the population issue in ways that might increase our understanding of the interconnections between population and politics.

Statistical and Conceptual Uncertainties

Many uncertainties exist concerning the nature of the population issue and its domestic and international implications. Equally impressive is the extent of disagreement as to the optimal approach or mode of analysis. The population question is inevitably defined in terms of referent variables — such as space, food, and resources — and the definition of the problem is viewed as one of levels, rates of growth, distributions, compositions, densities, and movements — all of which depend largely upon these referent variables.

Further complications arise from the fact that existing data on absolute levels and rates of change, and on projections and expectations, are fraught with uncertainties occasioned as much by the difficulties of compiling accurate statistics (and gauging the range of measurement error) as by the choices of intervening sociological or economic indicators. For example, United Nations projections are based upon the assumption of continuing progress in economic and social development and upon the continued availability of needed resources.[2] Variability in these assumptions inevitably colors the nature of the projections and, by extension, our assessments of the problem.

Adding further to a rapidly growing list of uncertainties are those which relate to potential constraints upon continuing population growth. The question of constraints is imbedded in the dual considerations of absolute global shortages of life's sustaining materials versus imbalances in regional distributions. In each case, experts tend to identify sources of potential dislocation with (1) food, (2) availability of resources (in terms of energy and mineral needs), and (3) general environmental resistance, as three distinct but highly interrelated dimensions of the earth's carrying capacity. Already the definition of the population issue assumes awesome proportions. And while there tends to be a general predisposition to view the constraints problem as one of distribution rather than of absolute shortages, there is in many circles a strong belief that the global "optimum" has long been surpassed and even that maximum world population has already been attained.

The concept of "optimum," so endemic to the issues at hand, is itself fraught with built-in conceptual and methodological difficulties, many of which are related to the referent variables — those variables against which population is viewed. The basic question is this: Optimum with respect to what? Since the economic optimum is not necessarily congruent with the political optimum, and since at the level beyond mere subsistence the optimum is culturally and sociologically defined, it is especially difficult to employ this concept as a useful measuring instrument for defining the population issue with any degree of precision. Any concept of optimum population must be viewed in the context of the goals or objectives against which such an assessment is made. For example, in any given society it may be that the optimum with respect to military capability is vastly different from the optimum with respect to political stability, or abundance of leisure, or the standard of living. This much we know from demographic and economic analyses and from the historical record, although we have little "hard" data on the subject.

Alternative Definitions of Population Problems

Statistical uncertainties and uncertainties pertaining to definitions of the "problem" are matched by uncertainties regarding the socioeconomic and political implications of added population or of continued growth. The basic Malthusian thesis that indefinite population growth would bring widespread poverty — applicable only under conditions of trade isolation, minimal standards of living, marginal flexibility in technology, and low energy output — is totally rejected by those espousing a Marxist perspective. These scholars define the problem in terms of distribution: If resources and technology were properly utilized and distributed, the entire population of the world could subsist on existing resources. The concept of overpopulation is in principle denied, and the problem is formally rejected.[3]

Many of these difficulties and contradictions can be attributed to the fact that missing from both the Malthusian and Marxist perspectives is sufficient appreciation of the implications of differential levels of technology and the associated repercussions on the available resource base and on the external environment. Also missing from these views is a necessary awareness of the social, economic, and political implications of added population for defining the issues at hand.

A non-Malthusian view, recently propounded by scholars like Jean Mayer, argues for a consideration of the relation between changes in levels of population to changes in level of wealth, and a case is made for population control on exactly the reverse of the basic Malthusian premise: Controlling the number of the rich is viewed as considerably more critical than controlling the number of the poor.[4] The vast differentials in the comparative impacts on the environment of peoples at different levels of development makes the non-Malthusian perspective one that must, by necessity, be taken seriously in any examination of the societal — and international — implications of population dynamics.

A Three-Dimensional Perspective: Population, Resources, Technology

The Malthusian, Marxist, and non-Malthusian perspectives suggest that different views of the problem result from different assumptions and different priorities. These perspectives suggest also that when viewing the consequences of population dynamics it is imperative to transcend simple demographic boundaries and that, at the very least, two other considerations must be taken into account: (1) the extent of resource availability, accessibility, and utilization of any society, and (2) the level of technology or knowledge and skills. A population with high resource needs is likely to make demands on the environment that are different from one with low needs. Since resource utilization is a direct correlate of development, the overall knowledge and skills of a society bear directly upon the environmental impacts that its population is likely to have. Because we now recognize that population growth occasions a nonlinear, negative impact on the environment and that population dynamics generate social and economic consequences which are not simply additive, it is therefore imperative that population be considered in conjunction with resources and technology.[5]

These considerations all reduce what is conventionally viewed as a population "problem" to one that must be defined in terms of the two companion vectors in any demographic calculus: resource availability and technological development. For our purposes, therefore, resources and technology are the most critical referent variables defining the political context within which population must be viewed.

Resources generally include the mineral and energy wealth of the country. Technology is most frequently defined as the level of knowledge and skills. Both these factors are exceedingly broad, and it is often difficult to develop operational indicators. Nonetheless, when placed in the context of level of knowledge and skills, it becomes apparent that the same population characteristics often give rise to different political implications, depending upon the nature of the resources available to the national leadership and to the population at large and upon their ability to sustain collective and organized action. When technology is defined more narrowly as tools (ranging from the hammer and the saw to sophisticated weapons), it becomes even more imperative to recognize that the consequences of alternative population dynamics depend very much upon the society's level of technology and on the resources at its disposal.

Although we do not argue for relegating population variables to secondary importance in the population/politics caluclus, it must be recognized that we still have very little sound knowledge on the relationship of population to resources and technology and the implications of different relationships for internal and external conflict. Elsewhere, we have compared in nonquantitative, though systematic, fashion twelve countries in terms of population, resources, and technology and have attempted to highlight in a qualitative manner the implications for international behavior.[6] Further work along these lines, however, must be done before we can cast these issues into sharper focus. The same types of general cross-national comparisons have not yet been undertaken with respect to the internal implications of alternative population, resource, and technology profiles. Such analysis is very much needed at this primitive stage in our knowledge of the sociopolitical implications of population dynamics.

Perceptions versus "Reality"

There is also a distinction to be drawn between the perceived versus the actual condition. While the relationship of population to resources, technology, food, or space is invariably occasioned by the hard, empirical realities of a situation, the actual definition of the situation by both analyst and participant is one that draws upon the subjective — upon perceptions and evaluations — regardless of the underlying empirical realities.

Political scientists readily admit that the definition of a situation by the actors involved is generally more indicative of potential outcomes than an analysis of empirical realities.[7] Thus, when we confront the different types of population variables as defined by demographers, it becomes immediately apparent that the perception-versus-reality problem is a critical issue regarding the implications and consequences of population dynamics.

Under ideal research conditions it would be desirable to identify what the empirical realities are, how these are perceived by the actors in question, and what the relationship is between the reality and its perception. Important information is undoubtedly contained in the nature of the gap between perception and reality. For this reason, terms like population pressure, excess, or equilibrium are difficult to analyze empirically, particularly since the perception of these variables often determines their effect.

Implicit in the above is the hypothesis that only when theoretical and operational linkages are made between hard realities and their perception by national leaders, policy makers, or the politicized population do population variables assume direct political relevance. But there are indirect effects. The alternative hypothesis appears equally plausible, namely that demographic realities are important in their own right by conditioning or constraining political outcomes — whether or not these are so perceived by the individuals in question. Without some assessment of how the subjective and the objective interrelate, it becomes exceedingly difficult to evaluate alternative perspectives on the social and political implications of population dynamics.

So far we have avoided repeated reference to a population "problem." Elsewhere, the present author has discussed in general terms some of the distinctly political implications of population dynamics and has expressed some definite views on the issue. Here we seek only to untangle various theoretical threads that may involve definitional issues or value judgments.[8]

Some Methodological Imperatives: The Requirements of Systematic Inquiry

Of the many critical methodological issues, four are particularly important: (1) definitional problems associated with key variables, (2) alternative perspectives on causal relations, (3) the manipulability of variables and the constraints imposed by parameters, and (4) identification of nonlinearities and system breaks. Because the most important factors in systematic research are replication, validation, and cumulative effort, explicit cognizance of these issues amounts to a fundamental methodological imperative.

Definitional Problems: Population Dynamics and Political Consequences

The definitional issue involves careful specification of population variables, of political (or other) consequences, and of the processes intervening between population and politics.

Population Dynamics: Some Conceptual Distinctions. At first glance it might appear that the population variables are so clearly defined by demographers as to pose no serious problem for scholars seeking to examine the consequences of population dynamics. It is also customary to speak of population as a composite phenomenon, without differentiating between the type of demographic factor in question and the level of aggregation at which the variable is employed.

At a point of departure we must distinguish among size, composition, and distribution, as distinct population variables, and between their absolute level and their rates of changes. Even in this simplified manner, we are confronted with the need to accommodate a two-dimensional perspective in terms of levels and rates of change.

Population size refers, of course, to the total number of people in a society or the total level. This number generates demands upon the environment, upon the society, upon governments, and upon the political system at large. The implications of these numbers differ according to the resources available and according to the level of knowledge and skills in a society. Any rapid change in this level may occasion added strains on the fabric of a society. Monitoring for departures from previous trends becomes an important task for students of political demography.

The composition of a population is conventionally thought of in terms of socioeconomic status, ethnic or racial divisions, and age structure. Rural-urban differentials are also viewed as composition variables, although they may also be viewed as distribution variables. A nonadditive perspective on the composition of the population would necessitate taking cognizance of all composition factors simultaneously. This is difficult to do without assistance of conventional statistical tools or without recourse to common modes of combining or aggregating data by categories. Sociologists and demographers, among others, excel in this type of activity, but political scientists have not yet become accustomed to treating the interactive effects of population variables in ways that shed light upon political considerations.

The same dimensionality issue pertains when viewing population distribution. Distribution is generally thought of in terms of spacial location or in terms of movement. There is also talk of population "density" and of "pressure." In each case population is viewed in the context of (a) the two initial referents, resources and technology, and (b) empirical realities and their perception by the population in question. Often what we might think of as "pressure" is nothing more than an unwarranted subjective interpretation of the realities at hand. In the same fashion, a situation that should on all empirical counts be viewed as one of "pressure" might not be perceived as such by the participants themselves. These potential discrepancies — pertinent to all aspects of the population issue — are especially relevant to distribution variables where the interplay among population, resources, and technology is the most pronounced. This distinction must be formally acknowledged by any investigator and taken into account in any sound research design.

The introduction of change highlights further complexity by drawing our attention to an important theoretical problem: The coincidence of any two or more of these simple population variables introduces computational and other methodological difficulties, the solutions to which are not always intuitively obvious.

The task of conceptualizing and defining population variables becomes even more complicated when complex population factors are introduced, variables that refer to population as well as to social, economic, or political considerations. For example, the term population *pressure* clearly involves some referent against which population is measured. The same may be said with respect to *over*population, *excess* population, population *equilibrium,* or population *differentials.* Complex population variables such as these call for specification of the referents or context against which population is evaluated.

Political Consequences: Some Conceptual Distinctions. Just as it is imperative that we define the population variables as clearly as possible, so too we must define the political (or societal) variables of interest. Here conceptual problems abound. It is difficult to identify, quantify, measure, or monitor societal considerations. And, while we must appreciate the complexities associated with measuring variables that come in natural units of measurement — numbers of people — these difficulties pale in comparison with those involved in conceptualizing and measuring nonmetric societal factors. The determinants of fertility, mortality, and morbidity are comparatively well understood by professional students of population. The other side of the equation — the consequences of population dynamics — is much less well understood and much less well conceptualized.

The concerns of the present author revolve around the conflict-related implications of population dynamics — with violence, with hostilities, and with warfare. My interests lie in tracing the origins of violence between states and determining the extent to which these may be located in population variables. The intent is not to search for — or expect to find — a direct link between population and politics or between population and violence, but to determine the ways (if at all) population combines with other variables to make violence more (or less) likely. This type of enterprise necessitates a careful assessment of the dependent variables and equally careful measurement, quantification, and eventually, statistical (or functional) analysis of relationships to the independent variables.

An appreciation of the variety of operational approaches to conflict and violence and the problems these pose is of important methodological concern. Indeed, definitional issues go a long way in accounting for the primitive state of our empirical knowledge concerning both causes and consequences of violence. And when population variables are introduced in this calculus, it becomes increasingly difficult to define the relationships that one seeks to clarify. Much of the existing empirical evidence regarding the population/violence calculus is almost entirely contingent upon the ways by which violence is defined. There are some thorny theoretical issues at stake which make it imperative to look closely at alternative operational measures of the dependent variables.

Political scientists have defined violent conflict in a number of ways, with different implications for systematic inquiry and with limited degrees of success. Some have developed underlying indicators of its manifestations, for example, Lewis Fry Richardson who talked of "deadly quarrels" generating casualties.[9]

Others have employed factor analysis as a means of identifying the underlying dimension of this societal mode of behavior.[10] Still others have recognized that violence cannot be isolated from the pool of actions and interactions among conflicting parties, that violence (or conflict) per se cannot be distinguished meaningfully from cooperation, and that the critical methodological (and conceptual) issue is not only one of degree but of dimension. Degrees of conflict can be identified, as can degrees of cooperation, but the two are analytically distinct.[11]

The different ways one might define violent behavior point to the difficulties involved: A sound perspective on the dependent variables — violence and manifestations thereof — is as important as refining our conception and measurement of the population variables. Methodological difficulties imbedded in these political variables necessitate a further differentiation of the dependent variables, in terms of a three-fold distinction: power relations among two states (population, parties, or groups), propensities for violence, and predispositions toward armed conflict or organized violence.[12] These three factors point to different perspectives and different manifestations of the political (and violence) variables. For research purposes, it is imperative that clear correspondence be established between the underlying concept, its indicator, and the operational variable.

Linking Population and Politics: Intervening Variables. Apart from space, food resources, and technology — which we have termed *referent* variables — there are also variables or processes mediating between population and its consequences. Such variables refer to the dynamics that translate the effects of population into particular types of outcomes. Referent variables define the context within which population must be viewed, or the nature of the population problem (if there be one), or the peculiarities of the situation which might propel populations toward political outcomes. By contrast, *intervening* variables refer to the ways by which the effects of population reverberate throughout the social system, generating distinctly political outcomes and sometimes even conflict and violence. Here the calculus becomes increasingly complex: Methodological problems abound as do conceptual ambiguities.

Once careful definitions of the population and political variables are made and the intervening variables specified accordingly, it is then necessary to think about the *dynamic processes* linking population and politics. A simple accounting of dependent and independent variables is only the point of departure; how they interrelate lies at the core of the problems at hand.

An illustration might be in order.[13] In recent studies of international behavior we have argued that the roots of conflict and warfare can be found in the basic attributes and characteristics of nations and that the most critical variables in that regard are population, resources, and technology, where technology refers to the level and rates of development of human knowledge and skills in a society. We have then attempted to specify the intervening sequences between these three sets of variables on the one hand and conflict and warfare on the other and have tried to identify the role of population in this complex process. On the bases of empirical and historical analysis, we infer that the chain of developments intervening between population and violence appears to be the following.

A combination of population and developing technology places rapidly increasing demands upon resources, often resulting in internally generated pressures. The greater this pressure, the higher will be the likelihood of extending national activities outside territorial boundaries. We have termed this tendency to extend behavior outside national boundaries *lateral pressure*. To the extent that two or more countries with high capability and high pressure tendency (and high lateral pressure) extend their interests and sociopolitical borders outward, there is a strong probability that eventually the two opposing spheres of interest will intersect. The more intense the intersection, the greater will the likelihood be that competition will assume military proportions. When this happens, we may expect competition to be transformed into conflict and perhaps an arms race or cold war. At a more general level of abstraction, provocation will be the final act that can be considered as the stimulus for a large-scale conflict or violence. But an act will be considered a provocation only in a situation which has already been characterized by high lateral pressure, intersections among spheres of influence, armament tensions and competitions, and an increasing level of prevailing conflict.

Major wars, we have argued, often emerge through a two-step process: in terms of internally generated pressure (which can be traced to population dynamics, resource needs and constraints, and technological development) and in terms of the reciprocal comparison, rivalry, and conflict on a number of salient capability and behavior demensions. Each process tends to be closely related to the other, and each to a surprising degree can be accounted for by relatively nonmanipulable variables (or variables that are controllable only at high costs).

Because these relationships rest upon the population variable, we find it necessary to understand the ways by which man is related to his physical environment and the ways in which added numbers impose added burdens upon that environment. Indeed, recently biologists have made explicit the extent to which each human being literally owes his life to the earth and ultimately to the sun, and how rapid increases in numbers — or changes in composition or distribution — generate commensurate (and often disproportional) effects on the environment. The task of political scientists is to identify the political implications of such changes and to specify the ways by which we may expect further changes in the environment to be generated by increasing numbers.

Because the inferences we draw and the analyses we undertake are almost completely predicated upon the assumptions we hold and the perspectives on reality that we espouse, it is necessary to examine the methodological implications of different ways of looking at the environment.

The Nature of Causal Relations: Alternative Perspectives on Reality

Perhaps the most important methodological problem involves the choice among alternative perspectives on causal relations.[14] One's beliefs about causality determine in large part the methodologies one adopts for investigating the linkages between population and politics and the type of values one chooses to accommodate. Social scientists concerned with the consequences of population dynamics impose upon their subject matter a causal sequence different from that employed by those concerned with the causes of fertility, mortality, and morbidity. This simple fact highlights the interdependence between the definition of the problem (or the nature of one's concerns) and definition of causal sequence.

There are at least five different concepts of causation with equally numerous interpretations of empirical realities. The most common view involves *time precedence:* One thing followed by another. But this is a rather simplistic notion, and philosophers of science tend to agree that causality in terms of asymmetrical relations is more realistic. Others maintain that causal relations involve unidirectional or recursive dependencies and that causality, by definition, cannot accommodate mutual relations. Conversely, still others argue that simultaneous relations are not inconsistent with causal notions and that the "real" world is of this nature. And, by way of accommodating such differing perspectives, some attempts have been made to think of causality in terms of mutual dependencies *and* in terms of unidirectional relations. This compromise is based upon a bloc recursive view of reality, a perspective that assumes that within a localized domain causal relations are unidirectional, but that these localized systems of relations are imbedded in larger structures characterized by simultaneous dependencies.

This last view amounts to the following: In international relations, for example, one can think of the domestic sources of foreign policy as a localized system composed of unidirectional influences — from the system to the leadership and eventually to the external environment — but these localized relations are influenced by external considerations (international alliances, ongoing armament competitions, and so forth) which themselves are fairly independent of the internal determinants of foreign policy. By the same token, the political implications of changes in the size of a population might have localized effects — in that greater demands may be placed upon the government for goods and services, greater strains are imposed upon the political system, and greater propensities for instabililty might result from these demands and strains — and these effects can be adequately thought of within a unidirectional perspective. Conversely, it is conceivable that added population means greater possibilities for channeling manpower into the military, which in turn might be perceived as a threatening factor by neighboring states, occasioning hostile exchanges, which then result in even greater stress upon increasing the number of men under arms. In such cases, a multidirectional perspective on causality would be more appropriate for purposes of systematic inquiry than one that is unidirectional. A bloc recursive view would also be acceptable and, in many cases, extremely desirable as well.

The choice of model type depends on several considerations: including underlying beliefs about the nature of the realities modeled (whether they can be represented in linear additive terms or not, whether they can be viewed in statistical rather than in functional terms, and so forth), the time perspective (whether one is concerned with the short-range or long-term dynamics), and the extent to which *linkage* between time perspectives and between levels of analysis is to be consciously undertaken as part of the investigation.[15] These three sets of considerations go a long way in determining the type of model employed.

In sum: Different models and different perspectives on causality serve different purposes, and since what we see depends upon how we look at it, we must appreciate the consequences of selecting one type of model, or one view of causality, rather than another.

Identifying the Manipulables: Variables versus Parameters

While population is a variable that can be counted, sorted, scaled, and ranked, we tend to assume that the same degree of quantitative precision cannot be imposed upon the political variables of interest. Recent developments in nonmetric and multidimensional scaling and the quantification of political actions and events, however, suggest that it is not unreasonable to expect a high degree of precision in the measurement of political variables.[16]

For policy analysis it is important to include in the research design variables that can be manipulated on short order or variables that can be subject to legislation, policy, or government action. In the same vein, account must be taken of factors that are variables in the short run but parameters in the long run. This is particularly relevant in population-related research where the effects of population variables make themselves felt in the long range — demographic considerations eventually become parameters of a situation — even though often considered as varying in the short range. The transition from variables to parameters corresponds to the change of a system (or of the dynamics under consideration) as the time perspective unfolds.

For operational purposes one must appreciate that different methodologies are appropriate for different time frames. The tools one employs to examine short-run implications of population dynamics are by necessity different from those employed to examine long-range factors. The recent controversy generated by *The Limits to Growth* is illustrative of the reactions modulated by short-term concerns (as is the case with economists, political analysis, and social critics), which are generally inappropriate to studies of long-term dynamics predicated upon a methodology suitable primarily for the analysis of system behavior in the long range.[17]

The dual issues of variables versus parameters and time perspectives have important implications for analyzing the consequences of population dynamics. We know that immediate short-range factors are imbedded in a larger societal context which is invariably conditioned as much by time as by habit, inertia, and social history. These conditions become the parameters of a situation in the shorter range. But in the long run, over years and decades, they change and take on new attributes and characteristics. Today's idiosyncracies become tomorrow's parameters. The methodological problem is this: If we can identify the conditions under which variables become parameters and if we can determine how it is and why it is that this change takes place, then we would resolve the problem of moving from shorter-range effects of population dynamics to long-range imperatives. The methodological task is to incorporate this information in the research design so as to alert us to the probabilities of change in the system under consideration.

Nonlinearities and System Breaks

A related question involves the identification of nonlinearities and breakpoints in the intervening processes and in the dependent variables.[18] A breakpoint represents a sharp change (which in regression analysis, for example, is exemplified by a change in the regression slope), but a non-linearity indicates a gentler departure from linearity, the nature of which can often be captured by conventional non-linear functions. Nonlinearities generally represent a functional relationship among variables. Complex systems — such as social systems — are invariably nonlinear. Thus if we expect linearities (however erroneously), we will sensitize our model and methodologies to search for linearities. The result will almost certainly be an invalid analysis. When it comes to the identification of breakpoints the situation is much the same. Because there is a tendency in the social sciences to confuse breakpoints with nonlinearities when observing system change, we must guard against the erroneous inference that what is in fact a nonlinearity may be interpreted as a system break. Because nonlinearities and system breaks abound in complex systems, monitoring for such changes becomes an important aspect of any research design. This is particularly true in social systems where population variables are undergoing rapid change and where *some* societal consequences are anticipated.

The critical political sectors where monitoring for system breaks occasioned by population variables has important implications for the society as a whole include the major institutions of society imposed by added population, potential changes in the nature of key institutions, changes in the distributions of goods and services, changes in resource allocations and utilizations, changes in patterns of budgetary allocations, changes in national priorities, and so forth. For example, almost every developing nation has, over the past several years, responded to increasing population by national plans of actions (development plans, family planning programs, health-care and delivery systems, and so forth), and in most cases the response has suffered from an absence of careful monitoring of demographic changes. This situation is in large part occasioned by the absence of reliable demographic statistics in many parts of the world, but also by a lack of appreciation of the importance of population dynamics for overall societal adaptation to the external environment, national as well as international.

Undoubtedly the most difficult conceptual and methodological problems encountered in examining the political (or societal) consequences of population dynamics involves an appreciation of the nature of a system *beyond* the change. For example, we referred earlier to recent studies tracing the origins of conflict and warfare to increases in levels and rates of growth in technological development and access to critical resources. Here we must emphasize that these aggregate societal factors provide the context within which day-to-day politics unfold and, in the long run, the parameters of a conflict situation where the belligerents confront each other in hostile stance.[19] A large-scale war represents a system break. And the question is: How does the system change following such a break?

If we look at population, resources, and technology carefully we might be able to put together the alternative scenarios upon which politics, governance, and structural considerations are predicated. Students of political demography are beginning to investigate the consequences of war for population dynamics in order to determine the nature of the system beyond large-scale breaks and to construct alternative futures based upon such analysis. There are important methodological implications of such concerns.

An illustration may clarify the issue. We know, for instance, that wars often affect the demographic composition of a state and that, since population characteristics are an important aspect of societal attributes, we can introduce in our research and analysis some consideration for the potential of changes in demographic characteristics. The same must be done for the other parameters of a situation. If we developed some systematic procedures for recording our expectations along these three dimensions concerning probable departures from system behavior occasioned by such breaks, and if this procedure were generalized to issue areas other than population, resources, and technology, we might begin to enhance our understanding of probable outcomes beyond system breaks.[20]

These methodological difficulties and problems only highlight the fact that a comprehensive research design should allow us to account for endogenous system change *without* any external intervention by the investigator. This is difficult to do. The point here is that a design could, by its very nature, incorporate those decision points at which a system change is likely to take place. This simple consideration will enhance the internal validity of the research in that factors external to the design itself — such as intervention by the investigator — would not be allowed to contaminate its outcome. It will then be easier to probe further into the weaknesses of the research design itself and isolate those problems resulting from the conception and conduct of the research and those that result from intervention by the investigator. This is not to suggest that all such intervention is undesirable but that controlled intervention must be distinguished from *ad hoc* manipulations.

These observations have the following methodological implications: How one constructs the research design, what one's assumptions are, and what notion of causality one chooses to espouse are of great importance. But it is more important by far to indicate the nature of one's decisions as explicitly as possible so as to communicate effectively with others engaged in similar research or with those concerned with translating the results of empirical investigations to practical use.

Research Alternatives: Costs and Benefits

At this point we indicate alternative research approaches to the analysis of population and politics and note the costs and the benefits of each. Our intent is to explore the alternatives before us and hopefully to render an educated judgment concerning the merits of different types of scholarly research.

There appear to be seven distinct modes of inquiry into the consequences of population dynamics:

The Case Study Approach

This method involves intensive analysis of one situation in which population appears to be related to the form of behavior or system change of interest to the investigator. The advantages are obvious: With research efforts concentrated on one case, it becomes considerably easier to investigate in depth the nuances and implications of the evidence at hand. But the disadvantages are equally obvious: Case studies, by their very nature, beg the issue of generalizability. One cannot draw inferences from one case to an underlying type of cases or to any other *single case*. Indeed, the expressed objectives of social science inquiry, namely the building of cumulative and consistent knowledge, is invariably defeated in single-case investigations. Even the "critical case" approach amounts, at best, to systematic description. Despite these obvious drawbacks we must recognize that in the absence of some overarching theory or guidelines for research, case studies do provide us with information which, if used judiciously, might shed some light on the problems at hand.

The Population Dynamics and International Violence Project at M.I.T. is currently undertaking four case studies seeking to identify the role of population variables in conflict situations. These include studies of the South African situation, the Arab-Israeli conflict, the El Salvador-Honduras war, and the Sino-Soviet dispute. We believe that case studies of this nature will add to our understanding, however unsystematic, of the role of population in contributing to warring outcomes.

The Comparative-Cases Approach

This method involves a rigorous comparison of several cases along prespecified dimensions. It includes, by definition, all the disadvantages of the single case study with few of the advantages. But it promises to generate information that is cumulative, comparative, and internally consistent. In order to obtain useful data, however, it is necessary to develop a conceptual framework — or at least some general rules of thumb or general queries — to guide the research as data for individual cases are compiled. This is not an easy task. And, given the state of the art as we have described it in the foregoing pages, it is extremely difficult to develop a theoretically sound and analytically precise context within which to place the relevant information, case by case. The object of the exercise might be, for example, to compare the El Salvador-Honduras case with the Arab-Israeli conflict or with any other conflict and draw some inferences that *within a certain probability range* would be expected to hold.

The M.I.T. project is undertaking a comparative analysis of fifty-two conflicts in less developed areas since 1945. What we gain in terms of the proprieties of social inquiry, we lose in terms of in-depth analysis and richness of information. The comparative case-study approach would, hopefully, allow us to draw some rough generalizations concerning population dynamics and violent conflict in the Third World from 1945 to the present. But we do not expect to obtain anything like closure on the issue.

The Critical-Theme Approach

This method is often termed "functional analysis" in that the emphasis is upon a functional representation (such as the role of ideology, or population policy, and so forth) and not upon a certain unit (such as country). The advantages are obvious: It allows the investigator to draw data, information, insights, and evidence from wherever possible without holding to the requirements of in-depth analysis or the rigor of cross-national comparability or of statistical propriety. But the disadvantages cannot be overlooked: Without some explicit theoretical or statistical control, it is difficult, if not impossible, to evaluate the information at hand or to assess its implications for the conclusions one is attempting to draw.

This mode of analysis is commonplace in traditional political inquiry, but students of population and political demography have not paid sufficient attention to this type of inquiry. Analytical description is often a useful, but initial, approach to a problem when the uncertainties and unknowns abound. For example, descriptive comparisons of alternative population policies and their role in national planning could be approached this way as a prerequisite for more systematic inquiry. Since we know very little about the consequences of population dynamics, critical-theme inquiries would provide worthwhile additions to the existing repertoire of research findings.

Cross-Sectional Quantitative Analysis

Two impressive studies — one by Douglas Hibbs, the other by Ted Gurr — illustrate this mode of analysis.[21] It amounts to statistical investigations of the relationships among variables (attributes and behaviors) for many nations (generally the entire population of independent states) for one or more time periods. The advantages include (a) the use of systematic modes of recording, processing, and anlyzing empirical data; (b) providing cross-national comparisons; and (c) allowing for the identification of "unique" cases, or those known in statistical parlance as "residuals." But the disadvantages are numerous. It is impossible to generalize findings from cross-national quantitative analysis to any one particular state or even to draw regional inferences (except perhaps by examining the residuals and identifying outliers). In this respect, at least, the costs and the benefits of cross-sectional quantitative analysis and of case studies converge: One cannot generalize from the aggregate to the single case, much as one cannot generalize from the single case to the aggregate. Both the Hibbs and the Gurr studies enable us to identify the role of population variables in domestic conflict. In each case the conclusion is that there appears to be no strong direct link between population and domestic violence. Hibbs suggests that the indirect links are too weak to allow for valid inferences. In each case, however, the caveats associated with the investigations necessitate a cautious assessment of these results: Cross-sectional studies do not allow for inferences concerning the single case, although the residuals provide important clues.

Quantitative Longitudinal Analysis

The Correlates of War Project at the University of Michigan represents this type of inquiry.[22] Essentially it involves quantitative analysis of demographic, economic, and political data (recorded every five years) from 1815 to the present. The investigations so far have been confined to correlations and the use of elementary statistical techniques. The advantage is that this approach involves, almost by definition, all the rigor required for quantification and drawing valid inferences in the social sciences. The disadvantages, however, are shared by all statistical or mathematical approaches to political analysis, namely that the process of quantification is undertaken at a level of abstraction that cannot capture the intricacies of the political process or of day-to-day politics. The proponents of this approach argue that a probabilistic interpretation of quantitative results (or, by definition, the yield from all statistical analysis) can be employed to capture that element of volatility interjected by human "nature," by politics, or by the political process.

In the long run this approach represents a worthwhile undertaking, but here we can only point to the numerous pitfalls and very real problems involved in such an effort given the present stage of the conventional wisdom regarding the implications of population dynamics for organized armed conflict or propensities for violence.

Theoretical Definition of a Problem, Subsequent Quantification, and Statistical Analysis

This somewhat unwieldy title refers to the type of research undertaken at Stanford University where the initial objective is to develop a theoretical framework which would then allow the investigators to identify the variables of interest, to develop quantitative measures, and to move systematically from simple correlational analysis to model-building and multivariate investigations.[23] The intricacies of the "real" world are rarely captured by any method of quantification – at least at the present stage in the development of statistical methodology – and it becomes extremely important to define as precisely as possible the variables of interest and the ways in which they are thought to interrelate.

The disadvantages of this approach are the same as those indicated with respect to the Correlates of War Project. The advantages, however, lie primarily in the fact that careful theoretical specification of expected linkages from population to war was undertaken before extensive quantitative and multivariate analysis, although, as is always the case, the results of earlier investigations serve to refine subsequent work and the underlying theoretical framework. This project, however, is not concerned with the relationships of *specific* population variables to organized armed conflict or to international violence. This is an area in which, to the best of our knowledge, no work has been undertaken to date. It is the strong belief of this writer that quantitative analyses of specific population variables as they relate to specific violence variables, internal and external, are called for as a logical extension of the present state of affairs in the population/violence investigations.

Quantitative, Statistical, and Longitudinal Analysis of a
"Critical Case"

This approach involves a combination of the foregoing. It pertains to statistical analyses of a case which has already been examined descriptively, theoretically, and analytically. The conceptual framework for quantitative analysis is therefore already developed. There are obvious merits to such an approach in that it allows for statistical rigor in conjunction with in-depth analysis. But there are also the disadvantages associated with case studies and with quantitative analysis.

The Population Project at M.I.T. is currently attempting to undertake two studies of this complex nature. The first involves relating demographic variables to casualties incurred in battle, with particular emphasis upon the Arab-Israeli conflict. The second is a statistical analysis of the effects of the demographic profiles along both sides of the Sino-Soviet border upon the conflict between these two powers. It is unclear at this point whether problems with Chinese population data provide insurmountable obstacles. Soviet statistics, however, are available, and developing demographic series over time that are moderately reliable and consistent appears to be a manageable task. But whether *statistical* analysis of the relationship between composition, distribution, size, and change along border areas, on the one hand, and Sino-Soviet relations, on the other hand, can be undertaken remains to be demonstrated. Under ideal research conditions we should be able to combine area expertise with statistical analysis in order to maximize our understanding of the role of population variables in Sino-Soviet relations. This is one of the many geographic areas where political analysts rarely examine the implications of demographic variables.

These several modes of analysis can be thought of as descriptive, inferential, and to some extent explanatory. But they are not in any sense predictive, nor do they allow for strong inferences concerning alternative and probable future outcomes. Other methodologies are more applicable for forecasting and simulation.

Furthermore, these modes of inquiry do not enable us to address ourselves directly to the policy implications of our research. Not only is it imperative that we increase our understanding of population dynamics, but it is also crucial that this understanding be translated into practical terms: The policy implications of our investigations must be made explicit.

The second perspective on the policy question involves the ways by which we may relate our research concerns to their implications for public policy and national priorities. The concluding section of this chapter addresses itself to these issues by stressing some research imperatives and policy implications.

Future Perspectives: Research Imperatives and Policy Alternatives[24]

The global implications of contemporary population dynamics can be fully appreciated only in the dual contexts of costs and feasibilities: What needs to be done and what the costs are likely to be. In political terms, the major demographic issues of the future concern population control and distribution in relation to the allocation and distribution of resources and technology. How this comes about, who develops the guidelines, and what institutional mechanisms are to be developed are all crucial questions which pertain directly to whatever type of international arrangement might be put forth for such purposes. However indispensable many of them may be, present international institutions are scarcely adequate for regulating the critical variables at the core of present population issues. Related obstacles involve existing discontinuities in national and international preferences and priorities and accompanying authority structures and processes. In those terms, at least, the evolution of congruent national, regional, and global priorities amounts to a major challenge.

A compelling difficulty emerges from the fact that the dynamics of our present predicament are not fully understood, nor are the long-range implications of proposed remedial action. Policies adopted to alleviate one kind of population problem all too often produce unexpected consequences. More than ever before it has become necessary to undertake long-range investigations of potential effects occasioned by alternative courses of action. In view of these uncertainties, it is important that we develop, refine, and apply methodologies *now* for analyzing relationships and interdependencies involving population dynamics, social organization and habit structure, acquisition of resources, pricing system, economic and social underpinnings, technological growth, and resulting environmental resistance.

But research and analysis represent only one side of the coin. The other and more critical imperative is to communicate the results of research to policy makers. The too frequent gap between academic and policy-oriented discourse is a luxury that can no longer be afforded.

The academic task is two-fold: (1) to specify and compile required data, and (2) to analyze the data in a critical fashion. It is necessary to develop priorities for the compilation of data on different aspects of the population issue. In some cases, data are indeed available and need only to be transferred to a format useful for analysis.[25] But this is not always so. Indeed, often we do not know what it is that we ought to be asking. But in many cases the problem is one of gathering data in primary form.

The situation with respect to analysis is more encouraging. A number of useful and extremely promising methodologies are now available for undertaking concerted analyses of long-range dynamics. Several of these have been noted in the previous section. But it is necessary to explore ways of communicating their policy-relevant implications to others outside of the academic community. In general, the imperatives at hand necessitate less the development of novel modes of analysis than the application of existing modes to problems of concern. The actual choice of method or research technique depends largely upon the specific problem encountered, on intellectual preferences, and on assessments of potential payoffs.

Research Alternatives and Policy Directives

By way of illustrating critical linkages between (1) long-range scientific research, (2) analysis of implications for policy making, and (3) translation from academic to operational contexts, we draw upon three distinct though complementary modes of analysis, each representing different manifestations of policy-oriented methodologies and designed to clarify different aspects of any one issue.

The first of these, System Dynamics, is both a philosophical orientation and a specific methodology for analyzing long-range implications of policies and decisions in complex, nonlinear, multiloop systems, of which social systems are the most complex. This type of analysis simulates the behavior of systems over a long period, sometimes going as far as 100 years into the future.[26] The kinds of data needed for analyzing long-range dynamics associated with environmental issues involve observations on population levels, economic performance, resource allocation and utilization, patterns of consumption, technological advances, and so forth. Indeed, considerable analysis of such data are already underway.

A major capability of System Dynamics as a research tool lies in the isolation of sensitive points in the system, as well as those points which contribute to future outcomes. The policy relevance of such information is obvious: If we can identify long-range implications of short-range decisions, it might be possible to ground our planning efforts on stronger footing, avoiding actions which appear to occasion benefits in the short term but in fact produce negative outcomes in the long run.

The second research approach, Decision Analysis, based on Bayesian statistics, represents an alternative to classical statistics and is designed to trace the probabilities associated with various outcomes occasioned by alternative decisions at key points. In the context of population dynamics, the data requirements involve information on demographic statistics, national preferences and priorities, alternative policies and programs, and so forth. This form assesses the probabilities attached to a range of proposed policies, thereby allowing for a critical evaluation of feasibilities.[27] However, as is also the case with System Dynamics, the cost factor is neither directly nor explicitly introduced in the analysis, a drawback that is not to be minimized for purposes of research.

The third of these research approaches, Policy Analysis of alternative allocations, deals specifically with cost considerations. It is addressed to different budgets based upon alternative preference structures and priorities. The data needed pertain to budgetary distributions as they relate to population issues. What emerges from this approach is the cost calculus attached to alternative modes of resource allocations.[28] The main advantage, therefore, is direct and explicit assessment of the cost-benefit equation, thus providing crucial information about the cost implications of proposed policies or, alternatively, setting up competing policies and observing their costs and feasibilities.[29]

Obviously, these three modes of research into present demographic predicaments differ considerably in terms of abstraction from reality. Of the three, System Dynamics is the most comprehensive, yet also the most removed from concrete day-to-day decisions that face policy-making communities. Decision Analysis and Bayesian statistics represent one step in the direction of political realism by providing probabilities attached to alternative paths and outcomes. Analysis of budgeting and resource allocations are the most specific, and they are also closely related to the stuff of politics and most directly concerned with linkages between national resources and national priorities.

To date, each of these methods has been applied in discrete fashion with little consideration for the possibilities of bringing these different scientific procedures to bear upon the development of policy alternatives, domestic or international, and even less consideration for systematic analysis of long-range implications. Through the judicious use of such methods for the analysis of appropriate data, it is now possible to construct in a laboratory setting realistic models of social systems which allow for experimentation with hypothetical situations and alternative futures. Drawing upon empirical data on population dynamics, resource constraints, and technological development, these techniques allow us to alter various values for key variables subject to different policy decisions and *allow us now to observe the changes that would take place over future time.* In addition we can begin to identify the manipulables of a situation, as well as the cost of manipulation.

Conclusion

Systematic research is no substitute for immediate and specific action. But at the same time, an incremental, piecemeal, or band-aid approach to global problems is no substitute for judicious investigation and systematic analysis.

Currently underway at M.I.T. are a series of computer-based simulations of the longer-range political and economic implications of population growth, technological developments, and resource constraints. A primary emphasis is on potentials for conflict and warfare. On the assumption that conflict might be avoided if the preventive action is undertaken early enough, these investigations have begun to raise a series of "what if" questions pertaining to alternative futures, costs, and feasibilities. For example, what would be the long-range implications for the United States (or other states) if population growth were curtailed significantly, or, alternatively, if consumption per capita were reduced, or if the costs of controlling external sources of raw materials and energy-producing fuels become too high, or if competition for resources becomes too intense?

Reports of these investigations are presented elsewhere.[30] Suffice it here to reiterate that appropriate technical skills and accompanying methodologies in addition to a certain amount of empirical data are presently available for an undertaking of extensive investigations of alternative futures and implications and consequences, both domestic and international. The transference of computer-based results from the academic community to the real world may be effectively undertaken through the application of Bayesian statistics in conjunction with policy analysis. The Bayesian paradigm would allow for the assessment of probabilities associated with different paths or policies that nations might pursue in seeking, for example, to assure continued resource availability or to minimize conflict-laden avenues of international behavior. The practical costs involved in adopting one policy over another can then be assessed in the context of overall national preferences and priorities by a judicious application of policy analysis, the most sophisticated and useful of such modes being represented by alternative budgeting analysis in the U. S. case as undertaken by the Brookings Institution.[31] In this context, the political and economic costs and consequences attached to the "what if" or "if . . . then . . ." questions can be identified and evaluated accordingly. Equally possible are systematic assessments of the political costs and feasibilities of modifying national priorities and habits, expectations, and institutions. The situation becomes considerably more complex when viewing the world as a whole and when assessing the viability of alternative international policies and institutions and their accompanying implications for relations among nations.[32]

Research imperatives for the present and immediate future are four-fold: (1) to examine systematically and objectively the longer-range implications of short-term actions and decisions; (2) to develop a whole series of alternative policies and alternative futures and examine their implications in laboratory and simulation settings; (3) to translate results in terms that are amenable to analysis of accompanying costs and feasibilities, economic as well as political; and (4) to devise means of disseminating information on methods, procedures, findings, and implications to national leaders and citizens alike in ways that are objective, valid, comprehensible, and believable.

98

Notes

1. The Commission on Population Growth and the American Future, *Population and the American Future* (Washington, D.C.: G.P.O., 1972).

2. United Nations, Department of Economic and Social Affairs, World Population Prospects as Assessed in 1963 (Population Studies no. 41), New York, 1966, p. 6.

3. See Nazli Choucri, "Population, Resources, and Technology: Political Implications of the Environmental Crisis," pp. 9-46 of David A. Kay and Eugene B. Skolnikoff, eds., *World Eco-Crisis* (Madison: The University of Wisconsin Press, 1972), for a critical discussion of Malthusian and Marxist perspectives on population issues.

4. See Jean Mayer, "Toward a Non-Malthusian Population Policy," Hearings Before a Subcommittee of the Committee on Government Operations, House of Representatives, 91st Cong., 1st sess., September 15-16, *The Effects of Population Growth on Natural Resources and the Environment* (Washington, D.C.: Government Printing Office, 1969).

5. See, for example, Paul R. Ehrlich and John P. Holdren, "Impact of Population Growth," *Science* 171, no. 3977 (26 March 1971): esp. p. 1212.

6. Nazli Choucri, Michael Laird, and Dennis Meadows, *Resource Scarcity and Foreign Policy: A Simulation Model of International Conflict* (M.I.T.: Center for International Studies, C/72-9, March 1972).

7. Herbert C. Kelman, ed., *International Behavior: A Socio-Psychological Analysis* (New York: Holt, Rinehart and Winston, 1965).

8. See n. 3.

9. Lewis Fry Richardson, *Statistics of Deadly Quarrels* (Chicago: Boxwood Press, 1960).

10. See Raymond Tanter, "Dimensions of Conflict Behavior within and between Nations, 1958-60," *The Journal of Conflict Resolution* 10, no. 1 (March 1966): 41-64; R.J. Rummel, "The Dimensions of Conflict Behavior Within and Between Nations," *General Systems Yearbook,* vol. 8 (1963), pp. 1-53; R.J. Rummel, "Dimensions of Dyadic War, 1820-1952," *The Journal of Conflict Resolution* 10, no. 2 (June 1957): 176-83; and R.J. Rummel, "Dimensions of Conflict Behavior within Nations, 1947-59," *The Journal of Conflict Resolution* 10, no. 1 (March 1966): 65-73.

11. For both sides of this issue, see Lincoln E. Moses, et al., "Scaling Data on Inter-Nation Action," *Science* 156, no. 3778 (July 1967): 1054-59, and Walter H. Corson, "Conflict and Cooperation in East-West Crises: Measurement and Prediction," Paper prepared for delivery at the Michigan State University Events Data Conference, April 15-16, 1970.

12. Nazli Choucri, "Population Dynamics and International Violence:

Propositions, Insights, and Evidence" (M.I.T.: Center for International Studies, September 1972, revised March 1973).

13. Nazli Choucri and Robert C. North, "Dynamics of International Conflict: Some Policy Implications of Population, Resources, and Technology," *World Politics,* Supplementary Issue, *Theory and Policy in International Relations* 24 (Spring 1972): 80-122.

14. For an extended discussion of these issues, see Nazli Choucri, "Forecasting in International Relations: Problems and Prospects" (M.I.T.: Center for International Studies, March 1973).

15. See especially Figure 1, "Integrating Forecasting Methodologies: An Illustration from Conflict Analysis," in Choucri (n. 14).

16. See, for example, Edward Azar, "Analysis of International Events," *Peace Research Reviews* 4, no. 1 (November 1970), entire issue, and Edward Azar, "The Dimensionality of Violent Conflict: A Quantitative Analysis," *Peace Research Society (International) Papers* 15 (1970): 122-67.

17. See Donella H. Meadows, et al., *The Limits to Growth* (New York: Universe Books, 1972), and the critiques of this study, in *Science* 175, no. 4027 (March 1972): 1197, in *New York Times,* Magazine Section, April 2, 1972, and in the Book Review Section on the same date. Also see the letters in *Science* 176, no. 4032 (21 April 1972): 109-13. The review in *Newsweek,* March 13, 1972, and the editorial in the *Saturday Review,* March 18, 1972, are also relevant. Another important review is by Carl Kaysen in *Foreign Affairs* 50, nos. 1-4 (October 1971-July 1972): 660-68. These reviews generally criticize *The Limits to Growth* for sins of omission rather than commission. They also point to the absence of empirical base for this analysis. The first criticism is, in the opinion of this author, unfair on theoretical, methodological, and scientific grounds. The problems of including pricing systems, technological innovation, and political institutions in any analysis of this kind are close to insurmountable. The second criticism is simply incorrect: *The Limits to Growth* is based on cross-national (cross-sectional) quantitative data. The major difference between their treatment of such data and the conventional wisdom in statistical and quantitative analysis is that they have not "estimated" their coefficients but simply used table functions instead. This is indeed a weakness, but it is imminently rectifiable and does not warrant the degree of criticism levied. The most important point about both the volume and its critiques, however, *is that it is basically a very conservative document,* and not a radical departure from current thought as many suggest. Indeed, the analysis in *The Limits to Growth* is extremely consistent with the studies sponsored by Resources for the Future. The major difference is that the authors of this controversial volume consider a much longer time span than do studies sponsored by Resources for the Future. It must also be pointed out that both groups employ the same empirical data on mineral and energy resources, namely, publications of the United States Government Bureau of Mines.

Regarding criticisms of the assumptions employed in the Meadows Study and in the earlier work by J.W. Forrester, *World Dynamics* (Cambridge, Mass.: Wright-Allen Press, 1971), see Robert Boyd, "World Dynamics: A Note," *Science* 177, no. 4048 (11 August 1972): 516-19, illustrating the extent to which the Forrester world model is sensitive to changes in assumptions.

18. Nazli Choucri, "Applications of Econometric Analysis to Forecasting in International Politics," *Peace Research Society (International) Papers,* in press.

19. See ns. 3, 6, 12, and 13.

20. See n. 14.

21. Douglas A. Hibbs, Jr., *Mass Political Violence: A Cross-National Analysis* (New York: John Wiley and Sons, 1973) and Ted Gurr, *Why Men Rebel* (Princeton, N.J.: Princeton University Press, 1970).

22. J. David Singer and Melvin Small, *The Wages of War 1816-1965: A Statistical Handbook* (New York: John Wiley and Sons, 1972).

23. Nazli Choucri and Robert C. North, *Nations in Conflict: Population, Lateral Pressure, and War* in preparation, revised version February 1973.

24. This concluding section is identical to that of an earlier article argued from another perspective; see n. 3 pp. 37-42. Some of the substantive arguments in this chapter have also been noted earlier: It is often difficult to divorce methodological concerns from their substantive context.

25. The extensive body of statistical data compiled by the United Nations since its inception is only one case in point.

26. See Jay W. Forrester, "Counterintuitive Behavior of Social Systems," *Technology Review* 73, no. 3 (January 1971): 52-68; Jay W. Forrester, *Principles of Systems* (Cambridge, Mass.: Wright-Allen Press, 1968).

27. See Howard Raiffa, *Decision Analysis: Introductory Lectures on Choices under Uncertainty* (Reading, Mass.: Addison-Wesley Publishing Company, 1968).

28. See Charles L. Schultze, et al., *Setting National Priorities: The 1972 Budget* (Washington, D.C.: Brookings Institution, 1971).

29. In this connection it becomes imperative to broaden our concept of cost to incorporate other than direct monetary considerations. For persuasive arguments, see Alice Rivlin, *Systematic Thinking for Social Action* (Washington, D.C.: Brookings Institution, 1971).

30. See n. 6.

31. See n. 28.

32. Robert C. North and Nazli Choucri, "Population and the International System: Some Implications for United States Policy and Planning," pp. 236-78 of A.E. Keir Nash, ed. (for the Commission on Population Growth and the American Future), *Governance and Population* (Washington, D.C.: Government Printing Office, 1972).

8 Theory and Method in Population Policy Research

Mair J. deVoursney

The chapters in this volume attest to a growing interest on the part of political scientists and other social scientists in population policy research. Even at this early stage it is important that practitioners and funding agencies be self-conscious about the nature and direction of research dealing with population policy. Recognizing a general need for a clearer view of research in this area, this chapter consists of four parts. The first aims to clarify what is meant by population policy research. The second considers the distinctiveness of the substantive area of population policy. The third evaluates the research approach which has been most widely used – the case study. The fourth advocates the use of comparative, cross-national, aggregate-data studies of the population policy process. Admittedly, this chapter offers no novel methodologies or substantive findings. The research approaches described have been sanctioned by widespread use in the social sciences. What is suggested is that these orientations and methods be applied to the study of population policy. Undergirding this presentation is a basic contention that population policy researchers should attempt to develop and test theories of population policy based on a general understanding of the policy process by using appropriate methodologies.

The Nature of Population Policy Research

The label "population policy research" is currently applied to studies that vary considerably in purpose and method. Studies cataloged under the heading "Population Policy" in the *Population Index* deal with such disparate topics as the evolution of population policy in single countries, problems encountered in the adoption of policy relating to family planning, ethical implications of a growing world population, compilations of governmental statements relating to population control, and descriptive accounts of demographic trends within a single country.

Lack of clarity about the nature of policy research is important since it can produce different expectations on the part of funding agencies and researchers about what constitutes the study of population policy. For example, many funding agencies want highly applied research into how-to-do-it studies on birth control programs or studies of the effectiveness of ongoing projects in family planning. The researcher, on the other hand, may be interested in more basic questions about policy determination. Another significant consequence of this lack of clarity is the attendant lack of attention given to assessing the strengths and weaknesses of different types of research. Too often proposals for funding are evaluated by reviewers not familiar with the policy sciences. While schooled in the methodologies and theories of their own fields (I am speaking here of demographers), these reviewers do not understand the potential for theoretical development in the area of policy. These reviewers are apt to view case studies as representing the "state of the art" in policy research.

A typology is presented in Figure 8-1 which differentiates among various policy studies. The four primary uses of this typology are to:

1. Delineate the field and order current and future work;

2. Clarify expectations on the part of individuals and institutions active in population policy research;

3. Distinguish among the research already conducted, enabling assessment of the relative merits of each type of research (Since limited resources are available for carrying out research in population policy, funding agencies and practitioners should apply some *a priori* notions about the inherent strengths and weaknesses of different research strategies.);

4. Establish the possibility for theoretically oriented work into population policy.

A variety of schemes could be developed to catalog research efforts. The typology here distinguishes on the one hand between basic and applied research and on the other between theory-oriented and atheoretical studies. Four types of research result from cross-classifying these dimensions.

Basic, Theory-oriented Population Policy Research. Despite considerable and persistent controversy, the so-called behavioral revolution in the social sciences has resulted in many social scientists coming to view social science as a science. With considerable individual variation in approach and interests, many social scientists have come to see the ultimate aim of social science to be the development of comparatively based, quantitatively tested, empirically validated theory. Within these broad commitments, some social scientists have spent their time in advancing theories and concepts, while others have chosen to concentrate on developing methods, creating indicators, gathering data, and testing propositions.

Confusion about the nature of social science exists because some social scientists spend a great deal of time addressing questions about specific public policies that are not of major theoretical interest within their own discipline. Others continue to employ traditional, nonscientific approaches in studying problems. My purpose here is not to say that social scientists ought not interest themselves in questions that are not of central significance within their own

Basic	Applied
Theory-oriented	1. i. conceptualization; definition; measurement of policy process, impacts, consequences; model-building; development of typologies ii. application of existing theory, developing theory iii. comparative, empirical analysis enabling generalizations about policy process and impact	2. i. application of basic research to specific cases ii. emphasis on "scientific" field research
Atheoretical-descriptive	3. i. "wisdom" literature ii. "bare foot" empiricism iii. the typical case study describing the policy process, usually producing recommendations for decision makers	4. i. application of descriptive research to field situations ii. review of policy recommendations by decision makers leading to policy adoption

Figure 8-1. A Typology of Population Policy Research

disciplines or that involve normative and prescriptive modes of thought; my purpose is to draw a distinction between discipline research — research directed toward the theoretical problems existing within a discipline — and other modes of research which, however valuable, are not oriented toward the theoretical problems of a discipline.

To date, little research into population policy has been discipline-oriented in the sense of being oriented toward basic theoretical questions. Few scholars have tended to conduct research on population policy with a view to what that research might contribute to theoretical questions in their own disciplines. Correspondingly, population policy researchers have not generally demonstrated familiarity with research results in such relevant fields as economic development, political development, comparative politics, and organization theory. More unfortunately, the emergence of policy science as a distinct area of social scientific concern with considerable advances in theory formation, conceptualization, and hypothesis testing [1] has tended to be overlooked by students of population policy. Simply stated, population policy researchers have tended to regard population policy as a discrete field with its own practical problems and have not regarded population policy research as a subspecies of a more general theoretical concern with the population process or social theory in general.

Applied, Theory-derived, Population Policy Research. Primarily concerned with the application of basic research to field studies, this may take the form of experimental field research, survey research, aggregate-data analyses, and assessments of deviant cases. Generalizations from comparative studies may be applied to specific cases. Frequently such studies, particularly of policy, are accompanied by an assessment of the implications for policy makers and specific recommendations for policy changes.

Basic, Atheoretical, Population Policy Research. This category includes the approach almost exclusively employed in population policy research — that of the case study. These studies lack generally both an explicit theoretical framework and conceptual rigor. Given the preponderance of this form of research in population policy analysis, attention will be paid later to the attributes of the typical case study and to the defects inherent in this form of investigation.

Studies of U. S. population policies and programs have consisted mainly of case studies of legislative process or of exploratory studies of decision makers. The researcher's goal has often been to generate hypotheses at the end of the study rather than to formulate explicitly a theory of change and to proceed to the testing of hypotheses derived from such theory.

Applied, Atheoretical, Population Policy Research. In this category one notes the application of descriptive, atheoretical research to field situations. Generalizations are derived from the single case study or from the sheer empiricism of quantitative work which lacks any guiding theoretical framework. Too frequently it is on the basis of atheoretical work that policy recommendations are made. Given the preponderance of atheoretical, descriptive research in the area of population policy analysis, decision makers are most frequently faced with advice which is not the product of adequate social science research.

The typology should suggest that a variety of research approaches are possible. The typology should focus attention on the methodological underpinnings of different research approaches. Research funding agencies, public and private, should be aware of the "status as knowledge" of proposals they are considering. Specifically, funding agencies should be conscious of the relative merits of what I have termed theory-oriented research — both basic and applied — and atheoretical-descriptive research. Such an examination should suggest the following research priorities:

1. Given the lack in consensus of theories of change, attention must be given to building theoretically based broad-range models or paradigms of the total policy process. Population policy analysis to this point is largely devoid of the development of paradigms. Such broad models would incorporate the societal context in which policies are made, the process whereby policies are adopted, the mechanisms of innovation, the implementation and outputs of policy, and the longer term outcomes and consequences of policy adoption.

2. Components of the policy process should be specified. These components require operationalization to allow the verification or rejection of the theoretical formulation.

3. Data in a form suitable for quantitative analysis should be more accessible. Of the information that has been compiled on the incidence and nature of family planning program development and the adoption of population-related policies,[2] presently much is not in a form suitable for the operationalization of population policy and the implementation of outcomes of that policy, or for the creation of indices of program development. Agencies such as the International Planned Parenthood Federation, the Agency for International Development, and the Population Council have done invaluable work in documenting information on country programs. However, considerable work has to be done before such information can be used in statistical analyses — for example, in the creation of additive or possibly cumulative scales of population program and policy development on an extensive cross-national scale. Unfortunately, while agencies that are working in this area regard the compilation of information on programs a routine task of their bureaucracies and expend considerable time and financial resources on compiling such information, their recognition of the needs of basic social science research in the policy area is lacking. This dearth of suitable data may well be a reflection of the poor communication between social scientists in identifying their research needs (both among themselves and to funding agencies) and the priorities of funding agencies in expending resources.

4. Comparative research should be encouraged. The investigation of single units cannot allow generalization to other units, nor is the single-unit analysis amenable to statistical procedures of testing. Population policy analysts have rarely employed the comparative method as envisaged, for example, by Durkheim, Nadel, and Murdock.[3]

5. The refinement of broad-range theories through the verification or rejection of hypotheses should be accomplished. Through empirical testing, a more precise formulation of the policy process can take place.

These considerations lead to the advocacy of broad-range, theoretically based, aggregate-data analyses at this research stage in the population policy area. Given the recency of policy research in this substantive area, the optimum expenditure of research resources is first to investigate the broader dynamics of policy change over several units of analysis. This stage should be accompanied by formulating data requirements for more refined social science research. Second, broad-range theoretical formulation, testing, and consequent refinement can be followed by more explicit identification of discrete elements of the policy process.

The Attributes of Population Policy

The neglect of the theoretical developments in the policy sciences by population analysts would be justifiable if researchers had established that population policies were in some way unique – that previous research by political scientists on policy could not be applied. If, however, population policy is held to be unique, it is still incumbent on these researchers to specify the theoretical basis for its uniqueness – that is, what theoretically sets it apart from other government policies and programs. With the exception of Lowi's innovative work,[4] the peculiar characteristics of population policies have not been identified.

Some justification may be found for regarding population policy as a distinctive policy arena. Five reasons follow.

Growth of Concern. Compared with other policy areas the growth of concern with population and the development of programs have been remarkably rapid. The interest and activity of international organizations, aid-granting countries, and national governments have increased dramatically. While not substantiated empirically, the time during which there has arisen an awareness of the problems consequent on rapid population growth would seem amazing. The years prior to 1960 did not see much international communication pertinent to either family planning or the broader facets of population growth. Except in a few cases such as funding by the UN specialized agencies of technical expertise and program aid in maternal and child health care and by the IPPF in its attempts to stimulate interest in private family planning programs in individual countries, little financial support was available for fertility-related programs from external sources. Commitment by individual governments prior to 1960 was similarly hard to identify or was absent. However, since 1960 population-related policies have been adopted and fertility-related programs have been implemented with unusual commitment on the part of the political elites of many countries. In the more affluent and industrialized countries population problems, until relatively recent years, have been considered the burden of the developing countries. It was mid-1972 before the United States published its first comprehensive consideration of its own population problems and policy recommendations.[5]

Over the last decade a consensus has developed on the part of the major multilateral, bilateral, and private aid-giving organizations in the area of fertility-related programs. This agreement has been reflected in: (a) the extension of training programs for personnel to work in applied family planning programs; (b) the offering of fellowships for studies in the country of origin and overseas; (c) the making available of technical expertise; (d) the dissemination of information on fertility control, sex education, maternal and child care; (e) the provision of contraceptive services; (f) the growth of both public and private institutions for controlling fertility-related behavior.

In contrast to fertility-related policies and programs, the incremental character of most policy implementation on a cross-national scale — such as the growth of social security programs, the provision of publicly financed medical programs, the growth of literacy programs, the malaria eradication programs — represents change over several decades. These programs have been financed largely by domestic budgetary allocations by individual countries. In a few cases — such as the support given by the UN special agencies to malaria eradication programs and the U. S. AID support of health programs — external sources of funds have been made available to individual governments. Some of these external funds have been offered through counterpart funding procedures, providing an incentive to recipient governments to increase allocations in a certain area. However, it is difficult to detect any uniform commitment — as indicated by the allocation of economic and social resources — by a large number of countries to any one of these programs. The commitment is present to a diffuse concept of improved health or to the attainment of modernization, but the interpretation of the means whereby to attain these goals varies widely.

One of the more severe problems of cross-sectional analyses of the variables antecedent to population policy adoption and program implementation stems from rapid changes in the substantive area. A comparison of a country at two points close in time may yield considerably different results. On the other hand, longitudinal analyses are hampered by the lack of sufficiently precise data and adequate indices to measure changes over time.

International Political Sensitivity to the Issue Area. Population policy is politically sensitive due to factors such as religious differences, perceived threats of racism, ethnic differences, and the sometime association of population size with national power. Yet there is a remarkable consensus of interest in the relationship between population growth rates and national economic, social, and political development, and between population growth rates and the quality of human life. It may be argued that this consensus of interest on the international level is in large part a response to: (a) economic pressures, and (b) the sheer flow of interpersonal and written communication related to the issue area. On the other hand, this is an era in which national governments react strongly to suspicions of political pressure such as the offer of economic aid contingent on the adoption of certain policies.

Intranational Political Sensitivity of the Issue Area. No less sensitive than international relations in the area of population programs are the domestic political relationships between individual national governments and their indigenous national populations. Irrespective of the differences in political systems, political, social, and economic elites rarely make explicit statements of policy in the area of population limitation. More often policies are implicit. Policy statements in this controversial area are little indication of what actually happens. In the latter situation, the analyst has to examine other social and economic policies – such as the permissiveness of abortion laws, policies allocating resources for the provision of contraceptive services, tax incentives or disincentives which might encourage or discourage larger families – to gauge the real intent of governmental elites.

Wide Distribution. The wide distribution of contraceptives through public and private channels is increasing rapidly.

Technological Advances. The last decade has witnessed considerable advances in contraceptive technology. During this period, more reliable contraceptives – the oral pill, IUD, condom, and chemical foam – have been made available for the first time in history to other than elite groups.

While these reasons somewhat justify regarding the development of policies and programs related to fertility behavior as atypical, these characteristics of population policies and programs do not preclude the operation of mechanisms attributed to the process of adoption, implementation, and impact of policies in other policy areas investigated in the discipline. Nor do these characteristics contradict theoretical developments in the policy sciences. Yet few of these developments have been generalized and investigated in the area of population policy.

The Case Study Approach to Population Policy

Perhaps the best way to illustrate the advantages of empirical theory building is to contrast comparative studies with the research method most commonly used in population policy research – the case study. But before embarking on this discussion, several qualifications must be made. First, case studies are not necessarily atheoretical. Deviant case analysis can stimulate theoretically oriented research and contribute new theoretical insights. Second, all case studies are obviously not the same. Many excellent, thorough, scholarly case studies have been conducted. But to the extent that these studies are case studies, they will share major methodological weaknesses that greatly reduce their scholarly contribution. Third, I am not suggesting that case studies are without heuristic value which might aid theory construction. I would only wish that instead of relying on the intuitive insights of their readers, the authors of these case studies would have been explicit instead of implicit in their theorizing. Fourth, a comparison between the case study and comparative, theoretical research should not be regarded as exhausting or defining the parameters of different approaches to research. Research efforts can be categorized in a host of ways, including units and objects of analysis employed, types of explanation, methods of data collection and analysis. Case studies and aggregate data analyses – to be described later – can both vary considerably.

The distinctive attributes of the typical case study include the following:

1. The identification and choice of the subject matter are primarily for reasons of intrinsic interest and availability. Less frequently is the subject matter chosen on the basis of a subjective impression of the typicality or the deviance/uniqueness of the case.

2. The case material investigated is dependent on the particular interests of the investigator — for example, in the population policy area interests may focus on the actors involved in making policy, the outcomes of decisions, the mechanisms whereby decisions are made, the identification of the influentials, the process of legislative change, the implementation process, and so forth. The investigator may have a commitment to thoroughness and detail, but rarely is this commitment related to theoretical interests, at least explicitly.

3. The focus of attention is restricted to one unit of analysis, be the unit a single country, a state, an individual, or a single piece of legislation. As such, apart from reasons of intuitive insight, the findings of the investigation cannot be generalized.

4. A variety of sources are used to supplement the collection of information. These sources may include historical data, newspaper articles, word-of-mouth information, hearsay, transcripts of meetings and conferences, and citations from social and economic journals.

At best, then, a single *political case* thus might be described as a "set of statements at a relatively low level of abstraction which describes something to be explained (the referents of dependent variables) and contains references to those factors and events hypothesized to be potentially relevant for the desired explanation (referents of independent variables)."[6] However, the interests of the behavioral scientist attempt to go beyond narratives of events and enumerations of relevant factors into searches for explanatory theory.

In constructing and in interpreting a single case there are several persistent problems which the analyst must face — which unfortunately are ignored frequently by case study analysts. These include questions about: (a) the boundaries of the case — what is to be included or excluded; (b) the level of case comparability to be sought — the extent to which the case method employed will permit replication and comparison; (c) the representativeness of the case — the universe of behaviors to which the case findings are hypothesized to apply; and (d) the adequacy of explanation — questions concerning the relative merits of competing explanatory hypotheses, including choices among internally induced and externally induced explanation.[7]

For the reasons given below, case studies as research tools possess a number of inherent weaknesses that severely compromise their usefulness.

1. Validity and reliability are low or completely lacking. The pursuit of an "understanding" of the variables is frequently cited as a major reason for

undertaking the case study. However, this contribution must be suspect for two reasons. First, reliability is low — for instance the replication of an investigation of the process of population policy adoption in Tunisia may produce quite different results. Not only will different investigators have different biases and perceptions in the selection and understanding of source material, but their reports will differ with the type of interpersonal contact with the political elites they encounter. Given the delicacy of the population policy area, the investigator more skilled in handling interpersonal relations may have a different impression of the influential decision makers. At the same time, that same investigator may become more personally involved with a select number of elites to the exclusion of other important inputs to the decision-making process. Biases such as these are almost inevitably "built in" to the case study, making controlled replication almost impossible to attain. Second, tests of validity are absent — as such, the findings of research cannot be generalized. The investigation is limited to a sample of one.

2. Basic to the generation of scientific evidence is the process of comparison or recording differences or contrasts — which the case study lacks. "Any appearance of absolute knowledge, or intrinsic knowledge about singular isolated objects, is bound to be illusory upon analysis."[8] Securing scientific evidence involves making at least one comparison. For such a comparison to be useful, both sides of the comparison should be made with similar care and precision.

As Holt and Turner acknowledge, "the goal of any science is to develop a valid, precise, and verified general theory . . . . If political scientists are to generate a body of theory and concentrate their efforts on making theory more general and valid, comparative cross-cultural research is essential."[9] Political scientists can hardly take issue with Murdock's conclusion that "there can never be any generally valid science of man which is not specifically adapted to, and tested with reference to, the diverse manifestations of human behavior."[10] It is in carefully designed comparative research that the social scientist, especially if he is concerned with macrosocial phenomena, finds something comparable to the controlled laboratory experiment of the natural scientist.

3. The absence of controls, in the words of Campbell and Stanley, means that there is "almost no scientific value in the case study."[11] Yet major expenditures of time and funds are invested in such investigations, and — more seriously — causal inferences continue to be drawn from the insights so gained.

In case studies in which a single group is studied only once, subsequent to some agent or treatment presumed to cause change, "a carefully studied instance is implicitly compared with other events casually observed and remembered. The inferences are based upon general expectations of what the data would have been had the change agent not occurred. Such studies often involve tedious collection of specific detail, careful observation, testing, and the like, and in such instances involve the error of misplaced precision."[12]

Unless the argument is made that the population policy area is unique, and the case study is used as an exploratory tool, the utility of the technique is limited. As previously indicated, no explicit argument has been made for the uniqueness of the policy area. As previously considered, there is some justification for regarding the policy area as distinctive but little reason at this stage of a research program for regarding the adoption, implementation, and impact mechanisms as different from those of other policy areas.

Speaking broadly, one can distinguish between analysts who have used data to try to understand the peculiarities of the political systems of one or two particular countries and those who have been more concerned with explaining broad patterns of association among variables across many countries. To a degree the identification of peculiarities implies that the broad patterns of association have already been identified — one can hardly identify the peculiar or the deviant case until the norm has been established. However, in the area of population studies, with few exceptions,[13] no attempt has been made to identify these broad patterns of association.

Given the identification of broad patterns of association, the so-called "deviant case analysis"[14] may involve — after locating the general patterns of association — a systematic study of those cases which are not well explained by the overall correlation in mathematical terms, that is, where the residual from the regression line is great. It is in this context that the case study can provide its most useful contribution at this stage in the development of a research program.[15]

The Uses of Comparative, Aggregate Data Studies of the Population Policy Process

In this fourth section, attention is given to some of the major uses of research based on aggregate data. My aim is not to present a full description of aggregate data analysis; excellent treatments exist elsewhere.[16]

It is relatively rare to find the use of purely aggregate data. Studies using aggregate data will frequently use global and contextual data. The following remarks on the uses of "aggregate data" analyses are therefore not confined strictly to the use of aggregate data, but rather to data based on other than individuals.

The uses of aggregate data analyses in population policy analysis include:

1. Testing for uniformities and regularities in political behavior. In an area which has not been much explored — such as the substantive area of population-related programs and policies — it would seem to be a rational research strategy to investigate the possible existence of broad patterns of association,

for example, the relationship between the adoption of population policies and various characteristics of the political system such as the political recruitment of elites, the degree of party competition, the existence of other social welfare policies. On the cross-national level, policy scientists such as Cutright and Aron[17] have investigated the relationship between certain types of policies and political system characteristics, using aggregate data. Dawson and Robinson,[18] using the American states as their unit of analysis, investigated the relationship between interparty competition and social welfare measures. Their research has led to additional research on the American states in an attempt to identify broad patterns of association between political system characteristics, socioeconomic characteristics, and policy outputs. However, with few exceptions,[19] little attempt has been made to conduct this type of research at the cross-national level on population-related policies and programs.

2. Aggregate data analysis can complement other forms of analysis:

(a) After broad patterns have been identified, research can become more focused. Critical variables with high predictive powers can be isolated. Deviant case analysis can facilitate explanation of those units that depart from the least squares line or where the residual from the regression line is great. Policy studies conducted in the United States have indicated the importance of economic growth on certain kinds of social expenditures.[20] Cutright and Aron have indicated a relationship between policy outputs and economic development on the cross-national level.[21] Where deviant cases arise from these patterns, the researcher has to seek for alternative explanations. For example, the presence of an antinatalist program, not otherwise to be anticipated on the basis of other social welfare policies, may be due to atypical historical circumstances such as certain colonial influences or bilateral relationships.

(b) Aggregate data analysis can alert the survey analyst to possibly critical correlations between variables and help him seek controls. Research, again in the United States, has suggested that while economic variables may be important in determining fiscal policies, political variables may be more useful in explaining other types of policies.[22] The relationship between competitive party systems and population policy adoption, when controlling for socioeconomic levels, may be considerable. The verification of such a relationship would highlight an area of study for the survey analyst such as the relationship between elite attitudes in the competitive party system and the adoption of anti- or pronatalist policies.

(c) Inferences can be drawn about groups through certain aggregate data. The composition of political elites may be reflected in the kinds of decisions these elites make. To my knowledge no cross-national studies in the area of population policy analysis have been conducted which attempt to measure the relationship between policy outputs and the characteristics of different elite groups.

(d) Research on elites need not be confined to survey research. Inferences can be drawn about the policy-making process through measurements of structure. For instance, concern with elite attitudes toward the adoption and/or implementation of family planning programs should not obscure the importance of elite structure (e.g., homogeneity, permeability, stability, differentiation) in the types of policy initiation.

3. Aggregate data are widely available: the relative ease of access and availability of aggregate data over long periods mean that various kinds of empirical analysis can be conducted inexpensively. A recognized function of governments has been to provide basic descriptive data for the major social and economic characteristics of national units. Exemplary of this material are data related to health — infant mortality, birth rates, death rates; data related to social life — linguistic diversity, ethnic composition, education; and data related to economic characteristics — gross national product, rates of industrialization and urbanization, the construction of communication networks. This array of aggregate data has been supplemented by historical data on such national characteristics as political system changes, leadership changes, rates of instability, internal domestic conflict, and interactions with other states.[23]

While acknowledging problems of reliability and validity of much cross-national data, the researcher interested in studying change cannot wait indefinitely until some arbitrary standard in data collection is achieved. Moreover, to suggest the postponement of quantitative research until higher standards of data collection have been attained indicates a lack of perspective on the substantive effect of random and nonrandom error.[24]

In contrast to the availability of aggregate data on various economic, social and political system characteristics, cross-national survey research data on individuals are not widely available. Of the data that exist — for example, the data on public opinion — most are not suitable for comparative analysis.

4. Various kinds of analyses may be conducted through the use of aggregate data.

(a) Studies of the diffusion of innovation, using aggregate data, attempt to explain systematically patterns of policy and program adoption. Walker's study of the diffusion of innovation in the American states investigates the influence of geographical contiguity and specialized sets of communications on the growth of certain programs.[25] In a cross-national study, Rogers and Cuyno are currently investigating the influence of geographical proximity, the communication of new ideas, and the receipt of assistance on the growth of population-related programs and policies.[26]

Since such programs and policies are primarily a phenomenon of the last decade, this latter study covers a limited time period. Such studies as these point to needed research in the area of population policy outputs and program adoption.

Research in this area raises questions such as: how do ideas spread among communities? how is information most effectively circulated? to what extent is the formulation of priorities among national elites a product of identification with certain abstract goals such as modernization? can the formulation of policy without a commensurate appropriation of funds for program implementation be explained through lip service to shared goals, again such as modernization? why are some population-related programs more successfully implemented than others — can this be explained through the "clustering" of factors conducive to program implementation such as historical circumstances, innovative elites, or attitudes conducive to change among the mass population?

(b) The American policy literature yields a variety of attempts to isolate the relative effects of socioeconomic and political variables on policy outputs in the area of social expenditures.[27] In two of the few cross-sectional analyses at the cross-national level, Cutright and Aron independently attempted to measure the effect of the type of political system on the nature of social expenditures.[28] Both found the level of socioeconomic development to be a more useful predictor of social expenditures than the difference in the political system. In a recently published article, Peters conducts a longitudinal analysis on economic and political effects on the development of social expenditures in France, Sweden, and the United Kingdom.[29] Such policy studies are rare in the cross-national area and deserve replication. In the substantive area of population-related programs and policies presently being discussed, there is a noticeable lack of such studies.

5. The population policy researcher has at his disposal aggregate data measuring the socioeconomic and political characteristics of a large number of countries, and aggregate data for subnational units are also available from a number of countries. As previously indicated, only limited data on population policies and programs are available for a large sample of nations. However, until researchers in the policy area can communicate a need for better cross-national data, and the funding agencies come to recognize the authenticity of requests for data improvement, research can proceed with somewhat less extensive funding on subnational units. Data on population programs and policies on subnational units such as the county are typically available in the more developed countries such as France, Sweden, the United Kingdom, and the United States. Given the range in terms of socioeconomic traits found among the subnational units of even the most developed countries, theories of change may be developed and empirically investigated in the more

developed countries in anticipation of the greater availability of data across a larger number of countries.

For example, many policy decisions on population-related programs are made at the county level in the United States. Considerable information exists about county program expenditures, personnel inputs, service levels, and the receipt of contraceptive services of various types. Sufficient information is available to construct indices of program development, making possible the use of sophisticated statistical tests in the exploration of theories of policy adoption and initiation and of policy implementation and outcomes. Yet to my knowledge, no comparative analyses have investigated either the initiation of such programs or the levels of support they receive. Nor have adequately designed comparative studies, again using the county as the unit of analysis, been conducted of the elites who have made the decisions or nondecisions to expend or withold financial support in this area.

6. Aggregate analyses can be conducted of the whole and parts of the whole. A number of social scientists such as Gregg and Banks[30] and Adelman and Morris[31] have suggested complementing global cross-national studies. A cursory view of regional characteristics does indicate different patterns of birth rates, death rates, incidence of family planning programs, population-related policies, and so on. However, attempts to explain population policies and programs exclusively on the regional basis may well lead to spurious conclusions. Limited commitment to family planning on the part of political elites has been variously interpreted, for example, religious factors have been considered an important limiting factor in the Latin American countries; many African countries express the need for population growth and hence a disinterest in family planning programs. However, investigations on a purely regional basis may result in undue emphasis being placed on regionally typical variables. Using the same rationale, to examine countries at similar levels of socioeconomic development again results in a bias in the range of socioeconomic variables. Where such variables are hypothesized to be important indicator variables — to so limit the population of countries being investigated or to so limit the range on the independent variable to the lesser developed countries — creates severe methodological problems.

7. Aggregate data are amenable to powerful statistical techniques. Aggregate data are found at, or may be converted into, several levels of measurement, allowing the use of various statistical routines in data analysis.

8. Research using aggregate data may be of practical value insofar as analysis may continue when other forms of investigation are suspect. Policy studies involving governments have become suspect in an era of growing national consciousness on the part of both old and new nations.

9. The informative value of aggregate data. The notion of informative value has been put forward in particular by Karl Popper, who speaks of the empirical

and informative value of scientific statements.[32] The empirical content of a statement increases with its degree of falsifiability; the larger the number of ways in which a statement can be proved false, the greater its empirical content, consequently the higher its informative value. The "ecological fallacy" has possibly diverted too much attention from questions of informative value. While there is probably general agreement with Robinson's contention[33] that ecological correlations cannot be used without strict qualifications as substitutes for individual correlations, there is also agreement that Robinson went too far in stating that ecological correlations are used simply and only as substitutes for individual correlations and that ecological correlations are subsequently less valuable than individual ones. Under certain conditions, the population policy researcher can use aggregate data to make inferences about the behavior of individuals and groups.[34]

In conclusion, this chapter has advocated the need for theoretical, empirical research into population policy. Brief reference has been made to the limitations of the approach most widely used in the study of the population policy process — the case study in its typical form. It was suggested further that survey research studies of elites are not an optimal research strategy at this stage in the development of paradigms of the total policy process. Lastly, in light of the limited research that has been conducted on the population policy process, a brief was presented for using aggregate data in population policy research.

Notes

1. This would include the theoretical and empirical developments in the areas of the policy-output literature, the diffusion of innovation research, and the community power studies; see for example *Public Choice* (a journal devoted exclusively to the policy sciences); Thomas R. Dye, *Politics, Economics, and the Public* (Chicago: Rand McNally, 1966); Ira Sharkansky, *Spending in the American States* (Chicago: Rand McNally, 1968); Richard I. Hofferbert, "The Relationship between Public Policy and Some Structural and Environmental Variables in the American States," *American Political Science Review* (henceforth *APSR*) 60 (March 1966): 73-82; Ira Sharkansky and Richard I. Hofferbert, "Dimensions of State Politics, Economics, and Public Policy," *APSR* 63 (September 1969): 867-79; Brian R. Fry and Richard R. Winters, "The Politics of Redistribution," *APSR* 64 (June 1970): 508-22; Jack I. Walker, "The Diffusion of Innovation among the American States," *APSR* 63 (September 1969): 880-99; Everett M. Rogers, *Family Planning Communications* (forthcoming); Theodore Lowi, "The Public Philosophy: Interest Group Liberalism," *APSR* 61 (March 1967): 5-24; Nelson Polsby, *Community Power and Political Theory* (London and New Haven: Yale University Press, 1963); Eulau, Wahlke, Buchanan, and Ferguson, "The Role of the Representative: Some Empirical

Observations on the Theory of Edmund Burke," *APSR* 53 (September 1959): 742-56; Peter Bachrach and Morton S. Baratz, "Two Faces of Power," *APSR* 56 (December 1962): 947-52; Robert A. Dahl, *Who Governs?* (New Haven: Yale University Press, 1960); Warren Miller and Donald Stokes, "Constituency Influence in Congress," *APSR* 57 (March 1963): 45-56; Terry N. Clark, ed., *Community Structure and Decision Making* (San Francisco: Chandler, 1968); Theodore Lowi, "American Business, Public Policy, Case Studies, and Political Theory," *World Politics* 16 (July 1964): 677-715.

2. The study of public policies related to population change includes both those purposely aimed at population change and those that indirectly influence demographic variables. As now conceived, population-related policies include those policies which relate to factors of mortality, migration, and fertility.

3. Emile Durkheim, *The Rules of Sociological Method* (Glencoe: Free Press, 1950), pp. 125-40; S.F. Nadel, *The Foundations of Social Anthropology* (London: Cohen and West, Ltd., 1951), pp. 222-27; and George P. Murdock, "Anthropology as a Comparative Science," *Behavioral Science* 2, no. 4 (October 1957): 249-54.

4. Theodore J. Lowi, "Population Policies and the American Political System," pp. 25-54 of Richard L. Clinton, William S. Flash, and R. Kenneth Godwin, eds., *Political Science in Population Studies* (Lexington, Massachusetts: D.C. Heath and Company, 1972).

5. Commission on Population Growth and the American Future, *Population and the American Future* (Washington, D.C.: G.P.O., 1972).

6. Glenn D. Paige, *The Korean Decision* (New York: Free Press, 1968), p. 10.

7. Ibid., p. 11.

8. Donald T. Campbell and Julian C. Stanley, *Experimental and Quasi-Experimental Designs for Research* (Chicago: Rand McNally and Company, 1963), pp. 6-7.

9. Robert T. Holt and John E. Turner, eds., *The Methodology of Comparative Research* (New York: Free Press, 1970), p. 5.

10. Murdock (n. 3), p. 249.

11. Campbell and Stanley (n. 8), pp. 6-7. See also E.G. Boring, "The Nature and the History of Experimental Control," *American Journal of Psychology* 67 (1954): 573-89; S.A. Stouffer, "Some Observations on Study Design," *American Journal of Sociology* 55 (1950): 355-61.

12. Ibid.

13. As for instance the ongoing research of E.M. Rogers and Cuyno, "An Aggregate Analysis of Population Policy Formation: The Case of Family Planning in Latin America, Africa, and Asia," in a forthcoming book edited by T.E. Smith; and Terry McCoy, "External Inputs and Population Policy in Latin

America," paper presented at the annual meeting of the American Political Science Association, Chicago, September, 1971.

14. As urged by Karl W. Deutsch in "Transaction Flows as Indicators of Political Cohesion," pp. 75-97 of P.E. Jacob and J.V. Toscano, eds., *The Interaction of Political Communities* (Philadelphia: Lippincott, 1964); and Bruce M. Russett, "The World Handbook as a Tool in Current Research," pp. 243-54 of C.L. Taylor, ed., *Aggregate Data Analysis: Political Indicators in Cross-National Research* (Paris: Mouton and Company, and the International Social Science Council, 1968).

15. There may be several variations on this theme, for instance Michael Haas takes note of the way the curvilinear regressions were used to isolate such cases in the *Handbook of Social Indicators,* then proceeds to a theoretical discussion of possible reasons for their deviance. See "Bridge Building in International Relations: A Neo-traditional Plea," in *International Studies Quarterly* 11 (December 1967): 320-23; and Frank Munger seeks to explain why Ireland should qualify as a stable democracy while rating so low, compared with other European states, on virtually all the economic development indices. See "The Legitimacy of Opposition: The Change of Government in Ireland in 1952," paper presented at the annual meeting of the American Political Science Association, New York, September 1969.

16. See for instance Taylor (n. 14); John V. Gillespie and Betty A. Nesvold, eds., *Macro-Quantitative Analysis* (Sage Publications, Inc., 1971); and Mattei Dogan and Stein Rokkan, *Quantitative Ecological Analysis in the Social Sciences* (Boston: M.I.T. Press, 1969).

17. Phillips Cutright, "Political Structure, Economic Development, and National Social Security Programs," *American Journal of Sociology* 70 (1965): 537-51; and Henry Aron, "Social Security in an Expanding Economy" (Ph.D. dissertation, Harvard University, 1963).

18. Richard E. Dawson and James A. Robinson, "Interparty Competition, Economic Variables, and Welfare Policies in the American States," *Journal of Politics* 25 (May 1963): 265-89.

19. See Rogers and Cuyno (n. 13).

20. See for instance Hofferbert (n. 1); Sharkansky and Hofferbert (n. 1); and Dye (n. 1).

21. Cutright (n. 17) and Aron (n. 17).

22. See Fry and Winters (n. 1).

23. See, for example, Rudolph J. Rummel and Raymond Tanter, *Dimensions of Conflict Behavior Within and Between Nations, 1955-1960* (Inter-University Consortium for Political Research, 1971); Charles L. Taylor and Michael C. Hudson, *World Handbook of Political and Social Indicators* (ICPR, 1971); Arthur S. Banks and Robert B. Textor, *A Cross-Polity Survey* (ICPR, 1963).

24. See Bruce M. Russet, "A Note on the Evaluation of Error and Transformation in Data Analysis," *APSR* 59 (June 1965): 444-46.

25. Walker (n. 1).

26. Rogers and Cuyno (n. 13).

27. See Fry and Winters (n. 1); Dye (n. 1); Hofferbert (n. 1).

28. Cutright (n. 17) and Aron (n. 17).

29. B. Guy Peters, "Economic and Political Effects on the Development of Social Expenditures in France, Sweden, and the United Kingdom," *Midwest Journal of Political Science* 16 (May 1972): 225-38.

30. Phillip M. Gregg and Arthur S. Banks, "Dimensions of a Political System: Factor Analysis of A Cross-Polity Survey," *APSR* 59 (1965): 555-78.

31. Irma Adelman and Cynthia Taft Morris, "A Factor Analysis of the Inter-relationship between Social and Political Variables and Per Capita Gross National Product," *Quarterly Journal of Economics* 79 (1965): 555-78.

32. Karl R. Popper, *The Logic of Scientific Discovery* (London: Hutchinson, 1959), pp. 119-21.

33. William S. Robinson, "Ecological Correlations and the Behavior of Individuals," *American Sociological Review* 15 (1950): 351-57.

34. Erwin K. Scheuch, "Cross-National Comparisons Using Aggregate Data: Some Substantive and Methodological Problems," pp. 148-56 of R.L. Merritt and Stein Rokkan, eds., *Comparing Nations: The Use of Quantitative Data in Cross-National Research* (New Haven: Yale University Press, 1966).

Political Science and Population Policy Analysis: Some Methodological Choices

Steven W. Sinding

Political scientists who have concerned themselves with the subject of population can be generally divided into two groups. By far the larger of these two groups is that which has investigated the relationship between population variables and political behavior. In most of the work that falls into this category, the effort has been to explain political behavior in terms of demographic factors.

The second group of political scientists concerned with population consists of those who have sought to understand the manner in which population policies are adopted and implemented. Most of the work in this area has focused, either explicitly or implicitly, on examination of factors which seem to explain the existence and the nature of national population policies or programs.

In this chapter, I attempt to examine the relative strengths and weaknesses of each approach to the study of politics and population, and to reach some conclusions regarding the utility of each insofar as international assistance agencies are concerned. As will become apparent below, the relative utility of each approach for donor agencies has very little to do either with the quality of the research which has been done or with its inherent scientific usefulness.

Population As a Determinant of Political Phenomena

Propositions about the impact of demographic variables on political phenomena have been in circulation for many years. From the earliest identification of a relationship between a nation's size and its power to very recent examination of the relationship between urban migration and political radicalism, students of politics have been interested in the interplay of politics and population. For convenience's sake, it makes sense to distinguish between investigation of the relationship between population and domestic politics and investigation of the relationship between population and international politics.

In the modern era of political science, it was students of international relations who first wrote seriously about the impact of a nation's population, in terms of both its size and structure, on its international behavior. Quincy Wright and the Organskis wrote about the empirical relationship between the relative

The ideas expressed in this chapter are my own and in no way reflect any official position of the U. S. Agency for International Development.

121

population size of nations and their power.[1] Later, Organski refined the concept when he wrote about the importance of what he called "effective population" in the size-power equation.[2] By "effective population," Organski meant that part of the population which is economically productive as a percentage of the total population. He argued that it is the size of a nation's "effective population," everything else being equal, which determines that state's degree of power in the international environment.

In recent years, students of international politics have tended to focus less on size alone and more on the impact of competition for scarce resources on relations between and among nations.[3] To what extent, it is asked, can one account for international conflict or cooperation (or the entire range of international relations) in terms of demographic variables and competition for natural resources? To date, the results of research on these questions have been rather tentative and inconclusive, as Nazli Choucri points out.[4] From her extensive review of the literature, one point stands out rather clearly; no systematic empirical research to date has discovered a direct relationship between international conflict and demographic variables. To the extent that population affects the nature of relationships between nations, it apparently does so only indirectly. Many variables intervene between population factors (density, growth rates, migration, etc.) and relations between nations. Population, in other words, may be a necessary but is never a sufficient condition of internation conflict.

An excellent review of the literature on the effects of population on domestic politics can be found in Myron Weiner's contribution to the volume, *Rapid Population Growth: Consequences and Policy Implications* edited by a committee of the National Academy of Sciences.[5] Without attempting to cover the same ground that Weiner does or with anything like the same rigor, I would point out here that most of the research on the domestic political effects of population change has focused on political stability and instability. Looking at such demographic variables as population growth rate, age structure, migration, and density, scholars (including remarkably few political scientists) have attempted to relate these variables to domestic political conflict, political stability and violence.[6] Of considerably lesser emphasis within this general literature has been research on the relationship between population and what Almond has called "governmental capacity."[7] Here the emphasis has been on examining the impact of population changes on bureaucratic capacity, on the relationship between local and central governments, and in general on the capacity of government to respond effectively to demands and to provide the sorts of services normally expected of political organisms.[8] As in the case of research on the relationship between population and international relations, study of the relationship between population and domestic politics has yielded only very tentative conclusions. As Weiner puts it: "there may very well be few if any uniform political effects of population growth; certainly the attempts so far to relate population growth to war, violence, political instability, revolution, etc. have not been very successful."[9] Weiner goes on to list ten areas in which it is reasonable to hypothesize important linkages between population and politics and which deserve far more systematic treatment by political scientists than they have received to date. Since most of the work on population and politics to date has been done by demographers, Weiner concludes by calling on political scientists to help refine such studies by bringing to them more precise and rigorous treatment of the political variables.

There is no question that the sort of research and the sort of theoretical inquiry described above are legitimate in terms of the way political science as a discipline defines itself. Indeed, the political scientist ought to be interested in the impact of demographic variables on various forms of political behavior. It certainly is reasonable to hypothesize that population change plays an important role in the determination of interstate and intrastate conflict, the presence and/or degree of political stability and instability, individual voting behavior, the behavior of groups, the decision-making process, and any number of other political phenomena which political scientists may specify. What is surprising is the extent to which political scientists have ignored population variables, even as environmental variables, in the construction of theories of politics. By "environmental variables," I mean those which, while not contributing directly to given political outcomes, do play an indirect role insofar as they affect those variables directly linked to politics. Hence, while it may be theoretically dubious to hypothesize that population density is directly related to violence, to hypothesize that rapidly increasing density produces competition for space, strains public services, leads to a sense of social alienation, and thus contributes to hostile and sometimes violent political manifestations is entirely reasonable and deserving of empirical investigation.[10]

In the search for theory, therefore, population variables ought to be included among the many other variables which political scientists have identified, or will in the future identify, as explanatory. For heuristic purposes or for the purposes of building "middle-range theories," political scientists may be interested in focusing expecially on population variables for one or both of two reasons: (1) to examine simple correlations between, for example, migration rates and conflict in urban areas; or (2) to seek to isolate the degree of variation in political phenomena that demographic phenomena are able to explain.

If one wants to construct middle-range theories of the impact of population on politics, or if one's goal is to build population variables into a multivariate theory of politics, then the methodological choices are clear. On the one hand the investigator may choose to work inductively. He may look at a single case (a nation, a subunit of a nation, a community) as an example of the phenomenon he supposes to be common to many similar cases. Out of this examination, a firm hypothesis may emerge. Confirmation of the hypothesis through the study of a single case is not possible, but replication of the initial case study over time or in a number of different settings would increase the investigator's confidence in the hypothesis, should the results of repeated case analyses correspond with the initial findings.

On the other hand the investigator may choose to work deductively, beginning with a full-blown theory, and "testing" it by looking at a large number of units simultaneously. In political science, the variables are normally difficult enough to measure so that gathering data of the sort one needs to accomplish a case study is not possible when one is looking at a number of cases simultaneously. However, enough aggregated statistical data exist so that the careful investigator can make inferences about the relationship of population and politics on the basis of published data which are more or less readily available. The quality of the data preclude his having absolute faith in the results of the analysis, and the nature of aggregate analysis precludes his making inferences about individual behavior, but the method does permit one to draw preliminary conclusions about the hypotheses without engaging in the much more arduous methodology of the case study.

Each approach has its shortcomings. The single case does not permit generalization to other cases, while aggregate analysis does not permit one to draw very firm conclusions. In the final analysis, only systematic comparison of a number of cases, including so-called deviant cases, can lead to greater substantiation of theory in political science.

Research Needs of International Agencies: The Determinants of Population Policy

We begin this section with a question: Should international assistance organizations, in the effort to achieve their stated goal of helping other countries deal with their population problems, support research in which politics is the dependent variable? This question suggests two subsidiary questions: How would sponsorship of such research affect the donor agencies' credibility? Would the sponsorship of such research contribute to the donors' chief mission?

If we start with the assumption that donor organizations sponsor research because they intend to make use of the results or because they anticipate that others will make use of the results, we begin to see that some research may be more useful to donors than other research. This distinction is usually made in terms of "basic" versus "applied." In the social sciences, the distinction is more difficult to draw than in the physical sciences. It is often very difficult to anticipate the possible applications of a piece of social science research — much more difficult than is the case in the physical sciences.

Nonetheless, I think that by making clear at the outset what possible uses *could* be made of a piece of social science research, whether basic or applied, one can begin to make distinctions between that research which is potentially useful and that which is not. The distinction between basic and applied, then, becomes less important than the determination of who might wish to use the results and how they might be used.

Let us return to the original question and the two subquestions posed above. It is conceivable that research involving population variables in which political variables are dependent could be used for purposes other than those of the donor agencies and by persons who see their mission in somewhat different terms than do such donors. To return to an example used earlier, how could the donor organizations make use of research on the impact of population density on domestic political violence? Who else might make use of such research and for what purposes? Certainly the donors and others could make use of such research by bringing it to the attention of leaders of other countries, particularly those countries with high population densities, in order to impress decision makers in such countries with the threat of violence that is hanging over them (assuming that a positive relationship between population density and violence were found). The implication of such a presentation would be that those countries ought to do something about their population growth rates or about their urbanization rates. In presenting such information, the donor organizations would be making explicit, therefore, a bias against political violence. Since I do not believe that such a bias, assuming that it exists, is legitimate (certainly not legitimate insofar as donors are concerned), I do not believe that research in which such a bias may be implicit ought to be supported by the donor organizations. Indeed, even if the bias does not exist, the credibility of the donors would be threatened, insofar as they sponsor such research, to the extent that other people might think the sponsorship of such research implies an antirevolutionary bias. One need only be reminded of Project Camelot (in which the ideological biases came to be quite clearly seen) to understand how research on political questions which is sponsored by public agencies can be interpreted.[11]

In a word, I am arguing that it is potentially very dangerous for organizations which define their function in terms of humanitarian assistance to sponsor research whose relationship to such assistance is questionable, at best. I think that research in which certain kinds of political variables (such as violence, internal partisan group or individual behavior, etc.) are dependent falls into that category.

That conclusion brings us to the question of which research strategies and which methodological approaches donors should support in the area of political science and population.

As a general rule, I feel that political scientists can contribute a great deal to the population-assistance organizations and to the countries with which they deal by concentrating their efforts on the population *policy* process. Although perhaps less appealing to those concerned with the development of theories of political behavior than research in which politics is the phenomenon to be explained, research on the population policy process has several virtues of its own.

First, insofar as the interests of political scientists are concerned, such research does have potential for providing a basis of information on which theories of public policy formation can begin to be built. Through case study or through cross-national analysis using aggregate data, the study of the process of public policy-making and the determinants of population policy, respectively, can make significant contributions to political science. Population is only one of several policy areas to which political scientists can apply themselves in their search for better understanding of politics and public policy. Certainly policy analysis is an underdeveloped enough field in political science to make population an attractive case area.

A second virtue of the policy approach is its potential usefulness to donors in terms of providing them with information about the sorts of population programs which are most likely to be acceptable to other governments. Careful studies of the political and ideological factors which impinge on the process of population policy development in any country would be very useful in helping donor organizations avoid making mistakes. All of the population-assistance agencies profess a need for far more sophisticated information than they presently possess concerning the policy milieu. Political scientists, who are among the best qualified to provide this sort of information, have been conspicuous by their almost complete absence from this area of inquiry.[12]

Finally, the study of population policy can be very useful to citizens or groups in the countries studied who are interested in advocating population policies but who lack information on how to operate in the political system. Such groups might include medical societies, private family planning associations, business federations, women's groups, and so on. As in many other policy areas, case study research in the population area can provide a far more sophisticated understanding than we presently have of who the actors are, what the distribution of influence among them is, what the ideological issues are, which strategies seem to work and which seem to fail, and so on. Replication of such studies can lead to a fairly good probabilistic assessment of the effectiveness of advocating population programs in different ways and by different groups. Studies of policy regarding social security, land tenure, and abortion have shown how effective good political science case analysis can be when it comes to policy advocacy.

Alternative Methodologies

This argument concludes with a reiteration of the methodological alternatives cited above for studies of the impact of population variables on political variables. In this section, however, those methodologies are applied to studies in which population policy is that which is to be explained.

The Country Case Study. The rigorous and systematic study of a single country, or the comparison of two countries along the same dimension(s), has been in ill-repute for a number of years in political science. The argument is made that such analysis does not permit one to generalize sufficiently to make any theoretically significant statements. I would argue that this is not necessarily the case. Obviously, the examination of a single case does not, in and of itself, provide sufficient information to give one substantial confidence about generalizing to other cases. However, a case study which begins from a theoretical posture, which "tests" hypotheses in a single case, can be used to work toward the verification of theories which have had *no* empirical referents. The single case will not, of course, verify the theory, but it certainly can provide evidence sufficient to disconfirm a hypothesis. By the same token, a theoretically based case study can provide evidence upon which to make decisions regarding the utility of generalizing research sufficiently broadly so that one can, in fact, verify an hypothesis. So much for this effort to make the case approach respectable. More important from the standpoint of the donor community is the information which case studies can provide on a country-by-country basis. Such research must be rigorous, not the anecdotal sort of pseudojournalism which gave the case study such a bad name in the first place. For the reasons cited earlier, country-specific information on the population policy process can be of great use to international donors and national advocates alike.

Cross-National Aggregate Analysis. If the case study represents a strategy of theory-building from the particular to the general, then the cross-national aggregate approach represents a strategy of beginning with the general in order to explain the particular. Elsewhere in this volume Mair deVoursney argues the case for aggregate analysis. Suffice it to say here that the systematic, aggregate level study of the "determinants" of population policy, while slightly different in emphasis than the case approach, can provide the sorts of general theoretical hypotheses upon which productive case examination can be built.

From the standpoint of the donors, I think the aggregate data approach is likely to be somewhat less useful than the case study approach. This seems to be true because the sort of information which the aggregate approach generates is not likely to be either firm enough or specific enough to imply action. Insofar as the development of theories of population policy formation is concerned, the aggregate approach has much to recommend it, but until such theoretical notions are confirmed by case analysis, they are not likely to be either precise enough or sufficiently confidence-inspiring to warrant action.

Analysis of the "Critical Case." Examination of what Harry Eckstein has called the "critical case" actually combines the two approaches just discussed. In effect, it means selecting for particularly careful study that case or those cases which either comparative case analysis or cross-national aggregate analysis have identified as "deviant." Supposing that in studying five countries in order to understand how population policy was formulated in each, four of the five looked pretty much the same, but the fifth case was so different that your theory did not permit you to explain what happened there. On the other hand, say that in a multiple regression equation you were able to account for seventy percent of the variance in population policy outcomes in sixty nations. By carefully inspecting the data you could identify those countries which caused the correlation coefficient to fall below 1.0. In either instance, according to Eckstein's prescription, you would select for the most rigorous analysis those cases which the theory does not explain. Until you could explain why those cases deviated from the norm, the theory would be incomplete. As long as the theory is incomplete, one cannot have full confidence in any action recommendations he might make or which others might infer from his research. Therefore, it is in the interest of political scientists and of the donor community to develop as complete a theoretical understanding as possible of the population policy process. For the donors, this importance derives from the possibility that in the absence of full understanding, they might make some awkward (or even disastrous) mistakes. In the case of political scientists, an adequate theory of population policy formation would be an important advance for the discipline, not because population was the substance of the inquiry, but because a major step forward was made in understanding the policy process in general.

Conclusion

In this essay I have tried to keep clear the distinction between the interests of individual political scientists and those of individual international population-assistance agencies. I do not pretend to speak for all donors, nor, I know, will all political scientists agree with what I have said. Whether or not a political scientist chooses to work in the population area is entirely up to him. Should he wish to work in the population area, how he carries out his professional activities is also entirely up to him. But insofar as he is interested in using his professional competence to make a contribution to the resolution of a grave, worldwide problem, I have tried to make a few observations as to how that competence might best be employed. There is nothing wrong with studying the effect of demographic variables on politics. Indeed, from the standpoint of disciplinary development, it might be the preferred way to treat these variables. On the other hand, I think I have shown ways in which the discipline of political science can be served *at the same time* that the eventual resolution of the world population problem can be served by the application of political science to the study of population policy.

Notes

1. Quincy Wright, *A Study of War* (2nd ed.; Chicago: University of Chicago Press, 1965); and A.F.K. and Katherine Organski, *Population and World Power* (New York: Alfred A. Knopf, 1961).

2. For the most recent formulation of this notion, see A.F.K. Organski, Bruce Bueno de Mesquita and Alan Lamborn, "The Effective Population in International Politics," in Richard L. Clinton, William S. Flash and R. Kenneth Godwin, eds., *Political Science in Population Studies* (Lexington, Mass.: D.C. Heath and Company, 1972).

3. Nazli Choucri and Robert C. North, "Dynamics of International Conflict: Some Policy Implications of Population, Resources, and Technology," *World Politics,* Supplementary Issue, *Theory and Policy in International Relations* 24 (Spring 1972): 80-122.

4. Nazli Choucri, "Population Dynamics and International Violence: Propositions, Insights, and Evidence" (M.I.T.: Center for International Studies, September 1972, revised March 1973). This review of the literature is undoubtedly one of the most complete, if not the most complete, in existence.

5. "Political Demography," pp. 567-617 of National Academy of Sciences, *Rapid Population Growth; Consequences and Policy Implications* (Baltimore: Johns Hopkins University Press, 1971).

6. Among the many examples of this work, see in particular Joan M. Nelson, *Migrants, Urban Poverty, and Instability in Developing Nations. Occasional papers in International Affairs,* no. 22 (Cambridge, Mass.: Harvard University Center for International Affairs, September 1969); Myron Weiner, "Urbanization and Political Protest," *Civilizations* 17 (1967): 1-7; and Irene B. Taueber, "Population and Political Instabilities in Underdeveloped Countries," in Philip M. Hauser, ed., *Population and World Politics* (Glencoe, Illinois: Free Press, 1958).

7. Gabriel A. Almond and G. Bingham Powell, *Comparative Politics: A Developmental Approach* (Boston: Little, Brown and Company, 1966), esp. ch. 8.

8. John D. Montgomery of Harvard University is presently working on the development of some research ideas in this relatively unexplored area. See his mimeographed paper, "A Strategy for Analyzing the Effects of Rapid Population Growth on the Administration of Public Services," prepared for a meeting on the effects of rapid population growth on political change in less developed countries, Department of State, February 17, 1972.

9. Weiner (n. 6), p. 608.

10. Such hypotheses have been advanced by Richard Lee Clinton, "Portents for Politics in Latin American Population Expansion," *Inter-American Economic Affairs* 25 (Autumn 1971): 31-46.

11. For a full discussion of this unfortunate episode in American foreign relations, see Irving Louis Horowitz, ed., *The Rise and Fall of Project Camelot* (Cambridge, Mass.: M.I.T. Press, 1969).

12. The few exceptions to this rule would include: Elihu Bergman, *The Politics of Population USA: A Critique of the Policy Process* (Chapel Hill: Carolina Population Center, Population Program and Policy Design Series no. 5, 1971); Richard L. Clinton, *Problems of Population Policy Formation in Peru* (Chapel Hill: Carolina Population Center, Population Program and Policy Design Series no. 4, 1971); Vivian Xenia Epstein, "The Politics of Population in Latin America," pp. 133-76 of David Chaplin, ed., *Population Policies and Growth in Latin America* (Lexington, Mass.: D.C. Heath and Company, 1971); and Pavao Novosel and Katja Boh, "Population Policy and the Slovenian Elite," paper presented at the second plenary meeting of the International Population Policy Consortium, Dubrovnik, Yugoslavia, October 1972.

10 Methodology and Policy

R. Kenneth Godwin

Several of the earlier chapters of this volume have indicated that the choice of research method will determine to a large extent what types of policy recommendations will be encouraged by the research. Thus certain types of research methods will encourage policies supportive of the status quo, while other methods may lead to more radical implications. In this chapter I would like to give an example of that process by examining how the use of attitude questionnaires such as those employed in knowledge, attitudes, and practice (KAP) studies has contributed to the support of family planning policies. I will attempt to show that the assumptions which generally underlie these studies almost inevitably lead to findings supportive of existing policies and existing socioeconomic relationships.

Frederick Stephen in 1962 discussed the difficulties of using attitude questionnaires to study the determinants of fertility. Stephen suggested that the measurement of fertility attitudes with a questionnaire tended to show these attitudes as more structured than is probably the case, ignored the complexity of the relationship between attitudes and behavior, and focused only on the individual's private attitudes rather than including the influence of the larger social group.[1] The result of these difficulties has been that KAP studies usually give a false picture of the private opinions of women concerning their desired family size and overemphasize the importance of these attitudes as predictors of behavior.

To show the probable extent of this distortion we need only look at the question from KAP studies: "How many children do you believe would be ideal for your family?" This question or some variation of it is invariably asked in KAP studies and is believed to indicate the number of children a woman would have if she had perfect control over her own fertility. Because there are important differences between the number of children a woman says would be ideal and the number of children actually born, and because the number "wanted" in the developing countries is usually substantially lower than the number born, it is implied that the knowledge about, and availability of, contraceptives could radically reduce the number of children born. Such an implication is only warranted, however, if the responses to this question tap attitudes which are both salient and well integrated with other important attitudes and beliefs.[2] In most of the developing countries these conditions are not met. For example, Mayone Stycos in his research with women in Peru found that a majority of lower-class women had *never* thought about how many children they wanted and that even among the upper-class women, one-third had never given the subject any thought.[3]

If the Peruvian results are at all representative for much of the rest of Latin America and the Third World, it is difficult to imagine anyone attempting to predict behavior or make policy on the basis of an answer to a question about which individuals rarely think. Of course, even more remote to most individuals would be such questions as:

> All things considered, do you think having a larger population would be a good thing or a bad thing for this country?

> All things considered, how would you feel about a birth control program to encourage people in your country to have fewer children — would you approve or disapprove of such a program?

Yet the United States Information Agency sponsored studies in twenty-two countries and collected data on 17,000 individuals asking these questions.[4]

If there is a reasonable doubt that attitudes as measured by questionnaires are not the best predictors of fertility behavior, why have social scientists continued these surveys and policy makers continued to rely on their results for the formulation and justification of policies? I believe there are three major reasons for this situation: (1) the law of the instrument;[5] (2) the prevailing ideology of individual freedom of choice which exists in the United States; and (3) the bias created by elites funding research which will support their own policies.

The Law of the Instrument

Abraham Kaplan has observed that if you give a young child a toy hammer he will soon discover that everything in his house needs hammering. In a similar manner when social scientists (and probably all other types of researchers) discover new research techniques or equipment they often find that the substantive problem they are interested in can best be studied through the use of these new "hammers." As most of the new instruments in the social sciences have been quantitatively oriented, the need for research techniques which provide quantitative data is obvious. The questionnaire, especially the closed-ended variety, has therefore become an attractive data-gathering instrument.

The attractions of the questionnaire are not limited solely to its quantitative qualities. Not only can we scale, code, punch, and factor analyze questionnaire data, we can also obtain our data relatively quickly and painlessly. In fact, it is usually more methodologically correct to let some other persons — well-trained interviewers — gather the data for us. In addition, the questionnaire is easily used in cross-cultural research, as it appears to require only a good translation and a qualified interviewing staff in the countries under examination to enable the gathering of comparable cross-national data.[6] Yet, since Richard LaPiere's famous study on racial prejudice in 1934,[7] study after study has shown the attitudinal data collected by questionnaires insufficient to predict behavior. LaPiere summarized the attractiveness and the limitations of the questionnaire as follows:

The questionnaire is cheap, easy, and mechanical. The study of human behavior is time consuming, intellectually fatiguing, and depends for its success upon the ability of the investigator. The former method gives quantitative results, the latter mainly qualitative. Quantitative measurements are quantitatively accurate; qualitative evaluations are always subject to errors of human judgment. Yet it would seem far more worthwhile to make a shrewd guess regarding that which is essential than to accurately measure that which is likely to prove quite irrelevant.[8]

Of course the questionnaire does have many valid uses. In the study of voting, in ascertaining many types of past behavior, and in some types of personality studies, the questionnaire has proved itself a useful tool. Unfortunately, however, too many researchers have used the questionnaire with little regard to the situational issues involved, thus impairing the reliability and validity of their results. More often than not, researchers studying fertility determinants have been among the most methodologically and conceptually careless in the use of the questionnaire.[9]

The Prevailing Ideology

A second major source for social scientists' reliance on questionnaires is, I believe, the ideology of individual freedom of choice which prevails in Western cultures. Although I have no ready empirical data to support this proposition, I would suggest that there is a mobilization of bias in nonsocialist countries which favors individual-choice indeterminism, just as there is a tendency in socialist countries to favor materialistic or situational determinism. Inevitably, a mobilization of bias will influence the choice of research strategies.

Although philosophers of science and others have for some time attempted to show social scientists that it is not possible to use personality traits as "causal" variables in the traditional sense of this term, we often continue to think of attitudes, beliefs, and values as causes of specific events. While we have, for the most part, given up explaining systemic events on the basis of personality variables[10] (e.g., the Nazi movement in Germany was "caused" by the authoritarian features of the Germans' personalities), we nevertheless continue to speak of attitudes and beliefs as causes on the individual level. B. F. Skinner has demonstrated the difficulties of using these personality characteristics as adequate explanations of behavior.

The conditions of which behavior is a function are also neglected. The mental explanation brings curiosity to an end. We see the effect in causal discourse. If we ask someone, "Why did you go to the theater?" and he says, "Because I felt like going," we are apt to take his reply as a kind of explanation. It would be much more to the point to know what has happened in the past, what he heard or read about the play he went to see, and what other things in his past or present environments might have induced him to go . . . .[11]

If we compared persons who attend the theater regularly with persons who do not, we might find that those who attend regularly have more favorable attitudes toward the theater. Does this mean that we could explain theater attendance by favorable attitudes toward the theater? I would suggest that this is not an explanation, as we would still need to know why these persons have favorable attitudes toward the theater. Such research would lead us to study the past consequences of previous theater attendance for both groups. In fact, if we knew this information the attitudinal data would add little or nothing in our ability to explain or predict attendance.

That previous consequences of past behavior are the major factors in predicting and explaining future behavior can be readily seen when we attempt to explain why one person who has favorable attitudes toward the theater did attend the theater on a given night, while another person whose attitude toward the theater is no less favorable did not attend. Quite obviously there are almost limitless reasons why the second person did not attend (e.g., weather, health, competing activities). We might say that for the first person the expected consequences of attending the theater were sufficiently rewarding that he was willing to pay the necessary costs, while the second was not willing to do so. We should not lose sight of the fact, however, that the expected utility of attending the theater was contingent not only upon the expected rewards and costs of theater attendance but also upon the expected rewards and costs of competing activities. (Actually the inability to participate in a competing activity can be viewed as a cost of theater attendance.) I do not think it unreasonable to assume that an individual's estimation of the rewards and costs of his possible activities is based primarily on past experiences with these or similar activities. Unfortunately, most attitudinal research gives us little indication of what the costs and benefits of any of these competing activities might be or how the individual calculates the utility of the behavior which is believed to be related to the attitude under examination.

If the study of attitudes is simply a surrogate for either the study of actual behavior or the study of the consequences of past behavior, why have we continued to study attitudes and continued to accept mentalistic causes of behavior? A part of the answer to this question was found in our discussion, "The Law of the Instrument." A second part of the answer is to be found in the allegiance of social scientists to the prevailing ideology of individual freedom of choice which is so much a part of the cultural and academic traditions of the West.

In his book *Beyond Freedom and Dignity* Skinner makes a strong case for considering freedom of choice and individual dignity as myths by arguing that present behavior is determined by the consequences of past behavior. If our present behavior is completely shaped by past reinforcements, and since we had no control over the reinforcements of our earliest behaviors, then it can be reasonably argued that both freedom of choice and individual responsibility and dignity are myths. This conclusion, though logical, reflects extreme reductionism.[12] From our Western liberal perspective, moreover, it smacks of materialistic determinism, hence we prefer to look to more mentalistic interpretations of behavior in spite of their explanatory and predictive shortcomings.

The Explanatory Bias in Population Policies and Research

If the ideals of individual freedom, responsibility, and dignity are important in the determination of research strategies, they are equally important in the determination of policy. As Marx so clearly showed, the prevailing values, ideologies, and myths in a society are normally supportive of the existing social structure. For this reason, policies will customarily reflect these ideologies. Existing population policies abundantly illustrate this generalization, for the term "population policy" has to date been little more than a euphemism for "family planning and/or population education programs."[13] Such policy measures are justified on the basis that they facilitate freedom of choice and parental responsibility. Persons can choose to have exactly the number of children they want. It is rarely mentioned, however, that family planning programs are supportive of the existing social and political structures, as they would not require any basic changes in the social structure for their success. Instead, the success of these programs relies upon technological innovations which make contraceptives more effective and easier to distribute.[14]

It is common knowledge that large amounts of money have recently been poured into the population field. The manner in which this money has been spent gives an indication of the bias of the public and private donor agencies. A look at the budget of the United States Agency for International Development, the largest funder of population-related research, yields some interesting findings. Of the $10,701,000 spent on research in 1971, 59 percent went toward the development of improved technological devices for contraception, abortion, and sterilization; 24 percent was spent on the development of systems to deliver these devices; while only 17 percent was allocated to the study of population dynamics and descriptive demography.[15] In this last category, approximately one-half of the funds were spent on descriptive demography (e.g., improved census reporting, determination of age structures, etc.), and one-half (8 percent of the total budget) was spent on studying attitudes and behaviors related to fertility.[16] The majority of this 8 percent was for KAP or other attitudinal studies.[17] Thus less than 4 percent of AID's budget in 1971 (and this is true of the entire 1966-71 period)[18] was spent in trying to determine the socio-economic conditions which influence fertility![19] These figures are also fairly representative of the private funding agencies.[20]

This pattern of spending should seem rather strange since past declines and increases in fertility have had little if any relationship to advances in contraceptive technology.[21] Rather, to the extent that fertility relationships are understood, they seem bound up with the individual's economic and personal interests.[22] Thus changes in socioeconomic situations rather than increases in technological capability would appear to be a more fruitful approach in the formulation of a population policy.[23] Why then have funding agencies concentrated on technical solutions to problems which appear to be social and economic in their causes? I believe Kingsley Davis answered this question most succinctly when he wrote that "as it is, reliance on family planning allows people to feel that 'something is being done about the population problem' without the need for painful social changes."[24]

In a very real sense, we can say that the AID budget is a rational response by policy makers to the demands placed upon them. Obviously, a major demand is that the program not violate the prevailing ideologies of individual freedom and responsibility. Because they rely on individual choice, family planning programs fulfill this requirement. Similarly the policy must not threaten either those persons who are demanding the program in the United States nor the elites being asked to implement the program in other countries. Given these inputs, the family planning policy is a rational output. As Eli Bergman[25] and Peter Bachrach[26] have demonstrated, the persons who have devoted the largest amounts of time, energy, and money to the population issue have been the economic elites, and these elites have been able to mobilize bias in favor of those policies which do not threaten the existing power structure. Of course, elites in other countries are also in favor of policies which do not threaten their power position. By implying that the only need is the invention and distribution of new technological devices, family-planning programs do not disturb the elites and are therefore more readily accepted by the host country.

The emphasis on technological research is not solely a result of the prevailing ideology and power sturcture. Given the severity of the population problem in some countries, the need for a rapid and simple solution seems imperative. Changes in the social and economic structure can be neither simple nor rapid. In fact, our experiences with programs such as the Alliance for Progress have shown that even those aid programs which were originally conceived to be change -oriented are not likely to be implemented in ways which require significant change. As Bernard Berelson discussed in his classic article, "Beyond Family Planning," policies which attempt to go beyond family planning usually go beyond the financial and governmental constraints existing in the lesser developed countries.[27]

Although family planning and other technologically based programs have the above attributes favoring their adoption, it is still necessary that the policy be perceived as effective. The research budgets of AID and other donor agencies greatly facilitate this perception. First, by concentrating research efforts in the technological and distribution fields, the budget rephrases the question from "What population programs will be effective?" to "How can we improve the effectiveness of family planning programs?" This rephrasing of the question becomes an example of the "nondecision" or "mobilization of bias in agenda building" described by Bachrach and Morton Baratz.[28] The more difficult original question, the question which might have implications which would indicate the need for painful social changes, does not reach the agenda.

As is the case with most policies, there are individuals who are not satisfied with current policies and attempt to reintroduce the original question. Among the most vociferous critics of family planning have been Kingsley Davis, Judith Blake, and Garrett Hardin.[29] Their criticisms have been based on the assumption that the existing motivations to have fewer children are not sufficiently strong to reduce population growth to an acceptable level. These critics argue that without this motivation, contraception offered on a voluntary basis will not sufficiently reduce the birth rates.[30]

It has been at this point in the debate over appropriate policies that social science research has played a significant role. If the family planners can show that persons are motivated to have fewer children, then they can refute the arguments of their critics. The questionnaire stressing mentalistic "causes" of fertility is the ideal weapon to wage this policy defense. The reason for this is that regardless of the outcome of the questionnaire, the outcome of the policy will be family planning and related activities!

Let us examine why this will be the case. In one of the more heated exchanges between the opponents and the defenders of family planning (Judith Blake, "Population Policy for Americans: Is the Government Being Misled?"[31] and Oscar Harkavy, Frederick Jaffe, and Samuel Wishik, "Family Planning and Public Policy: Who Is Misleading Whom?")[32] the debate centered in large part around the interpretation of fertility attitude questionnaires. Blake never had a real chance to change policy as long as the debate was on this battleground, as almost any interpretation could be used to support the family planners.

Few Children Desired. If the questionnaire shows that women tend to prefer fewer children than the present fertility rate, and the number preferred is around two, then the family planners can argue that the motivation already exists and all that is lacking is knowledge about, and availability of, contraceptives. This is because the attitudes and values which "cause" small families are assumed to be already present.

A Few Too Many Children Desired. If the questionnaire shows that women prefer three or four children, and the present average family size in the culture is five or more (a common situation in the developing countries), the family planners can argue that family planning is a vital first step in bringing about reduced fertility. (That the second step is not specified is not important to the continuation of the existing policy.) In addition to simply supplying the contraceptives, the family planner can argue that existing pronatalist attitudes and values must be changed. This is done by means of population education propaganda which will change those values and attitudes "causing" large families. As was discussed above, once we are within the realm of the questionnaire we tend to think in terms of individual choice and attitudinal determinism rather than materialistic determinism. Thus there is no need to change persons' life situations; only their attitudes.

Far Too Many Children Desired. If the questionnaire shows that women want as many as, or more children than, they are having, and they are already having more than those interested in population reduction feel are acceptable, then it is "obvious" that the attitudes and values prevailing in the society are inappropriate for reducing fertility. Thus a massive population education and propaganda campaign is necessary to change these attitudes.

Thus, regardless of the findings, family planning and population education are the answers to the problem. By accepting the methodology of the questionnaire, we have helped to insure that neither the existing mobilization of bias in the policy field nor the existing power structure in the society are challenged.

But how much of the variance in fertility behavior has been explained by changes in attitudes and better contraceptives? There have been several historical transitions from higher to lower fertility rates and a few incidences of lower to higher rates. Can these changes be attributed to changes in contraceptive knowledge and/or availability? Certainly the fertility declines in the United States during the depression and even earlier in France and Sweden cannot be attributed to technological advances in contraceptives. The postwar baby boom was not caused by decreases in contraceptive knowledge or availability. Similarly, in Asia the fertility declines of Japan, Taiwan, and China appear to be more closely related to increases in opportunities other than parenthood available to the citizens, especially the females, of these countries rather than to any increase in contraceptive efficiency or distribution. In fact, if changes in abortion laws are excluded, it is difficult to find any significant drop in a society's level of fertility which is attributable to family planning programs or improvements in contraceptive technology.

If advances in the technology of contraception and its distribution cannot account for the historical decreases in fertility, what can account for these decreases? When the methodology of the questionnaire and the theories of mentalistic determinism are accepted, we must look for changes in the values and attitudes of those persons who are having smaller families. An example of this type of thinking led to the Indianapolis Study of Social and Psychological Factors Affecting Fertility.[33] In their résumé of this study C. V. Kiser and P. K. Whelpton report:

There is good reason to believe that it is not socioeconomic status *per se* but rather the underlying attitudes and psychological characteristics that account for fertility behavior. And yet, whereas characteristic patterns of fertility differentials are found consistently in classifications by socioeconomic status, most classifications by psychological characteristics within socioeconomic groups fail to show such patterns.[34]

The above quote is particularly interesting in that the authors appear to have a very strong desire to hold to the psychological causes rather than socioeconomic causes, even though the empirical results indicate that individuals' life situations are more important in determining fertility behavior.

Just as there exist differential fertility rates among socioeconomic classes, the fertility differences between the more and less developed countries are also quite marked. Most industrialized societies have much lower fertility levels than less industrialized societies. Studies by William Clifford, John Williamson, and the present author have attempted to show that more "modern" attitudes and values lead to favorable attitudes toward smaller families.[35] In all three of these studies (which include samples from seven countries), the amount of variance explained by the more modern attitudes and values was less than 5 percent. When it is remembered that the expected relationship between modern attitudes and values is the two-step relationship shown in Figure 10-1, that the studies cited above were examining only the first step in this relationship (A→B), and that the strength of this first step was quite weak, then it would seem reasonable to assume that the relationship between A and C is extremely weak.

A	B	C
Modern Attitudes and Values	⟶ Fertility Attitudes	⟶ Fertility Behavior

Figure 10-1. Hypothesized Relationship between Modern Attitudes and and Fertility Behavior

Source: R. Kenneth Godwin, *Attitudes and Behavior Related to Modernization* (Chapel Hill: Carolina Population Center, Population Program and Policy Design Series, no. 6, 1972), p. 143.

Although the research cited above represents but a few of the many studies which attempt to relate attitudes to fertility, they are quite representative in their inability to explain and predict fertility behavior. Nevertheless, neither the majority of social scientists nor policy makers have been willing to look beyond mentalistic determinism and consider materialistic determinism.

Effects of an Alternative Methodology

Would an alternative methodology change the policy recommendations social scientists make? I think an affirmative answer to this question is highly probable. Once we change from mentalistic to materialistic determinants, we are looking at an entirely new set of causes. Instead of looking to the wrong attitudes as the causes of the wrong behavior, we see behavior as a product of the socioeconomic conditions within which individuals live. Motivation to reduce family size is no longer seen as the result of changes in a person's attitudes (and therefore highly susceptible to a massive information and propaganda campaign). Rather, this motivation is a result of opportunities for satisfaction outside of parenthood such as the opportunities which result from a better standard of living and greater equality.

Obviously, to say that fertility behavior is related to socioeconomic status or the level of development in a country is not a satisfactory explanation of this behavior. Socioeconomic status and country of residence are not variables or causes but are indicators of a large number of life experiences which are relatively similar for the many individuals within each class or country. Thus adequate explanations of fertility behavior would be those identifying the life experiences which are relevant to fertility behavior. If these life experiences can be identified, then policy recommendations would change. Again quoting Davis:

And if it were admitted that the creation and care of new human beings is socially motivated . . . by being a part of the system of rewards and punishments that is built into human relationships, and thus bound up with the individual's economic and personal interests, it would be apparent that the social structure and the economy must be changed before a deliberate reduction in the birth rate can be achieved.[36]

Such an admission would, however, require that policy makers face the probabilities of radical social change and/or overt coercion and that social science researchers reorient their methodologies so that the patterns of human behavior rather than attitudes and values can be studied.

Summary

All research methodologies bias their findings. In the social sciences the requirements of quantification and the ideology of individual choice have led us to a dependence on the questionnaire, and this choice of a research instrument has had the effect of further reinforcing both quantification and mentalistic explanations of behavior. This methodological bias has been quite congenial to the research needs of the apologists of existing population policies. These policies which are, by and large, family planning and population education, are themselves partially the product of the ideology of individual choice.

If, however, we view behavior as the result of past life experiences and the constraints of present situations, we are led to different methodologies which have radical implications for population policies. Both the failure of technological improvements in contraceptives to reduce birth rates in many areas of the world and the failure of previous attitudinal studies to show relationships between attitudes and fertility behavior indicate that now is an appropriate time to face these more radical possibilities.

Notes

1. Frederick F. Stephen, "Possibilities and Pitfalls in the Measurement of Attitudes and Opinions on Family Planning," pp. 423-31 of C.V. Kiser, ed., *Research in Family Planning* (Princeton, N.J.: Princeton University Press, 1962).

2. Beginning in 1934 with Richard LaPiere's article "Attitudes versus Actions," *Social Forces* 13 (1934), pp. 230-37, researchers have found that attitudes as measured by questionnaires are usually not predictive of behavior. Research on the salience and structure of attitudes has shown that only when an attitude is attached to other highly valued attitudes and beliefs will this attitude predict behavior. For a discussion of this research and fertility attitudes, see Chester A. Insko, et al., "Attitude Toward Birth Control and Cognitive Consistency: Theoretical and Practical Implications of Survey Data," *Journal of Personality and Social Psychology* 26, no. 2 (1970): 228-37; and R. Kenneth Godwin, "The Structure of Mass Attitudes in the United States and Latin America: Implications for Policy," pp. 113-34 of Richard L. Clinton and R. Kenneth Godwin, eds., *Research in the Politics of Population* (Lexington, Mass.: D.C. Heath and Company, 1972).

3. J. Mayone Stycos, *Human Fertility in Latin America* (Ithaca, N.Y.: Cornell University Press, 1968), pp. 115-58.

4. These were two of four questions which the United States Information Agency gathered from over 17,000 interviews in twenty-two countries, quoted in J. Mayone Stycos, "Opinion, Ideology, and Population Problems: Some Sources of Domestic and Foreign Opposition to Birth Control," pp. 533-66 of National Academy of Sciences, *Rapid Population Growth: Consequences and Implications* (Baltimore and London: Johns Hopkins Press, 1971), pp. 533.

5. Abraham Kaplan, *The Conduct of Inquiry* (San Francisco: Chandler, 1964), p. 28.

6. Obviously a cross-cultural questionnaire requires much more than a translation of a statement to its closest approximation in another language. If the questionnaire is to be accurate, the statement must tap similar situational responses in both cultures. Often a meaningful question or statement in one culture has either a quite different meaning in another culture or has no meaning at all. For a more complete discussion of this problem and a test of its

significance, see R. Kenneth Godwin, *Attitudes and Behavior Related to Modernization* (Chapel Hill: Carolina Population Center, Population Program and Policy Design Series, no. 6, 1972), ch. 4-6.

7. LaPiere (n. 2).

8. Ibid., p. 237.

9. Godwin (n. 2).

10. See, for instance, Neil J. Smelser, "Personality and the Explanation of Political Phenomena at the Social-System Level: A Methodological Statement," *The Journal of Social Issues* 24 (1968): 111-25.

11. B.F. Skinner, *Beyond Freedom and Dignity* (New York: Alfred A. Knopf, Inc, 1971), pp. 12-13.

12. Such reductionism is not necessary because personality characteristics — even though they may be largely determined by prior social experiences — are products of an extremely complex combination of biology, environment, and past information processing by the human mind. This means that although there may be regularity in the response of individuals to similar experiences, there is still a wide variety of responses. For an excellent summary of the relationship between social characteristics and personality characteristics, see Fred I. Greenstein, "The Impact of Personality on Politics: An Attempt to Clear Away Underbrush," *The American Political Science Review* 61 (1967): 629-41.

13. A.E. Keir Nash, "Making the World Population Problem Safe for American Democracy?" paper presented at the annual meeting of the American Political Science Association, Washington, D.C., September 1972, p. 18.

14. I will not attempt in this essay to show that family-planning programs are comfortable to the elites because they do not threaten the existing power relationships in our society, nor will I attempt to show that family-planning programs have been designed almost exclusively by the economic, social, and political elites with a virtual exclusion of mass inputs. These points have been discussed and documented elsewhere. See for example, Kingsley Davis, "Population Policy: Will Current Programs Succeed?," *Science* 158 (10 November 1967): 730-39; Elihu Bergman and William Flash, "The American Population Policy Process: Some Critical Insights," paper presented at the annual meeting of the American Political Science Association, Chicago, September 1971; and Elihu Bergman, "American Population Policy Making: The Politics of Do Good but Don't Rock the Boat!," pp. 41-70 of Clinton and Godwin (n. 2).

15. Agency for International Development, *Population Program Assistance: Aid to Developing Countries by the United States, Other Nations, and International and Private Agencies* (Washington: G.P.O., 1972), p. 37.

16. Ibid.

17. Ibid.

18. Ibid.

19. Ibid.

20. For example, see *The Population Council Annual Report, 1971* (New York: Population Council, 1972), pp. 96-114.

21. Davis (n. 14), pp. 735-38.

22. This argument is made by Davis, ibid., passim.

23. Ibid., p. 734.

24. Ibid.

25. Bergman (n. 14).

26. Elihu Bergman and Peter Bachrach, *Power and Choice: The Formulation of American Population Policy* (Lexington: D.C. Heath, 1973).

27. Bernard Berelson, "Beyond Family Planning," *Studies in Family Planning,* no. 38 (February 1969): 1-16.

28. Nondecision making, or the mobilization of bias, is a description of what happens when a problem area is not entered on the agenda of those who should be concerned with solving it. Perhaps the classic example of this was segregation in the South before 1954. Although it was obviously a problem, the decision makers never placed the issue on the political agenda. These concepts and examples are described by Peter Bachrach and Morton Baratz, "Two Faces of Power," *American Political Science Review* 56, no. 4 (December 1962): 947-52; and "Decisions and Nondecisions: An Analytic Framework," *American Political Science Review* 57, no. 3 (September 1962): 632-42.

29. Davis (n. 14); Judith Blake, "Population Policy for Americans: Is the Government Being Misled?" *Science* 164 (2 May 1969): 522-29; and Garrett Hardin, "The Tragedy of the Commons," *Science* 162 (13 December 1968): 1243-48.

30. Davis (n. 14)

31. Blake (n. 29).

32. Oscar Harkavy, Frederick Kaffe, and Samuel Wishik, "Family Planning and Public Policy: Who Is Misleading Whom?" *Science* 165 (25 July 1969): 367-73. A reply to this article by Blake can be found in the same issue, pp. 372-73.

33. For a résumé of this study see Clyde V. Kiser and P.K. Whelpton, "Résumé of the Indianapolis Study of Social and Psychological Factors Affecting Fertility," *Population Studies* 7 (1953): 95-110.

34. Ibid., p. 108.

35. William B. Clifford, II, "Modern and Traditional Value Orientations and Fertility Behavior: A Social Demographic Study," *Demography* 8, no. 1 (February 1971): 37-48; John B. Williamson, "Subjective Efficacy and Ideal Family Size as Predictors of Favorability Toward Birth Control," *Demography* 8, no. 3 (August 1971): 329-39; and Godwin (n. 6), ch. 7.

36. Davis (n. 14), p. 733.

11

Methodological Issues in
Population and Politics:
A Comment

Gayl D. Ness

This *potpourri* of articles offers something to suit any bias, to justify any research proposal, or to confuse any policy maker. Steven Sinding presents a modest donor's plea for critical case studies that will provide answers to the question, "what is to be done?" Mair deVoursney presents a case for aggregate analysis, denigrating case studies. Ken Godwin exposes some of the conservative biases in current research and action programs limited to contraceptive development and distribution and asks for a more radical approach to population problems. Nazli Choucri covers a larger portion of the waterfront, identifying uncertainties, focusing on political stability and instability, and surveying some of the problems of a rather comprehensive list of available research strategies.

The areas of disagreement in these articles are many and significant. Some of the more dramatic of these demand comment. Nazli Choucri reminds us that *population* is embedded with *resources* and *technology* (and from an older ecological perspective we might add *organization*) in a dynamic interrelationship. One need not be a strict technological determinist to observe that the recent development of noncoital specific contraceptive methods is a technological change of immense importance for population dynamics. Without such a technological change, specific direct-action programs for fertility limitation were among the least economic (showing the lowest benefit to cost ratios) of all the development programs a nation could adopt. With such a technology, fertility limitation programs become some of the most economic programs available. Two decades ago it could be argued that the resistance to investments in the development of contraceptive technology reflected powerful conservative or reactionary biases. Today it is possible for Ken Godwin to argue persuasively that AID's heavy investment in contraceptive development also reflects a powerful conservative bias. Now if technological development is an important component in population dynamics, and if investments for technological developments are radical at one point in time and conservative at another point, one might well raise a question of the utility and relevance of Godwin's argument. The identification of an ideological bias has utility if it assists in the prediction of behavior or policy. Although Godwin's identification might be accurate, it can also be considered of doubtful predictive utility.

The question of utility arises with another of Godwin's arguments. He points out that AID has concentrated a large portion of its noncontraceptive research budget in areas of descriptive demography, indicating an unwillingness to confront more fundamental issues of the relation between population and social structure. Again Nazli Choucri's observations present opposing implications. She points out that many development programs in general and family planning programs in particular suffer from a lack of technical and organizational competence for monitoring social change. Basic census materials and other forms of sustained data collecting capacities are often woefully underdeveloped and represent important weaknesses in any programs of planned social change. It is also apparent that in a number of national cases it was precisely census returns that provided policy makers with at least one important stimulus for turning attention to problems of rapid population growth. This implies that a case for improving local capacities in descriptive demography could be couched in quite progressive, if not radical, terms. Such capacities surely provide local elites with independent resources for decision making. The basic question here, of course, is not whether improvement of descriptive demography capacities is a good thing or not. The question I seek to raise is the utility of labeling AID investment in such improvement as conservative.

Mair deVoursney and Steven Sinding present some areas of agreement, on which I think they are both wrong, and some areas of disagreement, which are at least understandable. Both agree that case studies are of limited utility for the generalization that is necessary for the advancement of theory. For this and other reasons deVoursney argues for aggregate analysis; despite this, Sinding makes a plea for critical case studies. It is both fashionable and mistaken to argue that the findings of case studies are not generalizable. One need only call to mind such case studies as Tocqueville's *Democracy in America,* Selznick's *TVA and the Grass Roots,* Lipset's *Union Democracy,* or Tilly's *The Vendee* (the list of favorites will be as long and varied as respondents) to observe that case studies often provide powerful findings on the organic relations between variables in ongoing social processes. Some of the case studies available on processes of policy making for population limitation present highly generalizable propositions both about the processes and the substantive orientations of national development policies. A good case study of India's technological orientation in population control (the rejection of the oral contraceptive and the strong preference for vasectomy and condoms) would provide useful contributions to theories of the diffusion of innovation. In addition, of course, case studies can provide relevant information for the donor or other policy maker who must act in the present, usually under considerable constraint and with far less than adequate information.

Mair deVoursney's case for aggregate analysis has some curious inconsistencies and depends too much upon a denigration of case studies. The latter are argued to be lacking in reliability and validity. It is also recognized, however, that data for aggregate analyses often present the same problems, but the need for analysis is so urgent that we cannot wait for improvements in data quality. I think deVoursney does not give full recognition to the difficulties of much aggregate analysis, especially where nations are the units of analysis and data limitations force one to use cross-sectional rather than time-series data. Too often the results are merely plausible explanations for relations between indirect indicators of behavior. The power and utility of aggregate analysis constantly lead us to substitute more and more indirect measures of behavior for actual observations of behavior. Our ability to present measures for indicators with a few decimal points usually gives us a false sense of the accuracy of such measurements. It is difficult to think of any single measure, however, for which we could consistently claim error margins of less than ±10 percent, and for most measures for most countries the margins are usually much greater. Finally, the aggregate analysis tradition has its own horror stories: one analyst feeds his punched cards into the computer upside down, and still is able to provide plausible explanations for all the observed relations.

Ken Godwin also reminds us of Veblen's law of the instrument. Computers are instruments, too, and they have voracious appetites for data and for sophisticated mathematical processes. Their very power promotes aggregate analysis. They do not, by themselves, promote concern for data validity and reliability. It would be foolish to denigrate computer analysis on these grounds, however. When such analysis is done with good data and is informed by sensitive theory, it is powerful and useful. But to make a case for aggregate analysis in the area of population and politics by denigrating case studies and without paying close attention to some of the difficult problems of data and analysis is to invite a Luddite-like backlash.

Finally, the Sinding-deVoursney debate illuminates another intractable problem in research strategies or methods. The two sides of this debate represent institutional or organizational demands that are important limitations on rationality. Disclaimers notwithstanding, Sinding presents the plea of the donor in the curious worldwide business of aid giving. In the broadest sense, the aim of the donor is to achieve a given end by giving away resources wrapped in obligation packages. Usually very little is known about how to achieve the end or about what kind of behavior to require (or suggest) in order to achieve that end. The constraints on the process of obligation are even more severe and are also probably less stable. Relative levels of power or influence vary day by day and also from one type of activity to another. Even for the very limited, and probably conservative, end of fertility reduction, the problems of the donor are far from limited and simple. How does one induce a sovereign nation to make a policy decision for fertility control; or how does one provide support to those groups in a nation who favor fertility control as one way of dealing with a serious problem of rapid population growth? If there is a policy, what kind of program, technology, assistance, resources are best suited to the specific conditions? Even more important, how does one answer any of these questions, especially on a sustained basis? The immediate day-to-day problems of the donor understandably lead to a modest request for studies that will help provide *solutions,* or answers to the question, "what is to be done?" under severe constraints.

In contrast the plea for aggregate analyses reflects the interest of an academic institution. Scholars are more interested in providing understanding than solutions. Professional academic rewards are given more for elegance than for practicality. One could turn Godwin's ideological analysis on the scholars and note that the investment in ever more esoteric analytical techniques is self-serving in that it increases the power of the gatekeepers. But even if this argument is accurate, it tells us very little that is useful or relevant. It is far more important to note simply that the interests and demands of the donor and the scholar are likely to be different, and that there is little to be gained in conflict over which is better. There is much to be gained, however, by engaging in a dialogue that attempts to translate the experiences of the donor into the data of the scholar and to translate the findings of the scholar into prescriptions or guidelines for action by the donor. We could make the same argument if the term donor were replaced with policy maker. An arena in which the scholar faces a local mayor or a foreign prime minister will be one in which the same differences of interest and orientation will exist. If it were possible to have Sinding's and deVoursney's arguments directed toward one another rather than past one another, we might be able to provide some guidelines for resolving these differences in a constructive manner.

If these comments are called for by the disagreements in the chapters of this section, there are also some comments called for by issues that are not presented in them. Omissions are always almost unlimited, of course, but from my perspective three types of methodological issues require identification and further attention. One concerns *static* and *dynamic* analyses; a second deals with *sequence;* and the third raises the question of the appropriate *unit of analysis.* I shall deal with these three only briefly.

Except for Choucri's paper there is in this section a neglect of the dynamic character of the population-politics relationship. We are terribly bound up in the moment. We note countries with characteristics: population growth rates, types of governments, specific policies and specific relations with other governments. We tend to forget the recent past and look only to the immediate future. That is, we tend to present a dynamic process in static perspective. Rapid population growth is itself a recent phenomenon and has been widely identified as a serious problem only very recently. Even more recently we have experienced something of a mild epidemic of national policy decisions taking cognizance of the problem and mobilizing resources to deal with it. Both in any individual country and in the world as a whole the population-politics relationship is a dynamic one, almost constantly changing its character and values. There are important methodological issues raised in dealing with such dynamic situations, and it would be useful to see some attention given to these issues.

The world population-politics scene presents in addition some interesting sequential situations. Of the three major continental groups of new and developing nations, Asia experienced the earliest and most internally directed movement toward direct action in fertility control programs. A good portion of the argument and impetus for these programs came from economic planning agencies, which were *prior* in formation and activity. One can propose a sequence in which national independence gives rise to organized national effort to stimulate economic development. This effort is set in organizations that become increasingly competent to monitor the national economic and social environment. Such monitoring leads to the recognition of a serious problem in rapid population growth with consequent mobilization of effort to deal with the problem. From this observation a number of substantive questions arise. Is this an accurate identification of the Asian sequence? Will the same sequence occur in other regions? (Already Latin America suggests that the sequence may be quite different, though the importance of organized competence in economic planning may remain.) What are the organic connections between the various points or stages in the sequence? What are the policy implications: can stages be skipped or are they immutable? How is time to be measured? How are we to measure such things as the level or growth of organizational capacity for development planning? How do we separate the internal decision-making processes, which this model proposes to be of central importance, from external influences, both conceptually and in actual measurement?

Finally, all issues at some point touch on the units of analysis. For the papers of this section there is the implicit assumption that we are dealing with nation-states. This is made explicit in some of Choucri's concern with international conflict and stability. There is an obvious dilemma in the use of this nation-state unit of analysis. Its obvious advantage derives from behavioral and data concerns. Nation-states collect data and thus allow for an easy treatment as independent integral units. Further, nation-states do control boundary movements and do exercise some control over their internal populations, though to be sure both characterizations are of variables rather than of dichotomous attributes. There are, however, serious disadvantages in using nation-states as units of analysis. First, there are powerful regional units within and across the boundaries of nations that are not always recognized using national data. Second, there is the intrusion of other individual nation-states into the processes of boundary control and population mobilization. Godwin reminds us that AID is an organized activity of one nation-state attempting to influence the activity of others. And our characterization of fertility control policy decisions as epidemic since 1967 (when AID increased its efforts) indicates some success by the United States in influencing the action of other states. This adds another element to the sequential analysis discussed above, and once again it proposes that the analysis be kept dynamic.

There is one additional critical omission in dealing with nation-states. This is the rise of a worldwide community, with institutions for both participation in an interest-articulating body and for administering an increasingly worldwide communications and activities network. One cannot seriously deal with the rise of world interest in problems or rapid population growth without at the same time noting the work of international health services in reducing mortality or the signing of an international statement to promote fertility limitation in 1967. The epidemic of population policy decisions of the past few years is at least as much a reflection of the growing influence of the world community as a reflection of United States and AID influence.

How is one to approach this world community conceptually when dealing with the population-politics relationship? Certainly one of the major dimensions of variance in the community is the volume of communication, which reflects the extent to which events at one point are observed at another and affect behavior at another point. The scope and quality of communication also vary considerably. About a generation ago the information available for most of Asia and Africa consisted of trade statistics, reflecting only flows of commodities across the boundaries of colonial territories. The growth of uniform censuses and the increase in the quality of census data collection vastly increase the scope of behavior over which information is available. To suggest just one more dimension of variance, one can note the current interest in population and ecological issues, which follows closely on the heels of a more exclusive interest in economic development. Are these to be seen as mere fashions or fads, whose content varies randomly, or do they represent a more rational set of sequences in which various perceptive capacities are developed to be followed by attention to problems identified by those perceptive capacities? Additional issues could be raised, but I think this is sufficient to indicate some of the more critical areas that require attention.

The chapters of this section present a range of interests, points of view, and methodological problems. They provide both useful insights and useful arguments for particular research strategies. I have tried here to extend their utility by pointing to some critical areas of disagreement reflected in the chapters and to raise other issues that seem to me both important and somewhat neglected in what is otherwise an important contribution to the recent emergence of an old set of problems.

**Part Three
The Less Advantaged Countries and
Their Relations with
Advantaged Countries**

12 Population and Economic Development in Africa: A Critical Look at the Current Literature

The greatest single obstacle to the economic and social advancement of the majority of the peoples in the underdeveloped world is the rampant population growth.

Robert McNamara
President, World Bank Group

No other phenomenon casts a darker shadow over the prospects for international development than the staggering growth of population. It is evident that it is a major cause of the discrepancy between the rates of economic improvement in rich and poor countries.

"Partners in Development"
Commission on International Development

Osman S. Ahmed

A salient feature of the current development literature is the pivotal role assigned to population growth. It is becoming almost axiomatic that economic development in the poor countries will be all but impossible without slowing down population growth.

A citation of the monumental increases in world population during the last several decades, the portion of the increase accounted for by the poorer countries, the declines in mortality without corresponding decreases in fertility which resulted in high growth rates in the LDCs, and the observed doubling of the population every generation or so, have become a routine part of the writings on development in the LDCs. They will not, therefore, be repeated here. But an attempt will be made to answer some of the following questions: Conceding that population growth is an important factor to be considered in any development effort, how important is it *vis-à-vis* the myriad of other factors that affect development? Is the desired direction of population growth rates invariably downward? How genuine is the current interest of the richer countries in population matters of the poor? Could this interest be merely the

153

consequence of disappointment with results of development aid coupled with rising interest in population and ecology in the developed world?

The Case For Larger Population

Sparsely populated areas would benefit from larger populations because of the economies of scale, economies of complimentarity and proximity, and external economies. The cost of undertaking certain investments necessary for development might be so high in sparsely settled areas that development cannot occur. Population increase may so lower the per capita cost of these investments that the benefit that accrues as a result would more than outweigh the cost of the population increase. After a certain point, however, the economies of scale, of proximity, and of concentration would turn into diseconomies. This is in line with the often criticized theory of "optimum population." Social benefit will, according to this theory, be maximized at the point where the gains and costs of population growth are equal. The problem is that changes in nonhuman factors like capital accumulation and technological change would change the optimum point even with no increases in population. So instead of a point there will be an optimal "region" that gradually shifts to trace a path.

In spite of its shortcoming, the theory of optimum population does point out the often-neglected truism that you can't generalize for all the underdeveloped world and prescribe uniform policy measures. Yet a lot of this sort of prescription is evident in the population-development literature.

Rate of Growth and Economic Development

A distinction should be made at this point between population as a stock and as a flow. The latter is the rate of growth of the stock. Many non-Malthusian economists dismiss preoccupation with the stock as unimportant, but almost all agree on the adverse effect on the economy of a high rate of population growth.[1] Even if a country could benefit from a larger population, this argument runs, too high a growth rate would lead to a high dependency ratio which would reduce the rate of savings and thereby the rate of investment. Typically, such reasoning is developed in the following way. With a capital-output ratio of approximately four, 4 percent of GNP would have to be reinvested for a 1 percent increase in population in order to maintain the same per capita income. But because consumption has increased as a result of the population growth, less rather than more savings will be available for investment.[2]

There are several assumptions implicit in the above analysis, however, and the validity of the conclusions rests in the main on the realism of these assumptions. The principal ones are: (a) that resources are fully utilized; (b) that full utilization will be made of resources released as a result of lower rates of population growth; and (c) that the coefficient of productivity is constant.

That capital and resources are not fully utilized in any economy and least of all in the developing countries, where idle plant equipment and under-employment and unemployment of labor are acute – cannot be disputed. It is a paradox that "underemployment" and unemployment, which are alleged to be the result of population pressure in the LDCs are assumed away by those who are most concerned about population growth.

Assumption (b) is a corrollary of (a), and if the latter doesn't hold, there is no reason to believe that (b) would hold.

Assumption (c) *may* hold in some LDCs but would most probably be due to extraeconomic factors, particularly considering the transferability of technology from MDCs to LDCs.

In spite of these shortcomings, the rate of population growth obviously does have its place in anlyzing the problems of development. With high population growth the proportion of the *potentially* productive labor force would be lower than if the rate of growth were smaller, and governmental expenditures for educational and health facilities would absorb an increasingly larger share of the budget, leaving less for other development programs. Moreover, the tax base would be reduced, leading to the predicament of having to spend more with less revenue. Straight application of the dependency rate concept (as defined in the Western world) is, however, misleading when the vast majority of the employable and potentially productive labor force is unemployed partly because of the scarcity of capital or the capital-intensity bias of investments. Nor can standard definition of dependents as those under fifteen and over sixty-five be applied to Africa, where education is far from universal and where retirement at sixty-five has no relevance outside the government sector. Yet the literature on African population abounds in this and similar definitions of equally question-able applicability under African conditions.

Cost-Benefit Analysis of Population Growth

Benefits of Population Control

Various attempts have been made to quantify the economic gains to be achieved by slowing population growth. Among the most influential is Stephen Enke's attempt to estimate the negative value of an additional birth.[3] On the assumption that the relevant discount rate is 10 or 15 percent, Enke has shown that the present value of the consumption expenditures of a new child is more than his total productivity over his active life. This leads to the obvious conclusion that society would be better off economically without him.

Such an argument, however, is a straw man. Any future stream of income could be reduced to zero by picking an appropriate discount rate, and 15 percent is definitely high. A high enough discount rate would reduce any investment whether in population or in physical capital to a negative value in comparison to current consumption.[4]

A similar conclusion that the economic effect of a new child is negative could be reached by assuming that his marginal productivity is *zero*. A typical version of this approach is stated as follows:

$$\frac{Y}{P} = y,$$ where Y is total output, P total population, and y per capita income.

The implications of this simple equation are that by merely reducing the denominator, per capita income would automatically be increased.[5]

In sparsely populated areas where resources are currently underutilized (and many areas in the African continent would fall in this category), not only is the marginal product not zero but it might even be more than the average product. So a decrease in P would decrease Y by more than the decrease in P, thus leading to a smaller y. Of course, this is too simplistic an analysis, but it brings home the important point that as long as an area is not overpopulated (however imprecise the term), decreases in population could, other things being equal, lead to decreases in total output.

Cost of Population Control

The undervaluation of increments to total output as a result of an additional birth is accompanied by an undervaluation of the cost of preventing that birth. This means that benefits accruing to society as a result of the prevention of the additional birth, coupled with the low cost of preventing it, makes investments in population control appear very "profitable." Thus the assertion "that less than five dollars invested in population control is worth a hundred dollars invested in economic growth."[6]

Estimates of population control costs usually concentrate merely on the cost of delivering contraceptives. They take no account of the overhead or the publicity and motivation efforts that are necessary to the success of any population program.[7] The fixed cost component is particularly large at the beginning of a program, and any estimate that ignores this heavy start-up cost definitely underestimates the total cost.

The neat figures of the cost-benefit analysis of population programs are, therefore, at best unreliable. Moreover, there is a time lag between the launching of the program and the time the results are observed. This time lag introduces the possibility of other factors being operative, particularly when social and economic transformation is taking place, hence some of the births prevented could be entirely due to exogenous factors.[8] These complications make cost estimates extremely difficult if not impossible to undertake. Yet it is the impressive gains from population control which these analyses show that are used as a justification for adopting population policies. Population programs could very well prove to be of immense economic "profitability," but the priority level assigned to them should rest on a more justifiable basis.

Population, like any other variable in the development "equation," will assume different positions of importance in different regions. Yet there is always a persistent tendency to generalize or to impute universality to strictly local phenomena. Gabon and Ceylon do not have the same problems, hence the priority assigned to population limitation in their developmental programs will have to differ.

Priority Position of Population Control among Africa's Pressing Problems

In terms of material well-being, Africa lags behind the rest of the world. It has the highest death rate of any continent (23 per 100 compared with a world average of 16 per 1000), the highest illiteracy rate, and the lowest per capita income. But Africa is also potentially among the richest continents. Compared to the industrialized countries of Europe the per capita land area under cultivation is three times as high, livestock per capita twice as high, grazing land per unit of livestock seven times as high. It contains almost 40 percent of the world's potential hydropower, 12 percent of the uranium reserves, and 60 percent of the world's thorium. In summary, it has more than its share of the world's resources.[9]

The relevant question is how these enormous resources can be developed to alleviate the material deprivation of the African masses. The issue of population control and the high priority assigned to it ought to be viewed in this light. The hierarchical distribution of priorities is necessitated by the scarcity of resources, particularly highly trained manpower, which makes the simultaneous undertaking of many competing ventures (even if such ventures are complementary) an impossible task.

With the amelioration of the conditions of poverty under which the African masses live as the objective, population control should be viewed merely as a means and an indirect one at that. Moreover, the means and the end are connected by a set of assumptions which doesn't always hold: the effectiveness with which resources released as a result of a declining birth rate are utilized; the distribution of the increased per capita income; and whether in fact declining birth rate will, in the long-run, be economically beneficial to areas that are sparsely populated. The rampant inefficiency, the great disparity in income, and the sparsity of population in most parts of Africa indicate that these assumptions may not be warranted in many instances.

Undue emphasis on population growth as the main obstacle to development draws attention away from these more pressing issues at an inopportune time. African elites would naturally be prone to ratify a set of priorities that draws attention away from the real issue, which is a perpetuation of the system that favors them. In the long-run, moreover, undue concentration on population may prove to be a costly misallocation of the meager intellectual resources in the African continent.

A New Approach to Slowing the Rate of Population Growth

Even if fertility reduction is deemed priority number one, the mere dissemination of contraceptives and birth control information might not achieve any tangible results. Dissemination of contraceptives would have effect only when there is an appreciable unsatisfied demand. Even where demand exists, the inadequacy of qualified medical personnel to advise acceptors would lead to a high dropout rate. The immediate step, therefore, should be to appreciably increase the number of qualified medical personnel. But considering the acute shortage of personnel in all of Africa, this would be unfeasible. Where there is no demand for birth control methods, then the creation of that demand is a prerequisite to the delivery of contraceptives. But first, what determines the desired level of fertility and the demand for contraceptives?

According to Schultz, the frequency of births in a population can be understood in terms of three groups of factors that influence parents' desires for children. The three factors are: family size goal; the incidence of death, particularly among offspring, which necessitates a compensating adjustment in births to maintain the desired family size; and uncertainty in the family formation process.[10] The desired family size is the result of some kind of an optimization process whereby the subjective and pecuniary costs of having children are weighed against the pleasures of parenthood and the value of children as a source of income. Among the factors that affect the cost of children are: (a) the opportunity income of mothers, (b) child-labor practices, (c) family income, (d) education, (e) social welfare institutions, and (f) availability of contraception.

Following Schultz, let us look at these in turn. In devoting her time to her children, a mother foregoes the income she might otherwise earn and the other activities she might undertake. The greater the opportunities for women (or for that particular mother) outside the home, the greater the opportunity cost and, in general, the lower her fertility will tend to be.

Child labor is often an important productive asset to a family, particularly in LDCs. The assistance provided by an unpaid family member would, for instance, lower the cost of rearing children. Schooling would have the opposite effect. Not only does it deprive the family of free labor, but schooling is in itself expensive

Having children as "insurance" for old age is a recurrent point in the development literature. Parents have a socially approved claim on their offspring's earnings and so tend to have large families. A government policy that enforces school attendance and institutes support programs for the aged and the disabled would increase the cost of having children while simultaneously reducing the need for them. This would reduce the material desirability of large families.

After parents decide on the desired size of their family, this goal's achievement will partly depend on the availability of contraceptives and birth control information and the cost and inconvenience of taking contraceptives. Whether or not the desired family size is maintained will depend on mortality. Parents will, if they are still in the childbearing age, try to compensate for the incidence of death by increasing births. Under this hypothesis there is a certain lag period between a fall in the rate of mortality and the adjustment in the birth rate, perhaps of a generation or so, so that even if mortality falls parents will still continue to have as many children as before the onset of the decline in mortality until they make sure that the decline in mortality is not transitory but permanent.

Admittedly, the above factors do not reflect the totality of the environment that influences birth rates, but at least they go beyond the mere provision of contraceptives as a means of reducing fertility. Assuming that the above factors account for a significant portion of the family environment, then declines in birth rates will partly depend on improving health services, increasing educational facilities, providing greater opportunities for women outside the home, and the institution of some kind of old-age insurance. Obviously the provision of this kind of environment will most probably be concomitant with economic development, hence the question: Which is easier to achieve and more desirable, lower birth rates/economic development or economic development/lower birth rates? We have shown earlier in this chapter that economic development depends on a host of variables, with the demographic variable being only one of them. The importance of this variable will differ from place to place, but in sparsely populated areas where population is less than "optimum," or where at least the density aspect of population pressure is absent, reduction of population growth rates would be of secondary importance. As for the desirability of each sequence, it depends on whether one is interested in numbers or in people.

Conclusion

I hope the evidence presented here has demonstrated that the relationship between economic development and demographic change is more complex and less straightforward than the current literature would indicate. The neo-Malthusian approach of concentrating on the denominator of the $\frac{Y}{P}$ equation only holds if marginal productivity is zero. Even if marginal productivity is zero, however, it might be more because of institutional and other extraeconomic factors than due to limitations of the supply of land and capital. In sparsely populated areas, not only is marginal productivity not zero, but it might even be greater than average productivity, leading to the economic desirability of larger populations. The relevant question then becomes, at what rate should population grow? Assuming that total population is below the "optimum," how long should it take to reach that "optimum"?

High rates of growth increase the portion of total income devoted to consumption, leaving less for investment. The reason for this is the high dependency ratio that results from high rates of population growth. The dependency ratio, however, is only partially dependent on the rate of growth as long as a sizeable portion of the potentially productive labor force is either unemployed or underemployed and therefore dependent on the productive portion. But this is not to say that high rates of population growth would not swallow a lot of the potentially investable funds. Expenditures for health and educational facilities for children absorb an increasingly larger share of the budget. In the long run, however, this might prove to be a more than worthwhile investment.

The main argument for slowing birth rates in sparsely populated areas is that high growth rates would increase consumption and reduce savings and thereby slow down rates of capital accumulation. The very importance of capital accumulation in economic development is, however, being questioned. Simon Kuznets argues that the contribution of capital accumulation and direct labor account for less than 10 percent of the increases in total output.[11] The rest is largely due to improvements in the quality of the resources, to the effects of changing arrangements, to the impact of technological change, or to all three. If this is the case, and assuming that the young are more amenable to adopting change, then skewing the population curve in favor of the young makes a lot of sense. At least part of consumption would then have to be viewed as investment.

All the cost-benefit analysis of population control notwithstanding, there is no conclusive evidence that lower rates of population growth are invariably desirable. Even if they were, population control programs would have to be viewed in light of all the other pressing problems facing the poorer nations, and the priority position assigned to such programs would have to reflect the needs of these nations, not the sense of urgency they assume, or are made to assume, in the richer nations where, after all, the bulk of the development literature is produced. In a country where the number of persons per physician is above 100,000, it would make little sense to assign that doctor to a population control program. Yet the monetary inducements of the international agencies might do just that.

Because of disenchantment with conventional aid and a growing concern in their own countries about population growth, the richer nations and the international agencies which mostly reflect their concern are trying to impose their sense of priority on the poorer nations. The ready and prompt sponsorship of family planning programs, while funds for other development programs are difficult if not impossible to come by, is evidence of this imposition.

The problems of population "explosion" are also discussed on the environmental plane. An unmitigated rate of growth of population will ultimately lead to "overpopulation" with respect to the limited space and natural resources of the planet. Since the underdeveloped countries comprise over two-thirds of the present world population and will make up even more in the future because of the relatively high rate of growth in these countries, the prescription is to slow down the "monumental" increase of numbers in these countries. This reasoning doesn't stand, however, when one considers the environmental impact of the "explosion" in the production of consumer goods in the developed world with the consequent problems of waste disposal and resource depletion. Assuming that the production of artifacts is proportional to per capita income, then the incremental person in the United States will have sixty times as much adverse impact on the environment as a person in a poor country.[12] Even this might be an underestimation because of the cumulative nature of environmental deterioration So with the "explosion" in production of consumption goods unabated, problems of waste disposal and resource depletion will exert a pressure long before increases in human numbers do. Many cannot help but wonder whether this preoccupation with population is merely an attempt on the part of the Western world to protect its consumption patterns, since simultaneous increases in both people and goods might shorten the distance to destruction.

Notes

1. Goran Ohlin, *Population Control and Economic Development* (Paris: OECD, 1967), p. 25.

2. Charles P. Angwenyi, "The Effect of Population Growth on Economic Development in Kenya," paper presented at the Seminar on Population and Economic Development at the University of Nairobi, Nairobi, Kenya, December 14-22, 1969.

3. Stephen Enke, "The Economic Aspects of Slowing Population Growth," *Economic Journal* 76 (March 1966): 44-56.

4. Ohlin (n. 1), p. 113.

5. Agency for International Development, *Population Program Assistance: Aid to Developing Countries by the United States, Other Nations, and International and Private Agencies* (Washington: U.S. Government Printing Office, 1970), p. 1.

6. President Lyndon B. Johnson, Speech on the Twentieth Anniversary of the United Nations, 25 June 1965. Cited in Ohlin (n. 1), pp. 107-08.

7. Ibid., p. 109.

8. Ibid., p. 110.

9. M.A. Ghansah, "Population Growth, Family Planning, and Economic Growth in Africa," paper presented at the Seminar on Population and Economic Development at University of Nairobi, December 14-22, 1969.

10. P. Schultz, "Economic Model of Family Planning and Fertility," *Journal of Political Economy* (March/April 1969).

11. Simon Kuznets, *Modern Economic Growth* (New Haven, Conn.: Yale University Press, 1966), pp. 80-81.

12. Assumes that the per capita income in the U.S. is $3,000 and that in a certain LDC it is $50.

13

Population Policy in Client States: The Case of the Dominican Republic

Frank A. Hale

The feeling that the United States "has been and still is a major, continuing influence on Dominican society and politics"[1] is widely accepted and needs no further elaboration here. Given the client-state nature of the relationship between the Dominican Republic and the United States, it is reasonable to expect that some domestic public policy decisions there can be traced to external political actors.

Indeed, a review of the evolution of population programs in the Dominican Republic through 1971 indicates that the population policy formation process is deeply penetrated by individuals and organizations external to the Dominican polity and based in the United States. Moreover, while the basic strategy of the policy makers is to integrate family planning programs with established maternal and child health activities, which are valued in Dominican society, and thereby minimize political opposition, the main emphasis is on controlling fertility so as to reduce the rate of population increase.

Until recently population concerns were of little importance to the Dominican Republic. Analysis of census data from the post-Trujillo era, however, indicates that the society is currently doubling every two decades and that internal migration to urban centers is occurring at even faster rates. The country has experienced such rapid population growth in recent years that its age distribution heavily favors the dependent age groups under fourteen and over sixty-five which together comprise over 50 percent of the population compared with 37-38 percent in the United Kingdom, West Germany, or Canada.[2] This places a heavier burden on the economically active population and makes it more difficult for the country to sustain a viable economy.

Rapid population growth aggravates already substandard living conditions and largely voids efforts by the public sector to improve the "quality of life" of Dominican citizens through expanded service programs. Indeed, roughly measured, the demand-performance ratio appears to be on the increase because service levels are not keeping pace with population growth. A high official in the National Planning Office (ONAPLAN) has acknowledged that population expansion imperils economic growth and that the Dominican government aspires, even with increased resources, only to be able to maintain government services at their present low levels because of the demands produced by anticipated population increase. This has potential consequences for the political

163

system since there is great pressure for effective public policies to build and staff schools, modernize the economy, and provide community services.

Because population expansion imposes greater loads on the political system, and, in the short run, does not boost its distributive capacity, it exacerbates already existing pressures for change while simultaneously making change more difficult and costly in terms of resources needed. This dilemma affects not only Dominican political leaders but those outside the political system who wish to maintain these pressures at tolerable levels so that change may occur in orderly stable fashion and chaos be avoided. The threat of social turbulence is probably the major reason why the impetus for fertility control programs in the Dominican Republic has come from outside the political system through linkages between Dominican political and bureaucratic elites and North American private and government agencies. The result has been the creation and support of a special government agency, the Consejo Nacional de Población y Familia, within the Ministry of Public Health and Social Assistance to coordinate population activities and oversee the implementation of a national fertility control program.

Government population policies evolved from private sector family planning activities initiated by Protestant missionaries and the wives of some American Embassy officials. Between 1964 and the 1966 presidential elections, a number of private birth-spacing clinics began operations and a private Dominican Family Welfare Association (Asociación Dominicana Pro Bienestar de la Familia) were created. During the Balaguer administration the Dominican fertility control movement appeared to gain new vigor and increased momentum. The leading newspapers *Listín Diario* and *El Caribe* began to provide editorial support for family planning, and there was evidence that church leaders were becoming concerned enough to take action − especially with respect to sex education.[3] Moreover, the relative success of the Asociación had demonstrated that family planning was popular and could succeed.

So, although domestic political leaders were somewhat concerned over the population question, there is much evidence to suggest that the most important factor contributing to the development of a population policy involved the presence and cooperation of international expertise in project development and a willing source of funds for a fertility control program. Linkage politics are most evident through the activities of two coordinating external groups which were directly involved in the Consejo's formation: AID and the Population Council of New York.

AID officials gave encouragement in various ways to Dominican officials and were a key factor in developing a fertility control policy. Population matters have preoccupied the agency over the last several years,[4] in part because it has felt that overpopulation is a threat to stability. Moreover, the AID mission had felt pressure from Washington to promote family planning programs since the turmoil of 1965. On one occasion, Dominican AID Mission officials observed

unreliability of available statistics does not alter our basic conclusion that the growth rate is high, and family sizes depressingly large. Hence, economic and social progress, which has been dangerously slow and one of our major concerns, can be much more rapid if there is a sharp reduction in the population growth rate.[5]

Because many important documents concerning AID population activities in the Dominican Republic are "classified," information pertaining to United States involvement in the development of Dominican fertility control policies is limited. However, it can be argued that United States officials have encouraged attempts to limit rapid population growth in the Dominican Republic in three ways.

First, AID has worked to create among Dominican elites an awareness of the obstacles to development posed by rapid population growth. In April 1967, a number of Dominican leaders were invited to attend the Eighth World Conference of the International Planned Parenthood Federation (IPPF) in Santiago, Chile and, later in that same year, to go to a meeting in Caracas on Population Policies in Relation to Development in Latin America. Much of the expense involved in getting Dominicans to these meetings was allegedly borne by AID.

A second strategy for inspiring fertility control has involved financial support to family planning activities within the context of a broad maternal and infant care program administered through the Ministry of Health. This long-standing approach has provided the most policy leverage. A Population Council consultant's letter to the AID mission director following an April 1966 tour to confer with AID officials makes clear the rationale for this approach:

A national government policy regarding population and family planning in a Latin American country may not be feasible or desirable, and development of such a policy might be subject to attack and create an outright conflict with opposition groups. It is probably more important to develop family planning activities as an integral part of regular medical services such as the maternal and child health services of the country and to insure that what is done in this field is done on a voluntary basis. Thus, family planning clinics can be made a part of already existing services in health centers and hospitals throughout the country as part of an on-going program and therefore require "permissive approval" of reluctant government officials rather than active approval of a program.[6]

This strategy led to a policy of making AID funds available for maternal /child-health activities, providing that the Dominican government develop a family planning program. The result was that on April 15, 1969 the Dominican government signed a \$7.1 million maternal and infant care loan agreement for the purpose of "instituting a health program of maternal and infant care including the remodeling and construction of health facilities, procurement of equipment, education and training of personnel, studies, mass media materials, and technical assistance for the program."[7] The real goals of this loan were succinctly stated in a December 10, 1969, AID memorandum on population activities in the Dominican Republic:

The \$7.1 million loan will strengthen health infrastructure so as to permit the provision of a nationwide maternal/infant care service — including family planning — on a voluntary basis.

. . . After implementation is completed in about three years, results in terms of family planning are expected to be as follows: A MIC nationwide system will offer family planning services through about 30 hospitals, 30 sub-centers, and 75 rural clinics. Approximately 3,450 medical and paramedical personnel will have received training in family planning. While it is difficult to predict the demand for services, it is hoped that about 300,000 Dominican women or about 1/3 of those in the fertile cohorts will be participating in one or another family planning program.[8]

The strongest evidence that the MIC loan has as one of its principle goals the creation of a nationwide mechanism for the dissemination of fertility control information and assistance is contained in the "conditions precedent to initial disbursement" of funds:

(c) Evidence that Borrower has created a National Population and Family Council to serve as an advisory body to the Secretary of Health, to supervise all population matters within government hospitals, and to coordinate all family planning programs conducted in facilities other than government hospitals.

(d) Evidence that the National Population and Family Council is fully prepared to carry out its duties; such evidence shall demonstrate, *inter alia,* that sufficient staff has been hired, that all necessary equipment, including vehicles, has been acquired, that appropriate supervision of the existing rural clinics has been undertaken, and that a statistical reporting system for Project Services has been prepared.[9]

The third leg of the "country team" strategy has been an attempt to keep AID technical and advisory services well in the background in order to minimize the appearance of external United States involvement in the "sensitive" family planning area. Thus the details of the loan agreement were not made public by either AID or the Balaguer administration, and AID has encouraged participation by other donors:

As essential infrastructure moves into place and personnel are trained under the AID loan, we would hope that the international institutions, particularly the United Nations and PAHO, would carry an increasing proportion of the effort. We will, of course, continue to monitor and evaluate progress independently and suggest changes of strategy where called for.[10]

At AID's request the Population Council provided the Consejo with a technical assistance grant of $54,000 for a year's duration beginning in July 1968.[11] Since that time these two agencies have provided the bulk of the support required to keep the programs going. AID funds have been made directly available to the program either through PL-480 currencies generated by the sale of United States foodstuffs in the Dominican Republic or by supporting specific projects with grants-in-aid. It is estimated that about $625,000 has been provided via these channels.[12] Most of these funds have been used by the Consejo for clinic equipment and supplies (including contraceptives), office furniture, vehicles, and mass-media materials and propaganda such as message-oriented comic books.

The Population Council has sustained the administrative core of the Consejo since it began operations in 1968 under the initial $54,000 technical assistance grant.[13] Since the first year, the level of assistance has risen to $291,100, which is divided as follows:[14]

Administrative support for Consejo office, including staff salaries, travel, office supplies, vehicle maintenance, data processing, and meetings of Consejo members	$277,600
A 1968 grant for Lippes loops and inserters	3,500
A 1970 evaluation of various components of the program such as information and communication programs and service statistics activities	10,000

In some cases, the Population Council support funds have come initially from AID regional grants (this occurred in 1970), so that the Population Council itself is another channel for official U.S. government support of Dominican family planning programs. The Population Council does not wish to provide continuing core support and would like to see some other agency, preferably the Dominican government, take over that responsibility. It will, however, continue to channel support for needed research and evaluation activities including advanced training for individuals in this field.

The Dominican experience with fertility control programs ought to be considered a learning experience for donor institutions. For example, it may be argued that the Consejo was created as part of the strategy developed to implement a fertility-control program rather than in response to internally generated, broad-based demands for government involvement in population matters. Its architects sought to create an autonomous sluice for population funding to neutralize a perceived demographic threat to stability. Thus they designed the agency to achieve an immediate quantitative impact, measured in terms of operational clinics and number of family planning acceptors, and gave only minor consideration to long-range objectives related to the Dominican policy environment. Questions of integration and coordination of activities with other governmental and private groups, of strategies to make family planning meaningful in the context of Dominican social and cultural values, or of planning for the time when most program support could be internally generated, were largely ignored.

It seems plausible to assume that in the absence of foreign pressures to deal with the demographic crisis very little policy would have emerged in spite of President Balaguer's increasing awareness of population problems. While it is too early to evaluate completely the impact of fertility control, the results to date seem disappointing. The 1970 census counted 886,125 women in the fertile age groups (15-49).[15] At the end of the program's first three years of operation, approximately 5 percent of this total, or 46,992 patients, had been counted as first-time acceptors of contraceptive methods. This figure reflects patients who were ever enrolled in the program. The number of dropouts is not known, nor are there precise data available on the continuation and failure rates of patients who receive contraceptives through the clinics. It is very likely, however, that the number of women under contraceptive "control" is much less than the enrollment figure. In late 1971, the executive director of the Consejo estimated that the number of new patient acceptors was hovering around 1,500 per month or 18,000 a year.[16] This is only about 25 percent of the number of women who annually enter the reproductive age group.

Several obvious impediments to the program's success can be traced to the policy formation process: First, the program is permeated by a "numbers impede development" philosophy. While Consejo leaders have stressed that a reduction of demographic growth is not the only prerequisite for progress, the organization is perceived as primarily concerned with preventing births. The National Plan for a Population Program, which has guided the program in these early years, stresses the demographic objective of reducing the population growth rate rather than more broadly oriented goals which would appeal to more Dominicans. Thus the church has criticized the Consejo more for its failure to stress the family as a social unit and for its lack of attention to sex education than for reasons related to church doctrine. And the nationalist left has branded the program as "genocide" because it seeks to insure that there are fewer Dominicans. It is also evident from observing the program that concern with increasing the number of new patients served outweighs efforts to insure that once patients join the program they are motivated to continue.

Second, there has been little actual integration of family planning activities with related programs of other government agencies. The failure to do so can be interpreted as indicating that population growth is not considered a priority problem in domestic political and administrative circles. The actual relationship between the Consejo and the health bureaucracy to which it is attached is not clearly defined, and there is little operational integration of family planning activities with the ministry's related health programs, although the policy rhetoric indicates this to be central to the Consejo's program. At the personal level, some senior health bureaucrats interviewed voiced resentment over the occasional strains between Consejo personnel and Health Ministry employees.

Third, because external organizations were heavily involved in launching the Consejo and continue to support its activities, its family planning activities are viewed with suspicion by many groups and individuals both in and outside the government, and its legitimacy as a Dominican institution is not yet assured. The most significant external influence on population policy in the Dominican Republic has been the Agency for International Development, which can threaten to withhold program funds, if the conditions of the health loan with respect to fertility control activities are not met, in order to pressure the administration to support the Consejo. Many knowledgeable Dominicans believe that if United States funding were to disappear the program would cease to exist because the political leadership does not fully accept the relevance of family planning to economic and social development. While it is willing to give tacit support to a program that costs the country little in the way of resources, the Dominican administration is reluctant to budget funds for the negative economic goal of birth prevention, especially given the fact that an overly successful program would provoke political opposition from the nationalist left.

Thus, while the overall climate in terms of official and popular attitudes has not been overly antagonistic to fertility control, there are strong indications that important institutional and popular sectors of Dominican society lack a strong commitment to the program. Some officials and observers themselves question the intensity of the government's commitment to having a successful fertility control program. One anonymous cynic who had worked with the program told me that to understand the family planning program one must keep in mind that "the Dominican government is based on inertia, and if a good idea comes along that doesn't cost them money, the leaders will go along with it."[17]

Those closest to the operations of the Consejo insist that there is no guiding policy which governs their actions but rather a set of attitudes which are positive toward fertility control as long as it doesn't generate a lot of unfavorable political controversy. Consejo adminstrators cite the fact that the Executive Council of the Consejo has not functioned with any degree of effectiveness as evidence of the government's passiveness toward fertility control policy. One member of the Consejo complained:

The only real policy this country has is the policy of the leader trying to maintain himself. There is no other in the whole country. Everything is based on pragmatic expediency rather than planning to achieve objectives and make progress.[18]

Two general indicators of the government's attitude are the lack of emphasis on integration and coordination of the Consejo's activities with those of other agencies and its delay in supplying the Consejo with counterpart operating funds, as specified in the health loan, during a period in late 1971. The circumstances of that situation have not been revealed.

The opinions of three key individuals on the extent of Dominican official commitment in this area indicate that fertility control is not a high priority in the Balaguer administration. Mr. Jawdat Mufti, United Nations representative to the Dominican Republic, said that in his opinion the chief areas of interest to the Balaguer government were agriculture and education. He had not noted a strong commitment to family planning and population matters in the higher echelons of the government, although he felt that it was only a question of time before the concern would appear. Since it is the policy of the United Nations to become involved only on those priority areas of host nations, Mufti explained that little United Nations aid had been expended in this area.[19]

Mario Fernández Mena, former minister of health and a close advisor to the president, was asked if the Dominican government could take over financial support of the Consejo. Dr. Fernández Mena replied that with funds so scarce in the Dominican Republic, it would be best to search for some form of "international funding."[20]

The deputy administrator of AID in the Dominican Republic, Mr. John Bennett, knows first hand of the government attitude. He reported that at the time the Consejo was founded and the health loan arranged, AID was much more optimistic about the ability and the willingness of the country to make progress in these matters than it is now. Much of the loan has not yet been implemented, and the whole project has been quite discouraging. It was his personal opinion that Dominican leaders just didn't see rapid population growth as a significant obstacle to development.[21]

If these impressions are accurate, then it must be assumed that any significant fertility control activity will be the responsibility of other than Dominicans, and the burden of supporting fertility control activities will continue to rest on foreign groups. Dominican population policy will continue to be the product of linkage politics and internal political considerations. Heretofore the North American presence has been highly evident, but the current worldwide and hemispheric tendency to shift from bilateral to international assitance will diminish the vigor of the argument that in fertility control lie the seeds of "Yankee Imperialism." The need to educate and communicate in ways that have meaning for Dominicans will still exist, however, and it is to be hoped that a way is found to bring this most important of messages to those people in terms that they and their leaders can understand, appreciate — and accept.

Notes

1. Abraham Lowenthal, "The Dominican Republic: The Politics of Chaos," pp. 34-58 of Arpad von Lazar and Robert R. Kaufman, eds., *Reform and*

Revolution: Readings in Latin American Politics (Boston: Allyn and Bacon, Inc., 1969), p. 58.

2. Population Reference Bureau, "1972 World Population Data Sheet."

3. María Ugarte, "Gestionan Instituto de Educación Sexual," *El Caribe* (April 13, 1968), pp. 1 and 10.

4. AID assistance to population programs has expanded rapidly in the last five years from $4.4 million in fiscal 1967 to $95.9 million in fiscal 1971. U.S. AID, *Population Program Assistance* (Washington, D.C.: G.P.O., December 1971), p. 22. The fiscal 1972 Foreign Assistance Bill appropriated $125 million for population programs *as a separate line item in the budget.*

5. U.S. Agency for International Development, Memorandum on Population Activities in the Dominican Republic, December 10, 1969, p. 3.

6. Consultant's letter to Mr. Alex Firfer, Director USAID Mission, Dominican Republic, dated May 16, 1966, p. 2.

7. República Dominicana and U.S., Loan Agreement for Maternal and Infant Care, AID Loan Number 517-1-021, signed on April 15, 1969, p. 1.

8. U.S. AID Memorandum (n. 5), pp. 4-5.

9. AID Loan 517-1-021 (n. 7), pp. 4-5

10. U.S. AID Memorandum (n. 5), p. 10.

11. República Dominicana, Secretaría de Estado de Salud Pública y Asistencia Social, Consejo Nacional de Población y Familia, *Informe General del Secretario Ejecutivo del Consejo Nacional de Población y Familia* I (Santo Domingo: Julio-Diciembre de 1968), p. 35.

12. Richard A. Lemkin and Charles A. Lininger, "Assistance for Family Planning Activities in the Dominican Republic," unpublished paper, New York, January 25, 1972, p. 6.

13. Secretaría de Estado de Salud Pública y Asistencia Social, Consejo Nacional de Población y Familia (n. 11).

14. Lemkin and Lininger (n. 12), p. 8.

15. República Dominicana, Secretariado Técnico de la Presidencia, Oficina Nacional de Estadística, *Comentarios Sobre los Resultados Definitivos del V Censo Nacional de Población* (Santo Domingo: 29 diciembre 1971), chart 3.

16. Luis Gonzales Fabra, Executive Director, Consejo, private interview, Santo Domingo, October 17, 1971.

17. Private interview, not for attribution.

18. Private interview, not for attribution.

19. Jawdat Mufti, United Nations Representative in the Dominican Republic, private interview, Santo Domingo, March 30, 1971.

20. Dr. Mario Fernández Mena, presidential advisor, private interview, National Palace, Santo Domingo, October 12, 1971.

21. John Bennett, Deputy Director AID Mission, Dominican Republic, private interview, Santo Domingo, September 27, 1971.

14

The Rich, the Poor, and Population

Aaron Segal

Population problems should be viewed and understood as one aspect of the broader problem of relations between the rich and the poor. Population problems have a place in this relationship both between rich and poor nations and between the rich and the poor within a single society.

The terms rich and poor are deliberately employed here rather than the euphemisms developed and developing which serve to mask important realities. Whether capitalist or socialist, the rich countries' absolute and relative superiority in material standards of living is steadily widening over those of the vast majority of mankind. Some of the poor live in countries that are experiencing some macroeconomic development, the economies of other countries are stagnating or actually declining, while the phenomenon of "growth without development" has also been observed in various poor countries where the economic progress that does occur is largely confined to noncitizens and a tiny national elite. A similar process seems to be at work within certain rich countries, particularly the United States, where economic growth largely leaves the poor behind.

Since the time of Thomas Malthus it has been fashionable to describe excess fertility as one of the fundamental causes of poverty, whether among individuals or societies. One advantage of ascribing poverty to fertility is that it absolves the rich from any direct responsibility. As the Hammonds note in their study of town and country labor in England, "during the nineteenth century, all the social abuses — bad housing, bad sanitation, bad working conditions — could always be justified: if you did anything to improve the conditions of the poor, they would just have more children and, poor things, they would die of hunger."[1] Margaret Sanger, the crusading American founder of the birth control movement, started her career as a radical socialist. However, by 1920, as her movement began to be respectable and to attract support from the wealthy, she took the view that "the chief issue of birth control is more children from the fit, less from the unfit."[2] David Kennedy, the historian, notes that the U.S. birth control movement was converted "from a radical program of social disruption to a conservative program of social control."[3]

The belief that population growth is a basic cause of poverty, whether of individuals or of societies, plays a preponderant role in the thinking and public statements of some of the most active proponents of population control policies

173

and in the commitment of governments to the deliberate reduction of their rates of population increase. It is important to distinguish population control policies from those which advocate the use of government means to permit individuals to practice family planning. Although lines are often blurred, advocates of family planning primarily argue that it should be a responsibility of governments to facilitate individuals' deciding how many children they wish to have and when to have them. Population controllers argue that societies need to deliberately influence the choices of individuals about desired and actual family size in order to reduce fertility.

The United States government has provided funds to promote population control and family planning in other countries since 1965. Since 1967 substantial federal funds have been committed for family planning within the United States, although the Population Commission appointed by President Nixon in 1970 in its final report carefully steered clear of endorsing population control based on zero population growth or any other specific goal for the United States.[4] Official thinking, as reflected in a State Department briefing, is that "the U.S. and other nations providing aid are disappointed because rapid population growth consumes and nullifies two-thirds of our aid. Improvements in standards of living we hoped to see in a reasonably few years are taking much longer . . . . More aid will be needed just to maintain the present slow rate of progress. Congress and the public will be more reluctant to increase aid when so much goes to maintain more people at the same levels of poverty which now prevail."[5]

The private enthusiasts for population control are open and explicit in holding fertility responsible for poverty. Consisting largely of wealth businessmen and industrialists active in the Population Crisis Committee, which lobbies for increased government spending at home and abroad on birth control, an imposing array of mostly very rich Americans have signed their names to full-page newspaper ads claiming "Latin American Aid Nullified by Population Explosion" and that "America cannot long remain an island of prosperity in a sea of poverty and hunger. If corrective measures to check this human flood are not taken right here and now the resulting worldwide misery, strife, revolution, and wars will make our experience in Viet Nam appear minor by comparison."[6]

There is of course another view of the causes of poverty. It is reflected in the reply of Ernest Hemingway to the remark by F. Scott Fitzgerald that "the rich are different from us": "Yes, they have more money." The poor within rich countries and poor countries are more inclined to explain their poverty as a consequence of the policies and practices of the rich rather than of their inability to limit their own procreation.

The growing confrontation between these two views is at the heart of present thinking about population. On the one hand, rich donor countries have become increasingly disillusioned with foreign economic aid to poor countries or internal economic and social assistance to the poor within their own midst. The decline of the cold war, the Vietnam tragedy, the rapprochement between the United States and the Soviet Union and China, the belief that the poor countries do not affect global balances of power, frustration over the seeming lack of results from years of aid, and resentment at name-calling and other less-than-grateful acts by recipients of aid, have all combined to produce a steady deterioration in the qualitative and quantitative flows of assistance from rich to poor countries, particularly from the United States. One element of this deterioration has been the belief expressed by former U.S. Senator Clark that unless poor countries take measures to reduce their fertility "American aid would be poured down a rathole."[7] So great is the disillusion with aid that Robert McNamara, president of the World Bank, noted at the 1972 United Nations Conference on Trade and Development meeting in Santiago, Chile, that current and projected flows of official aid "at less than half their stated target, are wholly inadequate."[8] When it comes to trade and an easing of the heavy external debt that cripples numerous poor countries, the rich have shown themselves to be even less generous.

Together with the belief that rapid population increase undermines economic aid is a pervasive sense in rich countries that middle-class persons are being taxed to provide economic assistance for rich people in poor countries. This belief reflects the ghastly and often worsening income distributions in many poor countries. Some argue that the present trickle of aid helps to worsen those inequalities while being of no benefit to the ever fertile masses. Although the speeches of George Wallace put the case against aid in its crudest and simplest terms, more sophisticated versions of this reasoning are a major factor in the withering of the limited constituency for aid within rich countries, particularly the United States.

Similar attitudes and acts can be documented in the response to poverty in the United States. While support dwindles for programs intended to substantially raise the incomes of the poor, whether through income transfers or jobs, the President requests and Congress approves additional funds for birth control directed at the poor. Both at home and abroad if fertility causes poverty, then birth control is seen as considerably cheaper than economic aid, or spare us the thought, measures to redistribute incomes.

The relationships between population growth and economic development are complex and by no means clear or uniform for all societies. What can be safely generalized is that (1) lower fertility will, in and of itself, only slightly increase personal or family incomes, unless differences are on the order of four children per household versus eight; (2) lower fertility will mean fewer children entering school and adults the labor market and less demand on education and other government services; (3) lower fertility may, but does not necessarily, increase national rates of savings and investment, thus possibly leading to higher rates of economic growth; and (4) lower fertility has little effect on the short-run distribution of income within a society. High fertility is not a basic cause of poverty nor is its reduction a *sine qua non* of economic growth. However, lower fertility together with a number of other measures may make national and personal economic betterment easier. One source of conflict between rich and poor is the belief among many rich that high fertility is, in and of itself, a basic cause of poverty and that in the absence of fertility reduction economic growth cannot occur. The poor are more inclined to see high fertility as one of many contributory factors to the persistence of poverty and economic growth as the outcome of measures other than fertility reduction.

As the poor countries struggle to cope with rising debts, protectionist trade practices that restrict their access to the markets of the rich, and a declining flow of aid for everything but birth control, their frustration mounts. This frustration was aptly captured in an election poster displayed by the Communist party of India in a recent hotly contested election in the state of Kerala. Attacking the Congress party government of India for pushing population control, including accepting external aid for that purpose, the posters read "We want bread and they give us loops" (intrauterine contraceptive devices).

"We want bread and they give us loops" is the essence of the present crisis and confrontation between rich and poor countries and between the rich and poor within countries. Psychiatrist Robert Coles quotes a black American mother:

"To me, having a baby inside me is the only time I'm really alive. I know I can make something, do something, no matter what color my skin is, and what names people call me . . . . Even without children my life would still be bad — they're not going to give us what *they* have, the birth control people. They just want us to be a poor version of them only without our children and our faith in God and our tasty fried food, or anything."[9]

The paradox is that as the flow of assistance from rich to poor becomes a dried-up stream, funds for population control increase both absolutely and relatively. Globally, something on the order of $200 million was available from rich countries for birth control in poor countries in 1972, and this figure has been increasing by 25 percent annually since the U.S. government first provided funds in 1965.[10] Still a mere pittance compared to expenditures on arms or military aid, the population control item has come to represent between 5 and 10 percent of total U.S. foreign economic aid. At a time when most U.S. AID officials sweat out annually in Congress the survival of their agency and jobs, those in the population division accept an embarrassing largesse. During the last several years, while the U.S. Congress has taken a meat cleaver to general foreign aid requests, it has consistently voted as much or more money for population control as was requested.

The influential lobbyists of the Population Crisis Committee and other groups have done their job too well, earning for themselves the nickname of the "Population Mafia." Robert Black, an official of the Population Division of AID, admits that "we've let ourselves be trapped into a greedy acceptance of this proffered many millions from the U.S. Congress, and we are paying the price of having it identified so nakedly as assistance for population programs only, knowing that this will inevitably create some negative reactions, particularly in the developing world."[11] AID has tried to spend some of the $125 million a year it receives for population on manpower, education, and health services. It is anxious to establish that its programs are concerned with human beings and not just their reproductive organs. The United Nations Fund for Population Activities, the World Bank, and the more than thirty other international organizations in the birth control business profess similar aims.

In spite of the relatively small sums of money involved, it is apparent to many observers that the population control donors outweigh in numbers and enthusiasm the recipients. Bernard Berelson, president of the Population Council, the prestige research organization in this area, underscores the differing views of donors and recipients: "At present, if I am not badly mistaken, there is a discontinuity of will between the donor and the recipient agencies: they do not fully share the common objective of population control. The irony is that, with a few exceptions on each side, the donors are more committed than the recipients, yet it is the latter who must do the job. One cannot substitute its will for the other's."[12]

Berelson has tried to bridge the bread vs. loops clash by proposing a one billion dollar annual program to provide worldwide comprehensive maternal health and child-care services, including postpartum family planning. Like others he has contended that unless and until infant mortality falls in many countries, couples will continue to want many children in order to ensure that some will survive. (Infant mortality among the poor in the United States, incidentally, is twice as high as among middle- and upper-income groups.)

It is significant that the proposal to tie birth control to global maternal health has won little support in rich countries — such is the disillusion with aid. To those who believe in the population-poverty link, it has the disadvantage of serving to increase rates of population growth in many countries for a generation or two by reducing infant mortality at the same time it creates some of the long-term conditions for lower fertility. Nor have other proposals for non-reciprocal trade preferences from the rich to the poor, easing of debt burdens or providing poor countries with a limited share of the special drawing rights created by the International Monetary Fund as a new global currency reserve attracted much interest.

The world's wealthy nations — 25 percent of its people, but 80 percent of its wealth — have been susceptible only to the pressures of the handful of poor countries possessing reserves of oil and natural gas. Unfortunately, aside from heroin, opium, and marijuana, there are few other natural resources which the poor countries have and can use to extract more favorable terms from the rich. Nor has anyone come up with an effective way of assisting the poor without running the gauntlet of public and legislative opposition among the rich.

Whatever the actual or alleged advantage of multilateral as opposed to bilateral aid or trade, multilateral organizations including the World Bank are still ultimately dependent for funding on the governments and capital markets of the rich countries.

The net effect of this population overkill is that the national and international donor agencies have got far more money for population than they can efficiently or usefully spend in poor countries because most recipients want bread and not loops. Unable to deliver more bread, or even markets for the goods produced by the poor countries, and insecure in their own jobs and careers, the donor bureaucrats can only suggest to the poor that taking the loops may help somehow to produce more bread. There are of course some countries that are genuinely committed to population control and do want and need external aid in this area. There are many more who are willing to take the loops because that is what you have to do these days to have a chance to get other things. Often an interesting and complicated *double-entendre* game is played between local elites in poor countries and the officials of donor agencies. The local elites agree to see proposals and aid agreements drafted in such a way as to include some population control or family planning component wanted by the external donors as a means or condition of receiving other kinds of assistance the elites want.[13]

If and when accepting loops does not pay off in more bread, a new stage of confrontation between rich and poor may ensue. Just as more and more poor countries are openly or partially repudiating external debts which consume inordinate amounts of foreign exchange, so may some countries threaten to send back the loops (thus threatening the jobs of the donor-agency bureaucrats).

We are beginning to realize that aid for population control is different from other kinds of rich-poor country aid relationships and a new dimension in international relations. Foremost, it is an attempt on the part of rich countries, whether through bilateral or multilateral channels, to change the most sensitive and intimate private behavior of individuals in poor countries. There is a difference between providing assistance for contraception, with its direct effects on the sex lives, family structure, and daily behavior of millions, and providing a steel mill or hydroelectric project. The most suitable analogy is that of peaceful religious conversion. Historical evidence would suggest that the sending of persons or supplies from one society to change the religious beliefs of people in another society has not usually been successful unless backed up by high and sustained degrees of coercion. Since voluntary reductions in fertility depend on countless individual decisions, these new missionaries must perforce rely on local converts to reach the masses. This is almost entirely a function of genuine interest and commitment on the part of those converts, and external assistance can play only a marginal role in bringing that about.

Like other forms of external aid, population assistance is usually tied to the purchase of goods and services from the donor countries. This is particularly wasteful since the greatest costs of these programs are in local personnel, communications, and facilities. Lack of foreign exchange is seldom a major constraint on effective programs, and the availability of tied aid and foreign exchange for imports rarely resolves basic problems. For instance, no amount of imported pills, loops, or other contraceptive devices will be used unless someone whom they trust tells local people in a language that they understand about their availability. Nor are there many governments, no matter how pro-American or pro-Western, that are anxious to have on display contraceptives conspicuously marked "gift of the American people" in several languages, a condition that Congress has attached to U.S. material aid to ensure the presumably grateful poor know to whom to express their gratitude.

Another problem is that what little aid that is available these days is primarily in the form of loans rather than grants. Although many of these loans are "soft" with low rates of interest and long terms of repayment, the paying back of population loans poses particular problems. The preventing of births, with or without external loans, does not generate new incomes or revenues. At best what it does is to permit possible savings to occur to individuals and several years later to governments as there may be fewer children entering schools and using services. However, the loans have to be paid back out of scarce actual revenues, whether or not the births they may have prevented actually contributed to increasing personal incomes or government revenues. It is at least possible that a substantial portion of the "savings" to individuals in poor countries from their having fewer children will go right out of the country to pay for more imported consumer goods from rich countries. If this happens a government may find its foreign exchange situation and ability to repay loans worsening.

The tying of population aid to expenditures in the rich countries not only pushes up costs and decreases the real value of that aid but also sometimes results in countries being saddled with expensive imported mobile vans, medical equipment, and other material things which generate continuing local costs that aid does not meet. The donor agencies need to demonstrate to the "Population Mafia" that they are providing material objects, especially contraceptives, yet most of the time the real problem is to convince individuals to change their behavior to use these services, which is almost entirely a function of local costs and efforts. The result is dozens of countries in which 50 to 90 percent of the funds for birth control come from abroad as do most of the senior staff, who require housing, salaries, and equipment out of all proportion to national means.[14]

Population aid is often also given to private organizations within recipient countries in addition to, or as an alternative to, aid to governments. In many instances these private organizations have arisen in response to some local elites, primarily in the medical profession, perceiving that there was money available from outside if they set up an organization. The International Planned Parenthood Federation (IPPF), itself the recent product of the voluntary birth control movements of middle-class origin in North America, England, and Western Europe, has given "birth" to numerous recent affiliates in poor countries. Using U.S. government and other funds, IPPF shuttles funds into paper organizations which national governments view with indifference or with relief at being freed of the onus of accepting foreign aid for contraception.

Finally, in many parts of the world the willingness of a government to accept population assistance on a multilateral or bilateral basis has become one of several tests of whether or not it is pro- or anti-American, and/or pro- or anti-Western. Attitudes toward population assistance have become one of the yardsticks to measure the foreign policies of particular governments, both from within and abroad.

Not only do the population donors outnumber the recipients, but sometimes donors stumble over one another in their haste to spend their funds. Tunisia is an example of a politically moderate, pro-Western government committed to private enterprise with interested local elites and a national development plan that stipulates the desirability of population control. As a result, in 1971 in this country of five million, fifteen national governments, international organizations, and private foundations were engaged in the business of providing population assistance. Jamaica, with a population of three million and similar political attitudes, receives population assistance from twenty-three different sources.

Such is the shortage of takers that the population donor agencies with their excess funds exhibit a Pavlovian response whenever the grapevine indicates the likelihood of another population recipient. A competition ensues to see who can arrive first with the most contraceptives. In 1971 a small army of donors descended on the Philippines when President Marcos announced a population control policy and willingness to receive external aid. Taiwan, which has endorsed population control since 1964 and is one of the few countries where some of the fall in birth rates may be partly due to government programs, has had to develop an entire center just to handle international visitations from donor agencies.

Donor and recipient relationships in the field of population can be classified in terms of five types. The first type is one in which primarily, but not necessarily, in response to the availability of external resources, individuals within a poor country establish a private organization to provide purely voluntary family planning, usually by private doctors in the major cities. This first type occurred in most of the islands of the Caribbean, where there was a very close correlation between the severity of winters in the eastern United States and the willingness of representatives of certain donor organizations to visit their Caribbean clients.

The second type, which I call that of benign neglect, is characterized by the local, voluntary, private group beginning to make limited kinds of requests for assistance from its own government, such as duty-free import licenses for contraceptives, permission to promote birth control on radio or television, and so forth. Generally these requests are couched in terms of family planning rather than population control objectives, sometimes stressing combined programs of birth control and assistance to sterile persons wishing to conceive. Offering help to the sterile in societies where barrenness may place a terrible burden on women or families, especially in Africa, can make such a request much more palatable. Governments respond with benign neglect, purporting to ignore the activities of the voluntary group and their external donors. Unless and until basic political objections are internally overcome, countries may exhibit the first or second type of policies and programs in which voluntary, private, family planning bothers no one but reaches only a few persons.[15]

The third type involves a formal, public government commitment, usually in a national development plan, to the goal of population control as opposed to merely offering family planning.[16] External donors may be involved in assisting both governments and voluntary organizations. Often the donors are unable to coordinate their efforts, since they are themselves responsible to very different kinds of constituencies. There is consequent confusion, duplication, and chronic instability, since the donors worry incessantly that a change of government will mean a new regime dropping population control and sending the pills or loops back.

Although there are roughly thirty governments in the world, primarily in Southeast Asia, which have type three policies and formal commitments to population control, in most instances they represent a much lower priority for them than for the donor agencies. Local elites have opted to play the population game with donors because it has become synonymous with the aid game in these hard times. Playing the population game usually means that the donor agencies descend, the government makes a formal commitment to population control, and a politically weak, hopelessly understaffed and underequipped Ministry of Health that has thirty-seven tasks, most of which it does badly, is given the job of birth control. Within the Ministry of Health a special department or agency is created, some local people get trips overseas sponsored by the donor agencies, and some interagency rivalries and jealousies may be created.

The external donors are able to go back to their respective constituencies and justify further funds for population aid since another country has requested it. Apparently it matters little if external aid is expected to finance 90 percent of the national program or if the clinics that are opened and contraceptives that are dispensed are almost entirely confined to urban areas and to middle-income families. Since more takers have been found for money to prevent births, at least there is no risk that the donor agencies will be accused of its going down a rathole.

A fourth type of population policy causes acute embarrassment for the rich donors. In this type, governments pursue population policies based on ethnic or racial differences, favoring increase in numbers of some groups and decrease by others. The most flagrant examples of such policies and governments are the white minority regimes of Rhodesia and South Africa, which are anxious to increase fertility and immigration of whites and to promote birth control among blacks. Since these two particular governments enjoy low reputations among their own black populations, they have been particularly eager to have private, voluntary organizations spread the word of birth control rather than government agents. It is no credit to the IPPF that it has been willing to provide funds to such organizations under these circumstances.[17]

Elsewhere, where politics are organized on tight ethnic or racial lines, the key question has been which group is most likely to reduce its fertility and what will that do to the political balance of power. Only where governments have been convinced that their followers would remain more fertile than their foes have they been willing to accept external aid for population programs.

A fifth type is that of governments that have accepted the legitimacy of family planning as a basic human right of individuals to decide how many children they want, as well as the desirability of population control, and are seriously committed to a mass, national program to achieve both objectives. The seriousness of this commitment is reflected in the high priority given to the program at all levels of government, the willingness to commit scarce local financial and skilled manpower resources to the program, and the recognition that the fundamental problem is changing mass behavior, which involves efforts beyond family planning and the confines of the Ministry of Health. Sharp reductions in national fertility probably require generations rather than years. This means that the will to do the job, the funds and manpower available, and the commitment over time are largely the result of internal factors rather than external influences. The evidence suggests that at the present time Barbados, China, South Korea, Taiwan, Singapore, and India are about the only governments in the world — including the rich countries, most of which have type two policies — which are seriously committed to doing something about population control. It is conceivable that one of the features of type five behavior is that the Chinese people and society, whether living under Communist or capitalist regimes, are psychologically and socially moving toward the second stage of the historic demographic transition when fertility falls rapidly after mortality has fallen. Since the Chinese in all the countries in which they are resident total approximately 20 percent of the human race, this could be a profound development.

It is significant that type five governments display divergent ideological and political characteristics. In each instance elites have convinced themselves of the seriousness of national population problems and the need to act upon them. The Chinese, after ideological squabbles and administrative disputes, now seem firmly committed to reducing fertility, although totally without external assistance of any kind.[18] Barbara Ward notes that "the only conditions under which strong governmental policies will be introduced . . . is the perception, by developing governments themselves, that the pursuit of high population is as ultimately disastrous for the nation's well-being as a failure to try to increase productivity in farming or to introduce modern industry. No amount of rational or well-meant advice and offers of assistance from other governments or agencies can be effective until this essential internal decision has been taken. It can be particularly unwelcome when it is given by countries who, with less than a third of the world's population, consume over 75 percent of the world's income. But China and India are seeking to discourage large families in terms of their own self-interest."[19]

While the other four policy types generally entail extensive external involvement and inputs to prod local people to take population problems seriously, once the latter do so I suspect that they don't want foreigners messing around. John Lewis, former AID director for India, writes that "what foreign aid donors can contribute to population control in India is usually overrated by the donors. Foreign exchange has not been and is unlikely to be a significant constraint on this problem. Technical assistance projects of the traditional kind have a very limited future.... . The government of India repeatedly has shown that it is not very receptive to donor "leverage" on its policy choices in this complex and sensitive field. And the mandate the U.S. Congress has given AID to press funds on the government of India whether it wants them or not can be positively counterproductive in its impact on Indian program management."[20]

In most poor countries, however, even where some people are willing to play the population game, the basic concern is with bread and not loops. Nor is inserting loops believed to be an effective short-term means of internally generating more bread. As long as the donors and recipients see the population problem differently and accordingly assign it very different priorities, their misalliance is likely to be sterile. The loops may be accepted, but there is little prospect of national fertility being reduced as a result of their being used.

What elites in many poor countries are most worried about is massive urban unemployment of young persons already born. This is perceived as the greatest single political and economic threat. With nearly 50 percent of their total population under the age of twenty and urban populations increasing at 6 to 10 percent annually, it is no wonder that the politicians are frightened. What no one has been able to devise is a massive means of employing the unemployed to prevent births, either in rich or poor countries. (This might constitute a new job-training program for both poor countries and unemployed youth in rich ones.) Unless rich countries are willing to permit international migration of unskilled and semi-skilled persons on a substantial basis, there are no kinds of population external inputs that are going to make a significant short-term dent in the hundreds of millions of unemployed, semieducated, urban, young people in poor countries. (Effective migration out of the ghetto is also probably the only short-term means of cutting mass unemployment among young American blacks and Spanish-speaking persons.)

It is an easy task to use present rates of population increase, age distribution patterns, and dependency ratios to scare the hell out of politicians in poor countries. After all, if there are not enough jobs, schools or services for present populations, what will happen if natural rates of population increase continue at 2 to 3 percent per annum?

Politicians are often prepared to take population problems seriously, in addition to the trips abroad to attend conferences and meetings to discuss these problems. However, their concern is more jobs now, and the best that population control can offer is fewer children entering schools five years from now and fewer job-seekers fifteen years from now. This time perspective is too long in countries where political longevity may be measured in days or months rather than years. If the present unemployed can overthrow or help overthrow a government, then the prospect of their numbers being doubled in fifteen years unless births are prevented is of little relevance.

The relevant question for those in power who are presented with such scenarios is sometimes "what do you think is going to happen to the American dollar," or "do you think that it is wiser to invest in Switzerland or Miami," or "where can I go if and when I am out?" Politicians in poor countries can afford to take population problems and policies seriously only if they control their internal environment to the point of being reasonably confident of remaining in power to reap some of the long-term benefits, when the internal risks of such policies can be minimized through various strategies, or when external donors can promise and deliver bread and loops together.

The "Population Mafia" has oversold the U.S. Congress and the general public on fertility as the cause of poverty, making birth control a cheap substitute for tough concessions on foreign aid, trade, debts, and international monetary arrangements. The arguments used to get Congress to vote money for birth control are not the arguments needed to actually convince poor persons, whether in the United States or elsewhere, to reduce their fertility. Indeed, where the poor come to hear of these arguments they may be counterproductive. Having used one set of arguments to convince Congress and other organizations to appropriate funds, the problem now becomes delivering the results wanted, usually measured in neat tables and columns of numbers of births prevented. Except in a few countries like South Korea and Taiwan, which are already well advanced in terms of mass literacy, industrialization, and urbanization, the mere introduction of birth control services will not provoke their widespread acceptance. The determinants of human fertility are complex and interdependent, and all the evidence suggests that in most societies a number of changes that persist over time must occur before rapid voluntary fertility changes take place. This means investing on a long-term basis in a number of infrastructure programs before people are willing to begin to think about having fewer children. It may mean that where infant mortality is still high (as in most of Africa), mortality must fall and rates of population increase go up before fertility behavior may change. Instead of charts showing births prevented, the only meaningful results may be charts of infant deaths prevented.

Just as the rich countries tired of economic aid once they realized that it had no specific short-term end, so may they tire of population control when it begins to look like a long-term and expensive funding program that will not provide results for years or generations to come. As the numbers of prevented births fail to add up, the shrill voices may dismiss this program as "another rathole." As long as those poor people out there who breed too fast are not going to overrun us or drop nuclear bombs on us, or deny us their oil or natural gas, then we rich folks can't seem to convince ourselves of any good reasons for helping them on a long-term sustained basis. Humanitarianism is not enough, especially when it is their own fault that they are poor. Whatever political instability they may experience, as long as it does not directly threaten our welfare, may leave us indifferent.

At one time rapid economic development based on generous foreign aid was held to be an essential prerequisite for something called political stability (a term usually defined as producing governments acceptable to the donors). Then it was discovered that economic development itself could contribute to political instability through increasing expectations, discontent, income inequities, and other factors. The "Population Mafia" has argued that fertility causes poverty, instability, and even international unrest, although the arguments and evidence they have provided are most dubious. Once we fail to prevent sufficient births and wars continue, will we retreat to our rich enclaves, taking steps to ensure that the poor can do us no serious damage?

The road back to population sanity involves a few simple, unpleasant truths. These are:

1. That fertility does not cause poverty, war, or social unrest, although combined with other variables it can contribute to any or all of these occurring

2. That reducing fertility may leave the poor just as materially poor as before unless other kinds of assistance are provided and changes made

3. That the task of reducing fertility will have to be done by members of particular societies, with outsiders playing only a marginal role

4. That the determinants of fertility at the individual, societal, or global level are complex and mutually interdependent and that despite the assertions of one prominent AID official, the problem is not primarily one of bringing "to bear the heavy artillery"[2][1]

5. That, if we really wish to eliminate poverty, we had better find some more meaningful reasons for helping the poor than fear of what they may do to the rich

6. That trade, aid, immigration, income distribution, and maternal health may

have as much or more to do with reducing fertility as furnishing contraceptives (For instance, if we want to help some countries reduce their fertility, we might start in the United States by not recruiting a majority of their trained medical personnel to solve our own medical shortages; by accepting as permanent immigrants some of their unskilled young, much as Europe's population problems of the nineteenth century were partly relieved by the export of more than fifty million unskilled young persons to North and South America, Australia, and elsewhere; by giving poor countries a chance to sell us cheap manufactured goods which are labor-intensive, especially products which depend on employment of women; and by being willing to pay more for their agricultural exports. It would be helpful if the "Population Mafia" with their ample funds for publicity would mention some of these or other measures in their urgent messages to the American public and leaders.)

7. That we had better concern ourselves with the real causes of poverty within our own rich countries and not rely on birth control as a form of conservative social control

8. That we had better not ask others to do what we say rather than what we do (Until rich societies themselves adopt and take seriously population control policies they should avoid advising poor countries to do so. Instead they should wait for governments to take the initiative and keep external population inputs limited. The Chinese are in a better position, morally and materially, to convince Africans to take population problems seriously than we are.)

9. That we had better abandon the pursuit of coercive means of birth control (If we can't help create conditions at home or abroad in which individuals will want to voluntarily reduce their fertility, then we have no moral right to coerce them to do so.)

10. That we had better reexamine our own immigration policies so we can reduce the damage we are doing to poor countries through the brain drain. (This primarily means creation of incentives to encourage the skilled to return to their home countries, while enjoying regular opportunities to go abroad. Where possible, as in the United States for the Caribbean and the European Economic Community for North Africa, we should pursue immigration policies permitting a regular, permanent, legal immigration of young, unskilled persons and their families rather than the present illegal and temporary male migrant patterns.)

Notes

1. Quoted in Louise B. Young, ed., *Population in Perspective* (New York, London, Toronto: Oxford University Press, 1968), p. 63.

2. David Kennedy, *Birth Control in America* (Cambridge, Massachusetts: Harvard University Press, 1969), p. 115.

3. Ibid., p. 121.

4. Commission on Population Growth and the American Future, *Population and the American Future* (New York: New American Library, 1972).

5. Quoted in Barry Commoner, *The Closing Circle* (New York: Alfred A. Knopf, 1972), p. 324.

6. Quoted in Lawrence Lader, *Breeding Ourselves to Death* (New York: Ballantine, 1971). This book is a highly laudatory account of the life of Hugh Moore, originator of the Population Crisis Committee. A more critical view of the "population establishment" can be found in Elihu Bergman and William S. Flash, "The American Population Policy Process: Some Critical Insights," paper presented at the annual meeting of the American Political Science Association, Chicago, September, 1971.

7. Speech to the U.S. Senate on June 14, 1965.

8. Robert S. McNamara, Address to the United Nations Conference on Trade and Development in Santiago, Chile, April 14, 1972.

9. Quoted in Arthur J. Dyck, "Population Policies and Ethical Acceptability," pp. 351-77 of Daniel Callahan, ed., *The American Population Debate* (Garden City, New York: Doubleday and Company, Inc., 1971), p. 357.

10. Agency for International Development, *Population Program Assistance* (Washington, D.C.: G.P.O., 1971).

11. Remarks made at the Political Science/Population Workshop at Chapel Hill, North Carolina, May 4-6, 1972.

12. Bernard Berelson, "The Present State of Family-Planning Programs," pp. 201-36 of Harrison Brown and Edward Hutchings, Jr., eds., *Are Our Descendants Doomed?* (New York: The Viking Press, 1972), pp. 230-31.

13. Aaron Segal, *Politics and Population in the Caribbean,* Institute of Caribbean Studies, University of Puerto Rico, 1969.

14. Organization for Economic Cooperation and Development, *Population Assistance, Donor and Recipient Views* (Paris: OECD, 1970).

15. Most African and Latin American countries were representatives of types one and two in 1972, as were Middle Eastern countries except Egypt.

16. Dorothy Nortman, "Government Policy Statements on Population: An Inventory," Population Council Reports, February 1970, pp. 1-20.

17. See John Caldwell's paper on population policy in South Africa delivered at the Population Council Conference on Politics and Population in New York, October, 1970.

18. Pi-chao Chen, "The Prospects of Demographic Transition in a Mobilization System: China," pp. 153-82 of Richard L. Clinton and R. Kenneth Godwin, eds., *Research in the Politics of Population* (Lexington, Massachusetts: D.C. Heath and Company, 1972).

188

19. Barbara Ward and René Dubos, *Only One Earth* (New York: Norton and Company, Inc., 1972), p. 153.

20. John P. Lewis, "Population Control in India," pp. 243-65 of Brown and Hutchings (n. 12), p. 264.

21. R.T. Ravenholt, "Discussion of Dr. Berelson's Paper," pp. 237-42 of Brown and Hutchings (n. 12), p. 241. This heavy artillery refers to postconceptive measures.

15

Population Policy Research: A Personal Account

Robert H. Trudeau

This chapter is perhaps a bit unorthodox. In it, I will describe the unexpected effects (at least to me) of conducting research in the Third World, rather than the substantive results of the research project itself.[1] On the other hand, this is not an essay in ethics per se either. It is a personal account of my research experiences and what I learned from them. But I intend it to be more than that, for I will try to apply my experiences to a broader question, namely the normative implications of behavioral research in population policy questions.

Who I am and What I am Trying to Do

I initially became involved in this research project first of all because of a long-standing interest in things Latin American and secondly because of a recent recognition that demographic data can play a vital role in any analysis of political phenomena. I brought to the research project a mixed bag of values and preferences, of knowledge and experiences. Many of these will become apparent as the chapter progresses.

Since my days as a Peace Corps Volunteer, I have had a deep-rooted concern with the daily life of people in "less developed" areas. This concern has been reinforced by, and in turn has reinforced, much of my political thinking. You should be familiar with at least some components of this, if only so that the remainder of this chapter can be taken with the correct grains of salt.

I define political development (as well as any other kind of human development) in individualistic ways. While focusing on daily life rather than on formal or institutional variables, I usually observe those people who appear to me to be the most deprived in a given social grouping. I conceptualize deprivation in terms of basic human needs which aren't being satisfied. In observing an area and in thinking about it, I tend to focus first of all on the kinds of people I see around me, and only later (if at all) on the formal or informal political structures in their environment rather than *vice versa.*

In some ways this approach is psychologically oriented. Whether political processes be conceived of as a "system" and its "functions," as conflict resolution, as consensus-building, or whatever, I treat these processes as means and not as ends. For me, the ends are the daily life and psychological health of people as individuals not as statistical composites. My intellectual debt to Christian Bay and Abraham Maslow, among others, is obvious.

To the extent that I can see behaviorally oriented social scientists studying political processes rather than what I've described above as "ends," I find myself increasingly puzzled. I am confused by claims of value neutrality and also by the consequences of this alleged objectivity when it is put into practice in a research project. (My own project is a good example, as will be seen below). At the very least, it seems to me, these consequences include an overemphasis on political processes, *per se*, and an underemphasis on the direct, individual, human consequences of these processes. Most politics, in the words of Theodore Roszak, "is compounded of . . . reified hallucinations" such as "deterrence, gross national products, system stability" (otherwise known as "law and order"), and acceptable levels of unemployment.[2] (In a volume on population policy research, dare I add "population explosion" to the list?)

In any case, I've been interested by these kinds of questions for some time. It has occurred to me that political scientists might preclude dealing with them by their choice of research arrangements and methods. In part, this is the source of the impetus for writing this chapter. Recently, however, I have spent less time trying to tell other political scientists to reflect on issues such as value neutrality or the biases associated with behavioral research. Instead, I have been reflecting on my own behavior, heeding my own advice, as it were. This chapter is also the result of these ponderings and musings.

I recognize that these sorts of personal accounts are not a sufficient basis for any generalizations of scientific merit about the effects or research methods on political processes or on human development. Because of this, this chapter is perhaps more valuable to me than it is to any of you reading it. Nevertheless, I hope to raise and deal with issues that I think are salient, given my biases, and to propose relationships which I think are at least plausible. If this essay moves you to similar kinds of introspection, than its purpose will have been achieved. For with the exception of the assertion that to question one's research activities is a desirable thing, I have naught but questions with which to leave you.

Behavioralism and Political Demographers

So that the reader will have some reference points on which to base her/his interpretation of what follows, I would like to briefly raise some issues that seem to be part and parcel of the use of behavioral techniques in demographic research in political science. The treatment of these issues is neither inclusive nor exhaustive; I merely wish to place them on the agenda, for I have found the agenda to be singularly lacking in the consideration of these kinds of questions.

There are at least two levels at which questions about behavioralism can be raised. The first of these is generally acknowledged, and I mention it more in order to contrast it with another level of issues than to discuss these kinds of issues themselves.

Even while they assert the value neutrality of behavioralism *in toto* political scientists generally acknowledge the fact that the choice of research techniques can sometimes affect the outcome of the research endeavor. A good and widely recognized example is the controversy in community-power research between the advocates of the reputational and decisional approaches to the question of the existence of "power elites."[3] Using a reputational model, it is asserted, pretty much guarantees that the existence of a power elite will emerge from the research, though the precise attributes of the group will vary from one research situation to another. Similarly, at least partially predetermined results occur when a decisional approach is used: the existence of pluralistic politics is "proven."

By raising the issue of nondecisions, Bachrach and Baratz[4] (and more recently, Bachrach and Bergman)[5] revealed a whole set of normative and empirical questions that had been ignored by *both* approaches to community-power studies. Briefly, these were questions such as the mobilization of bias and agenda setting and their implications for political processes, democratic theory, and so forth.

I want to concentrate on a second level of issues, however. Bachrach and his colleagues have shown that although controversy and critical examination were taking place, broader questions were being ignored. Similarly, I'd like to note that arguing about behavioral techniques may be causing us to ignore larger issues arising from the use of behavioralism itself.

The adoption of a rationalistic, behavioral paradigm means, ultimately, epistemological reliance on a positivistic view of the world, with positivism's pursuit of measurement of those phenomena that can be regularly and empirically observed.[6] And so we can visualize, with Hampden-Turner, the behavioralist disappointedly reporting on the "Eureka-effect," observed when Archimedes interrupted the regular pattern of his bath — to run naked through the streets — and thereby reduced the regularity, orderliness, and predictability of his daily routine.[7]

To validly use the tools of the behavioral method seems to assure that those aspects of human existence susceptible to positivistic measurement will be reported.[8] In the absence of reports on other facets of human life, however, those that *are* reported become emphasized and accepted as complete: we begin to think that we are like what behavioral scientists say we are like. Following this a bit further, it seems to me that it is in this way that social scientists clearly aid us in defining ourselves. In the realm of political activity, for example, concepts such as "adaptation", "normal"; and "deviant" become normatively loaded and suggest definitions of "self" that are socially derived. To see certain kinds of activity as deviant and other kinds as normal is to help define what it is to be a normal person. Conversely, a definition of normal people implies a normal set of political procedures and activities for them to be a part of.[9]

Were these stimuli to occur in random directions, there would be no problem. But, it appears, no such randomness exists. In spite of the "problems" positivism is having in philosophical circles,[10] behavioralism continues to be the mainstream methodology in social science (although there is a growing postbehavioral group, especially in psychology). Consequently, to the extent that behavioralism presumes certain value positions, these are becoming more and more accepted as "normal". Every example of scientific verification, of "proof," available for the student to peruse seems to reinforce us into focusing on certain kinds of issues, data, techniques, and questions, - and away from others.[11]

Furthermore, the direction of this reinforcement is toward the quantifiable, the regular, the orderly, the measurable, the causal, the use of comparisons to explain variance; in short, toward the "normal" parts of the self that the scientific method can most easily deal with. Yet if major progress in knowledge is associated with "Eureka-effects" or with "new paradigms,"[12] then the direction of behavioralism is to retard and inhibit such nonincremental, discontinuous intellectual advances while at the same time marking progress in the ever-increasing collection of data and tested relationships, all of which are validly treated within the paradigm. I would like to hypothesize (and to see tested empirically) the following: as the collection of verified information grows, less effort — for a variety of possible reasons — will be spent questioning the paradigm itself.

I am not necessarily insinuating a malevolent "bandwagon" process. It could well be that a very subtle, subconscious set of assumptions are being adopted. In this methodological sense, behavioralism is conservative. Moreover, as it helps define people in ways that frown on deviance and thrive on observable regularity, behavioralism is also conservative politically.[13]

The quarrel here is not with the validity of behavioral techniques to test nomothetic hypotheses within the behavioral, positivist paradigm. Rather, it is with the tendency to see behavioralism as the path to objective truth and the consequent lack of attention paid to issues not easily susceptible to behavioral methods. The quarrel is important partly because of the importance of these issues and partly because of the philosophical problems facing logical positivism.[14]

I would summarize the foregoing as a two-pronged premise. The first part is that social scientists are affecting the reality they are a part of while they are studying it. This is so, whether or not it is intended, if only because of the definitions of self, normalcy, and deviance that researchers adopt. It also happens when researchers provide information for policymakers, which is a pretty direct involvement. But it also happens in indirect ways, somewhat akin to "agenda setting"[15] or to dignifying that which is studied as opposed to that which is studied as opposed to that which is not.[16]

The second part of the two-pronged premise is the nature of the involvement on the part of social scientists. Not only are social scientists involved in affecting the world around them (as everybody is), but social scientists of the behavioral persuasion are involved in a peculiar way that seems to simultaneously claim value neutrality while reinforcing conservative views of society and of people. I maintain that the first prong, involvement, is unavoidable. Consequently, I think that more attention needs to be paid to the second prong, the nature of the involvement.

I think that this is especially relevant to research in the area of population policy. Here, more so than in most other areas of political research, the agenda is in a state of flux; not only are data inconclusive and incomplete, the very nature of the questions to be asked is disputed. The personal nature of sexual mores makes this a particularly sensitive area in which to conduct systematic research, especially if one focuses on the individual outcomes of population policies rather than on the effects of these policies on some systemic indicator (by which I mean those "reified hallucinations" mentioned earlier.) Whether or not political demographers so focus in their research, it seems clear to me that population policies have direct impacts on daily life for many people, especially those who might be thought of as relatively deprived in a society.

Moreover, most people in the society are aware of and somewhat sensitive to, questions of population policy — however unsophisticated this awareness may appear to erudite social scientists from developed nations. It matters to most people, at one time or another in their lives and in a very personal sense, whether or not condoms are legally available, whether abortions are acceptable, what income tax deductions are allowed, and how many children they want or have. I do not refer here to the crusading kinds of concern associated with social reformers, but to the very personal awareness felt by individual people for their own options or lack thereof.

Because of this level of awareness,[17] political demographers engaged in research in population policy questions have a particularly strong responsibility to be aware of the role they have in shaping behavior in other people and in defining normalcy and deviance.

At this point, it may be useful to discuss, albeit somewhat parenthetically, the question of my megalomania, which arises when I assert that political demographers may have some sort of effect on the real world that is significant enough to justify writing about it. The two-step flow of communications theory has long been with us in the social sciences, and from it we can see, if not precisely measure, the possibility of the effects of creatures called opinion-leaders. This is especially visible when population policy research, for example, is discussed in the news media, although we all know that the president of the United States seems to have more of a short-run impact on popular thinking than a panel of prestigious political demographers would have, at least in the United States. The effects of political demographic research can also be seen in the adoption of its results in the action programs of public administrators. Not infrequently, moreover, the researchers become the administrators. Again, I accept the notion that the strength of the social scientist's impact is debatable. There are also effects, less measurable but nonetheless real, on the poeple who are studied — the interviewees — and finally, on the people with whom one is conducting research. If your bias is to focus on individual people, as mine is, then these categories become more important than the first two, for they become the categories somewhat susceptible to your personal scrutiny and control.

These effects of demographic research, plus the intensely personal and individualistic nature of the effects of population policies themselves, combine to produce (to my way of thinking) a research field in which political scientists should at least include — if not give primary emphasis to — consideration of these personal policy outcomes and of the directions in which our research, behavioral or otherwise, leads other people. By "personal policy outcomes," to repeat, I mean to include the personal effects of population policies (and of our efforts to study population policies) on individuals in society. These effects should be studied whether they are stated goals of policies or unexpected outcomes or both. The following section may help illistrate what I mean.

A Research Experience

Two paragraphs back, I listed four examples of ways in which political demographers could affect the reality around them, ending with the effects on coresearches and why I thought this was an important example. I would now like to expand on this by moving from the somewhat abstract discussion of the previous pages to a description of the research project I have been involved in recently in Puerto Rico. I will be focusing in this description on the nature of the relationships between the two North American researchers and the two Puerto Rican researchers, the consequences of these relationships, and the implications of all this for population policy research and for human development.

The focus of our project was the population policy process in Puerto Rico. A particular concern of the researchers was the level of political development in both the elites and in the masses of the populace in Puerto Rico. We conceptualized political development in individualistic terms rather than as characteristics of a policy, somewhat along the lines I described in the first section of this chapter. And, for reasons already given above, we saw population policy questions as a good way to get at these levels of political development. In designing and conducting the research, we made heavy use of such concepts as psychological independence, the absence or minimization of coercion and/or manipulation by elites of the masses, and self-reliance in important decision making occasions on the part of respondents. Final evaluation of policies and policy processes would depend in this schema on the perceived contributions of the policies and the processes to individual human development in Puerto Rico.

In addition to the substantive and conceptual arrangements, the procedural agreements among the four coresearchers were also important. We wished to avoid both the general pattern of colonial relationships between the United States and Puerto Rico and the expert *cum* field station relationship that had so often existed in research projects in Puerto Rico. We began the implementation of these desires by establishing complete equality in decision making in the project and by agreeing to cross-national coauthorship of any publications arising from the data collected in the project. No project decisions were to be made nor concepts adopted without general agreement. The research arrangement was designed to build consensus cooperatively rather than to make decisions hierarchically, and thereby to establish that cross-cultural teams could undertake and successfully complete research projects as equals.

Speaking for the North American contingent, my ideological position on these issues was simply that complete equality in the research arrangements was the best way to ensure the achievement of several goals I held to be important. Among these were the desire to help improve our project by having Puerto Rican cooperation rather than field-station subservience, to allow Puerto Rican researchers complete leeway, without any deference to the North Americans, in pursuing the directions they wished to pursue in a research project that in the final analysis involved their country, not mine. Additionally, we felt that the best way to increase research capabilities (in general) was to provide for equal participation by Third-World researchers. We adopted the notion that Third-World researchers know what is best for their nations and that cooperative research would do more to assure that research projects would aid in the implementation of these goals than would hierarchical arrangements that saw the local research institutions as a field station and the local scholars as assistants.

The kinds of research arrangements established in a project have been the subject of study by others. Robert Ward, speaking of field research in less developed areas (a normatively loaded approach to the topic), notes the importance of interpersonal relationships. He points out that researchers from the United States should try to understand cultural differences as well as the different approaches to social science analysis that may exist in other localities.[18] Ward's dependent variable in all this is successful completion of the research project. And though our definitions of "success" may vary, we also sought to establish research arrangements that would help us achieve certain goals.

As is so often the case, unexpected things began to happen. I began to see that the research arrangements had personal effects on the individuals involved as well as on the conduct of the project itself. I have only recently begun to integrate these happenings with my previously described ideological commitment to equality as both a means and an end.[19]

Several "facts" that we had apparently ignored began to assume some importance. The colonial relationships between North American and Puerto Rican researchers, although explicitly eschewed, had implicitly been internalized as "normal" by all four researchers. Consequently, the North Americans retained a sense of conceptual and methodological superiority which was accepted by the Puerto Rican researchers. Secondly, it became obvious that the fact of North American funding for the project was associated with a kind of deference that seemed to say: "okay, we will all participate in the decision making, but the final decision is the North Americans'."

I should add that neither of these "facts" was acknowledged verbally during the project. It is only with introspective hindsight — by studying our behavior during the project — that I can deduce these "facts."

We North Americans learned a lot about Puerto Rico, to be sure, by having associations with sophisticated Puerto Rican colleagues. But the conduct of the research project itself was not the consensus-building activity we had envisioned. Rather, it became a proselytizing process, in which the North Americans slowly but surely "educated" the Puerto Ricans in the ways of our "advanced" ideological and methodological approaches. While the project was being conducted, it was not a mutual learning process, though I have since learned many things as a result of the project, as I hope this account shows.

As the foregoing happenings occurred, and as I became conscious of them, I took great pains *not* to be a leader, in a situation in which the Puerto Rican scholars seemed to be waiting for the inevitable North American leadership to emerge, all verbal proclamations to the contrary notwithstanding.

I must emphasize, at this point, that most of the foregoing was subtle. And to the extent that it was all unplanned and unexpected, it was subconscious in origin. Furthermore, all that I have described is a very personal view; it is quite conceivable that none of my colleagues would agree with the analysis suggested here, or, for that matter, with the patterns of events as I have described them. Nevertheless, these "unexpected outcomes" are existentially real to me, though my descriptions probably differ from those my colleagues might offer.

At least two things, however, were neither subtle nor subconscious. One was the compendium of explicit arrangements and proclamations of equality, as described in the previous paragraphs. The second was that the research was proceeding at a very slow pace. I am convinced, in retrospect, that these delays were occasioned by the dissonance between our ideological positions and the reality of the situation in which we were functioning. By *reality,* I refer to the definitions of normalcy that were present in the minds of the four researchers and which were the result of previous experiences as well as the general nature of the colonial relationships between the United States and Puerto Rico. By *ideology,* I refer to the system of beliefs relating to research arrangements, as outlined above, which placed a premium on equality as a reaction to the hierarchical nature of past relationships.

After some introspection, I have concluded that we simply adopted the wrong tools to achieve our ends and that we did this because we had previously adopted an ideological (i.e., methodological) approach without seriously considering alternatives. Our ideological set was not appropriate for the situation we were in, but rather than to reassess it in the light of existing conditions we sought to shape our environment to meet our expectations. Such enterprises rarely succeed, and ours was no exception.

In less abstract terms, I would say that using equality as a method of establishing research relationships was not successful in helping us achieve our goal of equality between researchers. This is not double-talk. If normalcy includes hierarchy, then is it not plausible to maintain hierarchy by reversing it? That thought never occurred to me, nor as far as I have been able to discern, to any of the other researchers while the project was going on. For we all had adopted the notion that equality was the road to equality. It now occurs to me that a better road to equality may be to establish Third-World researchers as the leaders and to have researchers from supposedly more developed areas act as assistants. It is possible, and should at least be considered, that the way to help Third-World researchers develop research capability and decision-making ability is to let them do it with a minimum of assistance (and that upon their request) from the experts in the United States.

There are some implications that need to be mentioned. First of all, in competitive academic circles, it may be less desirable to note on one's personal resumé that he or she was a research assistant on a project in Puerto Rico than to be able to say "principal investigator." This issue (and its offshoots: prestige, likelihood of subsequent funding, promotions, recognition) needs to be faced. I suspect that it will be difficult for many researchers, if they are in competitive environments in their profession, to invest time in situations over which they have less control and which consequently jeopardize the commonly assured returns (on the time investment) that are needed to insure competitive advantage. Similarly, funding agencies may have to accept the notion of signing blank checks. More than that, they will have to take active, conscious steps — in both symbolic and substantive ways — to assure that recipients *feel* that the funds come as free of strings as needed.

Joining the Disjointed

What is to be made of all this? I contended in the early portions of this chapter that the behavioral approach to population policy analysis incorporates biases in the choice of issues, the conduct of research, and the political implications of findings. I am convinced, from an epistemological point of view (but more assuredly from an experiential point of view), that the positivistic system of logic and rationality ignores important aspects of human existence and that this becomes more noticeable as one concentrates on individuals in society rather than on society itself. There is a fundamental incongruence between the logic and world view (ideology?) of behavioralism and the human "reality" it seeks to describe. This dissonance practically precludes the attainment of the stated goals of behavioral population policy research, goals such as value neutrality, human development, peace, and the pursuit of objective Truth (the existence of which outside the self is another positivist assumption).

I have used my research experience in Puerto Rico as an illustration, by analogy, of the dissonance mentioned in the previous sentence. Behavioralism, as a method, seems to preclude consideration of certain vital questions. To me, it thereby becomes an ideology, not an objective tool. Similarly, the adoption of equality in research arrangements was the method we chose to achieve goals in Puerto Rico. This method precluded, at the time, reversing the normal hierarchical pattern and instead sought to abolish it. I have now concluded that it is at least possible that reversing hierarchical patterns while maintaining the existence of hierarchical arrangements may do more for "institutional development" in the Third World than "equality" in research arrangements can do.

The values built into an approach to solving a problem must be questioned. Further, it ought to be kept in mind that defining the problem is part of the approach to its solution. I have already suggested a plausible alternative to equality in cross-national research arrangements. I would like to do the same for behavioralism, the currently accepted way to scientifically investigate social problems.

While the ultimate value of objectivity as an end could be accepted for the moment, the value of objectiveness as a means must be challenged. (Were there more space, I would suggest why I think you should similarly question the value of discovering causality, of aspiring to prediction or to the reduction of uncertainty, and of the practice of laboratory emulation in general.) Within the realm of population policy dynamics, some heady issues have been raised, issues such as genocide, racism, sexism, the use of coercion by elites, and the use of the population "explosion" as a smokescreen to help elites preserve their position in society, both internationally and domestically. These problems are real, at least existentially, to many people. It seems to me they are worthy of some scholarly attention beyond polemics and ethics. Yet our behavioral approach must perforce focus on the objectively verifiable, not the existentially plausible. To do otherwise is to be unscientific, which is not desirable.

To the behavioralist, polemics and ethics are just as much an existential problem as objectivity is to the person who feels oppressed. Neither side's problems should be automatically dismissed by the choice of research methodology. Both sides' problems should at least be considered, and this demands some methodology that can provide for more than just one side. The "scientific method" seems to preclude becoming empathetic while conducting research, for example, although the ability to empathize is probably a crucial part of becoming a well-developed person.

As a result of my research experience in Puerto Rico and of having considered both hierarchy and equality in research arrangements as means, I am willing to at least *consider* abandoning equality as a means, simply because it did not help us achieve the goals, both personal and scholarly, we had intended to pursue. I think it is a good idea to so evaluate our research arrangements, that is, in terms of goals achieved and of outcomes that occur. We should do likewise with our methodology. Can researchers fully and unconsciusly committed to behavioralism consider such schismatic notions as empathetic involvement with research subjects as possibly conducive to achieving goals of human development? I do not wish to see the demise of behavioral research techniques, nor the universal adoption of some alternative, but I do wish to see an end to the automatic use of any single approach.

It seems to me that political demographers can become more value-neutral in fact as well as in aspiration if they will consider both value-free and value-laden issues, techniques, and conclusions, and I hope that by now you will see that this is more than semantics.

If, as I attempted to document early in this chapter, behavioral political demographers affect other people in a clearly nonrandom way, then an exclusive focus on behaviorally conceived issues and methods will eventually produce "Positivist Man," controlled by information holders and eminently predictable in behavior. To contribute to this eventuality is not to be "value free" in any sense that I can grasp, though I can understand, after reading John Stuart Mill, why such an eventuality might be desirous to some scholars and policy makers:

It is not much to be wondered at, if impatient or disappointed reformers, groaning under the impediments opposed to the most salutary improvements by the ignorance, the indifference, the untractableness, the perverse obstinacy of a people, and the corrupt combinations of selfish private interests armed with the powerful weapons afforded by free institutions, should at times sigh for a strong hand to bear down all these obstacles, and compel and recalcitrant people to be better governed. But . . . those who look in any such direction for the realization of their hopes leave out of the idea of good government its principal element, the improvement of the people themselves. One of the benefits of freedom is that under it the ruler cannot pass by the people's minds, and amend their affairs for them without amending them.[20]

A more contemporary source of the kind of thought in the quotation can be seen in much of the work of Maslow, wherein he refers to "self-actualization" in people as being associated with, at least in part, an increasing degree of self-reliance coupled with what might loosely be described as "social consciousness."[21] As a parenthetical point of comparison, Hardin, in "The Tragedy of the Commons," accepts competitiveness as an innate human characteristic and thereby concludes that autonomy and social consciousness are mutually exclusive.[22]

Concepts similar to Maslow's are again beginning to emerge in literature more closely associated with political science, as in Pranger's definition of "citizenship;" Lipsitz's analysis of the religious aspects of national politics; Bay's discussions of psychological, social, and potential freedoms; and Zinn's work on civil disobedience.[23]

But if (1) we are enmeshed in a value-free method, and (2) we are unaware of our entanglement, how are we to deal with these obviously normative issues when one of the values in our value-free approach is to eschew normativism? How can we avoid helping to produce "Positivist Man" if we are paradigmatically prohibited from using nonobjective research techniques?

Conclusion

In this chapter I have been trying to urge political demographers to question the implicit normative aspects of subjects we usually take for granted, namely the research methodology of behavioralism and the research arrangements we enter into with Third-World colleagues. My references to a particular research experience were designed to show the potentially fruitful consequences of the kind of questioning I'm suggesting we should undertake. I have focused more directly on means than ends — which may be a spurious although analytically useful distinction. I have evaluated by own experiences after analyzing actual outcomes and events, whether planned or unexpected, and I have urged political demographers to incorporate this (in addition to an analysis of stated goals) into the questioning process.

On the other hand, I have not sought to provide any alternative "goals," to "Positivist Man," for example. My aim has been to ask questions and to have questions asked. If the example of my research experience has stimulated you to question either research methods or research arrangements, then the goal of this chapter will have been realized.

Notes

1. At the time of this writing, this is an ongoing research endeavor focusing on population-policy processes in Puerto Rico, conducted in collaboration with scholars from the University of Puerto Rico, and coordinated under the auspices of the International Population Policy Consortium.

2. Theodore Roszak, *Sources* (New York: Harper and Row, 1972), p. 3.

3. The literature thereon is abundant. As examples, see Peter Bachrach and Morton Baratz, "Two Faces of Power," *American Political Science Review* 56 (December 1962): 947-52; Robert Dahl, "A Critique of the Ruling Elite Model," *American Political Science Review* 52 (June 1958): 463-69; and G. William Domhoff, "Where a Pluralist Goes Wrong," *Berkeley Journal of Sociology* 14 (1969): 35-37.

4. Bachrach and Baratz, (n. 3).

5. Peter Bachrach and Elihu Bergman, *Power and Choice: The Formulation of American Population Policy* (Lexington, Mass.: D.C. Heath, 1973), in which the notion of agenda setting and specification of issues is systematically related to population-policy processes in the United States.

6. For a scholarly description of behavioralism's ultimate reliance on positivism, see Eugene F. Miller, "Positivism, Historicism, and Political Inquiry," *American Political Science Review* 66 (September 1972): 796-817.

7. Charles Hampden-Turner, *Radical Man* (New York: Doubleday, Anchor Books, 1971), p. 9.

8. Ibid., p. 15.

9. George E. Marcus, "Psychopathology and Political Recruitment," *Journal of Politics* 31 (November 1969): 930-31.

10. Miller (n. 6), pp. 797-806.

11. I have discussed this in more detail elsewhere. See Steven Garland and Robert Trudeau, "Population Policy Research: A Critique and an Alternative," pp. 17-39 of Richard L. Clinton and R. Kenneth Godwin, eds., *Research in the Politics of Population* (Lexington, Mass.: D.C. Heath, 1972).

12. Thomas Kuhn, *The Structure of Scientific Revolutions* (2nd ed.; Chicago: University of Chicago Press, 1970).

13. Hampden-Turner (n. 7), pp. 15-16.

14. Miller, et. al., (n. 6); for an additional discussion, see Thomas L. Thorson, *Biopolitics* (New York: Holt, Rinehart, and Winston, 1970), esp. pp. 23-38, 176-78.

15. Bachrach and Bergman (n. 5).

16. Hampden-Turner (n. 7), p. 16.

17. A very preliminary look at data from our research in Puerto Rico (based actually on pretesting) supports the contention that more people think about population questions than, to use specific examples that were used in the pretesting, think about electoral reform or the status of Puerto Rico *vis-à-vis* the United States.

18. Robert E. Ward, "The Research Environment," pp. 26-48 of Robert E. Ward, et al., *Studying Politics Abroad* (Boston: Little, Brown, and Co., 1964), pp. 26-27.

19. The remarks that follow were originally delivered as part of a report to the second plenary meeting of the International Population Policy Consortium, Dubrovnik, Yugoslavia, October 1972.

20. John Stuart Mill, *Considerations on Representative Government* (Chicago: Gateway Editions, 1962), p. 55.

21. For work on or by Maslow, see A.H. Maslow, *Toward a Psychology of Being* (Princeton: Van Nostrand, 1962); A.H. Maslow, "Self-Actualization and Beyond," pp. 279-86 of James F.T. Bugental, ed., *Challenges of Humanistic*

Psychology (New York: McGraw-Hill, 1967); and Robert Theobald, *An Alternative Future for America II* (Chicago: Swallow Press, 1970), pp. 15-20.

22. Garrett Hardin, "The Tragedy of the Commons," *Science* 162 (13 December 1968), pp. 1243-48.

23. Robert J. Pranger, *The Eclipse of Citizenship* (New York: Holt, Rinehart, and Winston, 1968); Lewis Lipsitz, "If, as Verba Says, the State Functions as a Religion, What Are We to Do Then to Save Our Souls?" *American Political Science Review* 62 (June 1968): 527-35; Christian Bay, *The Structure of Freedom* (New York: Atheneum, 1965), esp. pp. 65-101; and Howard Zinn, *Disobedience and Democracy* (New York: Vintage, 1968).

16 Population Policy Research and the Institutionalization of Social Science in Latin America

David Chaplin

In the analysis of the development of explicit population policies in currently developing nations, obtrusive field research is unavoidable. Factor analyzing aggregate data from international yearbooks may clarify a few issues, but a serious study of how official population policies are adopted will require field studies in depth which, in turn, involve not only the institutional context in question but also that of local social science.

Before 1959 most foreign social scientists in Latin America were anthropologists or geographers whose work normally excluded the political at any level.[1] The 1960s saw the simultaneous explosive growth of social science research, expecially political, on Latin America and the inclusion of family planning as a high priority in U. S. foreign policy. These two developments have become even more interdependent as U. S. funds for nonpopulation research have been radically reduced, leaving population research, by default, the best supported area of U. S. social science field research in Latin America.

I will be considering not only U. S. social scientists working in Latin America (and the U. S. institutional influences on their work) but also the state of national social science in Latin America in terms of its effect on population policy field research and as a problem of intrinsic interest. My remarks should be understood as a response to such publications as Robert Ward's *Studying Politics Abroad* and Calvin Blair's *Responsibilities of the Foreign Scholar to the Local Scholarly Community* as well as to the way the Foreign Area Fellowship Program and the Social Science Research Council have implemented their suggestions. While I am very sympathetic to the goals being sought as well as to many of the means suggested, we also need to consider the development of disciplines to the extent that they can be separated from local nationalistic considerations *both* in the United States and in Latin America.

My conclusions on the present state and immediate future of social science in Latin America will be somewhat pessimistic. Just as Argentina and other countries are demonstrating that successful economic development is not inevitable in the immediate future, it may well be that social research will fail to reach its full potential in Latin America for many years to come. The essential reason for this is not that it has too little to offer the process of development but rather too much. It can yield invaluable data on which the more or less *planned social changes* now being attempted should be based. It is also

203

potentially useful to regimes of any ideology desirous of noncoercive techniques of social control. Sociology is second only to political public opinion surveys in political science (or the sociology of politics) in depending on *highly obtrusive research methods*. Unlike most economists, students of political behavior must generate their own data in the field by bothering, if not molesting, fairly large numbers of people who either see no reason to collaborate with such nosiness or who expect help or reform from such work which the researcher has no right to promise.[2]

Aside from this methodological handicap — which has already sharply reduced the feasibility of field studies on many topics in many countries (agrarian reform in Chile, demographic research in many countries, public opinion surveys on politics in most countries, etc.) — we must also deal with the institutional setting in the United States for foreign social science research as it affects Latin America.

U. S. Support for Social Science Research in Latin America

Two major sources of research funds for field research in Latin America became available during the post-Castro 1960s. The most notorious was the abysmal Camelot Project.[3] This source of money presumably was terminated in 1965, although some of its funds apparently still supported projects in Peru (Proyecto Simpático) and Columbia (Proyecto Colonia). It was replaced by AID funds made available primarily to more established centers of Latin American expertise. (One institutional "reform" which was supposed to have been carried out after this fiasco was a veto control by the State Department over all foreign research carried out through federal funds. Since this certification was to be conducted behind the scenes at some point in the project approval process, we cannot know how it operated. How many subsequent foreign research projects were turned down on the political grounds relevant to State's domain, rather than on the more scientific criteria presumably considered by the funding agencies? Were the criteria utilized by the State Department committee those the various professional ethics committees would agree with?)

Subsequently, the rising cost of the Vietnam war forced a diminution of foreign aid and hence a greater emphasis on family planning as, by Latin American interpretation, a cheap shortcut to economic development. President Johnson's widely quoted (in Latin America) statement at the UN in 1965 that $5 in birth control was worth $100 in economic assistance, signalled the increasing diversion of AID, Ford, and Rockefeller funds into family planning research and action programs.

Paralleling this shift was a bilateral disillusionment with the *Alianza* — especially the feasibility of the United States "bribing" or intimidating Latin American governments into carrying out the tax and other reforms agreed to at

Punta del Este. One reason for this failure, of course, was that pressure from the United States was not at all consistently in favor of such reforms.

The major shift was away from the desirability of redistributive agrarian reform in favor of higher agricultural productivity. This in turn meant (1) a decreased capacity for the agricultural sector to absorb rapid population growth since — although better seeds, fertilizers, etc., could constitute a labor-intensive type of investment in higher agricultural production per capita — the social infrastructure of agricultural credit (extension agents, etc.) was not sufficiently developed; (2) a decreased interest in social science research — other than in family planning — with greater emphasis on agricultural projects; i.e., "the green revolution."

Other sources of funds during the 1960s for North American social science field work in Latin America were the Social Science Research Council, the National Science Foundation, the National Institute of Mental Health, and the Ford funds given to Latin American programs. The current and future picture for such field work in Latin America seems relatively bleak with respect to both funds and the field feasibility of the projects themselves. The shrinkage of funds will, of course, be welcomed by those of us concerned about the "saturation effect" — especially of inadequately prepared graduate students imposing on inordinately high government officials (frequently at the expense of the reputations of their advisors and U. S. schools). Austerity can have its advantages if it forces a reform in the quality of work performed. In practice, however, it has strengthened the hands of the remaining sources of funds for field work — largely in favor of family planning. The extremely "mission-oriented" perspective of AID and other sources of birth control programs had effectively limited support largely to demographers and birth control delivery specialists. Other disciplines, however, such as mass communications, and, in the present case, political science, have recently been included in AID funded research in recognition of the many perspectives required for *understanding* as well as "delivering" a population policy.

Population Research and Latin American Social Science

Hale's chapter on the Dominican Republic deals with a very different situation from that of the African countries Ahmed has in mind. The Dominican Republic, as an island (together with Haiti) with very limited natural resources, would seem to be on the verge of "overpopulation" from almost any humane perspective (although its leaders, as Hale notes, still do not agree on this point). It is also one of the most dependent client states under U.S. influence. Not long after U.S. troops were removed from the island in 1965, the AID mission began its policy to persuade the government to institutionalize family planning nationally.

In spite of the extent of U.S. influence, however, the lack of genuine Dominican commitment to family planning has meant, as Hale notes, that the AID funds tied to compliance have not been fully disbursable. Family planning funds have probably been spent there, as in some other developing countries, on general public health needs rather than being concentrated on preventing births.

The institutionalization of social science in the Dominican Republic is not, unfortunately, dealt with by Hale. What is known to the present author on this issue is that, as in a number of currently developing countries, empirical social science field research was initiated there during the 1960s. The bulk of the funds for social surveys came from the United States and the United Nations, with family planning the predominant focus after 1965, as elsewhere in Latin America. Thus the first generation of national social scientists involved in field research was very likely to have been affected by the way this work was conducted.

Unfortunately the documents necessary to a proper study of this "side effect" of population research are not available for public scrutiny. The social research itself has been of two basic types: (1) basic demographic studies intended to dramatize the need for birth control; (2) evaluation studies of family planning delivery. The latter have generally lacked the national scope of the former, and hence, have avoided the critical issues of the societal reforms necessary to motivate people to desire fewer children. In several countries, research on certain issues (abortion in Chile, abandoned children in Caracas) has moved national elites to drop their resistance to family planning or actively to support it (Mexico). The critical factors in Mexico's case are not entirely clear, but the following appear to be relevant: (1) Mexico City's rapidly worsening problems of air pollution, water shortages, and sharply rising cost of mass transportation — all seen as a direct result of "overpopulation;" and (2) the personal influence of the president of Chile and Mrs. Allende on President and Mrs. Echeverría. The former, although "Marxist", are in favor of family planning. Often mentioned as well, but possibly counterproductive up to 1971, was pressure from the United States.

Population research in the Dominican Republic could be said to have failed in that it has been unable to discover any such "cause" which could legitimate family planning. Family planning funds have thus been accepted under pressure and apparently on a purely opportunistic basis. It has also failed in its institution-building function, partly because this was not one of its goals. Two major projects were carried out in the early 1970s, one a Cornell-based, Population Council-funded project with no ties to local academics and the other a direct AID grant to a national organization, UNPHU (Pedro Henríquez Ureña National University). The results of the latter's work are apparently not highly regarded by U.S. population funders, which will presumably mean that their sudden early affluence will end abruptly, leaving an embittered group of national social scientists, not only those cut off, but also those not in on the project. The point is simply that the crash development of local social science is not feasible. With this experience, the next U.S. project will probably find the local climate much less favorable.

As a policy-oriented project, family planning suffers from at least two shortcomings: (1) a simplistic technocratic model of human motivation, which assumes that all that is needed is the right device and an adequate "delivery system." While it is true that urban women of all classes are relying heavily on abortions, the availability of contraceptives could well lead to avoiding *that child* more humanely with therefore no effect on the birth rate. (2) The second limitation of family planning research in Latin America — and one could say policy as well — is its unwillingness to deal with systemic reforms which could hopefully reduce the total number of children desired.[4] This arises partly from the conservative sources of support for family planning in the United States as well as the exclusion until recently from the ranks of family planning researchers of social scientists other than demographers and some economists. The basic obstacle, of course, is the unwillingness of Latin American governments to be reformed from the outside. The U.S. government has to accept its declining ability to determine or even predominantly influence the development of other societies either through coercion or aid. Family planning may be our last effort before neoisolationism predominates.

There are some non-mission-oriented types of research in Latin America which can be loosely categorized. For obvious reasons, political scientists, modern historians, and sociologists of politics have found Latin America an especially interesting area for comparative work. It would make more sense, however, to discuss research on contemporary Latin America in terms of all of this type work rather than by disciplines since (1) within each social science discipline boundaries blur in foreign field work, and each social scientist finds (if he is seriously interested in an explanation in depth) that he must take economic, political, sociological, historical, and other factors or dimensions into account; and (2) various disciplines have focused on the same political issues, especially political science, sociology, anthropology, and modern history.

The first "generation" of post-1959 political studies was carried out by two different types of researchers: established Latin Americanists — largely historians and anthropologists — and major figures who wanted to add Latin America to their worldwide sample for comparative purposes. I have in mind especially Almond and Verba's *Civic Culture* survey and Lipset's *Elites in Latin America* and his other works which also include Latin American data. The first generation of personal field-work studies of Latin American politics awaited the arrival of the post-Castro generation of graduate students such as Maurice Zeitlin *(Revolutionary Politics and the Cuban Working Class)*. Although many of these studies on the left were generally sympathetic to socialist parties or regimes, none became as closely identified with a single party and local politics as did Harry Kantor (political science) in his *The Ideology and Program of the Peruvian*

Aprista Movement (1953). As the rush to study Frei's regime indicated,[5] political sympathies or antipathies continue to play a role in the choice of topic. This, however, need not lead to biased interpretations — after all, one's choice of a discipline as well as of a topic for study is unavoidably a matter of personal taste. (Spain continues to "enjoy" a high level of "freedom" from U.S. social science research owing, apparently, to a hangover of fascist stigmatization inculcated in current graduate students taught by faculty who went to college during the Spanish Civil War. British social scientists, however, have been increasingly active in Spain in recent years. Thus Spain — and Portugal — having neither a population problem nor a viable revolutionary movement, constitute "virgin terrritory" relatively free as yet of interest to U.S. foreign-policy strategists. They are nonetheless highly deserving of attention as a possible prototype — however one may evaluate their ethics — of the type of developmental policies Mexico, Brazil, and other Latin American countries are or may be pursuing.)[6]

Institution Building in Latin America

U.S. support for social science research in Latin America has not gone only to U.S. researchers. Increasingly, attention has been paid to "institution building" within Latin America. This could have been done through added U.S. support for the UNESCO centers in Santiago and Rio de Janeiro. But, implicitly, it would seem that these centers are not sufficiently "accountable" to U.S. patrons to be as "deserving" as certain private universities. Thus Ford has devoted most of its "institutional" support to such private schools in Lima as the Catholic University and the recently created (with Rockefeller and Ford help) private medical school, Cayetano Heredia. (Ford has reportedly tried to give funds to such politicized public schools as San Marcos, but student or faculty resistance prevented the school from accepting such support.) This disillusionment on the part of Ford with public universities in Latin America as unlikely to foster productive scholarship is hard to refute and seems to be one Latin American problem which cannot be blamed — directly, at least — on the United States. We must nevertheless expect a nationalistic backlash against this foreign favoritism for the private schools (already evident in Peru), expecially since they cater largely to upper-middle-class students.

The major lesson to be learned, it would seem, from our efforts to enforce our image of correct development priorities and desirable institutional steps toward this end, is that not only is direct military intervention no longer feasible, but neither is "soft coercion" via foreign aid. Given the neoisolationist mood within the United States and the future cost of defense ("no peace dividend even after Vietnam" — Secretary of Defense Laird), the level of our foreign aid, even if refunded, will be so low that, as in Peru during the 1960s, it will no longer give us control leverage but will serve primarily as a continuous source of irritation.

In cases where we could agree that U.S. interests are antithetical to those of Latin America, this decline in control via aid ("benign neglect") should be favorable. Latin Americans truly desirous of escaping external dependency should welcome aid-less austerity as an opportunity for reform just as some critics of U.S. education see a greater chance for pedagogic reforms thanks to the decline in funds for basic research within U.S. universities. Notwithstanding my criticism above of the family planning "establishment," however, I feel very strongly that both the diffusion of voluntary family planning services and a reduction of demographic growth are very much in the best interests of most Latin Americans — except, of course, for the old elite[7] and the terrorist left (and the latter are mistaken even in terms of their own goals). It is a tragedy of the highest order that so much public discussion in Latin American adopts an *ad hominem,* infantile Marxist, and paranoid nationalist style of reasoning when faced with the real significance of this action program. In terms of its logic — "If the United States is in favor of family planning — especially given the crass reasoning espoused by former President Johnson — then it *has to be* antagonistic to our interests" — this type of thinking can't comprehend good results arising from "evil" motives. In this connection, I fear that Ahmed's very brief but cogent discussion of the weaknesses in the case for birth control in the Third World also errs in its concern for the "genuineness" of Western interest in reducing population growth. Would it not be best if the leaders of African countries concentrated on the main issue of what rate of population growth would contribute most to the achievement of their own goals? Surely none will find 3-4 percent preferable to 1-2 percent, hence they could accept family planning aid without concern for the "real" motives of the donors.

As in the case of the institutionalization of social science in developing countries, the limits of U.S. influence are at issue. Is it desirable or possible for the United States to promote the system reforms Ahmed feels have a greater priority than family planning? Need African leaders view birth control as the top priority merely because some others do? What is to prevent their using our funds for this program while giving primary attention to the reforms he mentions, whose immediate necessity is often more political than economic?

The United States is rightfully faulted for supporting regimes which are not committed to the type of societal reforms which could provide a solid motivation for declining fertility. In such cases, promoting birth control could function to maintain an unjust and inefficient economy. (Even then, however, giving individual women the power to accomplish their desired family size and spacing seems intrinsically humane.) In the case of such dependent client regimes as the Dominican Republic, the inefficacy of family planning without system reform is very evident. In the majority of developing nations not as dominated by U.S. influence, however, the national governments must take primary responsibility for basic reforms.

Ahmed's most cogent point, I feel, is his focus on the resource (and energy) "crisis" as the primary reason for U.S. concern with "overpopulation." With Nixon's rapprochement with Peking and Moscow, the credibility of the Communist menace fades to be replaced by an obsession with maintaining the U.S. standard of living. Clearly U.S. affluence is far more relevant to the immediate causes of pollution and energy crises than is Third-World "over-population."

Segal's chapter also involves the issue of an individual-oriented family planning program and the aggregate goals of population controllers. To clarify this problem, let us separate the parallel issues of the motives of U.S. promoters and those of the users of birth control in developing countries from the more observable problem of the type of mass public arguments used in the United States and the LDCs. U.S. policy makers have been convinced of the need for birth control — first abroad, then at home — on the basis of the aggregate issues of "overpopulation." In many cases this has led to an effort to persuade *individuals* to have fewer children for the same type of reasons. Such a confounding of levels of action seems both impolitic and "immoral." In the latter sense, it implies obversely that people should *have* children for reasons of societal benefit, rather than a more appropriate individual "intrinsic" interest in childrearing. It is also "immoral" in terms of U.S. economic ideology in that it represents the surrender of an analogue of the market mechanism in linking individual self-interest decision making with a viable social system. Telling individuals to "have fewer children to save the environment" would be like asking them to "buy the economy out of a depression" by dissaving.

The most effective population policy would so restructure the decision-making environment (for example, by providing women with education and employment) that the personal types of motives most appropriate to fertility would lead to a lower birth rate. Therefore, Segal's confounding of promoter/user motives (as in his discussion of Rhodesia and South Africa) could be clarified by separating out the empirically testable question of what types of arguments (if any are viable without basic reforms) will *work*. If the above reasoning is correct, aggregate arguments by North American elites linking pollution or economic stagnation or revolution to overpopulation will not move the masses in LDCs — in fact, they would be counterproductive. Segal sees this clearly yet still devoted much space to castigating the United States for doing (presumably) the right thing for the wrong reasons. From this it follows that U.S. promoters could have the most dubious motives without necessarily damaging either the individual or collective welfare of the citizens of developing countries.

The same type of motivational issue is arising in our efforts to build better academic institutions in Latin America. Only here we may be overreacting to our past sins and thus abdicating responsibility for what we should know are the structural requisites for the development of social science.

The Underdeveloped State of Latin American Social Science

In Richard Schaedel's study of U.S. scholars in Chile,[8] he (I believe) overstresses the positive — for reasons, no doubt, of diplomacy — by playing down the lack of communication among competing social science institutes. (Chile has clearly the most highly developed social science milieu — Peru, the country I know best, exhibits a "pathological" absence of any national integration of sociologists; there is, as yet, no national sociological society, journal, or meetings. In fact, most of the departments in the late 1960s didn't even subscribe to journals published by other Peruvian schools.) The teamwork Schaedel admired in Chile functions only *within* schools or institutes not between them. Ford tried to sponsor a national organization of Chilean economists who, I am told, endured one "confrontation" and decided not to meet again.

We thus face a situation in which national social scientists are often more willing to collaborate with foreigners than with each other. As Schaedel noted,[9] Latin Americans find foreigners especially useful in gaining easier access to their own elites.[10] They too often have little respect for, or trust in, each other (I question the expressions of "professional respect" for their colleagues Chileans offered Schaedel, at least among social scientists. This could be a measure of their sophistication regarding our norms of universalistic evaluation rather than of their true feelings.)

The basic factor arresting the professionalization of social science in Latin America is, I feel, much more financial than "cultural." However prone Latin Americans may be to personalistic evaluations,[11] the objective lack of stable, adequately compensated academic positions and sufficient basic research funds would demoralize any nation's scholars. In fact, the arrested development of the social sciences in Latin America suggests a needed modification in the simple equation of bourgeois democracy as a prerequisite for the development of social science. As Russia, Eastern Europe, and Spain have demonstrated, most of the technical skills required for proficient social research can as well be developed in totalitarian or authoritarian societies *once* they renounce overt force and psychological terror as the primary instruments of social control. Since such a renunciation is a requisite for economic development, it follows that non-democratic regimes must manipulate mass behavior more subtly, which in turn requires giving the data gatherers "professional independence" from doubling as internal security and intelligence agents. Since knowledge is power, the results of social surveys can be used to control public behavior — but only on a group basis (as opposed to having a census interviewer turn over his data person by person to the police). Moving a step further from a totalitarian to an authoritarian regime we find that behavioral social science (largely sociology) is much more developed in Spain than in any Latin American country. It has reached this level of expertise by (1) serving as an instrument of public opinion feedback — as a functional substitute for meaningful elections (Instituto de Opinión Pública of the Ministerio de Información y Turismo) and (2) avoiding issues unacceptable to the government. This development of empirical social science in Spain is only a decade old, and already its leading figures are increasingly sympathetic to oppositionist causes. It would appear, however, that the Franco regime's strategy of gradual liberalization is proceeding more or less rapidly enough to accommodate these pressures, notwithstanding occasional reversals. The major institutional support for an increasingly independent (of the government) social science in Spain have been liberal elements in the church, especially the Jesuits and the Christian Democrats. The major enemies of social science remain the military. *Opus Dei* would appear to be splitting on this issue as on others, its liberals supporting critical social research, while its conservatives are not even happy with "in-house" governmental surveys.

It may be then that field research in social science will fare badly in Latin America's most democratic countries in the immediate future. The politicization and poverty of the universities make fruitful empirical work there unlikely except with foreign assistance. Governmental planning and research institutes are little better prospects, given the overwhelming commitment to legitimating action programs designed primarily for short-term political goals.

It is therefore possible, although not certain, that if a generation of Brazilian and Mexican and Argentine social scientists is willing to limit its range of topics in favor of honing its research skills on safe (but not necessarily insignificant) subjects, a considerable level of professional development may take place. I suspect, however, that, as in Spain — and historically in the United States (Columbia University's Bureau of Applied Social Research) — this generation of Latin American social scientists will have far greater research opportunities doing "commercial" and "contract" field research than "basic" research within universities, with the possible exception of UN institutes. This could also lead to corruption, as when political organizations manufacture survey data to support pet causes. But to the extent that the private sector develops objective measures of its own to evaluate the validity of commercial research, an external check on professional competence could be institutionalized.

Political abuse of commercial social research is not by any means limited to Latin American political interests. One of the best customers for the services of International Research Associates (IRA) has been the State Department and other U.S. agencies. On at least one occasion of which the author has first-hand knowledge, the State Department subcontracted a survey of Peruvian university students' cold war political orientations via the Roper Opinion Poll Center in Williamstown, Massachusetts. IRA then listed Roper as the sponsor, utilizing the implicit association with Williams College as an academic front. I don't know who was responsible for this deception, but, as always, it failed, and the real sponsors were eventually exposed — which, together with Camelot, made 1965 a miserable year to be attempting social science field work in Lima.

This project also illustrates the defect of irresponsibly managed and classified in-house research. To begin with, no responsible State Department official connected (presumably) with the design of the project was present in the field to oversee — even incognito — its execution. (Even then the filling out of at least 30 percent of the questionnaires by student interviewers with fictitious information in the comfort of their homes rather than in the slums might not have been caught.) Furthermore, since the results were never published for external disinterested evaluation, the State Department has no way of knowing if it even received its money's worth. This leads to the suspicion that — as was true of an earlier State Department survey of the Lima elite's view of the *Alianza* — a faction within the State Department was seeking prearranged corroboration of an already established course of action. Classified research is dubious in any country. The Russian intelligence fiasco in the Belgian Congo during the independence struggle was apparently due to the fact that they had relied on a single African Studies Institute at Leningrad, rather than permitting "duplication" through fostering several competing sources of African "intelligence."

The tragedy of the defective state of field research in social science in Latin America is that as these countries make ever greater efforts at planned, government-controlled social change, they badly need competent feasibility, monitoring, and follow-up evaluation studies. Development banks are helping to fill the gap by extending their own range of social science feasibility study teams beyond the disciplines of economics and engineering. Especially when "soft" loans to the public sector are involved, it is clear that the broadest assessment of a society's capital-absorptive capacity is called for.

Critique of Suggested U.S. Reforms

Finally, it remains to consider the implications of some of the reforms suggested by Adams and others — especially the requirement of the SSRC and Foreign Area Fellowship Program that all research projects be collaborative and therefore that U.S. researchers must receive permission from a Latin American colleague and institution in order to carry out the proposed project. This would appear to constitute precisely the national veto Adams insisted he was not implying.[12] However, everything else he suggested (most of which I agree with) does imply just such a veto. Perhaps one can justify such preventive medicine as an emergency measure to head off the type of licensing of foreign research now well established in Thailand and Colombia and under development in Costa Rica and Peru. (In the case of Peru, another "abortion survey" was being attempted, presumably hoping to replicate the "Chilean formula" for legitimating family planning. However, publicizing the high rate of abortion in Lima has been tried twice before with no success under the democratic Belaúnde regime, so there was even less likelihood of its working under the present military junta. Their more likely reaction to publicizing a higher abortion rate would have been to crack down on those having or providing abortions. The result of this survey was its termination when a general's wife fell into the sample. Thereafter all large-scale field projects in Peru have required the permission of the police, the Ministry of Foreign Affairs, and the "related" ministry.)

In many areas nowadays, "raw data," even those created by foreigners, are being treated like any other national resource. The rationale behind this policy is clearly a desire to maximize national gain from national resources — even when the data were entirely paid for by foreign funds and involve no loss of tangible assets. In practice, it is not only desirable, but also feasible, to code raw data and punch them on cards in the country studied, but efficient computer analysis is virtually impossible in Latin America or Spain as yet, owing to inadequate "software," that is statistical analysis programs.

Another danger arising from giving local colleagues veto power is a possible demoralization via affluence and overcommitment of the small number of competent and also institutionally powerful social scientists with whom foreigners would wish to affiliate. If such men charitably wished to avoid this veto role, they could sign on as collaborators for an irresponsibly large set of projects. The only way to avoid this would be for the U.S. donor to "ration" each Latin scholar to a "reasonable" number of U.S. colleagues. So, as always, the monied patron exercises ultimate control even if sincere in trying to divest itself of the power of its funds.

All of this implies treating data as just another raw material export which should either be held for national consumption or processed as far as possible prior to export to gain the fruits of the "value-added" in manufacture — or at least sold to the highest bidder for the maximum profit to a national enterprise. None of these policies is in the best interests of science.

The requirement that the subject country benefit from research done in and on it is harder to dispute. However, the sad history of the negative local reaction to the publication of many U.S. community studies should give one pause even on this point. No sociologist or anthropologist would yet be safe going back to Candor, New York (Vidich and Bensman, *Small Town in Mass Society*) or Newburyport, Massachusetts (Warner, *Yankee City*) to carry out obtrusive research. National researchers thus face the same issue. Historians twit us for falsifying the names of the communities we study. But they don't face the same feedback problems. It could well be irresponsible both professionally and humanely to "tell it just as it is" in studies on painful issues in an explosive political climate. It is one thing for a native of a country to describe a situation in such a way as to inflame it. The foreign professional will be much more constrained if forced to tell the people he studied what he found. Recall what happened to Oscar Lewis when *The Children of Sánchez* was made available in Mexico. Lewis was sued by the Mexican Society of Statisticians and Geographers for blasphemy, falsehood, and so forth. (He was subsequently exonerated but chose to shift his attention to Puerto Rico.) Mexico is evidently not yet ready for foreign — especially U.S. — criticism for its failure to live up to the rhetorical promises of its revolution.

Leaving data behind seems also indisputably proper, but suppose one were piously and naively to insist that they be left to a national data bank, as is increasingly customary in the United States, so that *any* scholar in that country — or of any nationality — could make further use of them. He would then find that no such open data repositories exist. (It is to be hoped that W.F. Whyte's exemplary openness with the massive amounts of data his community studies in Peru have yielded will not fall prey to the usual type of proprietary closure in which one's native associate regards himself — or at best only his institute — as the full local owner of such material.)

At this point it would be appropriate to respond to Trudeau's chapter on "Population Policy Research: A Personal Account." I am in full accord with his restatement of the implicit value implications of applied social policy research. However, his proposed solution to his own problem of relating himself to his Latin American colleagues I find unrealistic and probably incorrect in terms of the goal of either institutionalizing social science or successfully completing a project. To begin with, only if the Latin American colleague obtains the funds himself can he feel genuinely superordinate. This solution is being pursued by the Foreign Area Fellowship Program and some other U.S. foundations and agencies. But this does not solve the problem of United States, or any funder's, control as long as the *next* grant depends on whether the results of the previous one are acceptable to the donor, as Hale's chapter on the Dominican Republic illustrates. The best compromise would be such a long chain of international agency disbursement that the original donor would find it difficult to check up on the use to which its funds were being put. This is unrealistic in terms of the expectations of the donor countries' legislative budget committee. The only way the United States can come close to avoiding dominating Latin American research would be for a Latin American government to borrow the money as an apolitical commercial transaction and then give it to the research group. The quality of control likely to be exercised in such a case in most countires would probably not, however, be an improvement over U.S. control as far as the norms of science are concerned (given the above discussion of "in-house" research).

Trudeau's acquiescence to native hierarchial relations could also be viewed as antiprofessional. I believe a case can be made that collegial equality among researchers — expecially in social science research — is not an ethnocentric U.S. hang-up, but rather a requisite norm of sound social science. To surrender this in the interests of international good will could be a well-intended but unfortunate failure to "institution build."

It is also of interest that most U.S. foundations and government agencies today are moving away from "wholesaling" block grants to universities or research institutes for basic research. The current trend is very much for donor "retail" control of *who* studies *what* with the probable results preferably preindicated. The ultimate manifestation of this trend is away from research and toward the direct "purchase of services" and *implementation* with the attendant horrors of competitive bids based on the cheapest, fastest, and most predictably "responsible" results. In the face of these pressures, it seems even less likely that substantial funds will be given directly to foreign researchers, except perhaps for classified projects via commerical research firms.

The Cross-Cultural Validity of Social Indicators

There is yet another and quite different obstacle to the development of social science in Latin America or any other part of the world outside those few countries for which reliable social indicators are available. Most of the measures of individual values, attitudes, opinions, personality, intelligence, and other attributes and social skills were developed in the United States and have yet to be established as "culture free" universals. Some are patently invalid — such as the Srole index of anomie, relying as it does on "willingness to bring children in- to the world" as an indicator of faith in the future, an item confounded with piety in Latin America; or "distrust of the government" as a measure of alienation in countries where trusting the government would constitute an objective distortion of reality.

Among Latin American social scientists one encounters two extremes. Many trained locally or in Europe reject all of the theories and methods of U.S. positivistic social science as "irrelevant to Latin American reality" and an example of gringo intellectual imperialism. The other extreme arises largely from U.S.-trained technocratic "young turks" who too often uncritically try to replicate our measures and theories. The total rejection of U.S. theories is based on an antipositivistic stance, or a Marxist epistemology, or a misunderstanding of the difference between heuristically useful models or frameworks for analysis— such as the structural-functional model of society — and "causal" theories which specify a relationship between empirical variables — such as capitalistic entre- preneurship and successful economic development. Rostow's "take-off" model can well be rejected as irrelevant and/or incorrect even for the period for which it was derived, but it is not irrelevant to suggest that successful economic development requires more attention to the problem of productivity or to the population problem. The "Iron Law of Oligarchy" (Robert Michels) is highly relevant to understanding the P.R.I., Mexico's ruling political party. Latin American culture places a high value on the uniqueness of each individual and each nation, but this should not lead to an insistence that "no one has ever been this way before" and that each country must develop "its own sociology," "its own economics," and so forth.

At the theoretical level my response to a Latin American charge of irrelevant models is — politely — nonsense! One of the major problems in the development of social science, both within the United States and internationally, is the *rarity of replication* — the retesting of hypotheses in other settings. Thus if a model or theory is "irrelevant" — *if* the study has been properly conducted — its invalidity will be demonstrated. The related — and more justified — complaint that the topics chosen by foreigners are not always those of primary interest to national social scientists or patrons of research deserves two answers. (1) Foreigners have gotten into too much trouble already trying to concentrate on issues of high national interest. It makes more sense for us to specialize in noncontroversial topics which, if imaginatively interpreted, can usually shed some light on more "relevant" issues. (2) Is is hardly reasonable to fault us for trying to carry out espionage under the guise of scholarship on "hot" topics and then complain if we study "irrelevant" phenomena. Foreigners such as de Tocqueville, Bryce, and Myrdal have played a major role in U.S. intellectual history as critical analysts of the quality of American life. But the agonies of achieving self-respecting nationhood in Latin America may not leave a place for similar alien voices. As Díaz Plaja observed in *Los Siete Pecados Capitales de los Españoles* [The Seven Capital Sins of the Spanish], Spaniards have never been interested in the opinions other nations have of Spain. This may be one more element in Iberia's patrimony which will make Latin America's modernization more difficult, at least in the case of the development of social science as a means of generating self-critical social realism.

Summing up, it appears that nationalism both in the United States and in Latin America seems to be the major obstacle to the development of Latin American social science. Although as social scientists we recognize the reality and inevitability of Latin American nationalism, as Americans many of us have never felt less patriotic about our own country. It thus takes a positive effort not only to recognize but sympathize with patriotism elsewhere. Do we have to go through this agony of flag-waving patriotism as the "last refuge of scoundrels" all over again? Yet we also must recognize that much of it is in response to actions of our own government — aside from the fact that nationalism is apparently a necessary stepping stone to internationalism (a people apparently cannot move directly from tribalism — or subnational regionalism — to internationalism). In the process, however a social science seen as peculiarly strategic to the achievement of a realistic national identity is likely to suffer a long state of arrested development. Empirical social science research could be perverted to provide a "scientistic" legitimacy for the nation-building myths many Latin American countries now need. I would prefer that it languish until these countires are ready for the self-critical stage of political and cultural development since it is much more difficult to reform an established institution then to build anew.

218

Notes

1. Charles Wagley, *Social Science Research on Latin America* (New York: Columbia University Press, 1966).

2. Alejandro Portes, "Society's Perception of the Sociologist and Its Impact on Cross-National Research," mimeo paper for Institute for Comparative Sociology Conference, Bloomington, Indiana, April 8-9, 1971.

3. See Hopper's analysis of Latin American sociology in Wagley (n. 1), written in 1963 and published a year before the exposé of Camelot in 1965. See also Irving L. Horowitz, ed., *The Rise and Fall of Project Camelot* (Cambridge, Mass.: Massachusetts Institute of Technology Press, 1969).

4. See Kingsley Davis, "Population Policy: Will Current Programs Succeed?" *Science* 158, no. 3802 (10 November 1967): 730-39, reprinted in David Chaplin, ed., *Population Policies and Growth in Latin America* (Lexington, Mass.: D.C. Heath and Company, 1971).

5. See Richard P. Schaedel, "The Extent and Effect of U.S. Based Research in Chile: 1960-1968," pp. 45-80 of Calvin P. Blair, et al., *Responsibilities of the Foreign Scholar to the Local Scholarly Community*, Latin American Studies Association and Education and World Affairs, 1969, p. 62. See also Richard A. Lambert, *Language and Area Studies in the United States*, American Academy of Social Sciences and Social Science Research Council, 1973.

6. See Charles W. Anderson, *The Political Economy of Modern Spain; Policy-Making in an Authoritarian System* (Madison: University of Wisconsin Press, 1970); and Frederick B. Pike, *Hispanismo, 1898-1936; Spanish Conservatives and Liberals and Their Relations with Spanish America* (Notre Dame: University of Notre Dame Press, 1971).

7. See the concept of "Roman Exploitation" in Herman Daly, "The Population Question in Northeast Brazil: Its Economic and Ideological Dimensions," *Economic Development and Cultural Change* 18, no. 4, pt. 1 (July 1970), pp. 536-74.

8. Schaedel (n. 5).

9. Ibid., p. 60.

10. See David Chaplin, "Interviewing Foreign Elites," paper presented at the annual meeting of the American Sociological Association, 1968, and presently a research monograph in process.

11. Schaedel (n. 5), p. 61.

12. Richard N. Adams, "Introduction," pp. 5-10 of Blair, et al. (n. 5), p. 8.

Part Four
The Advantaged Countries with Special Emphasis
on the United States

17

Values and Choices: Some Anomalies in American Population Policy Making

Elihu Bergman

The Issues

Within the space of three days in the spring of 1972, two leading American newspapers published significant but contrasting material on national population policy concerns. On Sunday, April 30 the *New York Times* carried a twenty-eight page advertising supplement sponsored by a group of influential Americans endorsing the recommendations of the Commission on Population Growth and the American Future.[1] Two days later the *Boston Globe* carried a front-page story with the headline: "Hatred Drives Black Family from Dorchester Apartment."[2]

The Population Commission, whose work was endorsed by the influential Americans, had been appointed by the president two years earlier to "provide information and education to all levels of government in the United States, and to our people, regarding a broad range of problems associated with population growth and their implications for America's future."[3] The commission interpreted its mandate broadly, as evidenced by the chapter headings in its report, and explored the full range of causes and consequences of population change in the United States.[4] However, the commission did maintain a focus on population growth as a condition which could be manipulated to expand opportunities and suppress ills in American society. In introducing the report, the commission announced this priority:

Our immediate goal is to modernize demographic behavior in this country. . . . The time has come to challenge the tradition that population growth is desirable. . . .[5]

The emphasis on population growth was supported by the sponsors of the *New York Times* supplement. In his summation, William H. Draper, Jr., honorary chairman of the Population Crisis Committee, the sponsoring organization, said:

In this historic and far-reaching report, the Commission, established by Congress and appointed by the President, calls for population stabilization in the United States as soon as possible by voluntary means, through responsible individual action and enlightened governmental policies. . . . After two years of study the Commission has concluded that bigger is not better."[6]

221

The *Boston Globe* story described the demographic consequences of an American social ill which had nothing to do with population growth but rather conditions of population distribution. A black man named Harvey Holmes attempted to exercise the opportunity to live in a place of his choice by moving from an apartment in Roxbury to one in Dorchester. But Holmes' demographic behavior was frustrated by the social behavior of his neighbors. As the *Boston Globe* described the outcome: "Racial hatred drove Holmes . . . his wife and baby from Florida Street after four months of terror." The terror consisted of throwing rocks through the apartment windows (one of which narrowly missed the baby), demolishing Holmes' parked car, attempting to burn down the building, and firing guns outside the apartment. When Mr. Holmes sought protection, he was told by the police: ". . . if I valued my life, I should get the hell out of here. . . ."[7]

Those of us who live in the attractive suburban white communities surrounding Boston find it difficult to distinguish between Roxbury and Dorchester. Both are Boston central-city communities with all the inherent disadvantages. But to Harvey Holmes there was a difference. For him Dorchester, whatever we may think of it, was a step up.

Despite its interpretation of population growth as the immediate priority for American population policy making, the Population Commission addressed itself to a wide range of population issues, including the one of immediate concern to Holmes. The commission recommended that "action be taken to increase freedom in choice of residential location through the elimination of current patterns of racial and economic segregation and their attendant injustices."[8] But in contrast to its recommendations of specific dollar amounts to finance fertility control programs and specific organizational arrangements for population activities of the federal government, the commission recommended neither specific legislation, funding levels, a timetable, nor organizational arrangements to deal with the problem encountered by Holmes.

Earlier, a member of the Population Commission, Paul Cornely, deplored the assignment of priorities in the discourse on American population policy which is reflected in the tendency to talk about population exclusively in terms of numbers, for example, population size and population growth.[9] As an alternative he suggested that the discourse should evolve around a completely different set of referents more relevant to the condition of American society: values, stratification, and racism.[10]

Judging from the issues to which the Population Commission accorded priority, and on which it chose to be specific, Cornely's formulation of priorities was not employed. Likewise, solutions to the problem Holmes encountered in Dorchester, that is, population distribution determined by racism, though suggested, were held in abeyance until allegedly more immediate problems were treated, for example, excessive population growth.

This juxtaposition of priorities in the population policy area demonstrates how individual and group values are reflected in a policy-making process. It also begs the question of how particular values are associated with particular priorities, and how the particular priorities prevail.

For example, data released during the past year demonstrate a dramatic decline in American fertility rates. The average number of children born to women in the fertile age span (15-44) had dropped from 3.8 in 1957 to 1.8 in 1972.[11] This fertility decline goes below the average 2.1 rate, where births replace deaths. If this trend continues, the American population would stop growing in seventy years. Thus, because of "modernized demographic behavior," the problem of American population growth appears to be well along the road to solution.

Not so in the case of population distribution, however, as the experience of the Holmes family demonstrates. And beyond the limitations on Holmes' opportunities to move from one location to another in the central city, he would suffer the same constraints if he attempted to move out of the central city to the suburbs. John Kain has shown, for example, that residential choices in the suburbs are determined not by economic factors but by bigotry.[12] Yet the federal government consistently has resisted the utilization of its resources to remove racial obstacles to the exercise of free choice in housing. For example last year it was reported that "in developing policies to enforce the fair housing law, HUD Secretary George Romney has been careful to observe President Nixon's promise that Federal programs would not be used to force economic integration of the suburbs."[13]

Thus with growth far down the track to solution, and distribution hardly off the starting block, why the continuing preoccupation with growth? Could it be that issues related to growth are less threatening to the values and behavior of those who participate in population policy making than are the questions relating to distribution?

A New Look

Beyond the values that are projected into a policy discourse by those who participate in it or dominate it, there is the issue of selecting a framework in which the discourse is conducted. This too is influenced by the values of those who select the framework. The choice of growth or size as the starting point for a discourse on population policy can produce a different sort of agenda than would the selection of Cornely's referents: values, stratification, and racism. Indeed, in a separate statement on the commission report, Cornely says:

This Commissioner . . . firmly believes that population growth is indeed not the major problem in our society and that of more import is the need for a radical rearrangement of our values and priorities as well as the relationship of man to himself . . . many times throughout the Report of the Commission, the need to speak in terms of statistics about people, rather than about people themselves, may leave the impression that human beings are looked upon as things or chattel which can be equated in terms of numbers or quantities; what it costs to produce them, what is the supply and demand; and how they can be moved or rearranged.[14]

Thus for illuminating the American population policy-making process, or the policy-making process in any area for that matter, it is important to probe behind the agenda for the values that determine it. This is an ambitious and delicate project that awaits doing. Perhaps the new breed of population ethicists and political scientists interested in population matters could team up for the job. Politicial scientists could contribute to the enterprise by mapping out the policy-making process to identify the points at which to look for the values. And the mapping could begin with an identification of the participants in the process, their relationships, and the resources available to them, including the ingredients and exercise of power.

If Cornely's format were employed to guide the inquiry, a different set of questions might be raised about the causes and consequences of population change. Perhaps these questions might be equally or more relevant to the realities of American society than those posed by a format in which factors of size and growth are emphasized. As Cornely suggests, the issues would be posed in less quantitative and thus more complex terms. It is tempting to speculate that if Cornely's model had been employed to guide the commission inquiry, the report might have come to grips more directly and specifically with the sort of unsolved population problem experienced by Holmes, rather than with the apparently solved one relating to American fertility rates.

The question of why the Cornely format or for that matter other likely alternates less fixated on growth and size were not selected to guide the first comprehensive national inquiry on population is a political question. The selection of issues, questions, priorities, and the conceptual framework that organizes them is determined by the influence and power of those doing the selecting. And the choices expressed in the selection process are guided by the values of those involved. Thus the end product, the inquiry itself, results ultimately from an exercise of power.

At present, population policy is most frequently approached through the relationships between traditional demographic categories — size, growth, composition, and location — with various characteristics that make up the conditions of life experienced by groups of people. Thus the size of a group, the rate at which it grows, how it is physically deployed, and the characteristics that typify its membership — sex, age, education, occupation, etc., — are all related to the kind of life the group leads and the opportunities available to the group for changing or improving their conditions of life. Population policy is addressed to influencing this set of relationships (see Figure 17-1). If values, stratification,

A. *Demographic Characteristics*　　　　　B. *Conditions of Group Well-being*

A. Demographic Characteristics	B. Conditions of Group Well-being
Size	Nutrition
Growth	Health
Composition	Employment
Distribution	Leisure
	Shelter
	Education
	Civic
	Environment
	Etc.

MOBILITY　　　OPPORTUNITY

Figure 17-1. Perspective for Population Policy Making: Focus on Groups of People

Note: Population policy influences the reciprocal relationships between A and B.

and racism were added, what different sorts of questions might emerge from the new set of relationships, and more importantly, what different policy issues might be highlighted? (See Figure 17-2.)

For example, while distribution yields questions about racial obstacles to residential choices, it tends to pose the issue more in terms of physical deployment. Racism broadens the issue to include ingredients of socialization, cultural and religious norms, educational patterns, family influences, and other factors in a complex more immediately relevant to the questions of what prevents a distribution pattern which more closely conforms to the preferences of more Americans about where they might like to live. Thus an approach to distribution through the intervening condition of racism might yield a richer and more useful set of issues than would an approach through the medium of distribution alone.

Similarly, in the case of composition supplemented by stratification, composition is employed as an umbrella to differentiate the qualities of a group deemed useful to know, such as sex, age, religious affiliation, and political preference. Stratification highlights a narrower range of qualities that differentiate individuals within a group, principally those that determine their access to better opportunities such as educational attainment, income level, and occupational distribution. Thus for examining American population in the 1970s, stratification adds a sharp dimension to some rather compelling social issues.

Speculating on a linkage of values to size and growth is a tenuous enterprise. Values related to population size involve extrapolations from other concerns such as national power or environmental conservation. And values relating to

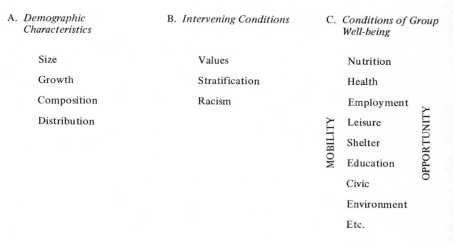

Figure 17-2. Perspectives for Population Policy Making: Focus on Groups of People (With Intervening Conditions)

Note: Population policy influences for the reciprocal relationships between A and C as mediated by B.

growth have to do with individual fertility choices and when these choices are made. They too are extrapolations of other hopes and fears, which principally involve an evaluation of the opportunity costs of various assets individuals enjoy or to which they aspire.

But values as intervening conditions are not linked to size and growth alone. They pervade all the relationships. In suggesting values as a concept relevant to the analysis of population issues, Cornely is probing deeper waters and calling for a focus on the norms evolving among the American population that influence the direction of American society, and for what purposes, and to whose advantage. This is an ambitious formulation, but perhaps one as relevant in a population policy discourse as in discussions of social theory, ethics, religion, and other areas that occupy themselves with a global approach to values.

Thus far values have entered the population policy discourse primarily insofar as they influence individual fertility behavior. But in the analytic format Cornely proposed, values can be examined in a much broader population perspective by linking them to the other ingredients in the format. Thus values, stratification, and racism exert a mutual influence on one another, and all together associate in a relationship with the conditions in which the American population lives. In a population policy discourse this mix generates issues and propositions certainly as worthy of debate as those produced exclusively by the traditional demographic variables.

Values, Power, and Policy Making

Beyond their significance in influencing the various population relationships, values influence group and individual assessments of the relationships themselves. Thus a certain value position held by an interested individual or group may propel a relationship between size and environmental conservation into the forefront of a dialogue, while another set may accord priority to the association of location and educational opportunity. For example, beyond the abstractions of egalitarianism and distributive justice, the immediate concerns of a suburbanite with preventing the overcrowding of schools and encroachments on conservation lands in his community would reflect values that influence his priorities in a population policy discussion. By the same token, a central-city black preoccupied with the deplorable state of schools and personal security in his community is likely to have other ideas about what should come first on a population policy agenda.

Indeed Cornely's formulation of the salient population referents in itself reflects a certain value position. An interesting political issue, of course, is whose values control the establishment of which priorities on which relationships, and how and why.

Despite evidence that suggests its decreasing relevance, then, the preoccupation with the factors of size and growth continues to dominate the American population discourse. During the past year American fertility rates declined below the replacement level, and if this trend continues, natural growth of the American population will level off during the next seventy years.[15] Of course the demographers are correct in pointing out that the current fertility decline is a period-specific happening and, like the weather, fertility rates can change, as historically they have done in the United States. Demographers are the first to admit that projecting fertility trends is like reading tea leaves. But on the basis of available tea leaves, one might be justified in reading that the lower fertility trends in the United States will persist largely because the lower fertility desires of the American female population can more readily be attained due to increasing knowledge and availability of contraceptive technology. Thus the emerging pattern of American fertility behavior and the greater availability of technology to sustain it are transforming the preoccupation with size and growth into an anachronistic concern in the American population discourse. As a result, we might well shift our priorities to other population issues more relevant to the current state of American society: Harvey Holmes' experience suggests one.

The report of the Population Commission symptomizes our reluctance to shift gears too quickly. I have speculated elsewhere about the inclination of those individuals and groups who participate in formulating American population policy to avoid the more controversial issues in favor of policy options around which a broad consensus is more likely to develop.[16] Indeed, the avoidance or suppression of conflict in policy making has been suggested as a prevailing style of American policy making generally.[17] The boundaries that are emplaced around a policy-making arena, including population, are established and maintained by those who enjoy the power to do so as a result of their intellectual, scientific, civic, and economic preeminence.[18] The boundaries or limitations on a policy-making process include the issues selected or avoided for debate, the format and substance of the policy agenda, and the differential access to the arena in which the policy debate is conducted. The particular interests, objectives, and values of the actors involved in policy making determine the content and configuration of the policy arena.

As a likely priority for the policy agenda, consider the grievance of Holmes and comparable experiences suffered by many like him. How frequently do we see thirty-eight-page advertising supplements in the *New York Times* advocating prompt and concrete action to guarantee the exercise of free choice in the selection of where to live? I have never seen such an advertising supplement, and I have been an avid reader of the Sunday *Times* for years. And why is it that the group of prominent Americans who sponsored this particular supplement chose to emphasize the message of population growth in preference to that of population distribution even though the commission had dealt with both issues?

I would suggest there was a screening of issues and an establishment of priorities which was influenced by the particular values of those in the preferred position to bring these matters to the attention of the *New York Times* readers. Appeals for the limitation of fertility and suppression of population growth are not calculated to influence the behavior of the *New York Times* readers or the sponsors of the *New York Times* public service advertisements. These constituencies are quite able to handle their own fertility and for the most part do so in a manner that does not contribute to excessive population growth. The message, then, must be intended to affect the behavior of a constituency "out there" — people who are nonreaders and nonsponsors — and for the most part unknown to the sponsors of the appeal. Thus insofar as the sponsors are concerned, their message enjoys a neutral quality; it does not affect them directly, except as they might see certain benefits for themselves in some of the consequences of reducing the fertility of others. The benefit that most likely attracted most of the sponsors was the satisfaction in discharging a civic responsibility by utilizing their influence to increase opportunities for a better life for the people "out there." But some who advocate fertility reduction "out there" may see other types of benefits accruing to themselves such as a reduction in welfare costs, a stabilization of social and economic discontent "out there," and a reduction of pressures to change familiar ways of managing the nation's affairs.

On the other hand, by assigning priority to the issue that concerns Holmes, the sponsors of the *New York Times* advertisement would have been entering an area less neutral and doubtlessly more controversial insofar as their interests and relationships are concerned. If they had assigned priority to this issue they might have called for prompt and vigorous action by the federal government to facilitate free choice of residence by all Americans, complete with the necessary enforcement mechanisms. If it were made, a plea of this sort would involve stepping on some toes; to begin with, the toes of the president and the Department of Housing and Urban Development, both having announced their intent to avoid this sort of action.[19] A strong position on free choice of residence, as contrasted to a mere declaration of intent, also could conflict with the immediate interests of construction enterprises and their financial institutions which understandably are interested first in maximizing their profits, not in expanding free choices of residence. Finally, an appeal of this sort by a group of influential Americans might be regarded as a threat by political subdivisions such as counties and localities, and by groups of citizens within them, sensitive about any change in the composition of their population. Thus the selection of population distribution as a priority, rather than fertility and growth, simultaneously would raise the level of conflict in the American population debate and threaten the preferences of those whose interests are more in common with the sponsors of the advertisement than with those who would benefit from the guarantee of free choice of residence. That the sponsors did not select this issue as a priority is not surprising. That they may not even have been conscious of it as an option of equal or better value for society is politically interesting.

A Challenge to Political Analysis

The foregoing discussion suggests that a political analysis of population policy making might focus on how the choices are sorted out both for those affected by and those involved in the policy-making process. We have depicted two sets of issues where choice is involved. The first of these sets reflects a juxtaposition of priorities suggested, on the one hand, by the experience of a man who was denied freedom in choosing the location of his residence and, on the other, by an example of support for selected population policy initiatives preferred by an influential group of citizens. The second set of political issues is derived from two contrasting analytical frameworks through which to view population policy issues: a set of traditional demographic concepts, on the one hand, and an alternative map which combines demographic and nondemographic concepts, on the other.

The selection of either of the priorities, or either of the frameworks, would lead ultimately to different sets of issues and policy choices. The priorities and frameworks selected are influenced by the values of those doing the choosing. And which particular option prevails, and thus becomes the basis of subsequent priorities and choices, is determined by the capacity to make it stick — power.

All of this is political subject matter whose exploration not only is revealing of the structure in which American population policy is made, but equally illuminating of the condition of American policy making generally. The mix is rich with ingredients and relationships that could generate propositions subject to empirical exploration. Some of the elements in this mix, as it pertains to policy making, have been suggested by the foregoing discussion, for example:

1. *The Composition of Power:*

   Resources — Position; knowledge; influence; money.
   Access — To policy making machinery.

2. *The Exercise of Power:*

   Decision making — Selecting the options.
   Predecision making — Arranging the agenda of options.[20]
   Nondecision making — Neglecting or excluding options.[21]

3. *The Actors:*

   Participants — Those involved in choice making.
   Nonparticipants — Those excluded from choice making.
   Objects — Those affected by choice making.

4. *The Apparatus of Policy-making:*

   Government institutions — Laws; legislative agencies; executive agencies; judicial agencies.
   Nongovernment institutions — Universities; private associations; mass media.

5. *Outcomes:*

   Scope — Coverage of the policy choice.
   Impact — With what costs and benefits for whom.

It is neither intellectually irresponsible nor lazy to depict values as a residual that permeates the entire mix of ingredients comprising a policy-making process. For values do, in fact, illuminate a most critical dimension of individual ingredients, combinations of them, and relationships among them. But the utilization of values in the analysis of policy making still is in a relatively primitive state. This is most likely because we still are groping for appropriate conceptual handles and empirical tools with which to deal with them. All the more reason, then, to persist in one of the most exciting challenges of political analysis, the systematic illumination of behavioral/normative linkages.[22]

In the matter at hand, moreover, a keener understanding of the role of values in American population policy making would better enable us to unravel some of the anomalies in the process. Indeed using the characterization *anomaly* itself reflects a value judgment that could stand some sorting out.

Notes

1. *New York Times,* April 30, 1972, section 12.

2. *Boston Globe,* May 2, 1972.

3. Public Law 91-213, S. 2107, 91st Cong., approved March 16, 1970.

4. Commission on Population Growth and the American Future, *Population and the American Future* (Washington, D.C.: G.P.O., 1972).

5. Ibid., p. 15.

6. *New York Times* (n. 1), p. 26.

7. *Boston Globe* (n. 2), p. 13.

8. *Population and the American Future* (n. 4), p. 120.

9. Paul B. Cornely, The Third Annual Fred T. Foard Jr. Memorial Lecture, The School of Public Health, The University of North Carolina at Chapel Hill, February 11, 1971.

10. Ibid.

11. Report in the *New York Times,* December 18, 1972, p. 1, based on Bureau of the Census publication "Projections of the Population of the United States, 1972 to 2020."

12. John F. Kain, ed., *Race and Poverty: The Economics of Discrimination* (Englewood Cliffs: Prentice Hall, 1969), pp. 22-27.

13. *Boston Globe,* January 30, 1972.

14. *Population and the American Future* (n. 4), p. 149.

15. *New York Times* (n. 11).

16. Peter Bachrach and Elihu Bergman, *Power and Choice: The Formulation of American Population Policy* (Lexington: D.C. Heath, 1973).

17. Theodore J. Lowi, *The End of Liberalism: Ideology, Policy, and the Crisis of Public Authority* (New York: W.W. Norton, 1969).

18. Bachrach and Bergman (n. 16), see particularly the discussions in chapters 1 and 6.

19. *Boston Globe* (n. 14).

20. For a development of this concept see: Roger W. Cobb and Charles D. Elder, *Participation in American Politics: The Dynamics of Agenda Building* (Boston: Allyn and Bacon, 1972).

21. This concept is developed in: Peter Bachrach and Morton S. Baratz, *Power and Poverty: Theory and Practice* (New York: Oxford University Press, 1970).

22. The value of this approach was suggested, among other places, in: David E. Apter and Charles Andrain, "Comparative Government: Developing New Nations,"*Journal of Politics* 30 (May 1968): 372-416.

18 Women and Population: Some Key Policy, Research, and Action Issues

Elsa M. Chaney

"For the first time in history, the purpose of women is not to preserve the race, because the race is preserving itself at the rate of 2.5 percent growth a year. If we're going to have the one- and two-child family and live to 70, you've got to give us something to do."[1] In these words, Barbara Ward graphically underscored the fact that humankind's pressing problem of overpopulation is tied to a complex and revolutionary redefinition of women's role in society. The following analysis will assess the key research and action issues related to alternative roles for women and will attempt to spell out the part that women themselves might play in population research, policy making, and the implementation of population programs.

At the political level we might well ask why there are so few women involved in a policy area which so intimately affects the lives of women. If women have made a few tentative inroads anywhere in government, it is precisely in the "feminine" areas of health, education, and welfare because women's participation could be justified as an extrapolation of their motherhood role to the arena of public affairs. What part do women actually play in the "population community" of physicians, task forces, government commissions, pressure groups, academics? Why are so few qualified women found in the disciplines from which population research and planning programs recruit? Should women play any greater part? Would women's involvement make any difference in policy outputs?

At the implementation level — in delivery services for birth control materials, for example, or in educational and media programs — are women enough involved as program administrators and field workers? As Moore has pointed out, U.S.-based international organizations active in family planning are almost entirely male-run operations.[2] Should women be more actively recruited? Does the key part played by the *matrona*[3] in Chile explain the apparent wide acceptance of that government's family planning program? Are male medical personnel really more effective except in regions where there is a positive prohibition of women being attended by a male physician? Is there greater or lesser confidence when women are instructed and attended by a male authority

The author is grateful to Dr. Kenneth Godwin, Dr. Miriam Keiffer, Dr. Mary Powers, and to Ms. Emily Moore for many insights into the issues discussed here. Helpful assistance also was given by Ms. Kathy Wall, graduate research assistant, and Ms. Mary Pat Farrell.

233

figure? What questions about birth control technology do we still need to ask? Should women have a part in deciding on techniques? If women were more involved, would greater progress be made toward developing male contraceptives? Would women's greater participation at the implementation level make any difference in effectiveness and acceptance of programs?

At the target level, what questions do we need to ask about women as the special "clients" of government and private programs? Do we really have any exact knowledge on the importance of smaller or larger families to women? What psychological conflicts may emerge in changing the image of woman's "proper role" in society? What social and economic factors influence women to want more or fewer children? What legal measures are necessary to encourage a basic reorientation of women toward new roles? Would attention to these factors make any difference in raising or lowering fertility?

Let us first concentrate on this last issue. The completed family size of women in many societies does appear to be related in some way to their status and opportunities. Some analysts now acknowledge this fact by calling for government and private efforts to increase the options of women as a necessary component of any broad population policy program. We know little about the links between women's involvement outside the home and lowered fertility; at this stage of research it would be risky indeed to assume any causal relationship. While we cannot say positively that participation of women in education, work, and professions is the variable *directly* linked to a smaller family size, recent research has uncovered impressive evidence across many cultures of a negative association between women's nonfamilial activities and their fertility.[4] The association between women's educational levels and family size seems to be the most firmly established.[5] We also know that in most countries studied, women who work not only have fewer children than those who stay at home, but that the longer the duration of her working life in relation to her married years, the more likely a woman is to have a smaller completed family.[6]

It seems that we ought to be asking more research questions precisely in these areas if we are interested in expanding government population policy "beyond family planning." The gross correlations noted above do not tell us, for example, whether opportunity to work actually influences women to have less children, or whether women who have less children from other complex motives take outside employment simply because they are freer to do so. Nor do gross statistics reveal whether most women who work at low-level jobs and in discontinuous fashion have higher fertility that those whom Tien has characterized as "working wives."[7] Does the small elite group of women who are committed to a profession and who take time off to bear children have fewer children than "working mothers" who take time off from raising their children to work?[8]

Many observers have already noted that increasing availability of birth control technology and rising indices of modernization do not automatically reduce population growth rates to acceptable levels. Mortality rates have gone down rapidly, but fertility continues at a high level or even increases in many developing areas where norms on family size have not changed.[9] Completed family size in Ghana, for example, averages seven children[10] and Poole believes that in most African countries the problem to the year 2000 is not one of achieving stable population, but of reducing families of six to eight children to families of four to six children.[11]

Governments of industrialized countries first entered upon *direct* programs to affect fertility when reproduction rates reached such a low point that they were viewed as a cause for alarm. Official fertility policy (as distinguished from planned parenthood efforts) in these countries was pronatalist before World War II, including those Fascist programs which advocated large populations as the basis of national power. In Eastern Europe (Czechoslovakia, Bulgaria, Romania, Hungary), a pronatalist policy apparently still is being pursued; in the USSR and the German Democratic Republic, policy has fluctuated.[12]

Since World War II, rapid population growth in the developing areas has influenced a number of governments to adopt antinatalist policies, usually in the form of recognition of, and support for, family planning and maternal health programs. The United Nations Population Division in a recently-issued report[13] listed as of mid-1969 thirty countries with policies of national family planning, representing 71 percent of the total population of the developing regions.

No one has yet come up with any real evidence that governments *can* effectively influence the birth rate. Nor is there any agreement on whether a "mix" of policies could be devised to influence fertility consistently in either direction. Birth rates are affected by many complex variables, some of which appear to encourage large families while others depress fertility. Perhaps all that governments can do (if they are not totalitarian) is to encourage the general societal changes which appear to be correlated with fertility decline. Much more research needs to be done precisely here: just what changes do have consequences for fertility, and in what direction? Very particularly, research effort must focus on the goals and aspirations of women. It is essential that policy makers at least try to answer Freud's famous question, "What does woman want?" because some governmental tinkering apparently has resulted in effects quite the opposite of those intended.

In Romania, for example, generous maternity leaves and benefits and a public system of child care were designed to encourage working women to have children in the face of a declining birth rate. The repeal of Romania's liberal abortion law in 1966 also was interpreted as a pronatalist measure (although some observers thought the government was interested, at least in part, in inducing women to adopt other forms of contraception — the high abortion rate having indicated that women were resorting to abortion out of habit because it was available before modern contraceptives were developed).

What has been the result of all these efforts? In 1966 the number of live births in Romania had reached an all time low of 14.3 per thousand. In 1967, in the wake of abortion repeal, births jumped to 27.4 per thousand, but in the two years following — as women switched to new contraceptive techniques — births again resumed their decline, dropping to 26.3 per thousand in 1968 and to 23.3 in 1969.[14] Since then, a further drop to 20 per thousand in 1971 has been reported.[15]

The factors at work here are admittedly unclear, but at least it would be interesting to investigate whether women who know that their jobs — at the same level of seniority and salary — are guaranteed them and who can count on inexpensive day care intend to return to work and, whether they in fact, do so. On the other hand, women who lose their jobs when they take "time off" to have a baby and who have no provisions for day care may find themselves trapped at home. They may go on to have three or four children simply because they must be at home anyhow, and they need some meaningful activity to prove their worth.[16]

What types of attitude surveys might uncover the vital information on options and services which should be offered to women? What kinds of pilot projects and controlled experiments could we set up to show us the directions in which policies should move? From what we know of the apparently limited results of government programs, particularly of legal measures such as raising the age of marriage in India[17] or unveiling women and sending them out to work — the device used by the Communist party in an attempt to break up traditional Muslim societies in Soviet Central Asia[18] — it seems unlikely that in either the developing or developed world women will increase or reduce their fertility on demand in response to overall government plans for socioeconomic development. It would seem that the polity must translate its general economic and social programs into terms of the family's — and particularly the woman's — personal aspirations and goals.

Probably very few students of the population question would hold to the view that availability of improved birth control techniques causes reduced fertility, although for persons who already have adjusted their goals to a smaller family size, effective techniques obviously are an important means to lowered fertility. But sometimes analysts and policy makers act as if they believe technology is everything — population policy programs often appear to be equated with national family planning programs.[19] Historical evidence, as well as the limited survey data we now have available, would appear to indicate that the key is not in techniques, but in individual and/or societal attitudes. When the connection between smaller families and the achievement of personal economic and social goals becomes salient enough to individuals, then fertility in a nation declines, and modern birth control techniques are not absolutely essential in slowing down the overall rates of population growth. When larger families continue to be the norm, fertility rates remain constant in spite of the availability of birth control technology. The baby boom was, after all, largely a white, middle-class phenomenon — and this group had birth control devices at its disposal which were far more efficient than those available to the French during their historic demographic decline of the last century (and no less efficient than the technology available to the low-fertility depression generation in the United States).[20] Much of the decline in the present U. S. population growth rate can be attributed to lowered fertility in this same white, middle-class group (although we know from 1970 census data that fertility also is declining among poor women and black women).[21]

How can we give women more significant alternatives and thus make smaller families salient to them? Barbara Castle, former Minister for Overseas Development in the United Kingdom, has written: "Family planning will never be accepted to the extent which is necessary until women understand that there can be a life available for them other than one of continual childbearing. . . . The two processes — the spread of knowledge about birth control and the creation of new professional lives for women — must go along in parrallel if both are to succeed. . . ."[22]

To create alternatives for women in the form of jobs (and expanded opportunities for education and training) is an attractive but not very realistic suggestion in labor-surplus economies where there are not enough employment opportunities for each family to have even one principal breadwinner steadily employed — male or female. Moreover, developing countries committed to capital-intensive, labor-saving technologies are not expanding employment opportunities quickly enough to take care of more than a modest percentage of the new workers entering the labor force each year.[23] Some measures to upgrade women's status, which may be desirable not only for their possible population effects, but for humanitarian (or huwomanitarian?) reasons, may be beyond the resource capacity of developing countries. It is not very helpful to recommend that to become developed, a nation must do things of which only a developed nation is capable.

Probably only the developed nations presently can afford the luxury of creating alternatives for women, broadening their educational opportunities, and convincing men and women to accept a new image of women in roles other than (or combined with) their motherhood role. It is important to note here, however, that level of economic development is not necessarily correlated with greater participation of women in the work force. Contrary to what is commonly supposed,[24] Japan modernized and industrialized with relatively low participation of women in education and work (although this situation now is changing). Even crude economic activity rates for women (in contrast to those for men) do not seem clearly affected by degree of industrialization.[25] Indeed, economic progress sometimes correlates negatively with levels of women's activity outside the home. Chaplin has suggested that women's participation goes through two stages in relation to industrial development.[26] In the first industrial revolutions in the West, when new occupations opened up which initially were "sexless" or unattractive to men, many women entered the labor force. Later (midway in the industrialization process, according to Chaplin), when relatively less labor was required and development brought more prosperity, women "retreated" to specialized roles as homemakers and consumers.

In Italy, for example, prosperity reduced Italy's labor force by more than one million women in the past decade. In 1961, 25 percent of all Italian women were working; by 1968 the number had dropped to 19.7 percent because husbands were earning larger salaries and their wives could give up their jobs.[27] In Peru and Chile, women workers in factories decreased not only proportionately but numerically from high points in the late 1940s and early 1950s,[28] as production became more mechanized and required technically skilled (and largely male) labor.[29] Hunt, in a study of feminine occupational patterns in the Philippines, Japan, and the United States,[30] finds that there is no direct relation between industrialization or urbanization and female employment patterns; along with other observers[31] he concludes that cultural and educational influences are much more effective in determining women's occupational roles in these countries.

All this evidence, and more which could be cited,[32] would appear to call into question the contention that economic development will solve the problem of women's participation.[33] There also is evidence to support the view that alternatives offered to women must be meaningful and challenging. Women will not find in low-level, repetitive, and underpaid jobs anything more than a temporary means to earn extra money, unless they are the sole support of their families. We touch here upon the revolutionary changes required in the structures of the world of work, changes which will affect men and women alike. In spite of the temptation of most developing countries to adopt the "latest available model" for their own development, these nations may have to reassess their strategies and deliberately choose labor-intensive technologies in order to give both men and women an opportunity to work. In capitalist economies, it is difficult to see how any increases in gross national product can otherwise be distributed.

None of these considerations affect those middle and upper-middle-class women in developing nations who took advantage of the increased opportunities for education and training; indeed, in societies where skill is in short supply, a qualified woman often finds more opportunity for work and advancement than her professional sister in developed economies. But professional women are too insignificant in numbers to affect the birth rate very much, even though the evidence suggests that they have smaller families.

Some evidence exists that feminine rates of activity in the developing areas might be influenced more strongly by demographic change than by economic progress. Ridley has explored the influence on women of sharp demographic transitions in countries which do not register high on indices of economic development.[34] Her data show that a decline in mortality is highly correlated with an increase of women in the labor force, while a decline both in mortality and the birth rate pushes women's activity rates even higher. If women live longer and (because of declining mortality rates) realize that they do not have to bear so many children in order to see some live to adulthood, they are far more likely to seek employment outside the home.

All these facts point to the conclusion that only within the context of a total mobilization effort are women given important tasks outside the home. As with blacks, the labor reserve of married women is tapped only in cases of acute labor scarcity. In the past, the pioneer woman of the American West had her counterpart in the *fazenda* (ranch) mistress on the Brazilian frontier.[35] In neither case, however, were they succeeded by the woman entrepreneur, senator, or professional, as might have been expected, but by the fainting, sheltered Victorian lady. During the two world wars many women were drawn into work outside the home. Shortages of males in the Soviet Union after World War II brought large numbers of women into the labor force and in addition, broke down sex stereotypes attached to certain jobs.[36] Klein found that married women in Britain — who for the first time in any country constituted the only labor reserve — finally were beginning to command equal pay, status, and promotions.[37] In present-day Cuba and China, labor-intensive modernization efforts are giving women new opportunities for productive work.

It remains to be seen if these newer mobilizations of women will result in any lasting advances. Societies accept women's help in an emergency, but their permanent and equal collaboration in work and professional life has yet to be legitimized or institutionalized in any country. In all these cases, there is strong evidence that women are drawn out of the home and into paid productive work only when the political elites consider women's participation essential to other (and higher) priorities. Purcell has made a convincing argument that this is the situation in Cuba today.[38]

It is difficult to see any "out" in this circular puzzle: women will go on having babies if they lack other alternatives and if they have no other way to affirm their existence and prove their worth. But the added population will outstrip development efforts and development will be doomed. Yet most poor nations cannot afford to invest in the costly effort to give women other alternatives — and in this case, development also will be doomed.

One suggestion (and here I return to my beginning) might be to involve more *women* in the policy research and planning, as we work together to find solutions. Women need to be involved in planning the total development agenda, but as a start it surely is not unreasonable to suggest that more feminine participation is urgent in these areas related to the family, maternal and child welfare, and population. I am not going to argue that only females can do effective research on women; only that women might add a missing dimension.[39] Women are, after all, the most important target group of population programs, and it is logical that they be involved at the policy making and implementation levels just as the blacks, the chicanos, the poor, have won the right to sit on the councils deciding their fate.

Presently, governments do not involve women to any great extent — nor do they see any pressing need to do so. The United Nations Commission on the Status of Women recently reported on replies to a questionnaire sent by the secretary general to governmental and nongovernmental organizations asking their views on the role women might play in the social and economic development of their countries. Answers showed that even where women participate actively in national life, their level of representation in policy making is low — while their participation in agencies related to planning, innovation, and social change is "practically non-existent".[40] So far as population is concerned, of seventy-seven states replying, only three stated that participation of women in decision-making even in the limited area of family planning programs was important (Barbados, Ceylon, and Malaysia), and only one (Barbados) expressed the view that women needed to be more involved at the national level in making population policy.[41]

Two recent studies on population policy elites also pointed up the fact that women are not very involved. Clinton, in selecting an interview group in Peru, identified 74 men and 7 women as involved or influential in population policy.[42] Bergman and Flash explicitly pointed to the absence of adequate female representation on the Commission on Population Growth and the American Future (4 of 25 members) and among the witnesses called to testify before the commission (18 of 111)[43] The latter figures are from the commission report.[44] In my own study of 167 women political leaders in Peru and Chile, only three women mentioned population as a national priority problem.[45]

The question of alternative, nonfamilial options and opportunities for women as part of a comprehensive population policy program remains an open one. Women — and men — might find here, if you will excuse the pun, a fertile field for research. The situation may never come to the point suggested by Moore, where gangs of forty-five-year-old women will roam the streets looking for something to occupy them.[46] Nevertheless, to end with Barbara Ward's plea, if women are going to produce one- and two-child families and live to seventy, "you've got to give us something to do."

Notes

1. Barbara Ward, "Barbara Ward Asks for 'New Morality,' " *Radcliffe News from the College* (Spring 1972), p. 8.

2. Emily Moore, "Population Problems from a Woman's Perspective," paper presented at a conference on the demographic challenge, International Population Program, Cornell University, October 16, 1970, p. 2.

As Moore also observes, some family planning programs rely heavily on women field workers and some use women physicians, especially in cultures where women will not accept a male physician. But few women are found in the command echelons; if the French and the Swedes find it suitable to have women program administrators abroad, she remarks, "it would seem that the American excuse — women wouldn't be accepted by the host country — is a feeble one."

3. The Chilean *matrona,* or midwife, is a university professional with four years training in obstetrics.

4. Data for the 1930s and 1940s on negative association between work-force participation by married women and their fertility is reported in United Nations, *The Determinants and Consequences of Population Trends* (New York: United Nations Department of Social Affairs, Population Division, ST/SOA/Ser. A./17, 1953). Andrew Collver and Elinor Langlois, "The Female Labor Force in Metropolitan Areas: An International Comparison," *Economic Development and Cultural Change* 10 (July 1962): 367-85, report on twenty countries *circa* 1950. More recently Steven W. Keele, "Controlling U.S. Population Growth," paper adapted from an address to the Western Psychological Association, San Francisco, 1970 (mimeo), using data available for the years closest to 1965, has shown the same trends for thirty-two countries. Other studies and discussions showing a negative relationship between education and/or work-force participation of married women and natality include: Jerzy Berent, "Causes of Fertility Decline in Eastern Europe and the Soviet Union," *Population Studies* 24 (March and July 1970): 35-58, 247-92; Judith Blake, "Demographic Science and the Redirection of Population Policy," *Journal of Chronic Diseases* 18 (November 1965): 1181-1200; Judith Blake, "Population Policy for Americans: Is the Government Being Misled?" *Science* 164 (May 1969): 522-29; David Chaplin, ed., *Population Policies and Growth in Latin America* (Lexington, Mass.: D.C. Heath, 1971), chapter 11; Kingsley Davis, "Population Policy: Will Present Programs Succeed?" *Science* 158 (November 1967): 730-39; Lincoln H. and Alice Taylor Day, "Family Size in Industrialized Countries: An Inquiry into the Socio-cultural Determinants of Levels of Childbearing," *Journal of Marriage and the Family* 31 (May 1969): 242-51; Jennie Farley, "Graduate Women: Career Aspirations and Desired Family Size," *American Psychologist* 25 (December 1970): 1099-1100; N. Federici, "The Influence of Women's Employment on Fertility," in Egon Szabady, ed., *World View of Population Problems* (Budapest: Akademiai Kiado, 1968), pp. 77-82; Ronald Freedman, "The Sociology of Human Fertility: A Trend Report and Bibliography," *Current Sociology* 10/11, no. 2 (1961-1962): 59-61; Ronald Freedman, "American Studies of Family Planning and Fertility: A Review of Major Trends and Issues," in C.V. Kiser, ed., *Research in Family Planning* (Princeton, New Jersey: Princeton University Press, 1962), pp 211-27; Murray Gendell, "The Influence of Family-building Activity on Women's Rate of Economic Activity," in *Proceedings of the World Population Conference, Belgrade, 1965,* vol. 4 (New York: United Nations, 1967); Murray Gendell, Maria Nydia Maraviglia, and Philip C. Kreitner, "Fertility and Economic Activity of Women in Guatemala City, 1964," *Demography* 7 (August 1970): 273-86;

A.J. Jaffe, *People, Jobs and Economic Development* (New York: Free Press of Glencoe, Inc., 1959); A.J. Jaffe and K. Azumi, "The Birth Rate and Cottage Industries in Underdeveloped Countries," *Economic Development and Cultural Change* 9, pt 1 (October 1960): 52-63; Stanley Kupinsky, "Non-familial Activity and Socio-economic Differentials in Fertility," *Demography* 8 (August 1971): 353-67; D. Peter Mazur, "Birth Control and Regional Differentials in the Soviet Union," *Population Studies* 22 (November 1968): 319-33; N. Krishnan Namboodiri, "The Wife's Work Experience and Child Spacing," *Milbank Memorial Fund Quarterly* 42, pt 1 (July 1964): 67-77; Lois Pratt and P.K. Whelpton, "Extra Familial Participation of Wives in Relation to Interest in and Liking for Children, Fertility Planning and Actual and Desired Family Size," in P.K. Whelpton and Clyde V. Kiser, eds., *Social and Psychological Factors Affecting Fertility*, vol. 5 (New York: Milbank Memorial Fund, 1958), pp. 1245-80; Jeanne Claire Ridley, "Number of Children Expected in Relation to Non-familial Activities of the Wife," *Milbank Memorial Fund Quarterly* 37 (July 1959): 277-96; Constantina Safilios-Rothschild, "The Influence of the Wife's Degree of Work Commitment upon Some Aspects of Family Organization and Dynamics," *Journal of Marriage and the Family* 32 (November 1970): 681-91; L. Tabah and P. Samuel, "Preliminary Findings of a Survey on Fertility and Attitudes Toward Family Formation in Santiago, Chile," in C.V. Kiser, ed., *Research in Family Planning* (Princeton, New Jersey: Princeton University Press, 1962), pp. 263-304; H. Yuan Tien, "Mobility, Non-familial Activity, and Fertility," *Demography* 4 (February 1967): 218-27; United Nations, *The Determinants and Consequences of Population Trends* (above in this note), pp. 79-80 and 88; Robert H. Weller, "The Employment of Working Wives, Dominance and Fertility," *Journal of Marriage and the Family* 30 (August 1968): 437-42; Robert H. Weller, "The Employment of Wives, Role Incompatibility and Fertility: A Study Among Lower- and Middle-class Residents of San Juan, Puerto Rico," *The Milbank Memorial Fund Quarterly* 46 (October 1968): 507-26.

For some disagreement on the meaning of negative association between working wives and their fertility, see Charles F. Westoff, Robert G. Potter, Jr., Philip C. Sagi, and Elliot G. Mishler, *Family Growth in Metropolitan America* (Princeton, New Jersey: Princeton University Press, 1961), pp. 301-304; Charles F. Westoff, Robert G. Potter, Jr., and Philip C. Sagi, *The Third Child* (Princeton, New Jersey: Princeton University Press, 1963), pp. 187-90; J. Mayone Stycos, "Female Employment and Fertility in Lima, Peru," *Milbank Memorial Fund Quarterly* 43 (January 1965): 42-54; J. Mayone Stycos and Robert H. Weller, "Female Working Roles and Fertility," *Demography* 4 (February 1967): 210-17; and Weller, "The Employment of Wives, Role Incompatibility and Fertility" (above in this note), pp. 518-20.

5. See United Nations (n. 4), p. 89 and United Nations, *Human Fertility and National Development: A Challenge to Science and Technology* (New York:

Department of Economic and Social Affairs, ST/ECA/138, 1971), p. 57 for some references; also Freedman, "The Sociology of Human Fertility" (n. 4), pp. 96-101; Jeanne Claire Ridley, "Demographic Change and the Roles and Status of Women," *Annals of the American Academy* 375 (January 1968): 16; and Weller, "The Employment of Wives, Role Incompatibility and Fertility" (n. 4), pp. 507-508.

6. Blake, "Demographic Science and the Redirection of Population Policy" (n. 4), pp. 1196-97; Freedman, "American Studies of Family Planning and Fertility" (n. 4), p. 223; Ronald Freedman, D. Goldberg, and D. Slesinger, "Current Fertility Expectations of Married Couples in the United States," *Population Index* 29 (October 1963): 376-77; Kupinsky (n. 4), p. 358; Pratt and Whelpton (n. 4), p. 1254; and Ridley (n. 4), p. 277.

7. Tien (n. 4), pp. 226-27.

8. Motives of women for taking jobs and the discontinuities of their work/career patterns are discussed in the following works: Elizabeth Faulkner Baker, *Technology and Women's Work* (New York: Columbia University Press, 1964), ch. 22; Eli Ginzberg, *Life Styles of Educated Women* (New York: Columbia University Press, 1966), pp. 5-14; Alva Myrdal and Viola Klein, *Women's Two Roles: Home and Work* (London: Routledge & Kegan Paul, 1956); Edna G. Rostow, "Conflict and Accommodation," in Robert Jay Lifton, ed., *The Woman in America* (Boston: Beacon Press, 1964): 211-35.

9. Ronald Freedman, "Norms for Family Size in Underdeveloped Areas," *Proceedings of the Royal Society* 159 (1963): 220-45; and Dudley Kirk, "Natality in the Developing Countries: Recent Trends and Prospects," in S.J. Behrman, Leslie Corsa, and Ronald Freedman, eds., *Fertility and Family Planning: A World View* (Ann Arbor: University of Michigan Press, 1969), pp. 75-98 summarize the principal studies offering evidence of continued high fertility in developing areas. Blake, "Demographic Science and the Redirection of Population Policy" (n.4), pp. 1197-98 discusses some of the reasons for "response lag" in adjusting birth rates to lowered mortality.

10. Walter Birmingham, I. Neustadt, and E.N. Omaboe, *A Study of Contemporary Ghana: Some Aspects of Social Structure* (London: George Allen & Unwin Ltd., 1967).

11. D. Ian Poole, talk at the Summer Institute of Demography, Cornell University, Ithaca, New York, July 23, 1971.

Birmingham and colleagues (n. 10), pp. 74-75 and 78 consider, however, that West Africa may have a level of fertility somewhat above the rest of tropical Africa. The authors estimate Ghana's intercensal growth rate between 1948-60 as 4.2 percent per year. For a discussion of current African population trends, see D. Ian Poole, "The Development of Population Policies," *Journal of Modern African Studies* 9 (January 1971): 91-105.

12. United Nations, *Measures, Policies and Programmes Affecting Fertility,*

with Particular Reference to National Family Planning Programs (New York: Department of Economic and Social Affairs, ST/SOA/Ser. A/51, 1972), pp. 61-64.

13. Ibid., p. 66.

14. Ibid., p. 43.

15. *New York Times,* "Population Growth Said to Slow in Countries of the Soviet Bloc" (February 5, 1972).

The same *New York Times* article gives different figures for Romania's birth rate fluctuations: 12 per thousand in 1966, to 40 per thousand in 1967.

16. For a further discussion of this question, see Keele (n. 4), pp. 13-15 and Berent (n. 4).

17. United Nations (n. 12), pp. 49-50.

18. Gregory J. Massell, "Law As an Instrument of Revolutionary Change in a Traditional Milieu: The Case of Soviet Central Asia," *Law & Society Review* 11 (February 1968): 179-228.

19. For an analysis which discusses population policy almost entirely in terms of contraceptive technology, see Dudley Kirk and Dorothy Nortman, "Population Policies in Developing Countries," *Economic Development and Cultural Change* 15 (January 1967), pp. 129-42. For an opposite view, see Davis (n. 4).

20. Day and Day (n. 4), p. 245, in an attempt to isolate sociocultural determinants of childbearing, compare levels of natality in twenty highly industrialized countries with populations of European origin where the technology of control over both mortality and natality has reached a high level. They consider that natality differentials among them indicate primarily "differences in readiness and motivation for limiting family size, rather than differences in biological constitution of their peoples or in their access to adequate methods of birth control."

21. As reported from a private study conducted by Planned Parenthood — World Population of Census Bureau data, in the *New York Times,* "Birth Rates Found in a Sharp Decline among Poor Women" (March 3, 1972).

22. Barbara Castle, "Women: Vital Force for Developing the Poorer Nations," *Freedom from Hunger* 7 (March-April 1966), p. 6.

23. For an extended discussion of this question and an up-to-date bibliography, see William C. Thiesenhusen, "Latin America's Employment Problem," *Science* 171 (March 1972): 868-74.

24. Chester A. Hunt, "Female Occupational Roles and Urban Sex Ratios in the United States, Japan and the Philippines," *Social Forces* 43 (March 1965): 410-11.

25. United Nations, *Demographic Aspects of Manpower, Report 1: Sex and Age Patterns in Economic Activities* (New York: Department of Economic and Social Affairs, ST/SOA/Ser. A/33, 1962), p. 6.

26. David Chaplin, "Feminism and Economic Development," occasional paper, typewritten (1969).

27. *Milwaukee Journal,* November 16, 1969.

28. David Chaplin, *The Peruvian Industrial Labor Force* (Princeton, New Jersey: Princeton University Press, 1967), pp. 187-95.

29. Blake, "Demographic Science and the Redirection of Population Policy" (n. 4) also touches on this issue in documenting how the Indian government appears to be discouraging rather than encouraging female employment. Censuses and other studies show, she reports, a decided decrease in the proportion of women working since the earlier years of this century. She says: "It is surprising that a country like India (where impressive amounts are being invested in family planning campaigns) is not taking advantage of this structural means of influencing family-size motivation." It should be pointed out that "premature" social legislation on behalf of women workers, making them more expensive to hire than male workers, sometimes militates against their employment in poor economies. This is especially true in the textile industry; in Peru, for example, after initially hiring many women, some textile mills have not taken on a single new woman employee in years because of the introduction of social legislation. See also an interesting discussion of women textile workers in India in R.C. James, "Discrimination against Women in Bombay Textiles," *Industry Labor Relations Review* 15 (January 1962), as quoted in Blake, "Demographic Science and the Redirection of Population Policy" (n. 4), p. 1199.

30. Hunt (n. 24).

31. United Nations (n. 25), p. 4.

32. Elsa M. Chaney, "Women in Latin American Politics: The Case Of Peru and Chile" (Ph.D. dissertation, University of Wisconsin, Madison, 1971, pp. 25-35 and 162-68).

33. For an expansion of this discussion on the variability of women's work participation rates, regardless of the level of economic development, see Collver and Langlois (n. 4), pp. 370-74.

34. Ridley (n. 5).

35. Gilberto Freyre, *The Mansions and the Shanties: The Making of Modern Brazil* (New York: Alfred A. Knopf, 1963), p. 75.

36. Participation rates for women tend to be much higher than the national average in the non-Moslem republics, which suffered a high loss of men in the war and where women still account for a large percentage of collective farm workers, and to be lower in the Moslem areas, reflecting demographic and traditional factors. See Norton T. Dodge, *Women in the Soviet Economy: Their Role in Economic, Scientific and Technical Development* (Baltimore: Johns Hopkins Press, 1966), pp. 32 and 262.

37. Viola Klein, *Britain's Married Women Workers* (London: Routledge & Kegan Paul, 1965), pp. 85-88.

38. Susan Kaufman Purcell, "Modernizing Women for a Modern Society: The Cuban Case," in Ann Pescatello, ed., *Female and Male in Latin America* (Pittsburgh: University of Pittsburgh Press, 1973).

39. As Moore (n. 2), pp. 1-2 has pointed out:

Missionaries learned long ago that mere translation of the Bible from the words of language A to those of language B is insufficient; the message often gets lost in the translation.

Social scientists, too, have found that you can't take a questionnaire designed for one culture, translate the questions and use it again in another culture without some specific adaptation.

And white sociologists are learning that in order to make a survey meaningful in a black community, their own language and terms of reference are often insufficient. Yet we still use questionnaires designed by men for application to women in the sensitive subjects of reproduction, sexuality, contraception, and abortion.

40. United Nations, *Participation of Women in the Economic and Social Development of Their Countries* (New York: Commission on the Status of Women, E/CN.6/513/Rev. 1, 1970), p. 4.

41. Ibid., p. 44.

42. Richard Clinton, *Problems of Population Policy Formation in Peru* (Chapel Hill, North Carolina: Carolina Population Center, Population Program and Policy Design Series, no. 4, 1971), p. 54.

43. Eli Bergman and William Flash, "The American Population Policy Process," paper presented at the annual meeting of the American Political Science Association, Chicago, Illinois, September 7-11, 1971, pp. 22-23 of the manuscript.

44. Commission on Population Growth and the American Future, *Population Growth and the American Future* (New York: New American Library, 1972), pp. 351-57.

45. Chaney (n. 32), pp. 473-75.

46. Emily Moore, "Changing Sex Roles, Alternate Life Styles, and Fertility Control," *Concerned Demography* 2 (March 1971): 8.

19

Population Policy and the Limits of Government Capability in the United States

Dorothy M. Stetson

Seeking to explain the capability levels of the United States political system in this study produces a set of questions which constitute an appropriate agenda for research in population policy in developed states. The answers to these questions will serve both the goals of political science and the goals of those interested in population policy problems.

Population policies are those policies which are directed toward affecting the size, fertility, mortality, immigration, distribution, or quality of a population. This study is concerned only with those population policies which directly affect the environment for reproductive behavior of citizens: fertility or "birth control" policies. While many policies may indirectly affect reproductive behavior or fertility, there are three direct targets for influencing reproduction: prevention of conception, termination of pregnancy, and sterilization.[1]

The population policy area offers a number of advantages for the development of concepts for comparative policy analysis.[2] In the first place, population policy is happening now. Unlike the process by which other types of policies of long standing such as social security and education were adopted, the population policy process can be observed first hand. Secondly, population policies are being considered and adopted in many countries. This problem is a pervasive policy concern, both in the more developed and less developed states. Therefore, it differs from other policy areas, such as zoning or economic planning, which may be found in only a limited number of states. With population policy, all nations in the world can be compared.

Thirdly, these attempts of governments to deal with population problems provide some intriguing political questions: How can a government go about successfully affecting such a personal matter as childbearing? Under what circumstances would various types of coercive, symbolic, or distributive policies be effective? How can government bridge the gap between individual choice in reproduction and the public's interest in population size and growth?

Fourthly, the United States government is concerned with obtaining more information about population problems. Government research programs appeal to political scientists for their attention. Political scientists may be able to contribute toward the formulation of effective policies in the population area, not only in this country but in other countries as well.

Capability Analysis

To make the study of population policy in developed states compatible with the pursuits of political scientists, a number of conceptual and methodological tasks need attention. First of all, there is great difficulty determining the population policy of any political system. This is partly due to the fact that there are a large number of policies that directly and indirectly affect population processes. The problem becomes more complex in federal systems such as the United States, since there are so many governmental sources of policies which directly affect fertility, mortality, and population distribution.[3]

For the purpose of this study, *population policy* is defined as action by governmental structures and leaders appearing to be directed toward affecting the environment for reproductive behavior of individuals: the conception and delivery of offspring. Policy activities of federal and state governments of the United States will be studied.

Once population policies are defined and collected, a framework is needed to give those policies meaning in comparative perspective.[4] The framework proposed here makes it possible to classify and compare policies according to some of their political characteristics.

All political systems produce policy outputs. The pattern of policy outputs of a system is its capability. The concept *capability* implies more than a description of a number of policy outputs; it refers to the political nature of a set of government actions in a domestic or international environment, rather than to the substance of the problem. Use of the concept suggests that governments differ as to their political capabilities regardless of the particular problem being considered.

To illustrate, actual governmental policies may appear substantively different from each other when one considers the wide range of governmental action. They differ as to source, such as executive decrees, parliamentary statutes, legal decisions, and statements by leaders. They differ with regard to content as well, such as the farm program, criminal codes, education, or the draft.

All policies are based, however, on a few types of political power or policy tools.[5] In selecting a course of action for responding to a policy demand, a government has a number of policy tools at hand; for example: coercion, money, legitimacy. Therefore, actual policy is based on the use of one or more of these tools. Policies which appear different from each other in content may be classified together because they are derived from the same policy tool.

A set of these policies represents government capability according to different types of political power used: regulation, distribution, and symbolism.[6] Each policy that is classified as an example of regulative capability primarily employs coercion as a policy tool. The government attempts to solve a problem or answer a demand by using its powers of "monopoly of force and control."[7] The distributive capability is based on the policy tool of spending. The government, through its distributive capability, attempts to solve a problem or to answer a demand by using its powers to "spend public money in the public interest." Symbolic policies are examples of government action in solving problems by appealing for support in the population for the political system. Because they constitute the government, officials benefit from being the society-wide "locus of authority and consent," and government actions which address problems by relying on the legitimacy of the system and its broad appeal are symbolic policies.

Capabilities of systems vary not only according to the types of political power or policy tools used but also in terms of the extent to which the political powers are employed. Not all policies represent the same amount of government commitment, energy, or power. The extent to which policy action represents different amounts of commitment, involvement, or power constitutes the varying levels of *capability performance.* For example, regulative policies and capabilities vary according to the amount of coercion and the frequency of application; distributive capabilities vary according to the amount of money spent, the number of people receiving benefits, and the amount of services delivered. Symbolic capability varies by the frequency and intensity of symbolic statements by political leaders.

How do we go about determining high and low levels of various types of capability? A usual practice is to classify on the basis of observations of a range of values found in a large number of observations.[8] For example, countries are classified into high and low levels of development on the basis of the highest and lowest values of development variables represented by the countries being studied. An actual observation may be high in one set of cases and low in another. Nigeria's GNP may be high in a set of African cases and yet low when compared with a set of European countries. Since there will be only one country considered in this study, it is necessary to develop a range of capability variations on the basis of possible population policy alternatives, sometimes called a *policy repertoire,* and then characterize U. S. capability in terms of the possible variations.[9]

Policy Repertoire

Table 19-1 presents a population policy repertoire which has been developed for this study as a standard for characterizing the capability of the U. S. government in the population area. It contains a classification of specific policy alternatives available to a political system in responding to a population problem that requires a change in the environment of fertility behavior. It is appropriate to a country which has previously had a pronatalist set of policies but which is making changes in that traditional stance.[10]

Table 19-1
Policy and Capability Types

Policy	Level of Capability Performance		
	Low	*Moderate*	*High*
CONTRACEPTIVE POLICY			
Regulative Capability			
Use of contraceptives	Allowed for some	Unrestricted	General fertility agent
Sale of contraceptives	Available from doctors only	Generally available	
Advertisement of contraceptives	Restricted to medical outlets	Unrestricted	
No. of children in family	Rewards/incentives to limit no. of children	Penalties for having more than N children	Sterilization after two children
Symbolic Capability			
Support of government for birth control	Neutral	Free choice in family planning desirable	Limitation of children encouraged
Information and education on family planning	Encouragement	Information available from government	Planned PR campaign
Distributive Capability			
Family-planning services	Available through public health	Government program for some	Family planning available to all
Research in reproduction	Part of general government research	Special program	Top priority commitment of funds

	Low	Moderate	High
ABORTION POLICY			
Regulative Capability			
Availability of abortions	Limited to special conditions	Available to all	Abortions required
Distributive Capability			
Subsidizing abortion	Part of general health care	Special funds for abortion for some	Everyone subsidized
Symbolic Capability			
Information and education	No statement or neutral	Information available	Encouraged
STERILIZATION POLICY			
Regulative Capability			
Availability	Limited	Available	Required
Symbolic Capability			
Attitude	Neutrality	Available information	Encouraged
Distributive Capability			
Subsidizing	Part of health care	Special funds for some sterilization	Everyone subsidized

The following points describe the features of the Table 19-1 and how it was constructed:

1. The left side of the table presents specific contraceptive, abortion, and sterilization policy concerns according to type of capability. The top of the table classifies the levels of capability performance — low, moderate or high — for each specific policy area (use of contraceptives, family-planning services, subsidizing abortion).

2. The *level of capability performance* columns refer to a range of possible government action, in this case, in the direction of lowering fertility. Policies are classified according to the extent of regulative, distributive, or symbolic power each represents. Moving from left to right, viewing possible policy alternatives in an area, the government's effort or performance in the direction of reducing fertility increases. All types of policy options have been limited to three levels of performance — low, moderate, and high.

3. The list of policy alternatives has been derived from the literature on population and family planning.[11] Individual policy suggestions found in the literature have been sorted according to the policy areas listed at the left side of the table.

4. Each cell of the table is an example of a particular policy alternative which represents government capability of a particular level. For example, when the policy of a government regarding use of contraceptives is to allow them for some groups in the society and not for others, it represents a *low* level of *regulative* capability.

5. Not all policies at each level of performance whether low, moderate, or high, represent the same amount of government activity or effort, nor does the table make allowances for variations within cells. If a government has officially taken action in any of the areas, it would be listed in a completed table for a country. The number of actions will be available. In in-depth comparisons of capability these categories could be refined. For this study, the nature of U. S. policies represented within each cell will be explained in the text. There is no attempt to view the policy where contraceptives are generally available to represent the same amount of government effort as might be involved in making information on family planning available from the government, although both policies are classified as moderate. The various policies are related to each other only horizontally, as expressions of alternatives in a similar policy area.

Capability of U.S. System Population Policies

U.S. Policies before 1960

The federal and state governments before 1960 had an official pronatalist policy.[12] The Comstock Act of 1873 defined contraceptives as obscene material and prohibited interstate distribution of them; all states but New Mexico had "Little Comstock Acts." Abortion had been illegal since the middle of the nineteenth century throughout the country, except to save the life of the mother.

In practice, the federal government was neutral on the issue. The courts had interpreted the Comstock Act so that contraceptives were available to doctors and drug stores. The state laws were mixed, some neutral and others pronatalist, restricting or prohibiting the sale and use of contraceptives. In general, then, contraceptives were available through doctors, in the case of diaphrams, and in drug stores, in the case of condoms. Abortions were also available but only illegally, since abortion laws prohibited doctors from performing them.

About half the states were silent on the matter of sterilization. Others permitted sterilization for eugenic reasons and allowed government officials to decide when it was appropriate. Although states seem to have been more liberal in the area of sterilization, it was not to curb fertility, but rather to affect the quality of the population.

Therefore, at the time when the problem of population growth became a public issue, federal and state governmental practices constituted a mixture of neutral and pronatalist policies. What policies have these governments adopted since 1960 that represent an antinatalist stand? And secondly, what level of system performance and types of capabilities are represented by these policies?

Policy Changes since 1960

A summary of policies and the capabilities they represent is found in Table 19-2.[13] Generally, the federal government has responded to population growth problems by exercising its low-to-moderate distributive and symbolic capabilities. Except through three court decisions and the repeal of the Comstock Act, it has not relied on the regulative capability. The states have also responded by a low-to-moderate distributive capability. By and large, the regulative performance has been low when the states have acted at all. One may wonder at this point why a set of policies generally referred to as "birth control" and implying regulation by government have, in reality, mostly been based on the distributive and symbolic powers of the government. Action to encourage fertility reduction has emphasized the spending powers of government rather than its "monopoly of force and control."

Federal Policies. Congress acted in 1971 to repeal the Comstock Act, thus destroying the fiction that contraceptives are obscene materials. This regulative action lifted restrictions on contraceptive use, sale, and advertisement on the national level. In addition, the Supreme Court has declared laws prohibiting the use of contraceptives *(Griswold* v. *Connecticut)*[14] and the sale of contraceptives to unmarried persons *(Eisenstadt* v. *Baird)*[15] unconstitutional under the Ninth

Table 19-2
Fertility Policy in the United States

Policy	Level of Capability Performance		
	Low	*Moderate*	*High*
CONTRACEPTIVES			
Regulative Policies			
Use of contraceptives	Allowed for some / Some restrictions on minors	Unrestricted / *Griswold v. Conn.* 1965[a] / *Baird v. Mass.* 1972[a]	General fertility agent
Sale of contraceptives	Available from doctors only / 22 states[a]	Generally available / Comstock Act repealed 1971[a]	Required
Advertisement	Restricted / 23 states prohibit advertisement[a]	Unrestricted	Government advertises
No. of children in family	Rewards/incentives to limit no. of children / *Dandridge v. Williams* 1970[a]	Penalties for having more than N children	Sterilization after two children
Symbolic Policies			
Support for family planning	Neutrality	Free choice in family planning desirable / 1965 Johnson statement[a] / 1965-67 Gruening hearings[a] / 1969 Nixon statement[a] / 1972 Commission Report[a]	Family planning encouraged
Information and education	Encouragement / A few states[a]	Information from government / 1972 Population Commission Report[a]	Planned PR campaign
Distributive Policies			
Family planning services	Available through health service / 1964 Social Security[a] / 1966 Public Health Act[a] / 1967 OEO Amendment[a]	Government family planning for some / 1970 Family Planning Act[a] / State grants to 43 states (limited)[a]	Government family planning for all
Research in reproduction	General research	Special programs / 1970 Family Planning and Population Research Act[a]	Top priority

ABORTIONS			
Regulative Policies			
Availability	Abortion limited 46 States[a] Supreme Court action[a]	Abortion available to all 1969 New York[a] 1971 Hawaii, Washington, Alaska[a] Advocated by Population Commission[a]	Abortion required
Distributive Policies			
Subsidies	Part of health care	Special funds for some	Everyone subsidized
Symbolic Policies			
Information and education	Moderate support 1972 Population Commission Report[a]	Information available	Encouraged
STERILIZATION			
Regulative Policies			
Availability	Limited Privately available for some	Available	Required 28 states for eugenic reasons
Symbolic Policies			
Attitude	No statement	Information available voluntary sterilization approved by HEW[a]	Encouraged
Distributive Policies			
Subsidies	Part of health care 1971 pilot federal project to subsidize vasectomies in Tennessee[a]	Special funds	Everyone subsidized

[a] Policy action — 1960-72

and Fourteenth Amendments. These policies are the only government actions representing moderate regulative capability in the area of fertility behavior.

Little regulative action has been taken to affect the number of children born to a family. Some states have taken action to limit aid to dependent children. In *Dandridge* v. *Williams* the Supreme Court upheld a state limit of $250 per family regardless of the number of children.[16]

Federal officials have responded to the population problem with statements supporting family planning.[17] Since Eisenhower's statement of 1959 that he "could not imagine anything more emphatically that is not a proper political or governmental activity or function or responsibility . . ." than family planning, government leaders have switched the official stance from one of noninvolvement to one of encouraging family planning. They are careful not to mention birth *control,* however. The chronology of symbolic support is as follows:

1960: Presidential candidate John F. Kennedy in a speech about his Catholicism indicated his support for information being made available for family planning. Later, of course, the Roman Catholic Church came out in favor of family planning, although it continued its stand against artificial contraceptives.

1965: President Johnson was the first president to indicate that federal support for family planning was being considered. In his State of the Union message in 1965 he stated: "I will seek new ways to use our knowledge to help deal with the explosion in world population and the growing scarcity of world resources." This statement seemed at the time to be directed more toward the foreign aid program than to domestic fertility.

1969: Nixon was the first president to deliver a special population message to Congress. He committed the nation to the support of voluntary family planning in all nations and pointed to the U.S. problem of unwanted children in poor families:

It is my view that no American woman should be denied access to family planning assistance because of her economic conditions. I believe, therefore, that we should establish as a national goal the provision of adequate family planning services within the next five years to all those who want them but cannot afford them. This we have the capacity to do.

He emphasized the need for guaranteeing freedom of choice and that the policy should not allow the government to infringe on anyone's religious convictions.

1972: The Commission on Population Growth and the American Future has made the strongest statement to date on the question of contraception and family planning:

The Commission believes that all Americans, regardless of age, marital status, or income, should be enabled to avoid unwanted births. Major efforts should be made to enlarge and improve the opportunity for individuals to control their own fertility, aiming toward the development of a basic ethical principle that only wanted children are brought into the world.

In order to implement this policy, the Commission has formulated the following recommendations:

— The elimination of legal restrictions on access to contraceptive information and services, and the development by the states of affirmative legislation to permit minors to receive such information and services.

— The elimination of administrative restrictions on access to voluntary contraceptive sterilization.

— The liberalization of state abortion laws along the lines of the New York State statute.

— Greater investments in research and development of improved methods of contraception.

— Full support of all health services related to fertility, programs to improve training for and delivery of these services, an extension of government family planning project grant programs, and the development of a program of family planning education.[18]

The federal government has responded to population growth most actively through the distributive capability, especially in dispensing funds for family planning services and research. These actions represent a moderate level of performance since they are limited in their availability and there is no commitment that all should be reached. Yet, the 1971 congressional act represented greater capability than earlier programs since it was specifically designed to relate to population and separated family planning services from general health administration.[19]

The Family Planning Services and Population Research Act of 1970 (PL 91-572) provided for an Office of Population Affairs in HEW to coordinate government population activities, grants for voluntary family planning projects, and grants to state health departments for family planning services. Priority is to be given to low-income families. It also provides funds for research in reproduction with the goal of developing better means of contraception, social and psychological explanations of high fertility in particular groups, and better family planning services. This research program represents moderate distributive performance as well. The 1973 budget for research and services does not meet the needs of the population according to the Population Commission report.[20]

The Supreme Court has been the only structure of the federal government to expand freedom of choice in childbearing by removing many of the state restrictions on abortions. At a time when many states had just completed reforms of their abortion statutes (see following section on state abortion policies), the Court ruled that states violate the Ninth and Fourteenth Amendments if they place any restriction on abortions, other than regulating medical conditions, during the first six months of pregnancy.[21]

While the Court has taken action to make abortions more available, other branches of the federal government have discouraged abortion as a means of family planning. President Nixon from time to time has expressed his opposition to legal abortion. The Family Planning Act of 1970 specifically prohibited the use of funds to subsidize abortion or encourage its use as a means of family planning.

There is no general federal law governing voluntary sterilization. HEW has approved voluntary sterilization and has developed a pilot project to subsidize vasectomies in Anderson County, Tennessee. This represents only the barest expansion of distributive powers to facilitate sterilization.

State Policies: Contraception. State laws restricting the use of contraceptives have been struck down by the Supreme Court.[22] States have been more conservative than the federal agencies in removing restrictions on the sale and advertisement of contraceptives. Some of the states (about twenty) have taken action to change laws restricting the sale and advertisement of contraceptives. Thus, less than half the states have responded to the problem by taking action to make contraceptives more easily attainable.

Many current policies represent low regulative capabilities in the direction of making contraceptives more available. In twenty-two states the sale of contraceptives in limited to pharmacists and doctors, prohibiting vending machines for condoms. In addition, advertisement of contraceptives is banned, and sales to minors are restricted. State laws permitting sale of contraceptives only to married people have been undermined by the decision in *Eisenstadt* v. *Baird.* States also vary in the extent to which they enforce the ban on sales of contraceptives to minors.[23]

The states have responded with distributive capabilities by offering family planning services, mostly through state and local departments of health. This represents a mixture of low-to-moderate distributive capability. State policies vary as follows:

1. No action
2. Statements authorizing family planning in public health clinics
3. Health departments distributing information
4. Health departments providing services only to welfare people and/or married people and/or adults
5. Health departments providing services to all regardless of economic condition, marital status, or age.

More than forty states receive funds for programs under the 1970 Family Planning Act.[24] Most of the states with operating programs have policies resembling Number 4, with eligibility for the service restricted in some way. Many of these programs serve only a city or part of a metropolitan area. These policies represent a moderate distributive capability.

State Policies: Abortion-Sterilization. Many states have acted to change century-old abortion laws. Only four, however, have used this regulative power to even a moderate degree to insure that abortion would be available for all who want it. Of the rest, at least fifteen passed the model bill of the American Law Institute (ALI) which allows abortions under certain conditions of pregnancy: (1) if the fetus is likely to be deformed; (2) if the life or physical and mental health of the mother are endangered; and (3) if pregnancy is the result of rape or incest. For several years the Supreme Court considered the state abortion laws one by one. Some were left alone and some declared unconstitutional. Then, in 1973, in a sweeping decision, the Court defined the circumstances under which states could regulate abortions, limiting such intervention to the time after the sixth month of pregnancy. States have since acted in various ways to bring their laws into conformity with the provisions made by the Court. States have not acted with regard to sterilization during the decade under study as far as can be determined. Laws in twenty-eight states requiring sterilization for eugenic reasons are directed toward affecting the quality of the population, not fertility. Existing state laws do not appear to restrict sterilization. Often, however, private physicians are reluctant to perform these operations for birth control purposes.

Research In System Capability And Population Policy

Government action in the population-fertility area in the United States has consisted of removing pronatalist laws and making the environment more conducive to freedom of choice in reproduction. Restrictions on that freedom still remain, however. Among the possible policy alternatives suggested by students of population and demography, the U.S. federal and state governments have opted for those that tend to be less rigorous, emphasizing distributive and symbolic capabilities rather than regulative ones. It seems evident that, on balance, the U.S. federal and state political systems have exercised limited capability in response to population problems during the last ten years.

For political scientists, the importance of this finding lies in the nature of the research questions that result from attempts to explain current system capability. Why did these types of policies come about at this time in this country? What aspects of politics and the policy process may explain these observations about U.S. population policy?

Three types of studies are suggested here that seek to explain capability in terms of policy process, issue areas, and forms of governments. A fourth area for research would involve the study of policy outputs in terms of the quality of knowledge available in the population field. In the remaining pages of this chapter, I will attempt to summarize the suggested research areas and then to give a detailed discussion of each.

1. One way to explain policy outcomes such as population policy is by examining the *policy process* involved in the particular issue or problem. If each issue tends to produce a particular policy process and outcome, then the capability represented by a set of policies may vary according to the issue being considered. The capabilities of government in the United States, according to this view, could be explained in terms of the nature of the policy process surrounding the population issue. The subject for research is to investigate that process to see if the capability can be traced to features of the policy process.

2. Another explanation for a particular system capability would direct the researcher to study the general policy *pattern* of a system. The system may respond to a general class of issues in a certain way. For example, the area of population problems may be similar to other sorts of social and economic problems such as family issues. Over time, a political system develops a pattern of response to social problems that is different from its response to foreign policy issues or to demands for participation and rights. For some types of issues, regulative solutions may be selected, while others are consistently handled in symbolic terms. The task for research is to determine whether such patterns of system capability exist and if they are associated with certain classes of issues. If so, it may be demonstrable that population policies are part of a general pattern of policy making.

3. According to a third explanation, various types of political systems respond to all problems by relying on certain types of policies and excluding others. For example, the United States is often classified as a representative government because its institutions operate according to certain procedures and values. As such, the U.S. capability may be more limited, regardless of policy area, than that of another system which relies on more authoritarian procedures and values. At the same time, a less developed political system may respond to problems exercizing a more limited capability than does the United States.

4. The last area for study turns from the policy process to the scientific basis for policy making with regard to fertility. The major thrust of policy has been in developing family planning programs and services, which constitute low-to-moderate distributive capability. The emphasis on family planning may be due to the belief that this policy is effective and humane for achieving lowered fertility and that it will work. This belief, in turn, arises from scientific information on reproductive values and behavior in the United States. It would be useful to know if distributive policies are designed and then adopted because of the published information on fertility. In addition, those studies need to be evaluated before one can be sure that adequate policies have been designed.

The Policy Process

Several aspects of the political process observed during the consideration of population matters may be useful in explaining system output. The steps in the policy process discussed here are cultural norms, definition of issues, interest groups and their controversy, and politics in the population/health bureaucracy.

Cultural Norms. Developed governments are reversing a tradition of many hundreds of years when they try to influence reproductive behavior in an antinatalist direction. Nearly all world civilizations have been pronatalist.[25] The mores of religious and other basic social institutions have been overwhelmingly oriented toward promoting childbearing. Until recently, government policies have tended to reflect or reinforce this dominant tendency. While during the last century social and cultural attitudes have been changing to favor the limitation of fertility in industrialized systems, many traditional cultural norms remain. To what extent do these traditional norms still have salience for the policy process and thus help to explain the limited response of American political leaders to suggestions for fertility control?

In the United States, social and cultural norms have been changing from encouraging unlimited childbearing to emphasizing the basic right of parents to choose the size of their families. Family planning accommodates the rights of people to have only those children they want and can care for. To do this they need family planning services and information from public health institutions. KAP (knowledge, attitudes, and practice of contraception) studies throughout the world and the U.S. fertility surveys show that people have larger families than they want. The exponents of family planning expect that people, if provided with the means, will voluntarily limit their own fertility.

The emphasis on freedom of choice may channel government activity away from regulating fertility. Decisions in the *Griswold* and *Eisenstadt* cases were based on this point. *Griswold* rested on the Ninth Amendment, specifically the right to privacy in childbearing and sexual behavior. American political theory finds the freedom of choice argument easy to accommodate.[26] Any increase in government regulation in the direction of fertility limitation, however, would require drastic change of cultural norms. Is it the case that in the United States birth regulation is not seriously considered by policy makers due to the cultural environment surrounding the issue?

Defining the Issue. The limited capability of the U.S. system in population policy may be explained in the way the issues were defined.[27] A brief glance at the Senate and House hearings on population in 1965-66 and 1969-70 demonstrated the various contradictory themes.[28] It is not clear exactly what the purpose of the legislation that resulted is, but the divisions on the nature of the issue may explain the lukewarm political response. HEW representatives emphasized family planning as part of an overall health program, not really related to population problems at all. Family planning was, of course, the prerogative of public health groups for many years until the population crisis people picked it up. HEW officials emphasized the burden of unwanted children and the fact that five million American women did not have access to family planning information. They spoke of the fact that high fertility and poverty seem to go together.

The population experts spoke of population, food, and the environment as well as the problem of unwanted children. General population problems are quite different from that of "unwantedness," but they are often treated as one and the same thing.[29] Congressmen addressed themselves much more to the latter in their statements than to the former, but much of the testimony of the hearing was on both subjects.

Still others testified about the health problems of poor women who are subject to frequent pregnancies and about the poor health and limited future of their children. These people did not see the problem as one of the unplanned-for child — a concept which assumes the ability of planning children on the part of parents. The pattern of behavior that concerned these people was that of the tremendously fertile human female, burning out her life through continual pregnancies.

Opposition to the bills further confused the issue. Few argued about family planning or health aspects of the problem. Most emphasized the evil effects of governmental involvement in the matter: "The minute the Government steps into it, it is no longer voluntary. We believe that people have a right to seek this information on a private basis."[30] Others argued against the population crisis experts. They opposed the need for fertility control by humans, saying that passing the gift of life is a precious activity and there will be enough land and technology to accommodate all the new people.

What was the problem Congress was expected to solve with the legislation of 1970: health? individual rights? right to privacy? poverty? social and economic burdens of unwanted children? population growth? the balance between population growth and food production? It may be that each of these proplems would require different policies relying on various types of capabilities, all not necessarily compatible with each other. It appears that the congressional committees selected the immediate health and poverty issues, not the larger problem of population growth. The resulting policy, which was entirely distributive, may be compatible with this limited definition of the issue.

This is only a brief view of the hearings on one family planning policy at the national level. Much more study could be made of the debates, reports, and media positions on the issue to determine the various points of view, how the problem was ultimately defined, and the effect of that definition on the policy outcome.[31]

Many of the population policies are to be found at the state level. Each state has different family planning policies and institutions, and these may be the result of varying policy processes. The issue is defined differently in the various states, resulting in numerous policy outcomes. Studies of state policies and processes hold forth promise for instructive comparative results.

Interest Groups. What sorts of interest groups are active on these population policy issues? At the national hearings, few groups represented an opposition to family planning policy. What happened to the opposition? Is there any opposition to population policies? If so, what is it and how does it affect the policy process? Is family planning an issue that has no opposition because it has few advocates, or because it doesn't do anything? In this case, is moderate capability the result of too much controversy or too little?

At the state level the questions of abortion and sterilization produce more well-defined arguments. Do the types of groups promoting repeal of abortion laws account for the fact that few states have selected that more drastic alternative? It may be that those groups which advocate broad family planning programs, child care and abortion-on-demand such as the women's movement groups are less effective than other types of groups, perhaps because legislators are less receptive to these groups. Would the system response be stronger if more acceptable groups advocated strong policies?

Politics of Bureaucracy. The involvement of one interest group, — the bureaucracy of the Department of Health, Education, and Welfare and associated groups of individuals — warrants special attention. The testimony of one HEW secretary after another opposed the family planning bill, although not family planning itself, because the bill specified structures for administration of the program. They said they didn't like to be handicapped by legislation specifying administrative procedures. There was also mention made during the hearings of the conflict among the various agencies involved in health and medical research, where heart, cancer, and tuberculosis research teams have had priority and resent the favorable treatment of a new research area in reproduction. Population and family planning had received funds before 1970, but HEW had not used them to provide services or support research to any great extent.[32] The level of capability of any government will be affected by the motivations of bureaucrats and the dynamics of administrative politics. The limited capability of the U.S. political system may be understood in part by the nature of the bureaucratic politics involved in the population issue. Of course, the bureaucracy, both as an interest group and as implementor of policy, can be studied at the state level as well.

These four areas of the policy process — cultural norms, issue definition, interest groups, and bureaucratic politics — have been suggested as fruitful for research into population policy capability by political scientists. Once this policy process has been adequately characterized by researchers, broader comparative questions can be considered.

Patterns of System Capability

Is the population policy process unique to this issue, or is it part of a general pattern of decision making and capability that can be associated with *types* of issues? Theodore Lowi has suggested that process and output patterns on types of issues develop over time in American politics.[33] He described the governmental response to social problems as "interest group liberalism." Is the pattern of policy making on population consistent with the theory of interest group liberalism?

Lowi states that decisions are made through bargaining among private interests, clustered around a portion of the public bureaucracy, especially the independent regulatory agencies. The line between the public and private domain becomes hopelessly muddled. In some areas such as agriculture, the private groups have taken over all the decision making. The role of Congress, the only formal democratic policy-making institution, has become that of outlining a problem area, appropriating funds, and letting the interested parties work out all the guidelines for their distribution.

Planning is impossible, almost heretical, to the tenets of interest group liberalism because of the emphasis on bargaining step by step. Only in times of crisis in the international sphere does direct strong action occur. Of course, Lowi is just one scholar analyzing the capability of the U.S. political system, but his work could serve as a comparative basis for studying the population policy process. If his is an accurate view, such an analysis would mean that control of population and planning for a stable population would be nearly impossible in the American system until the crisis is upon us. Comparing the theory of interest group liberalism with actual population policies would direct research toward the questions concerning the way funds are allocated in HEW for family planning and population research. Such research would test the concept of interest group liberalism as a tool for understanding American politics.

More and more studies are likely to appear attempting to characterize the policy process in terms of types of issues, policies, and capabilities. As they do, the study of population policy capability and its explanation can be classified as a way of determining if patterns of decision making are associated with various *types* of issues and interests.

System Capability and the Form of Government

To what extent is the capability of the U.S. political sysmen in response to population problems a result of the particular form of government and its supporting ideologies? Is the fact that the Unites States does not opt for regulative solutions to certain types of problems due to the fact that it is a representative system, based on concepts of limited government, individual liberty, and free choice? If so, it seems logical to expect greater regulative capabilities in more authoritarian political systems which have roughly the same levels of economic and social development. At the same time, limited distributive and symbolic capabilities would be the pattern expected in other developed representative systems with similar traditions of liberty and limited government such as Great Britain. These questions require research into the capabilities in the population policy field of other developed states.

Only a few studies of comparative policy outputs other than population have been completed.[34] One study of social security in the United States and the USSR indicated little difference in actual policy output despite the fact that the USSR has a different ideology and a more authoritarian government than the United States.[35] Cutright's study of social security failed to link variations in the content of social security policies to differences in forms of government.[36] Much work is needed in the area of policy analysis, and studies of population policies and system capabilities would contribute to the development of concepts and methodologies in this field. If there is little basis to support the contention that system capability varies with system characteristics, then further questions can be asked about similarities in attitudes toward reproduction in spite of variations in cultural norms and policy processes within systems.

Population Policy and Individual Behavior

A major part of U.S. population policy is providing family planning services to those who cannot obtain these services for themselves. This policy is distributive but limited in coverage. Opting for this policy may be attributed to the information available about the reproductive attitudes and behavior of American women.[37] Many advocate family planning as the most appropriate policy for affecting reproductive behavior because studies indicate that the general willingness of women to limit family size is hampered by unavailability of services. If current fertility studies are the basis for policy making in the United States, then it would be useful for policy analysts to evaluate their adequacy and suggest further necessary research for the design of the most effective policies possible in the area. Along these lines, further research into reproductive behavior in the United States and other developed countries would aid us in evaluating the ultimate effectiveness of family planning policies and help us in designing other policy alternatives of similar capability and level of performance, that is, moderate distributive capabilities.

In order to solve any public problem, the causes must be fully investigated to determine which measures will produce desired changes in behavior. If decision makers recognized and agreed that the problem of population was something to be concerned about and that it was necessary to design policies to limit fertility, they would be hard pressed to determine effective action to reach that goal. The state of our knowledge on fertility, reproduction, and childbearing makes this goal impossible. A brief examination of existing information about reproductive behavior suggests its limits as a basis for designing effective population policies.

To say that high fertility is caused by people having too many babies is a tautology. It is also an apt summary of present knowledge about human reproductive behavior. There are numbers of studies of fertility, it is true, but they *describe* the characteristics of groups with higher fertility compared with those of lower fertility. They seldom explore causes or attempt explanations by delving into reproductive behavior and the decision-making process involved in childbearing.[38]

Current fertility research emphasizes the relationships between social and economic characteristics — education, race, social status, income and class — and fertility characteristics such as family size and child spacing. These studies are useful, but they have not enabled us to say that some women have more children than others because they have less education, or because they are black, or because they are poor, or because they got married when they were fifteen. What processes of decision making are involved in having children, and under what circumstances are goals formed or changed with regard to family size? Most importantly, we need to know why people have children and what children mean to them.

Family planning programs are based on the assumption that people are willing and capable of planning their future time. This crucial assumption is questionable. It has not been systematically studied, and there is doubt that planning behavior is itself widespread, especially in young people. The first years of childbearing are crucial to the ultimate fertility patterns of women. Does the ability to plan change with age, or is it linked to personality characteristics or levels of formal education?

Important information on childbearing and planning cannot be obtained by using survey techniques alone. The knowledge, attitude, practice studies have severe limits, despite the fact that they have been used extensively on a worldwide basis.[39] The National Fertility Surveys in the United States, although more intensive, share the inadequacy of survey techinques in gaining complete information about reproductive behavior, the meaning of children, and the ability to plan. The matter of reproduction — childbearing — is extremely private and basic to one's life, hence extremely difficult to research.

It is likely that researchers, in designing fertility surveys, are structuring responses, since they do not know the respondents' frame of reference when dealing with the topics of sex and childbearing. This inadequacy may be just as true for studies done among many groups in the United States, as it is when American survey researchers tackle the problem in Latin America, Africa, or Asia. It may be necessary to supplement these techniques with other methods such as in-depth and specialized interviewing and participant observation, borrowing a page or two from the anthropologists' method book.

In sum, it may be quite mistaken to think that public agencies can develop policies that are effective in regulating this form of private behavior. Before a political system can opt for more extensive policies that represent greater system capability, there must be better evidence that the policies are based on a realistic understanding of relevant individual behavior. This type of research may not seem to be the proper business of political scientists. Yet, as students of politics and the policy process, we will be limited in our understanding of policies and their impact unless critical information about target populations is forthcoming.

Conclusions

The capability of the U.S. system in policy making with regard to reproduction in the last decade has emphasized moderate distributive and symbolic action, while utilizing regulative powers only to a limited extent. In seeking explanations for this policy response, several areas for research by political scientists have been suggested. The topics elaborated in this chapter were selected to pertain to the concerns of the political science discipline in testing propositions about policies in a comparative context. Therefore, information in any of these research areas would contribute to the further development of comparative policy studies and is certainly not of interest to the population field alone. At the same time, such information may aid the policy maker in his evaluation of programs affecting fertility in other developed countries.

One clear implication of this study is that sooner or later the scholar who travels down the path of research in the population field learns that he or she needs the help of colleagues in social psychology, economics, demography, geography, and anthropology. The entire area of population research, whether with regard to the problem of population growth, the effect of population patterns on policies, the policy process in population, administration and implementation of population policies, or the nature of reproductive behavior of target populations, requires the combined attention of all the social sciences.

Notes

1. Luke T. Lee, "Law and Family Planning," *Studies in Family Planning* 2, no. 4 (April 1971).

2. Comparative policy study is a new field. One of its immediate concerns is to complete the exploratory studies necessary to the development of compara-

tive concepts. See Richard Rose, "Why Comparative Policy Studies?" *Policy Studies Journal* 1 (Autumn 1972): 14-16.

3. In attempting to collect information on the actions of state governments, it soon becomes painfully clear that a central clearinghouse for state legislative and administrative action is needed. Otherwise, one can never be sure that all policies are included.

4. There are a number of studies of public policy, but most of them have been case studies with little attention to problems of classification and comparative analysis. An exception is Lewis Froman, "The Categorization of Policy Content," in Austin Ranney, ed., *Political Science and Public Policy* (Chicago: Markham, 1968); and "An Analysis of Public Policies in Cities," *Journal of Politics* 29 (February 1967): 94-108. Froman was limited in his work, however, by the inadequacy of the central concept.

5. Charles Anderson introduces the concept of policy tools based on the various sources of state power: as the locus of authority and consent, monopoly of force and control, the power to spend in the public interest, and the power to tax. He uses these concepts to classify policies dealing with economic development in *Politics and Economic Change in Latin America* (New York: Van Nostrand, 1967), pp. 47-67. Anderson further elaborates on the use of these policy tools in comparative policy analysis in "Comparative Policy Analysis: The Design of Measures," *Comparative Politics* 4 (October 1971): 117-32.

6. A number of theorists have developed classification schemes for capabilities. These concepts were used by Gabriel Almond and G. Bingham Powell, *Comparative Politics: A Developmental Approach* (Boston: Little, Brown, 1968). Almond and Powell had a fourth category, that of extractive capability. This type was not included in this framework because none of the policies studied employed the use of the taxing policy tool. Theodore Lowi has also developed a scheme for classifying policy that is slightly different from that of Almond and Powell. See his "American Business, Public Policy, Case Studies, and Political Theory," *World Politics* 16 (June 1964): 677-715.

7. Anderson, "Comparative Policy Analysis," (n. 5).

8. Ranking observations into low, medium, and high categories has limitations, because it does not allow for the variation within categories which is bound to occur. This is a simple classification to characterize the nature of a set of policies. A more detailed study would contribute fine measuring tools for policy variation.

9. Anderson, "Comparative Policy Analysis," (n. 5).

10. Many developed countries, including the United States, have had a predominantly pronatalist set of policies until the last decade. A set of pronatalist policies includes the strict control or illegality of the manufacture, use, and sale of contraceptives; prohibition of abortions; and sterilization viewed as a medical, not a reproductive, matter.

11. See especially Bernard Berelson, "Beyond Family Planning," *Studies in Family Planning*, no. 38 (February 1969) and Lee (n. 1).

12. Ray David Weinberg, *Laws Governing Family Planning* (New York: Oceana Publications, 1968).

13. There are a number of sources where information on state policies may be found; they are scattered through the literature about family planning in the United States. Some of the sources for this table were Weinberg, ibid.; Joseph Goldstein and Jay Katz, *The Family and the Law* (New York: Free Press, 1965); *Journal of Marriage and the Family* 30 (May 1968), entire issue. Other sources for U.S. policies include *Congressional Quarterly Almanac,* 1969, 1970; U.S. Senate, *Hearings,* Committee on Labor and Public Welfare, Subcommittee on Employment, Manpower, and Poverty, S 2993, 1966; U.S. Senate, *Hearings,* Subcommittee on Health, "Family Planning and Population Research," December 1969-February 1970, S 2108, S 3219; *New York Times Index.*

14. *Griswold* v. *Connecticut,* 381 US 479 (1964).

15. *Eisenstadt* v. *Baird,* 92 SCT. 1029 (1972).

16. *Dandridge* v. *Williams,* 397 US 471 (1970).

17. All statements in the following section were found in *Congress and the Nation,* vol. 2, and *CQ Almanac,* 1969, 1970.

18. Commission on Population Growth and the American Future, *Population and the American Future* (New York: New American Library, 1972), pp. 166-67.

19. Some family planning in the South had been available through Social Security programs since the 1930s. Other limited programs were included in the Comprehensive Health and Planning Act (PL 89-749) 1966, and the Amendment to the Equal Opportunity Act (PL 90-248) 1967. These programs served over one million women.

20. Commission on Population Growth and the American Future (n. 18), p. 182.

21. 93 *S. Ct.* 705, 1973.

22. See notes 14 and 15.

23. U.S. Department of Health, Education, and Welfare, "Selected Information on Projects Currently Funded by the National Center for Family Planning Services," June 1971.

24. Ibid.

25. D.V. Glass, *Population Policies and Movements in Europe* (London: Oxford University Press, 1967), esp. pp. 86-98; J.J. Spengler and Otis D. Duncan, *Population Theory and Policy* (Glencoe: Free Press, 1956).

26. A.E. Keir Nash, "Going Beyond John Locke? Influencing American Population Growth," *Milbank Memorial Fund Quarterly* 49 (January 1971): 7-31.

27. Elihu Bergman, *The Politics of Population USA: A Critique of the Policy Process* (Chapel Hill: Carolina Population Center Population Program and Policy Design Series no. 5, 1971), esp. p. 168.

28. Senator Gruening conducted Hearings in 1965 for the Subcommittee on Foreign Aid of the Senate Committee on Government Operations. The result is several volumes of testimony on the world population crisis and recommended government action. The 1969-70 Hearings were conducted pertaining to the Family Planning and Population Research Act of 1970.

29. This is especially the case when fertility studies done in the United States are cited. Because many mothers bear children they did not plan and do not want, one is tempted to advocate reduction in unwanted births as a means of fertility control, thus not having to face the more sensitive matter of actually reducing the fertility rate by government policy. See the controversy between Judith Blake and Harkavy, et al. in Daniel Callahan, ed., *The American Population Debate* (New York: Doubleday, 1971), pp. 298-359.

30. Testimony of Mrs. David R. Mogilka, Chairman, Reverence for Life in America, in U.S. House, *Hearings,* Interstate and Foreign Commerce Subcommittee on Public Health and Welfare, August, 1970, p. 242.

31. Bergman (n. 26) has done such a study at the national level.

32. Senators Gruening and Tydings, especially, delivered long indictments of HEW's record. The following report was also presented as evidence: Oscar Harkavy and Frederick Jaffe, "Implementing DHEW Policy on Family Planning and Population," September 1967.

33. Theodore Lowi, *The End of Liberalism* (New York: Norton, 1969).

34. J. Burkus, "Some Aspects of Income Distribution through Social Security in Four Western European Countries," *International Labor Review* 97 (February 1968): 167-90; Walter Galenson, "Social Security and Economic Development: A Quantitative Approach," *Industrial Labor Relations Review* 29 (July 1968): 559-69; John Miller and Ralph Gakenheimer, eds., *Latin American Urban Policies and the Social Sciences* (Beverly Hills: Sage, 1971); Gary Wynia, *"Policy and Bureaucracy in Central America: A Comparative Study,"* (Ph.D. dissertation, University of Wisconsin, 1970).

35. Gaston V. Rimlinger, "Social Security and Society: An East-West Comparison," *Social Science Quarterly* 50 (December 1969): 494-506.

36. Phillips Cutright, "Political Structure, Economic Development, and National Security Programs," *American Journal of Sociology* 70 (March 1965): 537-48.

37. There are many fertility studies of American women. One of the most recent and complete is the 1965 National Fertility Survey: Norman Ryder and Charles Westoff, *Reproduction in the United States* (Princeton: Princeton University Press, 1971). Data from the 1970 fertility survey are discussed in the 1972 Population Commission Report (n. 18).

38. There are some exceptions such as Lee Rainwater's *And the Poor Get Children* (Chicago: Quadrangle Books, 1960).

39. Kenneth Godwin, "The Structure of Mass Attitides in the United States and Latin America," in Richard L. Clinton and R. Kenneth Godwin, eds., *Research in the Politics of Population* (Lexington, Mass.: D.C. Heath and Company, 1972). Godwin evaluates KAP studies, discusses their inadequacies, and suggests alternatives. See also his chapter in the present volume.

20 Population Politics and Political Science in Developed Nations: Some Critical Observations

Michael E. Kraft

The development of the politics and population literature in the past two years has been distinctly impressive, both quantitatively and qualitatively. We now have more analyses of the interplay of population and political forces and of a higher quality than one would have guessed likely a few years ago. In particular, the thoughtful and sophisticated treatments in the present series of volumes and the efforts of political scientists involved with the Commission on Population Growth and the American Future represent a commendable quantum jump in an emerging aggregation of the discipline. This productivity in part compensates for the unfortunately belated discovery of the significance of population patterns by political scientists and bodes well for future accomplishments. Yet the literature most certainly has not realized its full potential and often seems to drift off into, in my view, less than desirable directions. The three chapters in this section indicate the valuable additions of recent work as well as the limitations of present lines of research. Reflection on their contents should clarify the objections I suggest and point to at least a few correctives.

A disclaimer of a sort is appropriate before venturing some criticism, praise, and suggestions for research. Much of the writing on population and politics by political scientists has come from individuals intimately plugged into profession- ally specialized channels. Some are associated with institutes for population studies, some have been involved with governmental commissions or agencies, and some are merely closely tied to such channels through collegial relationships. There are obviously advantages to such a condition (which is probably not all that unique in developing literatures), but the disadvantages go unnoticed. Certainly knowledge of population data and some degree of specialization are prerequisite for intelligent commentary. But professionalization also has its costs, as Bergman and Nash have noted so well with respect to the mobilization of bias in demographic and policy making circles.[1] Those of us falling somewhat more toward the amateur side of a population politics professionalism scale, while relatively deprived of the shared experience and conventional wisdom, may be more willing — or simply likely — to cast a more critical eye at the accumulating literature. Unburdened by the conceptual and normative biases of the professionals, we may demand, along with students and nonpolitical scientists, a more meaningful and utilitarian product than generally produced. We can learn a lot from students and population activists in this regard. They are

273

more likely than we are to ask simplistic, subversive, and embarrassing questions: Exactly what do you hope to accomplish through social science research? Why do you do the kind of research you do? To whom are you addressing yourselves? To other political scientists? To government officials? To a concerned public? What have you learned that is particularly valuable and worth the effort? What difference does political research actually make anyway? Who will read it and act on it? Wouldn't we be a lot better off if specialists in politics directed their attention to more practical political questions rather than engage in diversionary academic exercises? If you don't do that who will?

Although occasionally raised by those concerned with the normative dimensions of population politics, these kinds of questions are insufficiently addressed by many individuals deeply involved with empirical and analytic research, much as are similar questions in other areas of the discipline. In part as a consequence, the developing literature lacks clarity and purpose. Perhaps this reflects uncertainty and disagreement among practitioners over the function and utility of political research. Whatever the cause of this malady, we need to remind ourselves rather frequently of some basic questions: Do political scientists really have much to contribute to a dialogue on population and politics, or do we excessively rationalize the value of present accomplishments out of habitual professional immodesty? If we do have something to say, what needs saying? What do we need to know for what purpose? Or to state Robert Lynd's old question addressed to social scientists in general, "knowledge for what?"[2] And what research is of the highest priority? Since we cannot do everything, where should we concentrate our limited resources of time and energy?

Two recent — and I think fairly representative — statements on the direction of political research on population matters are relevant to such questions and to a review of the three chapters in this section. Both give partially wrong-headed advice, it seems to me, which may lead to an unfortunate waste of whatever talents political scientists do possess. In his introduction to the collection of political research reports for the Commission on Population Growth and the American Future, *Governance and Population: The Governmental Implications of Population Change*, A.E. Keir Nash comments that these essays

do not exhaust the potential ways of attempting to explore the ties between politics and population. Indeed, to use the jargon of contemporary social science, they are largely limited to looking at government and politics as dependent variables affected by changes in the independent variables of population and population policy. It would be quite proper to urge that matters could well work the other way around, to argue that government affects the characteristics of a population.[3]

Although, as Nash notes, other volumes for the commission take up the analysis when the relationship is reversed, it is instructive that these political scientists have approached the question in the way they have. There are good reasons for this result (the major one appears to be that this is what the commission wanted to know), and no doubt there is considerable value in projecting how governmental institutions and public services will be affected by population change. Following this approach does mean, however, that other questions are not being addressed or given the same degree of attention. It also seems to mean that population is accepted as a given, while we search for how best to manage the eventual problems. Charles Lindblom's criticism in another context of "policy analysis" (broadly defined) as "conservative and superficial" is appropriate here. Policy analysis is often conservative, Lindblom says, "because it does not ask radical questions about fundamental features of the social structure." And it is superficial "because it considers only those ways of dealing with policy that are close cousins to existing practices."[4] If there is a need to ask at least some "radical" and nonsuperficial questions, then the bias of these kinds of essays should be recognized, and some greater effort ought to be made to study the reverse of the equation to which Nash refers — and other matters which promise to be occasionally subversive. There has been precious little research to date, for example, on how the structure of political institutions, the nature of decision making, and the attitudes of political elites affect population change. And political scientists seem very reluctant to engage in "nonprofessional" strategic research on how to promote the achievement of national and international population policies, especially since there is no consensus on the severity of the problems or on acceptable policies.

The other statement to which I refer, by Terry L. McCoy, makes a number of useful observations on research needs and the capabilities of political scientists but in the process sets a goal which is equally challengeable.[5] McCoy seems preoccupied with the payoff such endeavors provide for advance of the discipline itself rather than for understanding and resolution of population problems. He reminds us that

while political scientists have problem-solving obligations and capabilities, they also have a responsibility to expand the general body of knowledge of their profession. In jumping from one crisis to the next, we often lose sight of our discipline. . ."[6]

He concludes by saying that in

tackling population or any other societal problem, political scientists should be self-conscious about their discipline. We should be guided by this question: What will we know of a general nature as a result of studying this particular problem which will enable us better to foresee and understand subsequent problems?[7]

Although the history of policy analysis and the controversial nature of population problems suggest some of the caution McCoy advocates, we ought seriously to question the notion that wherever there is no great disciplinary reward political scientists should keep hands off. Must all of us engage only or primarily in work which further refines the theoretical and methodological capacity of the discipline? It would be unfortuante if that were so. And it would be particularly regrettable if any sizable number of population researchers were diverted from more utilitarian interdisciplinary and problem-solving goals, whether those goals be critical evaluation of population proposals and policies or empirical studies of population policy making and strategies of change. I should think that contemporary norms in the discipline would guarantee sufficient theoretical research in any case. The more important concern as this subfield develops is to discourage overconcentration on rigid methodology and the building of analytic frameworks and theories to the neglect of creative, exploratory, substantive, and applied or "action" research.[8]

I mention these two comments on population research because they help put the Bergman, Chaney, and Stetson chapters and the question of research needs into a convenient perspective. In my mind the central questions are: How have governments responded to the challenge of population problems (particularly growth)? What accounts for the response (or nonresponse)? And what seem to be the conditions under which more "adequate" responses are likely? We want to ask how policy has been initiated, formulated, enacted, and implemented (and with what effects), and if no present population policy exists or if present policies are deemed inadequate, what policies are "necessary" or "desirable" and how they might be advanced toward adoption? In particular, what are the major obstacles or constraints throughout the policy process preventing adoption and effective implementation of such policies? If these are still important questions and insufficiently investigated at present — as I clearly think is the case — then perhaps the drift of research toward the impact of population growth on governmental services and toward primary concern for the development of the political science discipline should be reversed by a renewed emphasis on these basic concerns.[9]

Having said this much, let me turn to the three chapters which make up this section of the book. Since they are rather discrete efforts, a sensible procedure would be to discuss key questions arising with each, to note common concerns, and to ask what can be said in sum about light being shed on population and politics in developed nations, with, as might be expected, special emphasis on the United States.

Bergman's chapter "Values and Choices: Some Anomalies in American Population Policy Making," provides a good starting point since he directly challenges the notion that population growth should be our major worry. He faults the Population Commission and population activists for concentrating more or less exclusively on growth and thereby ignoring other important problems, for example, population distribution and residential mobility. The present allocation of attention and priorities is not trivial, he argues, because it reflects the dominant value orientation among establishment elites, demographers, and other populationists and contributes to the perpetuation of racism and injustice in American society through exclusion of these problems from the population agenda. Such exclusion restricts the agenda to safer, less controversial issues, helps avoid or suppress conflict, and protects the influence of present elites in the making of public policy.

Bergman associates himself with the position taken by one of the dissenting members of the commission, Paul Cornely. Cornely notes in the "Separate Statements" section of the report that he

firmly believes that population growth is indeed not the major problem in our society and that, of more import, is the need for a radical rearrangement of our values and priorities as well as the relation of man to himself, of men to each other, and to the earth from which we sprang.[10]

By offering a "new look" of political realism, by calling attention to the existence of "values, stratification, and racism," Bergman argues that we can more accurately appraise governmental actions on population problems as well as pose more meaningful research questions. Through attention to omnipresent value choices in public policy and to inequalities and discrimination in American society we can balance the distortion of apolitical, establishment, and technocratic visions of population policy making. And through recognition of the importance of agenda setting — how issues arise, how they are defined and by whom, and why policy makers concentrate their attention and energy on some issues and policy options and not others — Bergman suggests that we can add a new dimension to the study of policy-making processes and clarify the anomalies in those processes. Not only would the "structure in which American population policy is made" be revealed through such analysis, but there is likely to be a spinoff of propositions about the "conditions of American policy making generally." To this end he offers a conceptual framework with which such research can be guided, in general reflecting a systems approach to political decision making with special emphasis on predecision making, nondecision making, and the role of nonparticipants and nongovernmental institutions.

As in his earlier work on the mobilization of bias within the American population policy process, Bergman challenges our conventional wisdom about the democratic and representative character of policy making and the universality of concern and benefits.[11] He is asking "radical" and nonsuperficial questions and provoking us to rethink casual assumptions. By urging conscious attention to matters of values and the distribution of power in society and what, given that context of policy making, our research priorities should be, Bergman gets to the heart of some important questions. However, there are some difficulties with his analysis that deserve to be made explicit.

Along with a good many others, Bergman finds cause to alter his view of the seriousness of population growth in the United States in the data released in the past year by the Bureau of the Census. He notes that these data "demonstrate a dramatic decline in American fertility rates" to a point below the replacement level of 2.1 children per family. "If this trend continues," he says, "the

American population would stop growing in seventy years. Thus, because of modernized demographic behavior the problem of American population growth appears to be well along the road to solution." Several times he drives home the same point. The population growth problem is "apparently solved" and "with growth far down the track to solution, and distribution hardly off the starting block, why the continuing preoccupation with growth?" The argument is the chief one, it appears, justifying a switch to other policy questions and other research directions. Yet I am unpersuaded that present evidence of the decline in fertility rates is sufficient cause to leap to optimistic conclusions. Assuming a 2.1 child level were maintained for seventy years, a not necessarily safe assumption as demographers keep reminding us, the American population would level off at about 320 million people (without immigration).[12] Even if we could be assured that such a goal were possible within seventy years without governmental efforts, this begs the question of whether 320 million is beyond the "optimum" population for the United States, given our limited environmental "carrying capacity" and our ravenous appetite for energy and national resources. If sober and respected ecologists (and laymen) are alarmed over the environmental effects of our present 210 million people, we should raise the question of whether an additional 110 million (over 50 percent increase) is desirable or tolerable. I am not about to make great claims on the basis of present data and seventy-year projections, nor to claim that ecological criteria outweigh all others, nor that ecological problems should be "solved" through population limitation rather than through changes in technology and lifestyles. The point is, however, that neither can we afford the luxury of conjuring up optimistic visions of the spontaneous abatement of population growth and its consequences in the near future. And needless to say, arguments that growth is no longer a public problem hardly contribute to the development of public concern for, and policies on, population limitation.

A related point is made that the commission and other population elites consciously or unconsciously avoided raising controversial questions (e.g., of racial discrimination) and focused instead on "policy options around which a broad consensus is more likely to develop." Does this position imply that abortion was not controversial when the commission strongly (and with great, if unwanted, publicity) advocated liberalized abortion laws, given President Nixon's announced contrary position and the inevitable reaction of antiabortion groups? Or does it imply that advocating population stabilization itself was not a controversial position during a year in which the Population Stabilization Resolution in the United States Congress was defeated (due, it seems, to the intense opposition of antiabortion groups)?[13] To be sure, a number of population activists found the commission entirely too timid in its recommendations. Like most governmental commissions, this one was fairly moderate in its conclusions, and, like most, its impact may be less than political novitiates might imagine.[14] I concur with Bergman's point that racial controversies were downplayed and that the commission was on the whole moderate in its recommendations, but I must take issue with his assertion that a focus on growth represented a "safe" and inconsequential decision.

To the extent that Bergman is suggesting that by broadening our focus on population "change" and by widening the scope of political conflict we are better off both intellectually and morally, there is little reason to dissent. Expanding our definition of population problems and our awareness of the political and ethical ramifications of population policies is not undesirable, as Garland and Trudeau have argued at some length.[15] In fact, it is rapidly becoming unavoidable in an intellectual market where criticism of ecological and population change enthusiasts (e.g., the authors of *The Limits to Growth*) frequently turns on their presumed inattention to inequalities of wealth and status in the world and where population policies are assailed by minority groups having little to say in their formulation.[16] We ought to exercise some care, however, that the meaning of population policy is not so stretched that every other domestic problem becomes a necessary appendage. To say that racism, housing, poverty, and health care are also important political concerns is not to say that they must be tightly bound to population proposals. Rather, we should insure that the consequences of proposals, both intended and unintended, are thoroughly explored before pressing for their enactment. And decision-making processes should be sufficiently representative that bias is made less likely.

Let me note finally that Bergman's suggestion that an agenda-setting approach to population policy making has substantial analytic payoff is an important statement. Much of the significant behavior of American political elites can be understood through the use of concepts such as agendas, attention, definition of the problems, nondecision making, and the like, especially in the early stages of the policy process as a new issue develops and is taken up (or not taken up) by political actors. How problems are conceptualized has an important bearing on the nature and eventual outcome of conflicts.[17] Definition of the problem shapes the decision maker's perception of facts and values, his receptivity to information and advice, whose knowledge he considers expert, and how much attention he gives to various dimensions of a problem (e.g., population distribution). And given the fact that high-level decision makers are extraordinarily busy and normally beset with a very large number of competing significant demands and issues, and given their limited resources of time, energy, and attention, anything other than marginal and superficial attention to population issues would be unexpected. These very real limits are often unappreciated by analysts of the population policy process, some of whom see purposeful nondecision making (direct suppression of issues) rather than a more benign inattention. But before serious consideration of policy alternatives can take place, there must be a fairly high degree of attention and concern among policy elites, and this requires special motivation to pay attention to a problem (especially growth), which is low in visibility and which poses a seemingly distant and contingent threat of unknown dimensions. Under these conditions the chances are good that decision makers' (e.g., congressmen's) knowledge of population problems will be highly incomplete, their understanding of complex matters of public policy imperfect, and their perception of the facts distorted. They may well incline toward apathy, ignorance, and (consequent?) unwarranted optimism. The same can be said of the American public. With the exception of the abortion question, population problems are not especially salient, and the modest degree of concern shown in recent surveys has not been translated into significant political demand. With the recent well-publicized drop in fertility rates we might even expect a reduction in public interest in population growth. One could suggest, in short, that much could be learned about the politics of population by attempting to answer the question: Who pays attention to what, when, how, and why, under what conditions, and with what consequences for himself, for public policy, and for the larger social-economic-political-environmental system?[18]

Chaney's chapter, "Women and Population: Some Key Policy, Research, and Action Issues," is concerned with essentially two questions: (1) the level of involvement of women in population research, policy making, and the implementation of programs; and (2) the need for research and action on provision of alternative roles for women as a major means of affecting population growth. Like Bergman, she advocates more representative and democratic processes and is critical of the relative omission of "minorities" (women) from policy making. The argument is persuasive. Especially in a policy area "which so intimately affects the lives of women," she asks, why are so few women involved?

Women are after all, the most important target group of population programs, and it is logical that they be involved at the policy making and implementation levels just as blacks, the chicanos, the poor, have won the right to sit on the councils deciding their fate.

Beyond the justice of equal representation, Chaney poses an important question never fully answered: "Would women's involvement make any difference in policy outputs?" It would seem that a higher level of participation would make a major difference in those nations where women's roles are highly constricted at present. It is more difficult to say that generally increasing the number of women on commissions, task forces, and in policy-making bodies would result in greatly different policy outputs. Clearly, this depends upon whether women would bring a unique perspective to such discussions and upon who assumed such positions. One also wonders whether those who evince so much concern for "democratic" decision making resent the Supreme Court's recent resolution of the abortion issue[19] on the grounds that the Court is an elitist institution and not notably female in composition. The point is that we need not demand that all population decision making adhere to strict representational norms and need not assume that an unacceptable bias in results is inherent in situations of less than full equality (or female dominance).

The point is not worth quibbling over here, however. More important is recognition that the political role of women *is* significant and that their potential for exercising some influence over the direction of public policy around the world is not yet being realized particularly well. In addition to malrepresentation on commissions and task forces, the low level of participation of women in electoral and group politics is particularly curious. If consideration and adoption of policy proposals are strongly dependent upon sufficient public demand for action then women's groups constitute a highly significant political resource in the population movement, as the evolution (and apparent unsuccess) of the Equal Rights Amendment battle in the United States illustrates. Rather than fault governments for excluding women from active policy-making roles, however, we might ask of women — as of the public generally — why population policy is not of sufficient concern to motivate them to organize and make demands upon those governments. That is, the cause of nonparticipation in population politics — as in politics generally — surely lies as much in citizen inattention and unconcern as in conscious exclusion by ruling elites. Exclusion is far less likely when women constitute a powerful political force. The recent development in the United States of the National Women's Political Caucus and the National Organization for Women and their actions on the abortion and family planning fronts, for examole, indicate the potential for interest group activity and perhaps suggest how public unconcern and nonparticipation can be altered.

Of equal significance in Chaney's discussion of the need for alternative roles for women and the kind of immediate and "action-oriented" research which would clarify the feasibility and effectiveness of policy options. Since present evidence seems to indicate that "the key [to population limitation] is not in technique but in individual and/or societal attitudes" — in preference for smaller family size as a personal goal — a central manipulable variable in population policy is provision of "meaningful and challenging" alternatives to motherhood and home maintenance. But since we know little about the relationships between "women's involvement outside the home and lowered fertility," research on alternative roles, women's motivation, and the consequences of adopting governmental programs or of encouraging private efforts is indispensable to sound action. This would facilitate one of the most promising moves "beyond family planning" toward lowering the fertility rate.

Chaney raises a number of important questions in this regard and reviews some of the more reliable findings on the subject. As she points out, we really do not know if "governments *can* effectively influence the birth rate." Experience seems to indicate that women will not increase or decrease their fertility on demand of governments, an assumption inadequately confronted in the past. And the incredible complexity of social, economic, and political relationships adds to the difficulty of diagnosing policy requirements. Perhaps governments can only encourage general societal changes which seem to lead to lower fertility rates (economic development, increasing education and upgrading the status of women). Such considerations suggest that before advocating highly coercive policies of one type or another, we need to know the answers to these questions. It is entirely possible that population size can be maintained at "acceptable" levels with the proper mix of distributive and self-regulating policies. And there seems to be wide agreement that population problems should be solved, if possible, with maximum concern for individual freedom and democratic norms. More evidence on the effectiveness of such policies would promote the achievement of these goals and ward off otherwise inevitably more coercive and less democratic solutions.

Furthermore, we can hardly blame decision makers for not supporting controversial and possibly costly programs until they are given reasonable assurance that the programs will work — and are necessary. Accumulation of reliable knowledge on women's attitudes and motivation — and in particular on the effect of the availability of alternative roles — should at least take some of the uncertainty and guesswork out of policy making and thereby increase the likelihood that decision makers will be more responsive to policy needs. Governments and private organizations will still have to act in the meantime, however, and while engaging in detailed empirical research on the questions Chaney poses, perhaps social scientists can also hazard some professional speculation as policy advice. We will never know enough to make absolutely reliable predictions, but given the need for launching new initiatives we should be experimenting much more with pilot programs, even if based on an inexact policy science. All government programs are, after all, potentially subject to critical evaluation, review, and change.

Chaney's essay, in brief, while not as directly concerned with what governments have done or are willing to do and with power and political decision making as the Bergman and Stetson chapters, is highly "relevant" in discussing what policies and other actions will work to reduce population growth. By addressing itself to practical, important, and feasible topics, the essay indicates that there are alternatives to excessively theoretical and discipline-oriented research.

Stetson's chapter "Population Policy and the Limits of Government Capability in the United States," is the most comprehensive, systematic, and structured of the three chapters. Consequently, it poses a great many more questions than can be discussed here. I will of necessity, therefore, be highly selective in my remarks.

Stetson is especially concerned that a framework suitable for comparative policy analysis be developed. She suggests that comparative study provides the best means to address questions of the conditions for governmental action on population policy and the conditions for policy effectiveness and at the same time makes "the study of population policy in developed states compatible with the pursuits of political scientists." As a result, much of the chapter can be read as an attempt to set the stage for comparative analysis of population politics, certainly a desirable goal. And given that goal, her discussion is heavily directed to developing and defining concepts and to producing an analytic scheme with which she comprehensively surveys policy options, "levels of capability performance," and categories of variables which help explain governmental capability.

My major criticism of her approach is that it is geared more to the development of political science literature and to the concerns of the discipline than to the substance of population policy making (in the United States) and how that policy making might be made more nearly in accord with resolution of population problems. And I think this is not entirely due to her interest here in producing an analytic framework. It is a common characteristic of comparative political analysis as now generally practiced and even of comparative policy studies. But there are alternative ways to study politics and policy.

More than a hint of this orientation is evident in the conclusion, where she states that

the topics elaborated upon in this chapter were selected to pertain to the concerns of the political science discipline in testing propositions about policies in a comparative context. Therefore, information in any of these research areas would contribute to the further development of comparative policy studies and is certainly not of interest to the population field alone.

Why do we continually need to justify the study of "policy relevant" research by appeals to the significance of such work to the discipline? A major risk in encouraging this conception of the purpose of research is that political scientists might be dissuaded from making very good use of their considerable abilities to add an important dimension to substantive population dialogues and politics. And given disciplinary norms, expectations of academic employers, and the orientation of major professional journals, I think this a not unlikely outcome. But to whom should we address ourselves when analyzing population policies and the politics which surrounds them? Is there a basic incompatiblilty perhaps between speaking to a professional audience of political scientists interested in theoretical constructs and to governmental leaders and population activists with more practical and immediate concerns? If so, where do our research priorities lie? Without altogether abandoning theoretical research and the development of useful analytic schemes, we do need to be more realistic about the purpose and utility of research and finally get down to the task of engaging in empirical studies. As Nash has put it:

my bet is that we will be much further ahead a decade from now if we can avoid an almost endless proliferation of conceptual schemes which remain cumulating in a stratosphere of empirical virginity, and instead put far more emphasis on first picking out policy problems which are interesting . . . as problems and then choosing analytic modes which most clearly fit the problem to be 'solved.' Indeed I will be so bold as to declare that few things could be so helpful as to declare a five-year moratorium on the proffering of conceptual schemes attended by claims of the sort which were variously entertained by proponents of systems theory, group theory, and communications theory for them during the past generation or so.[20]

With that criticism, let me be more positive about the content of Stetson's chapter. The "policy repertoire" scheme, like earlier sketches by Nash and Lowi,[21] goes a long way toward clarifying policy alternatives in the three areas of contraception, abortion, and sterilization (Table 19-1). By distinguishing regulative, distributive, and symbolic actions and degrees of commitment, involvement, and power (capability performance), Stetson adds a higher order of sophistication to policy typologizing and provides an empirical and analytic basis for formulating and evaluating population policies. Similarly, the codification of U.S. fertility policy (Table 19-2) provides a convenient summary of wide-ranging governmental actions which in one sense or another constitute "policy."[22]

She also makes a number of suggestions for research, most of them organized quite properly around attempts to explain "current system capability." She recommends that we consider variables of the policy process (cultural norms, group politics, definitions of the issues, and bureaucratic politics), policy patterns (e.g., as Lowi has developed them), and forms of government (e.g., in the case of the United States, our representative system with its emphasis on individual liberty and limited government) in such a strategy. Whether these or other categories are used, the aim is to isolate the major factors or variables which explain why the U.S. government, for example, has and has not adopted certain policies, particularly why it has not adopted a higher order of national population policy.

This is, indeed, a central question upon which more of our research should focus. In pursuing this line of attack, however, the scope of investigations should not be too constrained by theoretical constructs and narrowing categories. We need to explore a wide range of questions and not prejudice the outcome by overly structuring variables in advance.

Substantively, we might want to know in much greater detail than now available why political elites or decision makers hold the values and attitudes they do; what their perceptions and definitions of the problems are; how well informed they are on the problems themselves; how they respond to policy advice (e.g., from population commissions and social scientists); why they are or are not motivated to devote scarce time, energy, and attention to population matters at all or to adopt particular policy preferences; what personal and political rewards attend commitment to, and action on, population issues; under what kinds of limitations or constraints they must operate (institutional, political, and behavioral); what kinds of policy leadership are provided by whom and with what effects; what major interest groups are active, and what strategies and tactics they use with what effect; what the roles of public opinion (especially the attentive public) and the media are; and so on.[23]

Present studies of policy making answer such questions in so general a fashion and so briefly — if at all — that we cannot really be confident of the explanations offered. And while in the United States, for example, data available in population newsletters (e.g., Zero Population Growth's *National Reporter* and its *Population Politics*) and in government documents (e.g., congressional hearings and the *Congressional Record*) can fill in certain facts of contemporary policy making, these data tell us very little about complex political dynamics, attitudes, and motivations. We have barely begun to apply the usual tools of the discipline to compile accurate and relatively complete explanations for the response of political systems to the population challenge. If we aspire to such investigations, which presumably serve as guides to criticisn and corrective action, then we have a long way to go. In comparison to what we know of the policy-making process in other issue areas, our knowledge of population politics is very skimpy indeed. By giving this focus the emphasis she has, Stetson helps encourage a more productive political science. Let us hope that her advice does not fall on deaf ears.

Conclusion

Criticism of the efforts political scientists have made at analysis of population problems thus far is extraordinarily easy. As rapidly as the literature has developed, it is still just beginning to come to terms with the most challenging questions and is bound to go through a stage of exploratory ventures and trial-and-error tactics. Compiling research agendas and holding out great promise for future political analysis are similarly easy tasks. We all do both endlessly, and we have something of a professional stake in justifying the worth of social science contributions. Much more difficult is evaluating what we can realistically hope to accomplish and what the effects are likely to be — either on the discipline or on population policy-making processes — as well as actually carrying out the research.

A good beginning has been made; but much remains to be done. The quality of future research depends upon our willingness to pose imaginative, significant, and utilitarian questions about population politics. That goal is best served by not imposing highly structured models and rigid boundaries on the study of population matters. We should instead encourage a diversity of approaches (including genuine interdisciplinary analysis), experimentation, and innovation. Above all, we need to be far more conscious of the social and political context within which we define research goals and within which resulting knowledge has an impact.

Notes

1. Elihu Bergman, "American Population Policy Making: The Politics of Do Good, But Don't Rock the Boat!" and A.E. Keir Nash, "Demographology in U.S. Population Politics," pp. 41-94 of Richard L. Clinton and R. Kenneth Godwin, eds., *Research in the Politics of Population* (Lexington, Mass.: D.C. Heath and Company, 1972).

2. Robert Lynd, *Knowledge for What? The Place of Social Science in American Culture* (Princeton, N.J.: Princeton University Press, 1939). Lynd's advice can still be read with profit.

3. A.E. Keir Nash, ed. (for the Commission on Population Growth and the American Future), *Governance and Population: The Governmental Implications of Population Change* (Washington, D.C.: G.P.O., 1972), p. 13.

4. Charles E. Lindblom, "Integration of Economics and Other Social Sciences through Policy Analysis," in James C. Charlesworth, ed., *Integration of the Social Sciences through Policy Analysis* (Philadelphia, Pa.: The American Academy of Political and Social Science, 1972), p. 1.

5. Terry L. McCoy, "Political Scientists as Problem-Solvers: The Case of Population," *Polity* 5, no. 2 (Winter 1972): 250-59.

6. Ibid., p. 250.

7. Ibid., p. 259.

8. For one list of applied research, see Lyle Saunders, "Action Needs: The Relevance of Political Research," pp. 1-14 of Richard L. Clinton, William S. Flash, and R. Kenneth Godwin, eds., *Political Science in Population Studies* (Lexington, Mass.: D.C. Heath and Company, 1972).

9. McCoy suggests in his overview of population and politics research that we already "know a fair amount about how policy is made," about the input side of policy making, including interest group activity, the attitudes of elites and the mass public, legislative bargaining and the like [McCoy (n. 5); p. 257]. There may be far more unpublished work than I am aware of on these matters, as McCoy says, but there is certainly not a great deal in print on the population policy-making process in the United States, for example. By way of illustration, two recent book-length treatments, Phyllis Tilson Piotrow's *World Population Crisis: The United States Response* (New York: Praeger Publishers, 1973) and Peter Bachrach and Elihu Bergman's *Power and Choice: The Formulation of American Population Policy* (Lexington, Mass.: D.C. Heath and Company, 1973), valuable as they are, hardly exhaust the subject, especially since a good case could be made that we have no explicit national population policy yet in the United States. McCoy rightly argues that we know so little about the *impact* of population policies that this focus deserves a great deal more emphasis. But since most governments have been reluctant to enact controversial public policies on population growth (especially if a degree of coercion is implied), it

would seem that most analysis of policy impact — direct and indirect — would have to be more speculative than empirical at present, as are, for example, Theodore Lowi's excellent essay on "Population Policies and the American Political System," in Clinton, Flash, and Godwin (n. 8) and Elsa Chaney's chapter in this section.

10. Commission on Population Growth and the American Future, *Population and the American Future* (Washington, D.C.: G.P.O., 1972), p. 149.

11. Bergman (n. 1) and Bachrach and Bergman (n. 9).

12. Projections are always subject to dispute. I use the figures from the latest Census Bureau estimates as reported in the *New York Times,* March 2, 1973, p. 41. It is also worth noting that since eventual stabilization presumably means curtailing immigration, obviously this involves a value choice with overtones of inequality similar to those which disturb Bergman.

13. Or so Zero Population Growth lobbyists and others have reported. The politics of the Population Stabilization Resolution in Congress illuminates many of the difficulties which population activists face. See Natalie Davis Spingarn, "Population Report/Fertility Drop Confuses Debate Over National Population Growth Policy," *National Journal* (November 20, 1971), pp. 2288-2301 and the hearings, U.S. Congress, Special Subcommittee on Human Resources of the Committee on Labor and Public Welfare, *Declaration of U.S. Policy of Population Stabilization by Voluntary Means, 1971,* 92nd Cong., 1st sess., 1971.

14. Study of the purposes and impact of such commissions has been considerably enhanced by Thomas R. Wolanin's "The Impact of Presidential Advisory Commissions, 1943-1968," paper presented at the annual meeting of the American Political Science Association, Washington, D.C., September 1972.

15. Steven Garland and Robert Trudeau, "Population Policy Research: A Critique and an Alternative," pp. 17-39 of Clinton and Godwin (n. 1).

16. Donella H. Meadows, et al., *The Limits to Growth: A Report for the Club of Rome's Project on the Predicament of Mankind* (New York: Universe Books, 1972). I say "presumed" because I think these criticisms are neither accurate nor fair.

17. Roger W. Cobb and Charles D. Elder, *Participation in American Politics: The Dynamics of Agenda Building* (Boston: Allyn and Bacon, 1972), p. 96.

18. This line of argument is presented in great detail in Michael E. Kraft, "Congressional Attitudes toward the Environment: Attention and Issue-Orientation in Ecological Politics" (Ph.D. dissertation, Yale University, 1973), esp. pp. 47-99. The most recent and useful political analysis of American attitudes toward population matters is Carl C. Hetrick, A.E. Keir Nash, and Alan J. Wyner, "Population and Politics: Information, Concern, and Policy Support Among the American Public," in Nash (n. 3).

19. *Roe* v. *Wade* and *Doe* v. *Bolton,* January 22, 1973.

20. A.E. Keir Nash, "Making the World Population Problem Safe for American Democracy? AID, IUD, and the Political Thought of R.T. Ravenholt," paper presented at the annual meeting of the American Political Science Association, Washington, D.C., September, 1972, p. 10.

21. See A.E. Keir Nash, "Going Beyond John Locke? Influencing American Population Growth," *Milbank Memorial Fund Quarterly* 49, no. 1 (January 1971), pp. 3-31; and "Population Growth and American Ideology," in Noël Hinrichs, ed., *Population, Environment, and People* (New York: McGraw Hill, 1971); and Lowi (n. 9).

22. It is worth calling attention to the fact that Stetson's definition of *policy* as "action by governmental structures and leaders appearing to be directed toward affecting the environment for reproductive behavior of individuals: the conception and delivery of off-spring" is more generous (or looser) than Lowi's. Lowi defines a *policy* as "a general statement by some governmental authority defining an intention to influence the behavior of citizens by use of positive and negative sanctions." (n. 9, p. 27). A single decision, statement, or action, however, is not a policy in itself.

A policy must possess the following three characteristics: (1) an official expression of intentions concerning desirable or undesirable conduct; (2) a provision for inducements, positive, or negative, or both; and (3) some provision of means of implementing the intentions and applying the sanctions. (Ibid.)

By this definition a fair number of governmental actions would not, strictly speaking, constitute public policy. The distinction is important because we are prone to call whatever outputs result from the political system "policy" even when they lack these necessary ingredients. If we do not yet have a national policy on population growth, effective political analysis and strategy depend upon recognition of this fact.

23. In one attempt to answer such questions I conducted a series of semistructured interviews in early 1970 with a highly selective sample of U.S. congressmen (most of whom were representatives) on seven environmentally significant subcommittees. Along with a content analysis of the *Congressional Record* for the period 1967-1970, these interviews indicated (unexpectedly) that population problems were not at all very salient for congressmen in the sample — even though they were officially "on the agenda" (the Population Commission bill had just been enacted and the Family Planning and Population Research Act of 1970 was under consideration at the time). In addition, few of the congressmen thought population growth in the United States particularly serious, fewer still seemed to connect population growth and environmental problems, and most demonstrated a remarkable degree of ignorance of the dimensions of population growth in the United States and worldwide. Most also heard very little from constituents on population problems — of 32 directly

asked, only two indicated that they received "quite a lot" of mail on population questions compared to other issues. Perhaps as a result of these conditions almost no sense of urgency existed. Not only were these congressmen inattentive and inactive, but they were little disposed to do much beyond supporting initiation of the Population Commission and continuation of modest efforts in the areas of research and family planning programs. Ideological and political considerations clearly shaped policy preferences and activism, and were as evident in the personal (and confidential) interviews as in the public record of policy discussions.

It is also of interest that members of the House especially concerned with and/or active on population growth issues were fairly distinctive. They were likely to come from the Far West or the Northeast, to be politically liberal (but equally Democratic and Republican), to be more knowledgeable than others on such issues, to be higher in seniority, to come from "safer" districts, and to have a national rather than local role-orientation. (More extensive discussion of these and other findings can be found in Kraft [n. 18] .)

Index

AID (Agency for International Development), 105, 107, 145, 146, 149, 150, 204; budget of, 135-36, 137; in Dominican Republic, 164-67, 169, 170, 205-6; and KAP, 135-36; and population control, 176-77; and U.S. Congress, 176-77, 183
Abortion, 207, 213-14, 235-36, 253, 257-59, 263, 278, 280
Academic institutions. *See* Universities
Adams, Richard N., 213
Adelman, Irma, 115
Africa, 115, 153-61 *passim,* 181, 184, 209, 213, 235; cost-benefit analysis of population control in, 155-57; new approaches to population growth, 158-59; priority position of population control in, 157-58
African Studies Institute (Leningrad), 213
Agency for International Development. *See* AID
Agenda setting, 137, 191, 192, 201 n.5, 223-24, 276-77, 278-79
Aggregate data analysis, 111-16, 127; of county data, 114-15; and diffusion of innovation, 113-14; of elites, 112-13; informative value of, 115-16; limitations of, 146-47; and testing for uniformities, 111-12
Ahmed, Osman S., 153-62, 209, 210
Alliance for Progress (*Alianza*), 136, 204, 213
Allende, Salvador, 206
Almond, Gabriel, 30-31, 122, 207, 268 n.6
American Law Institute (ALI), 259
American Political Science Association, 30
American Psychological Association, 9
Anderson, Charles, 268 n.5
Anderson County, Tenn., 258
Arab-Israeli conflict, 90, 93
Argentina, 203
Aron, Henry, 112, 114
Asia, 149
Attitudinal research. *See* KAP

Baby boom, 138, 236
Bachrach, Peter, 136, 137, 191
Bacon, Francis, 45
Balaguer, Joaquin, 164, 166, 168, 170
Banks, Arthur S., 115
Baratz, Morton, 137, 191
Barbados, 182, 240

Bay, Christian, 190, 199
Bayesian statistics, 95, 96, 97
Behavioralism, 29, 31, 190-94, 197-200
Beláunde, Fernando, 213
Belgian Congo, 213
Bell, Daniel, 48
Bennett, John, 170
Bensman, Joseph, 214
Berelson, Bernard, 136, 177
Bergman, Elihu, 136, 191, 240, 221-30, 273, 276-80
"Beyond Family Planning" (Berelson), 136
Beyond Freedom and Dignity (Skinner), 135
Birth Control. *See* Contraception
Birth control movement, 173, 179-80
Birth rates. *See* Fertility rates
Black, Robert, 176-77
Blair, Calvin, 203
Blake, Judith, 137, 270 n.29
Boston Globe, 221, 222
Boulding, Kenneth, 37
Brazil, 208, 239
"Bread vs. loops," 176, 177, 178, 183, 184
Brookings Institution, 97
Bryce, James, 217
Bulgaria, 235

Callahan, Daniel, 11
Camelot Project, 125, 204, 212
Campbell, Donald T., 110
Canada, 163
Candor, N.Y., 214
Capability analysis, 248-52, 259-67
Caracas, Venezuela, 165, 206
Caribbean islands, 180, 186
Caribe, El (Santo Domingo), 164
Case-study research, 89-90, 108-11, 127; vs. aggregate analysis, 146-47
Castle, Barbara, 237
Castro, Fidel, 207
Catholic Church, 10, 24, 27 n.17, 256
Catholic University (Lima), 208
Causation, concepts of, 85-86
Cayetano Heredia (Lima medical school), 208
Ceylon, 240
Chaney, Elsa M., 233-46, 280-82
Chaplin, David, 203-17, 237-38
Children: economic functions of, 53-54, 56-57, 159; education of, 158-59; marginal productivity of, 155-56

Nash, Leonard K., 42 n.11
Natalist policies, 24, 53, 235, 261, 268
  n.10
National Environmental Protection Act,
  46
National Fertility Surveys, 266
National Institute of Mental Health, 205
National Organization for Women, 281
National Plan for a Population Program
  (Dominican Republic), 168
National Planning Office (ONAPLAN)
  (Dominican Republic), 163
National Reporter, 285
National Science Foundation, 205
National Women's Political Caucus, 281
Nationalism vs. internationalism, 65, 208,
  217
Natural resources, 78-79, 157, 177
Nazis, 38, 133
Ness, Gayl D., 145-50
New Mexico, 253
New York State, 257
New York Times, 221, 228
Newburyport, Mass., 214
Newspapers, 164
Niebuhr, Reinhold, 4-5
Ninth Amendment, 253, 257, 261
Nixon, Richard M., 174, 210, 223, 256,
  258, 278
"Nondecision making," *See* "Mobilization
  of bias"
Nonlinearities and system breaks in popu-
  lation variables, 87-88
North Africa, 186
North America, "frontier mentality" of,
  24
Nuclear family, alternatives to, 46

Odum, Eugene P, 49 n.4
Ophuls, William, 45-49, 65-66, 68
"Optimum population," 34, 35, 77, 154,
  160, 278
Opus Dei (Spain), 212
Organski, A.F.K. and Katherine, 121-22

P.R.I. (Mexican political party), 216
"Partisan mutual adjustment," 46
"Partners in Development" (Commission
  on International Development), 153
Peace Corps, 169
Pedro Henríquez Ureña National Univer-
  sity (UNPHU), 206
Personality variables, 133, 142 n.12
Peru, 132, 204, 208, 211, 215, 238, 240,
  245 n.29
Peters, B. Guy, 114
Philippines, 180, 238
Pickard, Jerome, 32

Policy analysis, 96
Policy "tools," 248, 268 n.5
Political demography, 18
Political parties, 112
Political science: behavioralism and,
  190-94; demographic analysis and,
  31-32; as a discipline, 15-18, 66-67,
  70 n.24, 275-76, 283; growth of,
  30-31; models, 60-63; and population
  studies, 18-25; research, 65, 67; as a
  science, 29-32, 41 n.9
Political stability, 122, 164, 167, 185
Political Studies Association (Great
  Britain), 30-31
Poole, D. Ian, 235
Popper, Karl, 115
Population analysis, 148-49
Population Commission. *See* Commission
  on Population Growth and the American Future
Population control: in Africa, 157-58; cost-
  benefit analysis of, 155-57; in
  Dominican Republic, 163-70; foreign
  aid and, 173-86 *passim;* governments
  and, 55-56, 235-236, 264-65; non-
  Malthusian, 78, 154; opponents of,
  59-60; and population policy, 57-59
Population Council, 105, 164, 165, 167,
  177, 206
Population Crisis Committee, 174, 221
Population "density," 38-40, 81, 123,
  125
Population dynamics, 115; composition
  and distribution variables of, 81; concepts of causation in, 85-86; conflict
  and violence in 82-83, 90, 91; in international relations, 83-84, 85-86, 88,
  90, 92-93; intervening variables of, 83-
  85; Malthus vs. Marx on, 77-78;
  methodological imperatives of, 80-89;
  nonlinearities and system breaks in,
  87-89; political variables of, 82-83;
  population variables of, 79-82; referent
  variables of 76, 77, 78-79, 81; research
  alternatives in, 89-96
Population Dynamics and International
  Violence Project (M.I.T.), 90, 93
Population economists, 37
"Population explosion," 22, 52, 56, 161
Population growth rates, 36, 37, 46, 76,
  78; contraceptive availability and,
  54-55; cost-benefit analysis of, 155-57;
  and economic development, 154-55,
  175-76; mortality rates and, 52-53;
  and poverty, 173-76
Population "implosion," 22, 163
"Population Mafia," 176, 179, 184, 185,
  186

Population Policies in Relation to Development in Latin America Conference (Caracas, 1967), 165

Population policy: activism, 273-74, 276, 278, 287 n.13; attributes of, 106-8; avoidance of conflict in, 227-29, 276-77; capability analysis of, 248-52, 282-83; conflict of interests in, 6-7, 148; criteria for, 4-5; defined, 247, 288 n.22; donor agencies and prejudice, 180, 181-83, ethics of, 3-14; federal, 252-58; in Latin America, 203-17; mobilization of bias and, 136, 137, 138; political analysis of 229-30; political scientists and, 5, 6, 13-14, 15-25; and population limitation, 57-59; research and analysis of, 125-26, 148-49; research in system capability, 259-67; of states, 243, 258-59, 262-63; in U.S., 185-86, 221-30, 252-59; value terms and referents used in, 33-36, 222-26, 277; whole-systems analysis of, 45-48

"Population Policy for Americans: Is the Government Being Misled" (Blake), 137
Population Politics, 285
Population "pressures," 81, 82, 155
Population "problem," 55, 80; attitudes toward, 10-11; definitions of, 77-78
Population Stabilization Resolution (U.S. Cong.), 278, 287 n.13
Population stock vs. flow, 154
Population variables, 79-82; and political behavior, 121-23
Portugal, 208
Positivism, 30, 191-92, 197, 198, 199, 200
Postpluralist analysis, 35, 36
Pranger, Robert J., 199
Projections, 32, 36, 76, 278, 287 n.12
Protestant missionaries, 164
Proyecto Colonia (Colombia), 204
Proyecto Simpatico (Peru), 204
Puerto Rico, 194-97, 214
Punta del Este, Uruguay, 205
Purcell, Susan Kaufman, 239

Questionnaires. *See* KAP

Racial prejudice, 133, 181-82, 222, 223
Rainwater, Lee, 271
Rand Corporation, 36, 38
Rat behavior, 38-39
Reductionism, 45, 135, 142 n.12
Replication, 110, 126, 217
Research, 65, 67, 257; aggregate analysis, 111-16; basic vs. applied, 102-4,

124-25; behavioralism and, 190-94, 197-200; case analysis, 89-90, 108-11, 123-24, 126; conservatism of, 192-93; cost-benefit analysis of alternative methods of, 89-96; definitions and the individual, 190-94; equality vs. hierarchy in, 194-97, 198, 215; in Latin America, 204-8, and population studies/political science interface, 18-25; priorities, 104-5; reforms, 213-16; sponsorship of, 124-26; system capability, 259-67; technological, 135-37; typology of, 102-4
Resources for the Future, 99 n.17
Responsibilities of the Foreign Scholar to the Local Scholarly Community (Blair), 203
Revolution, 60
Revolutionary Politics and the Cuban Working Class (Zeitlin), 207
Rhodesia, 182, 210
Ridley, Jeanne Clair, 238
Richardson, Lewis Fry, 82
Rights, inalienable, 7
Rio de Janeiro, 208
Robinson, James A., 112
Robinson, William S., 116
Rockefeller Foundation, 204, 208
Rogers, E.M., 113
Romney, George, 223
Roper Opinion Poll, 212
Rostow, Walt, 216
Roszak, Theodore, 190
Rousseau, Jean Jacques, 9
Romania, 235-36, 244 n.15
Rural-urban differentials, 81
Russia. *See* U.S.S.R.

Sanders, Thomas G., 3-8
Sanger, Margaret, 173
Santiago, Chile, 165, 175, 208
Schaedel, Richard, 211
Scholars. *See* Investigators
Schultz, P., 158
Science, natural vs. social, 42 n.11
"Scientism," 30, 40 n.2
Segal, Aaron, 173-88, 210
Segregation, 143 n.28
Selznick, Philip, 146
Siete Pecados Capitales de los Espanoles, Los (Diaz Plaja), 217
Simulation, 93, 96-97
Sinding, Steven W., 121-30, 145, 146, 147, 148
Singapore, 182
Sino-Soviet dispute, 90, 93
Skinner, B.F., 133-34, 135

About the Contributors

Osman S. Ahmed is Associate Area Coordinator for Africa at the Carolina Population Center and a doctoral student in economics at Duke University. His principal interest is economic development. Prior to assuming his present position Mr. Ahmed was economist for Soul City, North Carolina.

Elihu Bergman, who holds the Ph.D in political science from the University of North Carolina at Chapel Hill, is Assistant Director of the Harvard Center for Population Studies. His professional specialization has been the management of development programs in the United States and overseas. He has worked with the Ford Foundation, VISTA, Development and Resources Corporation, and the Agency for International Development. His major research interest is in the political analysis of population policy. Dr. Bergman was an organizer and has served as Executive Secretary of the International Population Policy Consortium. A contributor to Clinton and Godwin, eds., *Research in the Politics of Population* (D.C. Heath, 1972), Bergman's most recent work, in collaboration with Professor Peter Bachrach, is *Power and Choice: The Formulation of American Population Policy* (D.C. Heath, 1973).

Elsa M. Chaney is Assistant Professor of Political Science and Director of the Latin American Program at Fordham University. She obtained the Ph.D. at the University of Wisconsin in 1970, and her major research and teaching interests are in the areas of Latin American politics, comparative politics, and women in politics. Professor Chaney has published articles and chapters in the *Journal of Marriage and the Family* and in edited works.

David Chaplin, who received the Ph.D. in sociology from Princeton in 1963, is Professor and Chairman, Department of Scoiology, Western Michigan University. He is the author of the *Peruvian Industrial Labor Force* (Princeton University Press, 1967) and numerous articles on Peru. Recently he has edited *Population Policies and Growth in Latin America* (D.C. Heath, 1972) and *Peruvian Nationalism: A Corporatist Revolution* (Trans-action Books, forthcoming). He is currently studying the development of population policy in Peru and Mexico.

Nazli Choucri, a Stanford Ph.D. (1967), is Associate Professor of Political Science at Massachusetts Institute of Technology. Her major research has involved international relations, forecasting, and international violence and has resulted in articles in *World Politics, Journal of Conflict Resolution, International Affairs,* and *International Organization*. With Robert North she is the author of a forthcoming volume entitled *Nations in Conflict: Population, Lateral Pressure, and War.*

Richard L. Clinton is Assistant Professor of Political Science at the University of North Carolina, Chapel Hill, where he earned the Ph.D. in 1971. His fields of special interest are Latin American politics, normative political theory, and the political implications of population change. One of the founding members of the International Population Policy Consortium, Professor Clinton currently serves as executive secretary of that organization. His articles have appeared in the *Journal of Inter-American Studies and World Affairs, Inter-American Economic Affairs,* the *Annals of the Southeastern Conference on Latin American Studies,* and *Alternatives* (Canada) as well as in several edited works. He was co-editor, with William Flash and Kenneth Godwin, of *Political Science in Population Studies* (D.C. Heath, 1972), and, with Kenneth Godwin, of *Research in the Politics of Population* (D.C. Heath, 1972).

Mair J. deVoursney is a doctoral candidate in political science at the University of North Carolina at Chapel Hill. During two field work assignments in India she was involved in population programming research. Her academic interests are public policy and political development, focusing on population policy. Her current research is an aggregate data analysis of the socioeconomic and political factors affecting national population policies.

Moye W. Freymann is Director of the Carolina Population Center at the University of North Carolina, Chapel Hill. He received the M.D. from Johns Hopkins University in 1948 and, after public health experience in Iran and India, completed the Dr.P.H. at Harvard in 1960. He has contributed chapters to a large number of books and reports.

R. Kenneth Godwin is Assistant Professor of Political Science at Oregon State University. He received the Ph.D. from the University of North Carolina at Chapel Hill in 1971. His research interests and publications are in the fields of Latin American politics and comparative political behavior, particularly the problems encountered in devising survey instruments and interpreting survey data. Professor Godwin was a co-editor, with Richard Clinton and William Flash, of *Political Science in Population Studies* (D.C. Heath, 1972), and, with Richard Clinton, of *Research in the Politics of Population* (D.C. Heath, 1972)

Frank M. Hale earned the Ph.D. in political science at Syracuse University in 1972 and is a research associate in the Department of Community Medicine, Dartmouth Medical School. His research on Dominican population policy was supported by a Fulbright-Hays Fellowship and by the Population Council. He is currently doing research on health policy and the organization of ambulatory care.

Michael E. Kraft, is Assistant Professor of Political Science at Vassar College. He received the Ph.D. from Yale University in 1973. His fields of interest include

American politics, political behavior, and the politics of ecology. Currently engaged in research on congressional politics and the environment, he has contributed articles to *Alternatives* (Canada) and the *Policy Studies Journal.*

Thomas C. Lyons, Jr. is a student of political phenomena. He has been with the Agency for International Development since 1967 and is currently Chief, Policy Development Division, Office of Population. Before joining AID he served as a foreign affairs advisor with the Library of Congress. He lectures in this country and abroad on population matters and foreign policy.

Terry L. McCoy holds the Ph.D. from the University of Wisconsin and is Assistant Professor of Political Science and Research Associate of the Mershon Center at the Ohio State University. His major areas of interest are Latin American politics, comparative policy analysis, and the politics of modernization. Professor McCoy is co-author of *Population and Politics in the Developing World* (Free Press, forthcoming) and editor of *The Dynamics of Population Policy in Latin America* (Ballinger, forthcoming). He has also contributed to *Polity, América Latina,* and *Inter-American Economic Affairs.*

A.E. Keir Nash received the Ph.D from Harvard in 1967 and is currently Associate Professor of Political Science, vice-chairman of his department, and president of the AAUP chapter at the University of California, Santa Barbara. During 1970-71 he served as Director of Political Research of the National Commission on Population Growth and the American Future, in which capacity he edited the Commission research volume, *Governance and Population* (Government Printing Office, 1972). He is the senior author of *Oil Pollution and the Public Interest* (University of California Press, 1972), and his writings have appeared in the *American Political Science Review,* the *Journal of American History,* the *Virginia Law Review,* the *Journal of Comparative Administration,* the *Milbank Memorial Fund Quarterly,* and *Mercurio* (Italy), as well as in edited works.

Gayl D. Ness is Professor of Sociology at the University of Michigan. He was awarded the Ph.D. in 1961 by the University of California at Berkeley. His principal research has dealt with social change and economic development in Southeast Asia. Professor Ness is the author of *Bureaucracy and Rural Development in Malaysia* (University of California Press, 1967) and *The Sociology of Economic Development* (Harper and Row, 1971) as well as of numerous articles.

William Ophuls is a candidate for the Ph.D. in political science at Yale University. A former Foreign Service Officer with postings in Washington, the Ivory Coast, and Japan, he is a specialist in the political implications of the environmental crisis and has published several essays on this topic, for example,

"Leviathan or Oblivion?" in Herman E. Daly, ed., *Toward a Steady-State Economy* (W.H. Freeman, 1973). His dissertation is entitled "Prologue to a Political Theory of the Steady State."

Thomas G. Sanders whose Ph.D. is in religion from Columbia University, has been Latin American representative of the American Universities Field Staff since 1968 in which capacity he has authored numerous reports on population problems and programs and their varying perception in the Hispano-Catholic milieu of different Latin American countries. Dr. Sanders is also the author of two books: *Protestant Concepts of Church and State* (Holt, Rinehart and Winston, 1964) and *Catholic Innovation in a Changing Latin America* (CIDOC, 1969).

Aaron Segal obtained the Ph.D. from the University of California at Berkeley in 1965 and is now Visiting Associate Professor of Political Science in Cornell University's Department of Government. Former editor of *Africa Report,* he is the author of *Politics and Population in the Caribbean, The Politics of Caribbean Economic Integration,* and co-author of *The Traveler's Africa.*

Steven W. Sinding is a political scientist with the Office of Population of the Agency for International Development. He earned the Ph.D. at the University of North Carolina at Chapel Hill in 1970 and taught at the Facultad Latino-americana de Ciencias Sociales and the University of Kentucky before joining AID in 1971. His major research interests are in political development theory and its application to Latin American politics. He is the author of several articles on Chilean politics and on population policy and is the editor, with Kenneth Coleman, of a text on the study of politics in Latin America (Dodd, Mead, forthcoming).

Dorothy McBride Stetson received the Ph.D. from Vanderbilt University in 1968 and is Assistant Professor of Political Science at Florida Atlantic University. Her major research interests are comparative policy analysis and system capability and effectiveness. She has completed studies of Costa Rican elites and of the Costa Rican Demographic Association. Publications by Professor Stetson have appeared in *Journal of Politics* and *Florida Planning and Development.*

Robert Trudeau is Assistant Professor of Political Science at Providence College and earned the Ph.D. at the University of North Carolina in 1971. His fields of interest include Latin American politics, normative political theory, and political development. He has done field research in Costa Rica and currently is conducting research into population policy processes in Puerto Rico. From 1964 to 1966 he served as a Peace Corps Volunteer in Honduras.